D1572907

PLACE IN RETURN BOX to remove this checkout from your record.
TO AVOID FINES return on or before date due.
MAY BE RECALLED with earlier due date if requested.

DATE DUE	DATE DUE	DATE DUE

6/01 c:/CIRC/DateDue.p65-p.15

FUNDAMENTALS OF TURFGRASS AND AGRICULTURAL CHEMISTRY

L. B. (BERT) McCARTY
IAN R. RODRIGUEZ
B. TODD BUNNELL
F. CLINT WALTZ

WILEY

John Wiley & Sons, Inc.

**To those who are chemistry-challenged,
we dedicate this text and sincerely hope it will help.**

Library of Congress Cataloging-in-Publication Data:

Fundamentals of turfgrass and agricultural chemistry / by L.B. McCarty
. . . [et al.].
    p. cm.
  ISBN 0-471-44411-1 (Cloth)

  1. Turfgrasses—Fertilizers. 2. Turf management. 3. Agricultural
chemistry. I. McCarty, L. B. (Lambert Blanchard), 1958–

  SB433 .F86 2003
  635.9′64289—dc21

                                            2002151180

CONTENTS

PREFACE

Maintaining sophisticated turfgrass and agricultural sites requires a basic understanding and working knowledge of fundamental chemical properties. The technical sophistication required of turf and agricultural managers when applying chemicals on various sites is increasing daily. Scrutiny from the general public and regulatory agencies to ensure the continued health and purity of the environment is also increasing. The purpose of this book is to address and explain many of the chemical reactions that occur in daily turf and agricultural management.

The authors have attempted to condense a wide and very technical subject, chemistry, into a practical, useable text. As such, detailed chemical theory has been avoided, as we focused on fundamentally applied topics and situations. Numerous examples and applied situations are included to further explain various chemical reactions. This book is intended as a teaching guide to students with no or minimal chemistry background and as a reference guide for golf course superintendents, assistants, club managers, greens committee members, agricultural managers, product salespersons, students, and regulatory agencies. The text is not intended as a detailed chemistry book, thus the scope or amount of information presented is much abbreviated from that typically found in a general chemistry text.

The reader should first thoroughly review Chapters 1 and 2 to understand the fundamental basis of chemistry which will be utilized in subsequent chapters. The remaining chapters will be much easier to understand after the first two have been mastered. Since biochemistry is based largely on carbon-containing compounds, the Organic Chemistry chapter should be covered in addition to Chapters 1 and 2 prior to covering the Plant Biochemistry chapter.

The information is as complete and up-to-date as possible. However, new products, regulations, and management techniques continually evolve, therefore the reader should strive to continue their education by attending various conferences, short courses, and workshops.

All chemicals mentioned are for reference only. Not all are available for turf use and may be restricted by some states, provinces, or federal agencies; thus, be sure to check the current status of the pesticide being considered for use. Always read and follow the manufacturer's label as registered under the Federal Insecticide, Fungicide, and Rodenticide Act. Mention of a proprietary product does not constitute a guarantee or warranty of the product by the authors or the publishers and does not imply approval to the exclusion of other products that also may be suitable.

Please go to www.wiley.com/go/mccarty for access to additional simple problems and other resources.

ACKNOWLEDGMENTS

The authors express sincere appreciation to C. E. Berry Jr., Michael Edwards, and Haibo Liu, for their thorough, critical review of the text.

AUTHORS

L. B. (Bert) McCarty is a Professor of Horticulture at Clemson University in Clemson, South Carolina specializing in turfgrass science and management. A native of Batesburg, South Carolina, he received a BS degree from Clemson University in Agronomy and Soils, MS from North Carolina State University in Crop Science, and PhD from Clemson University in Plant Physiology and Plant Pathology. Dr. McCarty spent almost nine years as a turfgrass specialist at the University of Florida in Gainesville. While there, he oversaw the design and construction of the state-of-the-art research and education turfgrass facility, "The Envirotron." He also was author or coauthor of the books, *Best Management Practices for Florida Golf Courses*, *Weeds of Southern Turfgrasses*, and *Florida Lawn Handbook*. In 1996, he moved to Clemson University and is involved in research, extension, and teaching activities. He has published over 300 articles dealing with all phases of turfgrass management and has given over 500 presentations. He is currently coordinating author of the books, *Best Golf Course Management Practices*, *Managing Bermudagrass Turf*, *Southern Lawns*, and *Color Atlas of Turfgrass Weeds* and is active in a number of professional societies.

Ian R. Rodriguez is a PhD candidate in the Department of Horticulture at Clemson University in Clemson, South Carolina, and an Instructor at Lake City Community College, Lake City, Florida. He was born and raised in Tampa, Florida and received a BS in Environmental Horticulture from the University of Florida in 1994. After working in the landscape design/build/maintenance field for two years, he returned to the University of Florida and received an MS in Environmental Horticulture in 1998. His areas of research have included new methods of turfgrass fertility management, rapid turf tissue analysis methods, and methods of reducing the effects of heat stress in creeping bentgrass. After completing his education, he plans on pursuing a teaching career in academia.

B. Todd Bunnell is currently a Graduate Research Assistant pursuing a PhD in Plant Physiology (turfgrass emphasis) at Clemson University. A native from Lexington, Kentucky, he received his BS degree at the University of Kentucky in Plant and Soil Science, and MS degree at Clemson University in Horticulture. His research interests include soil atmospheres of golf greens and light quantity on warm-season turfgrasses. Mr. Bunnell has published numerous articles and presented research findings at conferences worldwide. Following completion of his PhD degree, he plans to pursue a turfgrass-related career in industry or academia.

F. Clint Waltz is an Assistant Professor of Crop and Soil Sciences at the University of Georgia in Griffin. He received his MS degree in Horticulture, with an emphasis in turfgrass, from Clemson University in 1997 and a PhD in 2001 in the Crops and Soil Environmental Science with an emphasis in soils. Prior to arriving at Clemson University to pursue his graduate degrees, he worked in golf course maintenance for over 2 years at the Augusta National Golf Club. It was this experience that inspired him to further pursue the applied principles and practices involved in maintaining high-quality turfgrass. His long-term objectives involve applying scientific principles to solve practical problems associated with turfgrass maintenance and being an advocate for the environmental benefits of turfgrass and golf courses.

CHAPTER 1

FUNDAMENTALS OF CHEMISTRY

INTRODUCTION

Chemistry is the branch of science which studies matter—its composition, properties, and changes. Scientists attempt to discover and describe matter, then determine why these kinds of matter have particular characteristics and why changes in this matter occur. The discoveries of chemistry have greatly helped expand the life span of mankind, increase crop yields, and produce thousands of products that facilitate a higher standard of living. Most of today's medicines, plastics, synthetic fibers, alloys, pesticides, fertilizers, and many more products that enhance our lives are from the many discoveries of chemistry. Chemistry provides the foundation for the study and understanding of the biological sciences because without chemical reactions, life would not exist. Neither food nor clothing would be available. The energy needed for the human body to move and operate as well as all other biological processes would not exist without chemical reactions. Likewise, all processes involved in plant culture such as soil reactions, plant growth and development, pest management, and water use and quality, involve chemical reactions.

In developing a useful knowledge of chemistry, it is important to have a solid foundation and understanding of the fundamentals of chemistry. This foundation depends on a good understanding of the nature of elements and compounds and their relationships. The first three chapters of this book cover many of the concepts necessary to build this foundation required for turfgrass and agricultural managers and from which subsequent chapters are based and expanded upon.

Chemistry may be subdivided into several branches (Chart 1-1). These branches are not separate but overlap considerably.

Analytical chemistry deals with the separation, identification, and composition of all kinds of matter. Within analytical chemistry, *qualitative analysis* deals with the *separation* and *identification* of the individual components of materials while *quantitative analysis* determines *how much* of each component is present.

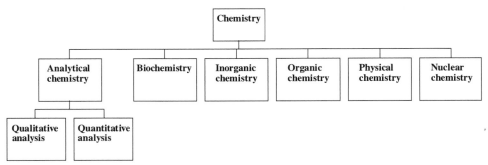

Chart 1-1. Branches of chemistry.

Biochemistry includes the study of materials and processes in living organisms.

Inorganic chemistry covers the chemistry of elements and their compounds except those containing carbon.

Organic chemistry is the study of carbon-containing materials.

Physical chemistry investigates the laws and theories of all branches of chemistry, especially the structure and transformation of matter and interrelationships of energy and matter.

Nuclear chemistry deals with the nuclei of atoms and their changes.

Turfgrass and agricultural science and management deals with all branches of chemistry with the possible exception of nuclear chemistry. This chapter introduces basic chemical concepts and topics necessary to use chemistry in agronomic practices covered in subsequent chapters.

ATOMS

The smallest particle of an element that has the properties of that element is an **atom** (from the Greek *atomos,* meaning "indivisible"). **Molecules** are groups of two or more atoms held together by the forces of chemical bonds (Figure 1-1). Molecules are electrically neutral (no net charge). **Ions** are atoms or groups of atoms that carry positive or negative electrical charges.

An atom consists of two parts, the nucleus and the electron cloud. Every atom has a core, or **nucleus** (plural: nuclei) which contains one or more positively charged particles called **protons.** The number of protons distinguishes the atoms of different elements from one another. For example, an atom of hydrogen (H), the simplest element, has one proton in its nucleus; an atom of carbon (C) has six protons. For any element, the number of protons in the nucleus of its atoms is referred to its **atomic number.** The atomic number of hydrogen is one and the atomic number of carbon is six (Table 1-1).

Atomic nuclei also contain uncharged particles of about the same weight as protons called **neutrons.** Neutrons affect only the weight of the atom, not its chemical properties. The weight of an atom is essentially made up of the weight of the protons and neutrons in its nucleus. The **atomic weight** of an element is defined as the weight of an atom relative to the weight of a carbon atom having six protons

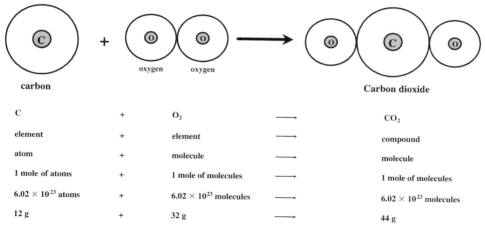

Figure 1-1. Relationship between the number of atoms, molecules, moles, and grams when carbon (C) combines with oxygen (O_2) to form carbon dioxide (CO_2).

and six neutrons and a designated atomic weight of 12. Because these atomic weights are relative values, they are expressed without units of weight. Similarly, the **atomic mass** of an element is the mass of an atom relative to that of a carbon atom with a designated atomic mass of 12. The atomic structures of some elements are shown in Table 1-1.

atomic mass (proton + neutrons) − atomic number (or protons)

= number of neutrons in the nucleus

The remainder of an atom lies around the central nucleus and is called the electron cloud (Figure 1-2). The electron cloud gives an atom its volume and keeps other atoms out since two objects cannot occupy the same space simultaneously (often referred to as the *law of impenetrability*). Within the electron cloud, electrons revolve about the nucleus similar to the planets revolving about the sun, in orbits of various diameters dependent upon the available energy.

An electron cloud is composed of negatively charged particles, called **electrons** (Figure 1-2). Electrons are attracted by the positive charge of the protons. The number and arrangement of electrons determine whether an atom will react with itself or other atoms, and the manner in which the reaction will occur. Due to their opposite charges, protons attract electrons, and all atoms have an equal number of protons and electrons; thus all atoms are *electrically neutral*.

atomic number = number of protons = number of electrons

The Atomic Theory

An **atom** is the smallest unit of an element that can exist either alone or in combination with other atoms like it or different from it. In 1803, John Dalton attempted to explain why elements always combine in definite proportions and always con-

TABLE 1-1. Atomic Structures and Electronegativity of Some Essential Plant Elements

Element	Symbol	Common Oxidation (Valence) Numbers	Nucleus: Atomic Number (Number of Protons)	Number of Neutrons	Number of Electrons: Total	Shell or Orbital 1 (K)	2 (L)	3 (M)	4 (N)	Atomic Weight	Electro-negativity
Essential Elements for Plants											
Hydrogen	H	+1	1	0	1	1	0	0	0	1	2.1
Boron	B	+3	5	6	5	2	3	0	0	11	2.0
Carbon	C	-4, +4	6	6	6	2	4	0	0	12	2.5
Nitrogen	N	-3, +5	7	7	7	2	5	0	0	14	3.0
Oxygen	O	-2	8	8	8	2	6	0	0	16	3.5
Magnesium	Mg	+2	12	12	12	2	8	2	0	24	1.5
Phosphorus	P	-3, +5	15	16	15	2	8	5	0	31	2.1
Sulfur	S	+6, -2	16	16	16	2	8	6	0	32	2.5
Potassium	K	+1	19	20	19	2	8	8	1	39	0.9
Calcium	Ca	+2	20	20	20	2	8	8	2	40	1.0
Manganese	Mn	+2, +3	25	30	25	2	8	8	7	55	1.5
Iron	Fe	+2, +3	26	30	26	2	8	8	8	56	1.8
Copper	Cu	+1, +2	29	35	29	2	8	8	11	64	1.9
Zinc	Zn	+2	30	35	30	2	8	8	12	65	1.6
Molybdenum	Mo	+3, +5	42	54	42	2	8	8	18[a]	96	1.8
Other Elements											
Sodium	Na	+1	11	12	11	2	8	1	0	23	1.0
Aluminum	Al	+3	13	14	13	2	8	3	0	27	1.5
Chlorine	Cl	-1	17	18	17	2	8	7	0	35	3.0

[a]Molybdenum has 6 additional electrons in a 5th shell.

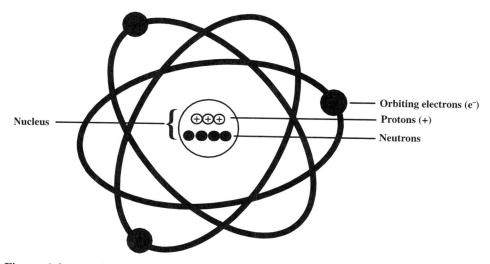

Figure 1-2. Atomic structure of lithium (Li). Atoms are made up of a relatively heavy, compact, centrally located nucleus which contains positively charged protons and neutrally charged neutrons. Lighter, negatively charged electrons orbit about the nucleus at varying distances from its center.

form to the Law of Conservation of Matter. Basically, for each element there is a chemical or reactive unit, called an *atom,* which has its own characteristic weight. In chemical reactions these unit particles are merely rearranged, they are not destroyed. This is referred to as the **Law of Conservation of Matter.**

Summary of Dalton's Atomic Theory

1. All substances are composed of small, dense, indestructible particles called atoms.
2. Atoms of a given substance are identical in mass, size, and shape.
3. An atom is the smallest part of an element that enters into a chemical change.
4. Molecules of a compound are produced by the combination of the atoms of two or more different elements.

ELEMENTS

Matter is anything that occupies space. A **substance** is a distinct kind of matter consisting of the same properties throughout the sample. All matter is made up of **elements** (Chart 1-2). Elements are substances that cannot be broken down into other simpler substances by ordinary chemical means. There are 92 naturally occurring elements on Earth, each differing from the others by the number of protons in the nuclei of its atoms. These are referred to as *natural* elements. Examples of natural elements include iron (Fe), oxygen (O), mercury (Hg), copper (Cu), aluminum (Al), hydrogen (H), sodium (Na), gold (Au), silver (Ag), sulfur (S), and carbon (C). Hydrogen (H) is the lightest element with only one proton in its nucleus while uranium (U) is one of the heaviest at 92. Currently, 113 total elements exist, including those that are man-made (*artificial* elements) with new ones periodically being synthesized.

Elements are composed of a single kind of atom; if it is composed of different atoms in a fixed ratio, it is referred to as a **compound.** Water (H_2O) is a compound composed of different atoms. It can be separated into simpler substances, thus it is not an element. It separates into two different gases, oxygen (O_2) and hydrogen (H_2), which are elements.

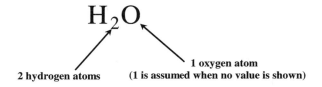

Table salt (NaCl) is also a compound composed of the elements sodium (Na) and chlorine (Cl). Table sugar or sucrose ($C_{12}H_{22}O_{11}$), is a compound formed from a combination of the three elements—carbon (C), hydrogen (H), and oxygen (O)—in a distinct ratio. Important characteristics of a compound are:

(a) Compounds are made from simpler substances called elements, and can be decomposed into elements by ordinary chemical means.

(b) The elements of which a compound is composed (its components) are combined in a definite proportion by mass. This proportion is the same in all samples of the compound.

(c) The chemical and physical properties of a compound are different from those of its components.

Of the more than 100 known elements, eight make up more than 98% of the Earth's crust [oxygen (O), silicon (Si), aluminum (Al), iron (Fe), calcium (Ca), sodium (Na), potassium (K), and magnesium (Mg)].

A **mixture** consists of two or more substances (elements or compounds) physically mixed together but not chemically combined like in a compound. A **solution** (also called a mixture) with no visible differing parts (e.g., a single phase) is referred to as **homogenous.** Sugar dissolved in water produces a single phase homogeneous mixture (or solution) of sugar water. A **heterogenous** mixture has visibly different parts (or layers or phases). Most salad dressings, for example, have visible different parts no matter how thoroughly they are mixed and can be separated by ordinary physical means (Chart 1-2).

Metals and Nonmetals. Most elements fall into one of two groups—*metals* or *nonmetals* (refer to the Periodic Table inside the front cover of this book). Metals conduct heat and electricity readily and reflect light (have luster) (Table 1-2). Most metals are quite ductile (capable of being drawn into wires) and malleable (capable of being hammered into sheets). These properties exist because electrons in metals are continually exchanged between atoms and are not restricted to fixed positions.

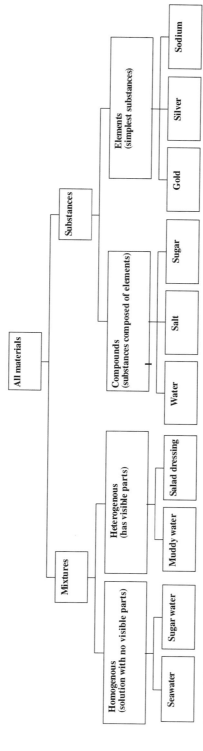

Chart 1-2. Classification of materials. Through chemical reactions, elements combine to form compounds. Through physical changes, substances are mixed to form mixtures.

TABLE 1-2. Properties of Metals and Nonmetals

Metals	Nonmetals
Have a luster (shine)	Have low luster
Good conductors of heat	Poor conductors of heat
Good conductors of electricity	Poor conductors of electricity
Malleable (capable of being hammered into sheets)	Nonmalleable
Ductile (capable of being drawn into wire)	Nonductile (brittle)

This property is referred to as the "sea of electron" effect. Metals also have fewer electrons in their outer shells than nonmetals. Examples include copper (Cu), platinum (Pt), silver (Ag), aluminum (Al), mercury (Hg), magnesium (Mg), tin (Sn), zinc (Zn), and gold (Au).

Nonmetallic elements typically have opposite characteristics of metals. Nonmetals are generally lighter in weight than metals; they are brittle (not malleable); not ductile; vary in color; and are poor conductors of electricity and heat (Table 1-2). These properties are due to nearly complete or filled outer shells with electrons that are held relatively rigidly, and thus tend to be somewhat less reactive. Examples include sulfur (S), chlorine (Cl), carbon (C), nitrogen (N), and oxygen (O).

Except for the noble gases, no element in the free state possesses the stable, complete outermost shell. All elements with incomplete outer shells tend to combine with other elements and thereby undergo significant bonding under ordinary conditions. Therefore, the completeness of the outermost shell is a factor in determining bonding capacity of an element; that is, the ability of its atoms to combine with other atoms and will be discussed in further details later in this chapter.

Naming Elements. Elements are often named after the discoverer. Different symbols are used to designate each different element. The symbol of an element is either the first letter of the name or the first letter followed by some significant other letter. The first letter of the symbol is always capitalized and the second letter (if used) is always lower case. For examples, the symbol of carbon is C; the symbol of calcium is Ca; the symbol of chromium is Cr; and, the symbol of cobalt is Co. The symbols of some elements are derived from languages other than English. For example, the symbol for gold, Au, is derived from the Latin word, *aurum*; sodium (Na) is from *natrium*; while iron has the symbol Fe, from *ferrum*.

Grouping Elements—The Periodic Table. One of the great milestones in chemistry's evolution was the arrangement of elements into groups with similar properties. The **Periodic Table** or chart shown on the inside front cover of this text illustrates this grouping of elements. In this table the metallic elements are located on the left side of the heavy line that runs diagonally across the table while the nonmetals are located to the right.

The periodic table is read like a newspaper, from left to right and down the page. Each horizontal row of the periodic table represents a **period** or **series.** An electron is added to the valence (outer) shell of the atoms of each element as one moves from left to right within each of the seven periods.

The vertical columns of elements in the periodic table are called **groups** or **families.** In older periodic tables, a Roman numeral and a capital letter were used to identify each group. Today, numbers from 1 to 18 are used to identify these. In general, elements in the same group have similar properties and have the same number and similar arrangement of outer-shell (valence) electrons. Each element is located within a square containing the symbol, relative atomic mass, and atomic number of that element. The elements in several of the groups have family names. These are:

Group IA (1), the Alkali (or Sodium) Family. These are highly reactive metals, silvery in color, with relatively low densities. They are easily oxidized (corroded) in air and react vigorously with water to form hydrogen gas and a class of compounds called **bases** (OH^-).

$$\underset{\text{alkali metal}}{2X(s)} + \underset{\text{water}}{2H_2O(l)} \rightarrow 2X^+(aq) + \underset{\text{base}}{2OH^-(aq)} + \underset{\text{hydrogen gas}}{H_2(g)}$$

where X represents any of the alkali metals (Group IA, or 1).

Due to this oxidation tendency, special storage techniques for these elements in their pure state or form are needed. Many are stored under light oil to keep air and moisture away. These atoms all have only one electron in the outermost shell. Hydrogen (H), sodium (Na), and potassium (K) are commonly used members of Group IA and their reactivity in this group increases from top to bottom of the group in the periodic table. Because of their great reactivity, the compounds they form are more important than the metals themselves, e.g., sodium chloride, sodium hydroxide, sodium carbonate, sodium silicate, and potassium chloride.

Group IIA (2), the Alkaline-earth (or Calcium) Family. These are also silvery metals which react with oxygen-forming oxides and acids to release hydrogen gas. Since the Group IIA (2) metals have two electrons in the outermost shell of their atoms, these are not as reactive as the alkali metals (Group IA, or 1). Like the alkali metals, the reactivity of the alkaline earth metals increases from top to bottom of the group in the periodic table. Magnesium (Mg) and calcium (Ca) are commonly used members of Group IIA. Mg is the lightest metal used for construction and Ca compounds are used as common liming sources.

Group IIIA (13). Aluminum (Al) is the major commercially important element of Group IIIA. Al is the most abundant metal in the Earth's crust, making up 8.3% by mass. Al-containing minerals, such as feldspars, weather to form clay, a major component of soil. Aluminum, of course, is also an important lightweight, corrosion-resistant metal used in many applications of modern life. Boron (B), another member of Group IIIA, is an important micronutrient needed in minor amounts for most plants.

Groups IIIB-IIB (3–12), the Transition Metals. These elements are metallic and include many common metals such as iron (Fe), copper (Cu), gold (Au), and silver (Ag). The oxidation states of these elements may vary depending on energy considerations. Most of the transition elements have more than one kind of ion – for example, iron forms iron(II) ion, Fe^{+2}, and iron(III) ion, Fe^{+3}. Most of the transition metals also have high melting and boiling points and high densities and are hard and strong. Iron (Fe) has many manufacturing and construction uses, while gold is used in jewelry, dentistry, electronics, science, and as a monetary unit. Titanium(IV) oxide is a white-colored member of this group and is used as a white pigment in paint, a coating on paper, and as a filler in plastic and rubber.

Group VA (15), the Nitrogen Family. Nonmetallic members of this group are nitrogen (N) and phosphorus (P), while bismuth (Bi) is metallic, and arsenic (As) and antimony (Sb) have both metallic and nonmetallic (called *metalloids*) properties. The atoms of each of these elements have five electrons in the outer shell and a very stable inner shell. Nitrogen and phosphorus are two major nutrients for plants.

Group VIIA (17), the Halogen Family. Halogens, which means "salt formers," are relatively reactive nonmetals. Seven electrons are found in the outer shells of the atoms of these elements. The reactivity of the halogens decreases from top to bottom of the group. At room temperatures, fluorine (F) and chlorine (Cl) are gases, bromine (Br) is a liquid, and iodine (I) and astatine (At) are solids. Iodine vaporizes easily and forms a violet gas that is highly corrosive. When in their elemental gaseous state, the halogens are found as diatomic (two-atoms) molecules, e.g., F_2, Cl_2, I_2, etc. All of these gases are considered poisonous. Chlorine is the most used halogen for bleach, to purify water, vinyl (plastic) production, and to manufacture other organic and inorganic chemicals. Fluoride is used to fight tooth decay, while iodine is a necessary micronutrient often added in commercial salt sources.

Group O (also referred to as Group 18 or VIII), the Noble Gases. They include helium (He), argon (Ar), krypton (Kr), xenon (Xe), and radon (Rn). These are nonmetals that rarely react with other elements, and are gases at room temperatures. These elements, with the exception of helium, have eight electrons (called an **octet**) in the outer shell, which is the largest number of electrons found in an outer shell, and therefore are virtually unreactive (very stable). Helium's (He) outermost shell (K or 1) is complete with two electrons (a pair), making it stable. When the outer shells are completely filled, the electrons shield, or screen, the positive charge of the nucleus, thus making it extremely difficult for such atoms to combine with others. As a result, the noble gases occur in nature as single atoms. The noble gases were referred to in the past as *inert gases* because they were thought to be chemically inert. However, in 1962 several of these have been made to react to some degree with fluorine and with oxygen. The lack of reactivity of helium and argon, the most common noble gases, is the basis for their main use—as an inert atmosphere for high-temperature processes such as arc welding. Although twice as dense as hydrogen, helium is also used to fill balloons and blimps since it is nonflammable.

Inner Transition Elements, the Lanthanides and Actinides. These are metallic elements listed in the two long rows beneath the table. Uranium (U) and plutonium (Pu) are generally the most widely recognized elements in this group. Almost all of the remaining elements have been synthesized in nuclear reactions and are characterized by their radioactivity and are not found naturally in the Earth's crust. Uranium and plutonium are used in nuclear power plants and in nuclear weapons.

Changes in Matter During Reactions

Chemical and physical changes occur in matter during reactions. Physical changes are those in which certain identifying properties of a substance remain. Examples are freezing, boiling, and dissolving. Chemical changes are those in which different substances with new properties are formed. Reactions that absorb energy as they proceed are **endothermic.** Reactions that liberate energy are **exothermic.** The rates of some chemical reactions can be accelerated by a **catalyst,** which is a substance that speeds up or slows down a chemical reaction without itself being consumed.

In nature, a basic tendency is for processes to occur that lead to a lower energy state. Another basic tendency is for processes to occur that lead to a more disordered or more random state. **Entropy** is the property that describes the disorder of a system. The more disordered the system, the higher its entropy.

Atomic Structure

Electrical forces hold the nuclei and electrons together in an atom. Each electron carries a unit of negative electrical charge, and each proton has an equal sized unit of positive electrical charge. Neutrons carry no charge. The net positive charge of the nucleus is offset by electrons. The electrons of an atom are not distributed uniformly around the nucleus, nor are they distributed randomly. They occupy certain regions of space determined by their energy, usually referred to as **orbits, shells,** or **energy levels.** These orbits can contain a fixed number of electrons. This arrangement of a nucleus and its electrons is referred to as the **atomic structure** (Figure 1-2). Electrons found at different distances from the nucleus have different energies. This ring model helps visualize the energy levels of an atom, helps keep track of the number of electrons in each energy level, and shows how atoms are likely to interact.

Electrons move about the nucleus with different energies. Electrons fit only into specific orbitals and energy levels around the nucleus, and depending upon this energy, some arrangements are more stable than others. This arrangement is similar to an orbiting satellite around the earth except gravitation forces hold a satellite in orbit, whereas electrical attraction of oppositely charged particles holds electrons in an atom. The somewhat random orbiting pattern of electrons is also synonymous to the random flight pattern of bees around a bee hive where no two bees fly exactly the same pattern but overall circle the hive in varying shaped orbits.

An atom is most stable when all of its electrons are at their lowest possible energy levels (called its **ground state**); in other words, closest to the nucleus. However, the attraction between an electron and a nucleus turns into a repulsive force if they approach too close. This repulsion keeps the electrons and nuclei from colliding. The atoms remain stable when the attraction between nuclei and electrons is sufficient to overcome the forces of repulsion.

Orbital Designation

Shells or Energy Levels. Seven principal shells are known and are designated numerically 1 through 7 or previously, alphabetically as K, L, M, N, O, P, and Q. Although seven shells exist, most elements involved in the plant sciences have only four. In the order listed, the letters (or numbers) represent increasingly greater distances from the nucleus and, therefore, higher energy levels. The electrons of an atom fill the energy levels (or shells) in order: the first is filled before the second, the second before the third, and so on. Each shell surrounding the nucleus can accommodate only a fixed number of electrons. The simplest atom, hydrogen, has a single electron that moves around the nucleus in the first energy level, while helium has two (Figure 1-3). Atoms with more than two electrons must have at least two shells to hold these. The first shell (designated as 1 or K) can hold only two electrons, and the second (designated as 2 or L), eight (Table 1-1). Every outer shell similarly can hold no more than eight electrons, except with unusual elements. Eight electrons in an outermost shell is extremely stable and is referred to as an **octet.**

Since the first energy level for most elements is filled by two electrons, additional electrons must occupy higher energy shells, farther from the nucleus. The second

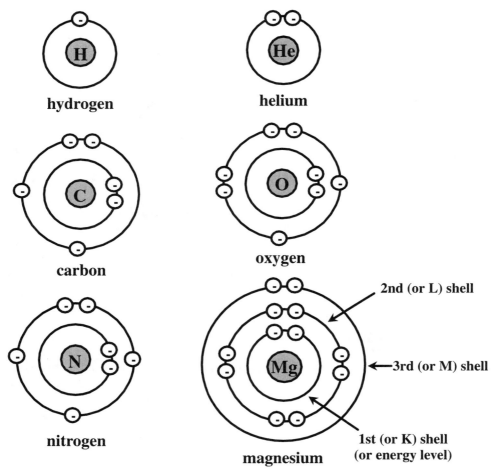

Figure 1-3. Electron configurations for the atoms of several elements found in biology. Refer to Table 1-1 for the number of electrons per shell for each element.

energy level can hold up to eight electrons, and so can the third energy level of elements through atomic number 20 (calcium). Carbon, nitrogen, and oxygen nuclei have six, seven, and eight protons, respectively (Table 1-1), and they exert a much stronger attraction for electrons than hydrogen. In the atom of sodium, for example, 11 electrons occur, two in the first shell, eight in the second, and one electron in a third (designated as 3 or M) shell. For elements of higher atomic number than 20, the pattern becomes more complex.

The outermost principal energy level of any atom is called the **valence shell.** The electrons in this outer shell are called **valence electrons.** The chemical nature of an element depends largely on the number of valence electrons, which varies from 1 to 8. Refer to Appendix A for additional information on electron (or orbital) pairs.

Electrons and Energy. The distance between an electron and the nucleus around which it moves is determined by the electron's potential energy, or *energy of position.* The more energy an electron has, the farther it moves from the nucleus. Thus an electron with a relatively small amount of energy is found close to the nucleus and is said to be at a low energy level. An electron with more energy is farther from the nucleus, at a higher energy level. With a sufficient input of energy, an electron can move from a lower to a higher energy level, but not to an energy state somewhere in between. An atom that has absorbed sufficient energy to boost an electron to a higher energy level is said to be in an *excited state.* As long as the electron remains at the higher level it possesses the added energy. When it returns to the lower energy level (or *decays*), as it tends to do, the added energy (often as radiation) is released. The most stable state of an atom is called its *ground state* and has this lower energy.

Isotopes. Although all atoms of a particular element have the same number of protons in their nuclei, atoms of the element may contain different numbers of neutrons. These different forms of the same element, differing in atomic weight (number of neutrons) but not in atomic number (a.k.a., number of protons), are known as **isotopes** (*iso*—meaning "same"). For example, the most common isotope of hydrogen may be shown using the symbol ^1H. This isotope contains one proton and no neutrons in the nucleus. The total number of protons and neutrons is shown as a superscript. Deuterium (or heavy hydrogen, ^2H) is another isotope of hydrogen that contains one proton and one neutron. Tritium (^3H) is a third hydrogen isotope that contains one proton and two neutrons (Figure 1-4). The atomic weight of an element having two or more isotopes is a weighted average value calculated for the naturally occurring mixture of isotopes.

Some isotopes (for example, tritium, ^3H) are *radioactive.* This means the nucleus is unstable and emits energy as it changes (or decays) to a more stable form. The energy (particles or rays) released by **radioactive isotopes** (also called **radioisotopes**) can be detected by various means, such as with a Geiger counter or on photographic films. The rate of decay of a radioisotope is measured in terms of **half-life,** which is the time in which half the atoms in a sample lose their radioactivity and become stable. Half-lives vary widely; for example, the radioactive nitrogen isotope ^{13}N has a half-life of 10 minutes while tritium (^3H) has a half-life

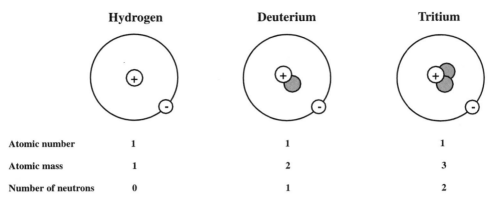

	Hydrogen	Deuterium	Tritium
Atomic number	1	1	1
Atomic mass	1	2	3
Number of neutrons	0	1	2

Figure 1-4. The three isotopes of hydrogen differ due to the number of neutrons. Since they have the same number of protons, the three isotopes have the same atomic number. Neutrons only cause atoms to acquire additional electrons to move at similar speeds.

of over 12 years. For certain radioactive elements, their half-lives are quite long. For example, uranium 238's half-life is 4.5×10^9 (or 4,500,000,000) years, which causes a major problem in handling and disposal of its radioactive "waste."

Radioisotopes are widely used in biological research. They are used to *date,* or determine the age of fossils. They are also used as *tracers* to trace or follow the course of many essential chemical reactions in living systems. For example, radioactive carbon dioxide ($^{14}CO_2$) was used to elucidate the pathways of photosynthesis, since isotopes of an element, ^{14}C in this case, have the same chemical properties as the nonradioactive isotope. Isotopes are also used in **autoradiography,** a technique where a sample of material containing a radioisotope is exposed to a sheet of photographic film. Energy emitted from the isotope leaves traces on the film and so reveals the exact location of the isotope within the specimen. Herbicides containing radioactive carbon are often applied to plants, and the treated plant is then exposed at various timings to photographic film to determine the uptake and translocation properties of the herbicide within the plant.

The Basis of Chemical Reactivity

Atoms react by losing, gaining, or sharing electrons. The manner in which an atom reacts chemically is determined by the number and arrangement of its electrons. As discussed, an atom is most stable when all of its electrons are at their lowest possible energy level. Moreover, an element having atoms with a completely filled outermost energy level is more stable than an element having atoms with a partially filled outer energy level. Oxygen, for example, requires eight electrons to achieve a neutral charge. Two of these are in the inner shell and six are in the outer shell. Oxygen, therefore, needs to gain two electrons to stabilize its outer shell to eight. This gain of electrons, thus attaining a more negative oxidation state, is called **reduction.** Magnesium (Mg) has two electrons in its outer shell. When Mg loses these two electrons, its outer shell contains eight electrons and the resulting ion has an excess positive two charge. The loss of electrons, thus attaining a more positive oxidation state, is called **oxidation.** In another example, helium (atomic number 2), neon (atomic number 10), and argon (atomic number 18) have completely filled outer energy levels and so tend to be unreactive. This also results in equal numbers of electrons and protons, so the atoms are electrically neutral.

The outermost shell of electrons, called the **valence shell,** determines the chemical behavior of most elements. The Lewis Dot system is often used to simplify electron structures of atoms and allows for visualizing where the electrons are lost, gained, or shared by different atoms in the formation of compounds or molecules. It is often diagramed as a dot system when writing chemical structures and equations to indicate the number of only the valence (outer shell) electrons. The symbol of the element is used and the electrons (designated as dots) are distributed along the two vertical and two horizontal surfaces of an imaginary square. Begin at the top and proceed clockwise. Distribute the first four dots around the chemical symbol before putting two dots next to each other. This essentially conforms to four orbitals which can each contain a maximum of two electrons and thus, accommodate all the eight valence electrons needed for chemical stability. All the elements in the same group of the Periodic Table have the same notation since they all have the same number of outermost electrons. For example, the Lewis Dot diagram for a sodium atom is the same as that for a lithium atom and the diagram for an oxygen atom is the same as that for a selenium atom as they are both members of group VIA (or 16). The Lewis symbols of the first 20 elements of the periodic table are shown below.

Ḣ							Ḧe	Ḣ							Ḧe
L̇i	Be·	Ḃ·	·Ċ·	·N̈·	·Ö:	·F̈:	:N̈e:	L̇i	Be	Ḃ·	Ċ·	·N̈·	·Ö:	·F̈:	:N̈e:
Ṅa	Mg·	Al̇·	·Ṡi·	·P̈·	·S̈:	·C̈l:	:Är:	Ṅa	Ṁg	Al̇·	Ṡi·	·P̈·	·S̈:	·C̈l:	:Är:
K̇	Ċa							K̇	Ċa						

| **Ground State** | **Exited State** |

In their ground state or unexcited state, electrons usually pair up. However, in their excited state, electrons are unpaired where possible as shown.

The Lewis Dot system indicates the number of electrons that can be lost, gained, or shared. There are two possible structures for carbon, which accounts in part for the large number of carbon compounds possible. The number of bonds that an element usually forms in compounds equals the number of unpaired electrons. For example, H can form 1 bond, Be—2, B—3, C—4, N—3, O—2, F—1, and Ne—0.

A simple method of producing Lewis Dot symbols in the excited state is to place one dot representing a valence electron on each side or face of an imaginary square if four electrons are available. If not, place only the number of valence electrons available. If there are more than four electrons, start pairing them up on the faces.

Electron transfer using the Lewis Dot system for formation of ionic compounds can be demonstrated for the formation of sodium chloride (table salt):

Example:

$$\overset{\bullet}{Na} \xrightarrow{\text{oxidation}} Na^+ \quad + \quad \bullet \text{ (1 electron)}$$

$$:\overset{\displaystyle ..}{\underset{\displaystyle ..}{Cl}}\cdot \;\; + \quad \bullet \xrightarrow{\text{reduction}} [:\overset{\displaystyle ..}{\underset{\displaystyle ..}{Cl}}:]^-$$

The ionic compound formed (NaCl, sodium chloride or table salt) would be shown using the Lewis Dot system as:

$$\overset{\bullet}{Na} \qquad + \qquad :\overset{\displaystyle ..}{\underset{\displaystyle ..}{Cl}}\cdot \longrightarrow Na^+[:\overset{\displaystyle ..}{\underset{\displaystyle ..}{Cl}}:]^-$$

The formation of sodium chloride also represents an oxidation-reduction reaction since sodium loses an electron (is oxidized), while chlorine gains this electron (is reduced).

In atoms of most elements the outer energy level is only partially filled, which is an unstable arrangement. These atoms tend to interact with other atoms in such a way that, after reaction, both atoms have completely filled outer energy levels. Some atoms lose electrons while others gain electrons. Sodium has an atomic number of 11, which represents two electrons in its inner shell, eight in its second shell, and one in its third shell. As a consequence, the sodium atom has a tendency to lose this odd electron (or become oxidized), achieving a stable electron configuration of eight in what then becomes its outer shell. The loss of this electron gives sodium a net positive charge of 1. Using chemical symbols, an atom of sodium is represented as Na and a sodium ion which has been oxidized is Na^+. Chlorine, with an atomic number of 17 and 7 electrons in its outer shell, needs to gain one electron in order to stabilize its outer shell to 8. In gaining an electron, the Cl atom acquires a negative charge (is reduced) and becomes Cl^-.

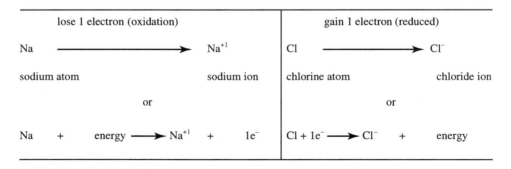

It may be easier to visualize this process by actually counting the number of electrons and protons during an oxidation-reduction reaction. For example, a magnesium (Mg) atom has 12 electrons and protons. During oxidation it loses 2 electrons

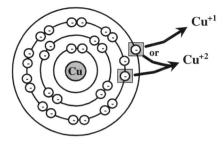

Figure 1-5. The normal electron structure of the copper atom is 2-8-18-1, resulting in an oxidation value of +1. However, an electron from the next-to-outermost shell (designated as the 3 or M shell) can also act as a valence electron, thus giving the atom an oxidation charge of +2.

from its outer shell and has two more protons than electrons. The magnesium ion then has a net 2 positive charge and is indicated by the symbol Mg^{+2}.

ⵔⵔⵔⵔⵔⵔⵔⵔⵔⵔⵔⵔ   lose 2 electrons   ⵔⵔⵔⵔⵔⵔⵔⵔⵔⵔ

⊕⊕⊕⊕⊕⊕⊕⊕⊕⊕⊕⊕ (+ energy) ⟶   ⊕⊕⊕⊕⊕⊕⊕⊕⊕⊕⊕⊕   +   ⵔⵔ

a magnesium (Mg) atom   (oxidation)   Magnesium(Mg^{+2}) ion   +   2 electrons

The number of electrons an atom or molecule must gain or lose to attain a stable configuration in its outer shell is its **oxidation state** which in the past was referred to as its **valence** (Table 1-1). From the examples above, magnesium ions (Mg^{+2}) have an oxidation state (or valence) of $^+2$ because it has lost two electrons, and chlorine ions (Cl^-) have an oxidation state (or valence) of $^-1$ because it has gained one electron.

Some metallic elements may have more than one oxidation state (or valence). Such elements are heavier atoms that have three or more filled shells and in which an electron may move from one shell to another. Iron (Fe), for example, can have a charge of $^+2$ or $^+3$ depending on the energy available in the reaction while copper (Cu) may have a charge of $^+1$ or $^+2$ (Figure 1-5). Copper not only has only one electron in its outermost (valence) shell, it also has loosely bound electrons in the next-to-outermost shell. This loosely bound electron can move to the outer shell and when combined with certain elements, copper gives up one electron, forming Cu^+ (formerly called cupr*ous*). While with other elements, higher energy in the reaction is necessary for an additional electron loss and copper gives up two electrons, forming Cu^{+2} (formerly called cupr*ic*). This is an important property in its biological activities.

Example:

The formation of magnesium chloride required 2 chlorine ions for each magnesium ion:

Step 1:

$$\overset{\bullet\,\bullet}{Mg} \longrightarrow Mg^+ \; + \quad \bullet \; (1 \text{ electron})$$

$$:\overset{\bullet\bullet}{\underset{\bullet\bullet}{Cl}}\bullet \; + \quad \bullet \longrightarrow [:\overset{\bullet\bullet}{\underset{\bullet\bullet}{Cl}}:]^-$$

Step 2:

$$\overset{\bullet}{Mg^+} \longrightarrow Mg^{++} \; + \quad \bullet \; (1 \text{ electron})$$

$$:\overset{\bullet\bullet}{\underset{\bullet\bullet}{Cl}}\bullet \; + \quad \bullet \longrightarrow [:\overset{\bullet\bullet}{\underset{\bullet\bullet}{Cl}}:]^-$$

Chlorine, in nature, is found as a diatomic molecule (Cl_2) which requires two electrons from Mg to form magnesium chloride ($MgCl_2$). The loss/gain of electrons may be summarized as shown:

$$\overset{\bullet\bullet}{Mg} \; + \; 2\bullet\overset{\bullet\bullet}{\underset{\bullet\bullet}{Cl}}\bullet \longrightarrow Mg^{++} \; + \; 2[:\overset{\bullet\bullet}{\underset{\bullet\bullet}{Cl}}:]^-$$

$$\quad\quad\quad \text{(oxidized)} \quad\quad\quad\quad\quad \text{(reduced)}$$

This leads to a foundation for writing formulas for compounds.

Some of the chemical elements have a higher affinity for their electrons than others. These elements have a tendency to share their electrons with other atoms rather than give up or accept electrons in order to obtain an octet or complete outer shell. This sharing results in the formation of molecules or compounds that are covalently bonded. Hydrogen (H^+) is one such element along with oxygen, nitrogen, and members of the halogen family (members of vertical column VII-A [or 17] on the periodic table). These elements share electrons with unpaired electrons of other elements as well as with like atoms.

The gaseous elements on the periodic table with the exception of the noble gases form covalent bonds in this manner with atoms of their own kind. This results in the formation of diatomic molecules (2-atom molecules). These gases are found in this molecular configuration in nature (H_2, O_2, F_2, etc.).

Example:

Lewis dot structures for several covalent molecules:

F_2 :F̈:F̈: or **F–F** NH_3 **H:N̈:H** or **H–N̈–H**
                                              H   **H**

HF   **H:F̈:** or **H–F** H_2O **:Ö:H** or **:Ö–H**
                                          H   **H**

The electron-dot structure can be used to indicate shared electrons; however, chemists frequently use a dash (–) such as shown above for water (H–O–H) and other molecules. This dash represents a pair of shared electrons. This type of formula is called a *structural formula,* while the *molecular formula* (e.g., H_2O for water) indicates only the actual composition (ratio) of atoms in the molecule.

Electronegativity. The atomic nuclei of different elements have different degrees of attraction for electrons in their chemical bond. The affinity of an element for electrons to move to the most stable possible configuration in a covalent bond is known as its **electronegativity.** Since an element that gains electrons is acting as an oxidizing agent (gains electrons), electronegativity is also a measure of the oxidizing strength of an element. Atoms having high ionization energies and high electron affinities, that is, atoms that lose electrons with difficulty and gain electrons readily, are very electronegative. Electronegativity is expressed on a scale of 0 to 4, with helium and other noble gases having electronegativity of 0 and fluorine having an electronegativity of 4 (Table 1-1). In the periodic table, electronegativities for elements increase from the bottom of the table to the top and from left to right. Fluorine (F) in the upper right-hand corner in the periodic table, for example, is a stronger oxidizing agent than any other element.

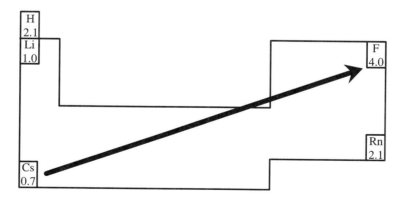

Electronegativity of the elements increase from bottom left of the periodic table to the upper right. Fluorine (F), in the upper right-hand corner, is a stronger oxidizing agent than any other element.

A higher value means a stronger tendency to retain the electrons, that is, the more polar (has a slightly positive and negative region) the bond becomes. Differences in electronegativity between two atoms can identify the nature of the chemical bond, whether a bond is more ionic or more covalent. The shorter distance between the nucleus and outer shell electrons causes this greater affinity. For example, a molecule with a mixture of nuclei tends to be negative near the nitrogen and oxygen nuclei, and positive near the carbon, hydrogen, phosphorus, and sulfur nuclei. With water (H_2O), the hydrogen of one water molecule is attracted to the oxygen of the neighboring water molecule because of their slightly opposite charges. The resulting hydrogen bond gives water many unique properties such as being a universal solvent, having high surface tension, and having relatively high boiling and low freezing points that render it readily available for earthly processes.

When writing formulas, the element furthest to the left in the periodic table (less electronegative) is usually written on the left side of the formula. If two elements are from the same group, the one lower in the column in the periodic table is usually written first. Note: notable exceptions include methane (CH_4) and ammonia (NH_3).

IONS, MOLECULES, AND CHEMICAL BONDS

Except for the noble gases such as He, Ar, Kr, Xe, and Rn, no element in the free state possesses the stable, complete outermost shell. The noble gases are not assigned values because of their relative inertness since their outer shells are complete. Elements with incomplete outer shells tend to combine with other elements and thereby undergo significant bonding. Most elements found in the Earth's crust are in a combined state. The abundance of oxygen primarily accounts for this. Therefore, the completeness of the outermost shell is a factor in determining bonding capacity of an element; that is, the ability of its atoms to combine with other atoms. Only a few metals such as gold (Au) and silver (Ag) are found in a free state in nature.

All atoms are electrically neutral since they have an equal number of positive protons and negative electrons. Atoms can interact to achieve completely filled outer energy levels in different ways—by losing electrons, by gaining electrons, or by sharing electrons with each other. The gain or loss of electrons produces charged atoms, called **ions** (from a Greek word meaning "to go"). An ion is an atom or group of atoms that carries an electrical charge. Ions are symbolized with a superscript to indicate the number and sign of the excess charges. For example, K^+ indicates the potassium ion with one more proton than the number of electrons; the oxygen ion, O^{-2}, has two more electrons than protons. The charge carried by an ion determines how many oppositely charged ions are combined with it in a compound. **Cations** are positively charged ions (for example, K^+) while **anions** are negatively charged ions (for example, O^{-2}). The sharing of electrons produces new, larger particles called **molecules,** which are assemblies of atoms held together by chemical bonds. **Diatomic** molecules contain two atoms including many of the gaseous elements such as hydrogen (H_2), oxygen (O_2), nitrogen (N_2), and chlorine (Cl_2). Some elements such as neon (Ne), argon (Ar), and helium (He) are unreactive under normal conditions. They do not combine with each other or with other elements and consist of only one atom. These are referred to as **monatomic.** The elements sulfur (S), and phosphorus (P) occur as multiatomic molecules in nature, e.g., S_8, P_4, etc.

When an ion is composed of more than one kind of atom, it is called a **polyatomic ion.** For example, a sodium ion (Na^+) is a cation, a chloride ion (Cl^-) is an anion, while a sulfate ion (SO_4^{-2}) is a polyatomic ion because it consists of sulfur (S) and oxygen (O) molecules. The charge carried by an ion determines the ratio in which it combines with other ions. A list of common positive and negative ions is found in Table 1-3. As mentioned earlier, some elements, such as iron (Fe), can exhibit more than one oxidation state (or charge) such as Fe^{+2} and Fe^{+3}.

When different elements combine or mix in a definite and constant proportion and are held together by chemical bonds, the product is a **chemical compound.** Examples of chemical compounds are water (H_2O), table salt or sodium chloride (NaCl), carbon dioxide (CO_2), and glucose ($C_6H_{12}O_6$). The formula of a chemical compound consists of the symbols of the chemical elements involved and subscripts indicate the number of each element. The subscript one ($_1$) is not used since the symbol represents one atom. For glucose, its chemical formula, $C_6H_{12}O_6$, indicates six atoms each of carbon (C_6) and oxygen (O_6) and 12 atoms of hydrogen (H_{12}). For copper sulfate, $CuSO_4$, the formula shows that this compound has the proportions of one copper (Cu) atom, one sulfur (S) atom, and four oxygen (O_4) atoms.

Writing Chemical Formulas

When writing chemical formulas, the first step is to recognize the symbols of the elements in the compound. These can be found in tables such as Table 1-3. From this, the ion notations (including their charges) are written in the order named. The number of each kind of ion is then adjusted to provide a net total positiveness (valence $\times$ subscript) and negativeness (valence $\times$ subscript) charges of equal but opposite magnitude. This is referred to as assigning oxidation numbers (see box). For example, sodium chloride (NaCl) is represented by positively charged sodium ions, Na^+, and negatively charged chloride, Cl^- ions. When writing formulas for ionic compounds, the total charge of the first element (valence $\times$ subscript) must be equal and opposite the total charge (valence $\times$ subscript) of the second ion found in the compound. For sodium chloride, the charge of one sodium ion is equal ($^+1$) and opposite the charge of one chloride ion ($^-1$).

For polyatomic ions containing oxygen, these have four different forms and remembering the -*ate* form of each eliminates memorization of the other three. Some of the more common polyatomic ions include chlor*ate,* ClO_3^-, sulf*ate,* SO_4^{-2}; carbon*ate,* CO_3^{-2}; nitr*ate,* NO_3^-; phosph*ate,* PO_4^{-3}; and bor*ate,* BO_3^{-3}. Oxidation numbers involving these and other ions will be discussed later.

Using the Periodic Table to Determine Oxidation Numbers. When using the periodic table, some general rules can be followed.

1. The algebraic sum of oxidation numbers (total charges) of all atoms in a formula is always zero.
2. The oxidation number in the periodic table for Groups IA (or 1) = $^+1$; IIA (2) = $^+2$; and, IIIA (B and Al only) = $^+3$. F = $^-1$. For example,

TABLE 1-3. Some Common Cations (Positively Charged Ions) and Anions (Negatively Charged Ions)

+1	Name	+2	Name	+3	Name	+4	Name
NH_4^{+}	ammonium	Ba^{+2}	barium	Al^{+3}	aluminum	Ce^{+4}	cerium(IV)
Cu^{+}	copper(I)	Cd^{+2}	cadmium	As^{+3}	arsenic(III)	Ni^{+4}	nickel(IV)
H^{+}	hydrogen	Ca^{+2}	calcium	Ce^{+3}	cerium(III)	Sn^{+4}	tin(IV)
Li^{+}	lithium	Cr^{+2}	chromium(II)	Cr^{+3}	chromium(III)	Ti^{+4}	titanium
Hg^{+}	mercury(I)	Co^{+2}	cobalt(II)	Co^{+3}	cobalt(III)		
K^{+}	potassium	Cu^{+2}	copper(II)	Fe^{+3}	iron(III)		
Na^{+}	sodium	Fe^{+2}	iron(II)	Ni^{+3}	nickel(III)		
Ag^{+}	silver	Pb^{+2}	lead(II)	Au^{+3}	gold(III)		
Au^{+}	gold(I)	Mg^{+2}	magnesium				
		Hg^{+2}	mercury(II)				
		Ni^{+2}	nickel(II)				
		Sn^{+2}	tin(II)				
		Zn^{+2}	zinc				

−1	Name	−2	Name	−3	Name	−4	Name
$C_2H_3O_2^{-}$	acetate	CO_3^{-2}	carbonate	AsO_4^{-3}	arsenate	$Fe(CN)_6^{-4}$	ferrocyanide
HCO_3^{-}	bicarbonate	CrO_4^{-2}	chromate	AsO_3^{-3}	arsenite	$P_2O_7^{-4}$	pyrophosphate
HSO_4^{-}	hydrogen sulfate	$Cr_2O_7^{-2}$	dichromate	BO_3^{-3}	borate	SiO_4^{-4}	orthosilicate
HS^{-}	hydrogen sulfide	O^{-2}	oxide	PO_4^{-3}	phosphate		
Br^{-}	bromide	O_2^{-2}	peroxide	$Fe(CN)_6^{-3}$	ferricyanide		
Cl^{-}	chloride	SO_4^{-2}	sulfate	N^{-3}	nitride		
ClO_3^{-}	chlorate	S^{-2}	sulfide				
ClO_2^{-}	chlorite	SO_3^{-2}	sulfite				
CN^{-}	cyanide	$S_2O_3^{-2}$	thiosulfate				
F^{-}	fluoride	HPO_4^{-2}	monohydrogen phosphate or biphosphate				
OH^{-}	hydroxide						
NO_3^{-}	nitrate						
NO_2^{-}	nitrite						
MnO_4^{-}	permanganate						
SCN^{-}	thiocyanate						
$H_2PO_4^{-}$	dihydrogen phosphate						

$$Na = +1 \text{ from IA (or1)}$$
$$Mg = +2 \text{ from IIA (or 2)}$$
$$Al = +3 \text{ from IIIA (or 3)}$$

Elements in IVA (or 4) do not always comply with the above statement. The values of +4 or −4 should be considered but there are many exceptions. Group VA (15) is usually +3, −3, or +5; Group VIA (16) is usually −2; Group VIIA (17) is usually −1.

3. $H = {}^+1$ except in binary compounds with metals where $H = {}^-1$, such as with NaH where $H = {}^-1$.
4. $O = {}^-2$. Nonmetals in group VA to VIIA (5 to 7) usually have negative values because they accept electrons. These elements can also share electrons. When writing formulas, the value of the Roman numeral above the group can be subtracted from 8 (8 electrons complete the outer valence shell) to determine the magnitude of the negative charge. For example,

$$F = -1 \text{ from VIIA (or 7)}$$
$$O = -2 \text{ from VIA (or 16)}$$
$$N = -3 \text{ from VA (or 5)}$$

Another reason to determine oxidation numbers of a substance is because an increase in acidity is common with increasing oxidation numbers. For example, the sulfur in sulfuric acid, H_2SO_4, has an oxidation number of +6 and is a stronger acid than the sulfur in sulfurous acid, H_2SO_3, which has an oxidation number of +4.

Example:

Which is the stronger acid,

a. HNO_3 or HNO_2?

oxidation number of each element	+1	?	−2	+1	?	−2
formula	H	N	O_3	H	N	O_2
total oxidation number of each element	+1	+?	−6 = 0	+1	+?	−4 = 0
		? = +5			? = +3	

For N in HNO_3; +1 +? −6 = +5 and for HNO_2; +1 +? −4 = +3; therefore, HNO_3 has a higher oxidation state for its N (+5) than in HNO_2 (+3), which indicates HNO_3 is the stronger acid.

b. $HClO_3$ or $HClO_4$?

oxidation number of each element	+1	?	−2	+1	?	−2
formula	H	Cl	O_3	H	Cl	O_4
total oxidation number of each element	+1	+?	−6 = 0	+1	+?	−8 = 0
		? = +5			? = +7	

$HClO_4$ has a higher oxidation for its Cl (+7) than in $HClO_3$ (+5), which indicates $HClO_4$ is the stronger acid.

Determining Formulas from Names. Knowing oxidation numbers also can be used in writing chemical formulas from names. For example, with lead(IV) oxide, the Roman numeral IV indicates an oxidation number of +4 for the lead (Pb) in this compound. Since the sum of oxidation numbers must equal zero, the sum of oxygen in lead(IV) must equal −4. According to rule 4 for assigning oxidation numbers, the oxidation number of oxygen is −2, thus two oxygen atoms are present to total zero, leaving,

$$+4 \text{ (from lead(IV))} + [2 \times -2 \text{ (from oxygen)}] = 0$$

Therefore, the formula for lead(IV) oxide is PbO_2.

Example:

Determine the formula of the following compound names:

a. **Lithium chlorite.** From the assigning oxidation rule 2, lithium is a member of the IA periodic group, thus has an oxidation value of +1. From rule 4, oxygen has a −2 value. Therefore, to algebraically equal zero, +1 (from lithium) + −2 (from oxygen) leaves +1 for chlorine, $LiClO_2$. Alternatively, from Table 1-3, chlorite is shown to be ClO_3^-, thus requires a +1 oxidation value from one lithium (Li) ion to sum zero.
b. **Sodium sulfite.** From Rule 1, IA group members, such as sodium, have a +1 oxidation value. From Table 1-3, sulfite is SO_3^{-2}. To algebraically equal zero, two sodium (+1) ions are needed for the −2 value from sulfite (SO_3^{-2}), and the formula is Na_2SO_3.
c. **Aluminum sulfate.** From Table 1-3, sulfate is SO_4^{-2} and from Rule 2, aluminum (Al) is +3. Since these do not sum zero (+3 + −2 ≠ 0), the lowest common denominator for 2 and 3 is needed which is 6. Therefore, the aluminum oxidation value equals +6 and the SO_4 is −6. To accomplish this, two Al ions are needed ($2 \times {}^+3 = {}^+6$) and three SO_4 ions are needed ($3 \times -2 = -6$), thus the formula is $(Al)_2(SO_4)_3$.
d. **Potassium nitrate.** From Table 1-3, nitrate's formula is NO_3^- and from Rule 2, potassium's oxidation value is +1. Since these sum zero (+1 from K + −1 from $NO_3^- = 0$), the formula is KNO_3.

When compounds are composed of ions that are not equally charged, these compounds must be adjusted so that the algebraic sum of the oxidation numbers is equal to zero. For example, calcium chloride, $CaCl_2$, is composed of the calcium (Ca^{+2}) ion and chloride (Cl^-) ions. For the algebraic sum of the ions to be equal to zero, two chloride ions are needed for each divalently charged calcium ion. The subscript '$_2$' indicates two chloride ions are needed for one calcium ion in calcium chloride. No subscript is required for Ca since only one Ca^{+2} ion is represented in the formula $CaCl_2$ and when this occurs, the symbol represents one atom and eliminates the need for the subscript$_1$.

For more complex compounds consisting of polyatomic ions, parentheses are used around the ion and subscripts are placed outside and to the right to indicate more than one ion. For example, a common fertilizer, ammonium sulfate, is composed of two polyatomic ions—ammonium, NH_4^+, and sulfate, SO_4^{-2}. In order for the $+$ and $-$ charges to be equal, two NH_4^+ ions are required for each SO_4^{-2} ion. This is represented in the formula by enclosing the NH_4^+ ion in parentheses with the subscript '$_2$' outside. The final empirical (simplest) formula is then written as $(NH_4)_2SO_4$.

Another example involves calcium nitrate, also a popular fertilizer source. From Table 1-3, the calcium ion is Ca^{+2} while the nitrate ion is NO_3^-. Again, the total positive and negative charge represented in the formula must be equal to zero. Because the positive charge is 2 (Ca^{+2}) and the negative charge is 1 (NO_3^-), two nitrate ions are needed to make the algebraic sum equal to zero. The formula is written as $Ca(NO_3)_2$.

Examples:

Assign oxidation numbers to each element in the following:

1. P_4 With any free element (those not bonded to any other element), the oxidation number of each atom is zero, therefore the oxidation number of P = 0.
2. H_2SO_4 Since the oxidation of H = $^+1$ and O = -2 and the sum of all elements in the formula must equal zero, this can be deduced by writing the oxidation number over each element and the total oxidation number for that element underneath it.

$$\text{oxidation number of each element} \rightarrow +1 \quad ? \quad -2$$

$$\text{formula} \rightarrow H_2 \quad S \quad O_4$$

$$\text{total oxidation number of each element} \rightarrow +2 \quad ? \quad -8 \ = 0$$

The oxidation number of H = $+1$; since two H^+ atoms are present, the total oxidation number of all H^+ is $+2$. Similarly, the total oxidation number of O is -8 ($-2 \times 4 = -8$). To determine the oxidation number of S, algebraically add the total values to equal zero:

$$+2 \text{ (from } H_2) + ? \text{ (S)} + -8 \text{ (from } O_4, 4 \times -2) = 0; \quad ? = +6$$

Since there is only one S atom, $+6$ is the oxidation number of S.

$$\text{oxidation number of each element} \rightarrow +1 \quad +6 \quad -2$$
$$\text{formula} \rightarrow H_2 \quad S \quad O_4$$
$$\text{total oxidation number of each element} \rightarrow +2 \quad +6 \quad -8 = 0$$

3. $Au(NO_3)_3$ In this example, the oxidation number of Au and N are not known. However, from Table 1-3, it is seen that the total oxidation value of $NO_3 = -1$, therefore, the oxidation value of N can be found.

$$\text{oxidation number of each element} \rightarrow ? \quad -2$$
$$\text{formula} \rightarrow N \quad O_3^{-1}$$
$$\text{total oxidation number of each element} \rightarrow ? \quad -6 \ = -1$$

For N; $? + {}^-6 = -1$. Thus, the oxidation value of N must be $+5$. To determine the value of Au, set up the whole equation:

$$\text{oxidation number of each element} \rightarrow ? \quad -2 \quad -2$$
$$\text{formula} \rightarrow Au \quad (N \quad O_3)_3$$
$$\text{total oxidation number of each element} \rightarrow ? \quad +15 \quad -18 \ = 0$$
$$\text{For Au, } ? = +3.$$

Naming Inorganic Compounds

Many rules and exceptions are involved when correctly naming inorganic compounds. These are listed and explained in Appendix B.

IONS AND IONIC INTERACTIONS

Chemical bonds are the forces holding atoms together in elements, compounds, and metals. When chemical reactions occur, chemical bonds break in the reactants and form in the products. The two major types of chemical bonds are **ionic bonds** and **covalent bonds,** which are formed by the transfer and sharing of valence (or oxidation) electrons, respectively. **Valence electrons** are the electrons in the outermost, or valence shell. All elements in a group usually have the same number of valence electron(s) in the valence shell. For example, the elements in Group 17 have seven valence electrons. Possession of the same number of valence electrons by all members of a group is the reason the members of a group have similar properties.

Atoms tend to stabilize or complete their valence shells and remain in a lower energy state. For many atoms, the simplest way to attain a completely filled outer energy level is to gain or lose one or more electrons. The following example involves aluminum ionizing where Al^0 contains 3 electrons in its outer shell. To remain in its lower energy state, the Al^0 will lose the 3 valence electrons:

$$Al^0 + energy \rightarrow Al^{+++} + 3\ electrons$$

In another example, a chlorine atom (atomic number 17) needs one electron to complete its outer energy level which contains seven electrons; a sodium atom (atomic number 11) has a single electron in its outer level. If an atom of sodium approaches an atom of chlorine, there is a tendency for the outer electron of the sodium atom to be attracted and added to the outer shell of the chlorine atom which has the higher electronegativity. Each atom would then have a stable electron structure. This outer electron of sodium (Na) is strongly attracted by the chlorine atom (which is highly electronegative, Cl), and a transfer from the sodium atom to the chlorine atom occurs (Figure 1-6).

Although an atom such as sodium may have a strong tendency to lose an electron, electrons do not fly off into space; instead, they are transferred from one atom to another during a chemical reaction or are returned to the original atoms where the energy is lowered. As a result of the transfer, the sodium and chlorine atoms have outer energy levels that are completely filled. Each atom now has an unbalanced (or unequal) numbers of electrons and protons: the sodium ion has 11 protons and 10 electrons (an extra positive charge, designated as Na^+); the chlorine ion has 17 protons and 18 electrons (an extra negative charge, designated as Cl^-). Such interactions involving the mutual attraction of oppositely charged ions (positive and negative) are called **ionic interactions,** and form **ionic bonds.** An ionic bond is a chemical bond resulting from the mutual attraction of oppositely charged ions (e.g., Na^+Cl^-). Metals, with relatively low ionization energies, transfer electrons to nonmetals (with high electron affinities) to form positive and negative ions, respectively. Potassium (atomic number 19) also has a single electron in its outermost energy level and reacts with chlorine to form potassium chloride (K^+Cl^- or KCl).

The calcium ion (Ca^{+2}) is formed by the loss of two electrons; it can attract and hold two Cl^- ions, forming calcium chloride ($Ca^{+2}Cl_2^-$ or $CaCl_2$) (the subscript 2

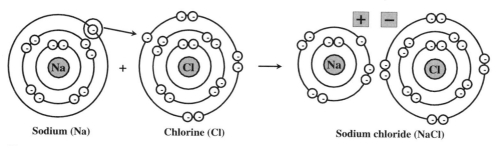

Sodium (Na)   Chlorine (Cl)   Sodium chloride (NaCl)

Figure 1-6. The formation of an ionic (attraction of opposite charges) bond where transferring a single unpaired valence electron gives sodium a stable arrangement (2 + 8) and gives chlorine the electron it needs to have all its energy levels full (2 + 8 + 8). Sodium attains a stable configuration by acting as an electron donor, passing a single outer shell electron to chlorine (an electron acceptor) in order to gain stability. In this process, sodium acquires a positive charge and chlorine a negative charge.

indicates that two atoms of chlorine are present for each atom of calcium). Similarly, magnesium has two valence electrons (two electrons in its outermost or valence shell); thus, one atom of magnesium can combine with two atoms of chlorine, giving up one electron from each to form magnesium chloride, $Mg^{+2}Cl_2^-$ or $MgCl_2$.

Small ions such as Na^+ and Cl^- make up less than 1% of the weight of most living matter, but they play crucial roles. For instance, Na^+ in minute quantities helps regulate stomatal opening and closing in plants but excessive amounts are often toxic. K^+ is the principal positively charged ion in many organisms, and many essential biological reactions occur only in its presence. Mg^{+2} is an integral part of chlorophyll, a molecule in green plants that traps light (radiant energy) from the sun and produces food in the form of glucose. Cl^- is also believed to be required for photosynthesis in chloroplasts.

When writing ionic equations for reactions in solution, strong electrolytes are indicated as being fully ionized, while nonelectrolytes and weak electrolyte formulas are written in the molecular form. Since insoluble substances and escaping gases do not ionize (form separated ions), they are also shown by molecular formulas.

1. Molecular form:

$$NaCl + AgNO_3 \rightarrow NaNO_3 + AgCl\downarrow$$

Ionic form:

$$Na^+ + \mathbf{Cl^-} + \mathbf{Ag^+} + NO_3^- \rightarrow Na^+ + NO_3^- + \mathbf{AgCl\downarrow}$$

2. Molecular form:

$$Ca(OH)_2 + 2HCl \rightarrow CaCl_2 + 2H_2O$$

Ionic form: a neutralization reaction where water as a product is always shown in molecular form

$$Ca^{+2} + \mathbf{2OH^-} + \mathbf{2H^+} + 2Cl^- \rightarrow Ca^{+2} + 2Cl^- + \mathbf{2H_2O}$$

3. Molecular form:

$$NaNO_3 + H_2SO_4 \rightarrow NaHSO_4 + HNO_3\uparrow$$

Ionic form:

$$Na^+ + \mathbf{NO_3^-} + \mathbf{H^+} + HSO_4^- \rightarrow Na^+ + HSO_4^- + \mathbf{HNO_3\uparrow}$$

Molecules and Covalent Bonds

Another way for atoms to complete their outer energy levels (form chemical bonds) is by sharing electrons with other atoms that also seek an octet instead of being transferred between atoms as with ionic bonds. Chemical bonds formed by sharing

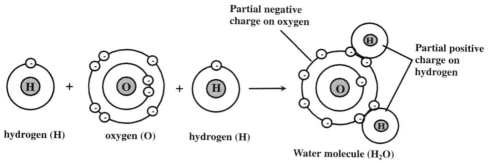

Figure 1-7. Covalent bonds from the mutual sharing of electrons between hydrogen (H) and oxygen (O) atoms to form water.

one or more pairs of electrons in overlapping orbitals are known as **covalent bonds.** With ionic bonds, an electron donor reacts electrically with an electron acceptor. With a covalent bond, each electron spends part of its time around one nucleus and part of its time around the other and they are treated as if they were in the valence shell of each atom. Thus, the sharing of electrons completes the outer energy level of each atom. For example, with water (H_2O), each hydrogen atom needs one more electron to complete its outer shell (Figure 1-7). Each oxygen atom has eight protons and eight electrons. Two of the electrons are in the first shell and six in the second shell, so oxygen needs two more electrons to stabilize its outer shell. If two hydrogen atoms share their electrons with one oxygen atom, the requirement of all three are satisfied and water is formed.

Another example is ammonia, NH_3, where its nitrogen atom has seven protons and has seven electrons, two in the inner shell and five in the outer shell (Table 1-1). Nitrogen needs three electrons to fill its outer shell to achieve an octet (eight); hence, it combines with three hydrogen atoms to form NH_3 which shares its three electrons with the three unpaired electrons of nitrogen.

Elements that form two-atom (or diatomic) molecules with a single covalent bond are H_2, F_2, Cl_2, Br_2, and I_2, O_2, and N_2.

Carbon-Atom Combinations. Of primary importance in living systems is the capacity of carbon to form covalent bonds. Carbon (atomic number 6) has four electrons in its outer energy level. It can share each of these four valence electrons with another carbon atom(s) or with other atoms, forming covalent bonds and producing a stable, filled outer energy level (8 electrons). In methane (CH_4), for example, one carbon atom shares one electron with each of four hydrogen atoms and in carbon dioxide (CO_2), four electrons are shared with each of two oxygen atoms (O::C::O or O=C=O), forming two double covalent bonds. Because carbon is neither strongly electropositive nor strongly electronegative, the covalent bonds formed may be with different elements, most often hydrogen (H), oxygen (O), phosphorus (P), sulfur (S), nitrogen (N), or with other carbon atoms. In fatty acids, the first carbon in the chain bonds with three hydrogen atoms and the next carbon atom. The next carbon atoms share two electrons with each of two hydrogen atoms and each of two more carbon atoms. A carboxyl group (–COOH) is attached to the end of this chain. An example involves stearic acid, a 18-carbon containing fatty acid obtained from animal fat, designated as $C_{17}H_{35}COOH$ or $CH_3(CH_2)_{16}COOH$.

Stearic Acid

Because carbon reacts so readily with other carbon atoms, it can form long chains as well as more complex ring structures. This element can also form double and triple covalent bonds with another carbon atom(s).

Types of Covalent Bonds. Atoms can form three types of covalent bonds, single, double, and triple bonds, depending on how many other atoms it shares electrons with. There are various ways in which atoms can form covalent bonds and fill their outer energy levels. In the water molecule (H_2O) one of the oxygen electrons participates in a covalent bond with one hydrogen atom and the other in a covalent bond with a different hydrogen atom (remember that hydrogen atoms need only two electrons). Two **single bonds** are formed, and all three atoms have filled outer energy levels.

Note that oxygen has two unpaired electrons in its excited state, allowing it to form two bonds with hydrogen ions.

The bonding situation is different in another familiar substance, carbon dioxide (CO_2). In this molecule each oxygen atom is joined to the carbon atom by two pairs of electrons (four total electrons). Such bonds are called **double bonds** (e.g., $O=C=O$). Carbon atoms can form double bonds with each other as well as with other elements, as in ethylene, $H_2C=CH_2$, a fruit ripener and growth regulator, and the components of some fats and oils. Although somewhat rare, carbon atoms can also form **triple bonds** (in which three pairs of electrons are shared), such as with acetylene ($HC\equiv CH$), a fuel in welding and cutting of metals.

Single bonds are flexible, allowing the bonded atoms to rotate in relation to one another. Double bonds are much more rigid, restrict the relative movement of the bonded atoms, and have a higher bond energy than single bonds. Carbon-carbon triple bonds, however, tend not to be very stable as its electrons have a great deal of energy and are typically broken easily.

The nitrogen diatomic molecule (N_2) contains a triple bond that is extremely strong. Lightning with its tremendous energy passes though the atmosphere and will break these bonds as well as those of oxygen. The strong antiseptic smell present after an electrical storm is due to the formation of ozone (O_3) and nitrogen/oxygen combinations. Nitrogen makes up 78% of the air and acts as a dilution agent for the more chemically active oxygen. Oxygen reacts with most substances causing oxidation (rusting) and supports combustion. Without the nitrogen dilution factor, an apparent increase in the oxygen concentration would increase the ease in which matter burns. The friction from walking might cause shoe soles to burn, while a golf ball rolling across a green might catch itself and the grass on fire.

Polar Covalent Bonds. As noted previously, elements differ in electronegativity (their attraction for electrons). In covalent bonds between atoms of different elements, the electrons are not shared equally between the two atoms. The shared electrons tend to spend more time around the nucleus of the more electronegative atom. As a consequence, this part of the molecule has a slightly negative charge, and the region around the less electronegative atom in the molecule has a slightly positive charge.

Covalent bonds in which electrons are shared unequally are known as **polar covalent bonds.** Such bonds often involve oxygen, which is highly electronegative. In molecules that are perfectly symmetrical, such as carbon dioxide, the unequal charges cancel out and the molecule as a whole is nonpolar. However, in asymmetrical molecules such as water, the molecule as a whole is polar, with regions of partial negative charge and regions of partial positive charge. Many of the special properties of water, upon which life depends, result largely from its polar nature.

Using the Lewis Dot system to construct molecules gives clues to the shape of a molecule and also helps to determine if the bond is polar or nonpolar.

In summary, ionic interactions, polar covalent bonds, and nonpolar covalent bonds may be considered as chemical bonds that differ widely in electronegativity between combining atoms. In ionic interactions, there is no electron sharing but rather an electrostatic attraction between oppositely charged ions (e.g., Na^+ and Cl^-). If the electronegativity between two elements is >1.6, the bond is ionic. In polar covalent bonds, electrons are shared, but, because of a difference in electronegativity between bonding atoms (e.g., H and O), they are shared unequally. The greater the electronegativity difference, the more polar the bond will be, as long as this difference is not greater than 1.6. In totally nonpolar covalent bonds, electrons are shared equally; such bonds exist only between identical atoms, as in H_2, Cl_2, O_2, and N_2.

Molecular and Structural Formulas

The properties of molecules depend on their three-dimensional structure—the shape and volume of space occupied by electrons in their outermost energy levels (orbitals). Chemists have developed methods for representing molecules on paper that allow them to keep track of all the atoms and bonds. *Molecular formulas indicate the number and types of atoms in a molecule; structural formulas show the way in which the atoms are bonded to one another.* Sometimes two or more compounds can have the same molecular formula but different structural formulas; such compounds are called **isomers.** Glucose and fructose are one such example, with both having a chemical formula of $C_6H_{12}O_6$ while having different structures.

Isomers

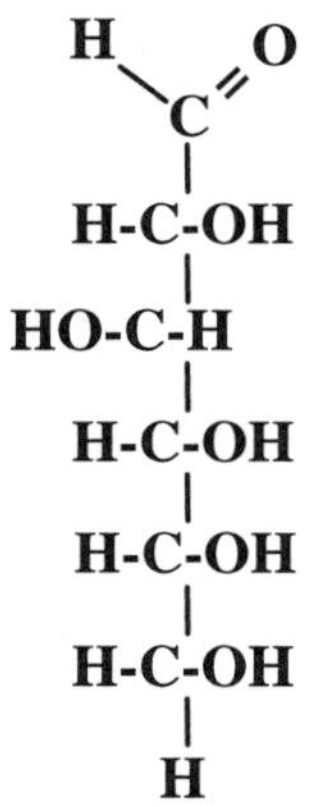

H   O
 \\   ⁄⁄
   C
   |
H-C-OH
   |
HO-C-H
   |
H-C-OH
   |
H-C-OH
   |
H-C-OH
   |
   H

Glucose Formula

H
|
H-C-OH
   |
 C=O
   |
HO-C-H
   |
H-C-OH
   |
H-C-OH
   |
H-C-OH
   |
   H

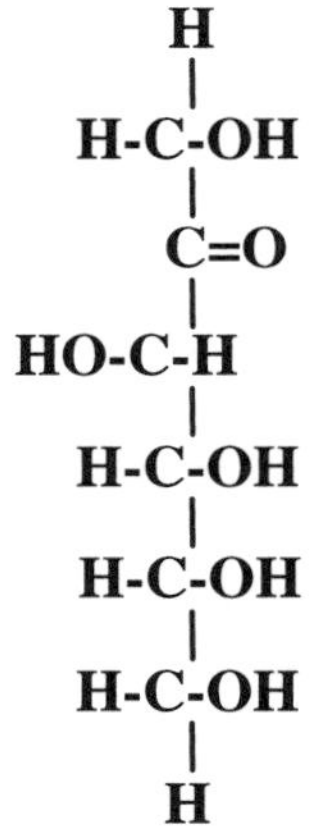

Fructose Formula

SOLUBILITY

Aqueous (water) solutions may contain a wide spectrum of substances. A **solution** (also called **a homogenous mixture**) is a uniform mixture of molecules or ions of two or more substances. The substance present in the largest amount, usually a liquid, is called the **solvent**; whereas, the substances present in lesser amounts are called **solutes.** For example, vinegar is a solution containing 3 to 5% acetic acid by weight and the rest is water (both are liquids): acetic acid is the solute and water is the solvent. In another example, salt is the solute in seawater (Table 1-4). The number of solute molecules in a given volume of solvent is the **solute concentration.** The terms *dilute* and *concentrated* refer to relatively low and high solution concentrations, respectively, but are indeed arbitrary.

The actual solubility of a substance depends on the nature of the solute, the nature of the solvent, temperature, pressure, and other factors which are sometimes difficult to predict. The dissolving of any solute in any solvent provides an illustration of equilibrium. When a solid is placed in water, solute particles immediately go into solution and may be dispersed throughout the solution. As the process continues, the concentration of solute in solution increases, and the rate at which

TABLE 1-4. Types of Solutions

Solute	Solvent	Example
Gas in a	Gas	Air
Gas in a	Liquid	Carbonated beverages [CO_2(g) in H_2O(l)]
Gas in a	Solid	H_2(g) in palladium (Pd(s))
Liquid in a	Liquid	Vinegar [CH_3COOH(l) in H_2O(l)]
Liquid in a	Solid	Dental amalgam [Hg(l) in Ag(s)]
Solid in a	Liquid	Seawater [NaCl(s) in H_2O(l)]
Solid in a	Solid	Brass [Zn(s) in Cu(s)]

solute particles dissolve increases until a state of equilibrium is reached. Equilibrium occurs when the rate at which the solute particles are going into solution equals the rate at which they are returning to the solid state and the solution is then referred to as **saturated.**

Not all substances form true solutions in water. If clay is mixed with water, very little clay actually dissolves. Particles of clay are huge compared to molecules of water. The result is a muddy, heterogeneous mixture called a **suspension.** Some mixtures appear to be true solutions; however, upon close inspection small particles are revealed which seem permanently suspended. These particles are bombarded from all sides by water molecules (referred to as the **Brownian motion**), and this molecular action keeps them from settling out. Mixtures of this type are called **colloidal suspensions. Colloids** are substances that, when mixed with water, do not pass through semipermeable membranes. A simple way to distinguish between a true solution and a colloidal suspension involves passing a beam of light through each. A true solution is transparent, while the particles in a colloidal suspension appear cloudy or milky as the suspension disperses light much like dust particles in a beam of light or water particles in fog in a car headlight. This scattering of light by colloidal dispersions is called the **Tyndall effect.**

Types of Colloids. Various types of colloidal dispersions exist based on the physical states of the colloidal particles and of the homogenous mixture (Table 1-5). Water is the most important dispersion medium followed by air and other solvents and gases.

Emulsions are colloidal dispersions of liquid in liquid. Ordinarily, mixing two immiscible liquids will not produce a stable emulsion unless a third substance, called an *emulsifying agent,* is added. Kerosene and water, for example, normally do not mix but will if some soap or gelatin is also present. With pesticide formulations, *emulsifiable concentrates* are oily (or nonpolar) liquids that form emulsions (droplets of oil surrounded by water) in water (polar) instead of forming true solutions. The *emulsifying agent* acts as a binder-coupler between the oil-water surface, reducing interfacial tension and allowing the tiny droplets of oil to remain in suspension. This allows water-insoluble pesticides to be uniformly dispersed in water, even though each maintains its original identity. After emulsifiable concen-

TABLE 1-5. Colloidal Dispersions (Modified from Umland and Bellama, 1999)

Name	Colloidal Solute	Medium	Examples
Foam	Gas	Liquid	Whipped cream, shaving cream, suds
Foam	Gas	Solid	Foam rubber, marshmallows, sponge, Styrofoam, Ivory Soap, pumice
Aerosol	Liquid	Gas	Fog, clouds, aerosol sprays
Aerosol	Solid	Gas	Smoke, airborne viruses
Emulsion	Liquid	Liquid	Homogenized milk, mayonnaise
Emulsion	Liquid	Solid	Butter
Gel (sol)	Solid	Liquid	Gelatin (Jell-O), cream, milk of magnesia, mud, detergents, paints, toothpaste
—	Solid	Solid	Many alloys, ruby glass

trate compounds are added to water, the resulting emulsions are milky colored and require mild agitation to keep the pesticide uniformly suspended in the spray tank.

Soaps and detergents are colloidal particles made up of clusters of small particles. They clean by a colloidal phenomenon. Soaps consist of molecules with long hydrocarbon chains attached to negative (polar) groups. They form colloidal dispersions in water where the negative ends of the molecules are soluble in water and attract the positive ends of water molecules. The other end of the hydrocarbon chains are nonpolar and attach themselves to organic particles, such as grease droplets, in the water. This forms a roughly spherical **micelle** cluster around the grease particle, with the hydrocarbon chains extending inward and the negative ends at the outside of the sphere. The water then removes the organic particle from the soiled object and carries it away (refer to Figure 2-2).

Detergents and soaps are **surfactants** or *surface-active agents.* Surfactants concentrate at the surface of water and reduce surface tension (hydrogen bonding between water molecules) and expand the surface area. Thus, surfactants make water-wet surfaces better. Surfactants are used in many chemical solutions to increase the surface area covered by the spray solution (reduce surface tension). Soaps and detergents are discussed further in **Chapter Four.**

A true solution is formed when a solute, consisting of molecules or ions, is dispersed throughout the solvent to form a homogeneous mixture. A true solution exists in a *single phase.* The solute is said to be soluble in the solvent. A colloidal suspension, meanwhile, is a *two-phase system.* It has dispersed particles rather than a solute, and a dispersing medium rather than a solvent. The system consists of finely divided particles that remain suspended in the medium. Molecular motion (kinetic energy) of water molecules keeps particles dispersed for a period of time until gravity causes particles to settle because of their density.

Increasing the rate at which a solid dissolves in a liquid depends on the nature of the solid and liquid involved. In general, the rate of solution of a solid in a liquid can be increased by: (1) stirring to bring fresh portions of the solvent in contact with the undissolved solid; (2) grinding the solid into a powder which greatly increases the surface area being exposed to the liquid; and (3) heating the solvent to increase the kinetic activity of the solute particles. Stirring is a common means for turfgrass and agricultural managers to help suspend various materials in spray tanks. The stirring device, called an agitator, circulates water through the tank to help maintain a suspension, thus preventing settling of suspended particles.

For most solutes there is a limit to the concentration of solute molecules that a given solvent will accept at a given temperature. A solution is **saturated** when this limiting solute concentration is reached, and often excess solute molecules aggregate to form masses such as crystals. A solid that separates from a solution is called a **precipitate.** It may be possible to heat such solutions and allow more solute to dissolve. If all the solute dissolves and the solution then cools, recrystallization may not occur as the excess solute remains in solution. If this occurs, a **supersaturated** solution has formed. A supersaturated solution is so unstable that shaking a sprayer containing a supersaturated solution may produce enough shock to cause the excess solute to recrystallize, or adding more solute to this solution may cause recrystallization, leaving a saturated solution.

The formation of solutions usually increases the disorder (or entropy) of a system. In addition, energy changes always accompany the dissolving of a solute. It is not easy to predict whether the overall solution process will be endo- or exo-thermic. Energy is always required to separate particles that are attracted to each other, and such forces of attraction exist in any solid. Temperature is a common factor that disturbs a system in equilibrium. Increasing the temperature of a satu-rated solution often dissolves more ions, affecting the solubilities of different com-pounds at various temperatures. The solubility of gases dissolved in liquids decreases as temperature increases. This is why bubbles of gas usually form inside a beaker of water as it is heated. Since the water was saturated with air at the lower temperature, and the solubility of the gas decreases as the temperature rises, some of the gas will leave the solution by forming bubbles, as the temperature rises.

Pressure also influences the amount of gas that dissolves in a given quantity of a liquid at a given temperature. *An increase in pressure increases the solubility of a gas.* This is known as **Henry's Law.** In a bottle of carbonated beverage, for example, a certain amount of carbon dioxide is dissolved at a given pressure. If the cap of the bottle is removed, the pressure above the contents immediately drops to atmospheric pressure. Since the solubility of CO_2 is lower at this lower atmos-pheric pressure, some of the gas in the solution escapes as bubbles and the solution becomes saturated with the gas at a lower concentration corresponding to the lower pressure. If the bottle remains open, CO_2 continues to diffuse into the surrounding air and is replaced by air. Eventually the pressure of CO_2 inside the bottle drops to the very lowest level of this gas naturally in the atmosphere (about 0.04%) and the beverage now tastes "flat," or "sweet."

Henry's Law

At a given temperature, the solubility of a gas is in direct proportion to the pressure above the solution:

$$Cg = kp_{gas}$$

where Cg is the concentration of the dissolved gas,
     k is the constant characteristic of the gas,
     p_{gas} is the pressure of the gas above the solution.

Solubility and Polarity. The nature of the solvent and solute are important in the solution process since a substance dissolves when its particles mix freely with those of the solvent. In general, polar molecules dissolve in polar solvents; nonpolar molecules dissolve in nonpolar solvents. In other words, "like dissolves like" is true. Not only does the solute weaken hydrogen bonds between water molecules but charged ions are attracted to the polar regions of the solvent. The electrostatic attractions of these polar ions are strong enough to separate the water molecules from one another, thus intermingling of the particles can occur and a solution results.

In nonpolar substances, such as fat and gasoline, the molecules are held by weak van der Waals (intermolecular) forces. These substances do not dissolve in water because their attractive forces are too weak to separate water molecules from one another. However, if nonpolar substances are mixed together the molecules are able to intermingle freely to form a solution because they are attracted by similar weak forces, and are separated.

Alcohols have polar bonds at the hydroxyl end of the molecule and nonpolar bonds within the hydrocarbon end. They are able to dissolve both polar and nonpolar solvents. For example, the alcohol ethanol has the molecular formula of $CH_3—CH_2—OH$, with the OH being the polar end and the CH_3 having nonpolar bonds.

SOLUTION CONCENTRATIONS

A number of ways exist of quantitatively expressing the relative amounts of solute and solvent or of solute and solution. Solution concentrations may be expressed in terms of weight percentage, molarity, molality, parts per million, millimoles, and equivalents. Each method has advantages when used for specific purposes.

Molecular Weights and Concentrations

When dealing with a solution, the concentration depends upon the relative proportions of solute and solvent. The more solute dissolved in a solvent, the more concentrated the solution becomes. Meanwhile, the more solvent added, the more dilute the solution becomes. The weight of solute per 100 grams of solvent in this solution is known as its **solubility.** At a given temperature, the terms dilute and concentrated are qualitative and chemists have developed several methods for expressing solution concentrations quantitatively.

Molecules, as well as atoms, are measured in units called **moles.** A mole is a specific number of chemical particles. One mole of any substance contains the same number of particles (atoms, ions or molecules) as 1 mole of any other substance. This number, 6.022×10^{23}, is known as **Avogadro's number.** For example, 1 mole of sodium contains 6.022×10^{23} atoms of sodium; 1 mole of chloride ions contains 6.022×10^{23} Cl^- ions; and 1 mole of water contains 6.022×10^{23} molecules of water. One can think of moles in the same way as a pair or a dozen, since each represents a numerical quantity.

$$1 \text{ pair} = 2 \text{ objects}$$

$$1 \text{ dozen} = 12 \text{ objects}$$

$$1 \text{ mole} = 6.022 \times 10^{23} \text{ particles}$$

One mole of gold, for example, contains just as many atoms as one mole of lead, just as there are as many socks in a pair of socks as there are shoes in a pair of shoes. The **molecular weight** of a substance is the sum of the atomic weights of all the atoms in a molecule. For example, the molecular weight of carbon dioxide, CO_2, is the sum of the atomic weights of one carbon and 2 atoms of oxygen; $12 + 16 + 16$, or 44 g. For a brief review of the metric system, which is used exclusively in chemistry, refer to **Appendix C.**

One mole of a substance weighs an amount, in grams, that is numerically equal to its atomic weight (or molecular weight). For example, the molecular weight of

$CaCl_2$ is 111 g; therefore, 111 g of $CaCl_2$ is one mole (contains 6.022×10^{23} molecules) of $CaCl_2$. Also, one mole of sodium weighs 23 grams, and one mole of water (H_2O) weighs 18 grams. In another example, to obtain 5.0 moles of oxygen (O_2) molecules, 5.0×32 g = 160 g of oxygen must be measured. To obtain 5.0 moles of hydrogen (H_2) molecules, 5.0×2.0 g = 10 g of hydrogen must be present. These two quantities, 160 g of oxygen and 10 g of hydrogen, contain the same number (6.02×10^{23}) of molecules.

The mole is useful for defining quantities involved in chemical reactions. In order to form water, for example, 2 moles of hydrogen atoms and 1 mole of oxygen atoms combine to produce 1 mole of water molecules as shown: $2H_2 + O_2 \rightarrow 2H_2O$. Similarly, to make table salt (NaCl), 1 mole of sodium (about 23 grams) would combine with 1 mole of chlorine (about 35.5 grams) to form 1 mole of NaCl which weighs 58.5 g as shown: $2Na + Cl_2 \rightarrow 2NaCl$.

In another example, one mole of carbon atoms (12 g of C) reacts completely with one mole of oxygen molecules (32 g of O_2) to form carbon dioxide in the reaction: $C + O_2 \rightarrow CO_2$, because one mole of carbon and one mole of molecular oxygen contain exactly the same number of carbon atoms and oxygen molecules.

Determining Empirical Formulas. The empirical formula for a compound consists of the symbols of the constituent elements in their smallest whole-number ratio (e.g., H_2O or NaCl). The first step in determining the empirical formula of a compound is to convert the gram ratio of each element to a mole ratio. The mole ratio is then adjusted to its simplest whole-number ratio.

Example: What is the empirical formula of a compound containing 75 g C and 25 g H?

Step 1: convert gram ratio of each element to mole ratio

for
$$C: 75 \text{ g C} \times \frac{1 \text{ mole C}}{12 \text{ g C}} = 6.25 \text{ moles C}$$

for
$$H: 25 \text{ g H} \times \frac{1 \text{ mole H}}{1 \text{ g H}} = 25 \text{ moles H}$$

Step 2: adjust mole ratio to a simplest whole-number ratio by dividing the mole ratios by the smaller value. If a whole number does not appear, it is necessary to multiply each number in the ratio by a value that will create the simplest whole number ratio.

$$C = \frac{6.25}{6.25} = 1 \qquad H = \frac{25}{6.25} = 4$$

Therefore, the empirical formula is C_1H_4 or CH_4, which is a gas, methane. To successfully understand and work with various units (e.g., weights and volumes) within chemistry, refer to Appendix D on Unit Analysis.

Example Problems:

1. What is the simplest formula of a compound containing 20 g Ca, 6 g C, and 24 g O_2? The molecular weights of Ca = 40 g, C = 12 g, and O = 16 g. Ca = 20 g/40 g = 0.5 mole; C = 6 g/12 g = 0.5 mole; O = 24 g/16 g = 1.5 mole, therefore, $Ca_{0.5}C_{0.5}O_{1.5}$ or $CaCO_3$.

2. What is the weight (or mass), in grams (g), of 3.50 moles of copper atoms? First, determine the atomic weight of copper which is 63.5 g, then insert the following:

$$3.50 \text{ moles} \times \frac{63.5 \text{ g Cu}}{\text{mole}} = 222 \text{ g Cu}$$

3. What percentage of nitrogen (N) and potassium (K) are in the fertilizer, potassium nitrate, KNO_3?

Step 1: determine the molecular weight of each element in KNO_3

$$K = 1 \times 39 = 39 \text{ g}$$
$$N = 1 \times 14 = 14 \text{ g}$$
$$O_3 = 3 \times 16 = \underline{48 \text{ g}}$$
$$\text{total } 101 \text{ g}$$

Step 2: Now determine the percentage of each element in KNO_3 by dividing the total weight of each element by the total formula weight of the compound. To express the value as a percent, multiply the results by 100.

$$K = \frac{39 \text{ g}}{101 \text{ g}} = 0.386 \text{ or } 38.6\%$$

$$N = \frac{14 \text{ g}}{101 \text{ g}} = 0.139 \text{ or } 13.9\%$$

$$O_3 = \frac{48 \text{ g}}{101 \text{ g}} = 0.475 \text{ or } 47.5\%$$

Therefore, pure KNO_3 contains 38% K, 14% N, and 48% O. To check the results, add up the percentage of each element in the formula. This should equal 100 (38 + 14 + 48 = 100).

4. (a) How many moles of atoms are in 6.20 g of phosphorus? The atomic weight of P is 31 g, thus,

$$6.20 \text{ g P} \times \frac{1 \text{ mole}}{31 \text{ g P}} = 0.20 \text{ mole}$$

(b) How many moles are contained in 900 g of glucose, $C_6H_{12}O_6$?

Step 1: Determine the molecular weight of glucose.

$$C_6 \ (6 \times 12 \text{ g}) + H_{12} \ (12 \times 1 \text{ g}) + O_6 \ (6 \times 16 \text{ g}) = 180 \text{ g}$$

Step 2: Calculate the number of moles in 900 g.

$$\text{moles} = 900 \text{ g} \times \frac{1 \text{ mole}}{180 \text{ g}} = 5.0 \text{ moles of } C_6H_{12}O_6$$

5. (a) How many moles of oxygen are in 8.0 g of O_2?

$$8.0 \text{ g } O_2 \times \frac{1 \text{ mole}}{32 \text{ g } O_2} = 0.25 \text{ moles } O_2$$

(b) How many molecules of O_2 are in 8.0 g of O_2 gas?

$$0.25 \text{ mole } O_2 \times \frac{6.02 \times 10^{23} \text{ molecules}}{1 \text{ mole } O_2} = 1.5 \times 10^{23} \text{ molecules } O_2$$

6. What is the empirical formula of a compound containing 92.3% C and 7.7% H? C = 12 g/m; H = 1 g/m.

Step 1: calculate the number of moles in each element.

$$\text{Moles of carbon atoms} = \frac{92.3 \text{ g}}{12 \text{ g/m}} = 7.7 \text{ moles}$$

$$\text{Moles of hydrogen atoms} = \frac{7.7 \text{ g}}{1 \text{ g/m}} = 7.7 \text{ moles}$$

Step 2: determine the mole ratio of each element in the compound.

Mole ratio for carbon: $\qquad \dfrac{7.7}{7.7} = 1.0$

Mole ratio for hydrogen: $\qquad \dfrac{7.7}{7.7} = 1.0$

Therefore, the simplest formula is C_1H_1 or CH.

7. Determine the simplest formula for a compound with hydrogen = 2.04%, sulfur = 32.65%, and oxygen = 65.31%.

	atom percent of compound	÷	atomic weight	=	relative no. of atoms	÷	least common denominator	=	whole no. ratios
H	2.04	÷	1	=	2.04	÷	1.02	=	2
S	32.65	÷	32	=	1.02	÷	1.02	=	1
O	65.31	÷	16	=	4.08	÷	1.02	=	4

Therefore, the simplest formula is H_2SO_4.

8. Determine the weight of the following.
   (a) 1.0 mole of $Na_2S_2O_3$

$$Na = 2 \times 23.0 = 46.0 \text{ g}$$
$$S = 2 \times 32.0 = 64.0 \text{ g}$$
$$O = 3 \times 16.0 = \underline{48.0 \text{ g}}$$
$$\text{total } 158 \text{ g/m}$$

(b) 0.50 mole of CO_2

$$0.50 \text{ mole} \times \frac{[12 + 2(16) \text{ g}]}{\text{mole}} = 22 \text{ g}$$

(c) 1.0×10^{-3} mole of $C_{254}H_{377}N_{65}O_{75}S_6$

$$C = 254 \times \quad 12 = 3048$$
$$H = 377 \times \quad 1.0 = 377$$
$$N = \quad 65 \times 14.0 = 910$$
$$O = \quad 75 \times 16.0 = 1200$$
$$S = \quad 6 \times \quad 32 = \underline{192}$$
$$\text{total } 5727 \text{ (or } 5.73 \times 10^3) \text{ g/mole}$$

$$1.0 \times 10^{-3} \text{ mole} \times \frac{5.73 \times 10^3 \text{ g}}{\text{mole}} = 5.73 \text{ g}$$

(d) 3.60 mole of $Pb(NO_3)_2$

$$3.60 \text{ mole} \times \frac{[207 + 2(14) + 6(16) \text{ g}]}{\text{mole}} = 1.19 \times 10^3 \text{ g}$$

9. How many moles of phosphoric acid (H_3PO_4) are needed to neutralize 0.9 mole of sodium hydroxide (NaOH)? $H_3PO_4 + 3NaOH \rightarrow Na_3PO_4 + H_2O$ a 3 to 1 ratio exists between NaOH and H_3PO_4; therefore,

$$0.9 \text{ mole NaOH} \times \frac{1 \text{ mole } H_3PO_4}{3 \text{ mole NaOH}} = 0.3 \text{ mole } H_3PO_4$$

Calculations Based on Chemical Reactions

A chemical formula indicates the number and kind of atoms that make up a molecule of a compound. Since each atom is an entity with a characteristic mass, a formula also provides a means for computing the relative weights of each kind of atom in a compound. In a balanced chemical equation, the coefficients show the relative number of moles of each substance involved. The combined weight of the reaction products is exactly equal to the combined weight of the original reactants. The ability to balance and interpret equations should enable calculations involving the relative masses of substances involved in chemical reactions, if we understand mole, mass, and volume relationships. These are known as **stoichiometric calculations.** For the following reaction:

$$A \rightarrow B$$

$$\text{mass of } A \times \frac{1 \text{ mol } A}{\text{gfm } A} \rightarrow \text{mol } A \times \frac{b \text{ mol } B}{a \text{ mol } A} \rightarrow \text{mol } B \times \frac{\text{gfm } B}{1 \text{ mol } B} \rightarrow \text{mass of } B$$

Mass-mole conversion   Mole ratio from   Mole-mass conversion

balanced equation

A = given quantity of a reactant or product,
B = wanted quantity of a reactant or product,
a = number of moles of G in the balanced chemical equation,
b = number of moles of W in the balanced chemical equation,
gfm = gram-formula mass.

For the reaction of hydrogen and oxygen to form water, the equation may be read as 2 moles of hydrogen react with 1 mole of oxygen to form 2 moles of water. Also, since the weights of a mole of hydrogen and of oxygen can be readily determined from the atomic weights, the weight relationship between reactants and products can be calculated:

$$2H_2 \quad + \quad O_2 \quad \rightarrow \quad 2H_2O$$

2 moles   1 mole   2 moles
4 g   32 g   36 g

The equation describes the ratios of moles that react when different amounts of substances are involved. If 65 moles of oxygen are available, then:

$$130 \text{ moles } H_2 + 65 \text{ moles } O_2 \rightarrow 130 \text{ moles } H_2O$$

Steps for solving limited (stoichiometric) chemical reactions include:

1. Write a balanced equation for the reaction (if it is not given).
   (a) Write what is given and what is asked for.
   (b) Write the formula masses needed.
2. If quantities of more than one reactant are given, determine which reactant is limiting. The quantity of the limiting reactant determines the amount of product formed and the amounts of other reactants that react.
3. Set up and perform the calculation(s):
   (a) Use formula masses to convert grams of the given quantity to moles by using the numerical value of the formula mass.

(b) Use the equation for the reaction to write conversion factors for converting moles of one substance to moles of other substances.
(c) Use formula masses to convert moles to grams. Be sure to include formulas of substances in labels.

Example:

Show the calculations on how many grams of oxygen are needed to produce 36 g of water from the following reaction:

$2H_2$	+	O_2	$\rightarrow$	$2H_2O$
? g		? g		36 g
2 moles		1 mole		2 moles

A = given quantity of a reactant or product, = H_2O
B = wanted quantity of a reactant or product, = O_2
a = number of moles of A in the balanced chemical equation, = 2
b = number of moles of B in the balanced chemical equation. = 1

The basic steps in the calculations are:

$$\text{mass of } H_2O \rightarrow \text{mol of } H_2O \rightarrow \text{mol of } O_2 \rightarrow \text{mass of } O_2$$

$$\text{Mass of } A \times \frac{1 \text{ mol } A}{\text{gfm } A} = \text{mol } A$$

or

$$36 \text{ g } H_2O \times \frac{1\text{mol } H_2O}{18 \text{ g } H_2O} = \begin{matrix}2 \text{ mol}\\ H_2O\end{matrix}$$

$$\text{mol } A \times \frac{b \text{ mol } B}{a \text{ mol } A} = \text{mol } B$$

or

$$\begin{matrix}2 \text{ mol}\\ H_2O\end{matrix} \times \frac{1 \text{ mol } O_2}{2 \text{ mol } H_2O} = \begin{matrix}1 \text{ mol}\\ O_2\end{matrix}$$

$$\text{mol } B \times \frac{\text{gfm } B}{1 \text{ mol } B} = \text{mass of } B$$

or

$$\begin{matrix}1 \text{ mol}\\ O_2\end{matrix} \times \frac{32 \text{ g } O_2}{1 \text{ mol } O_2} = 32 \text{ g } O_2$$

gfm = gram-formula mass.

Table 1-6 can be used to solve any stoichiometry problem. In short, this table represents that in order to find the mass of a reactant or product, the number of moles in the balanced chemical equation must be determined as shown above:

TABLE 1-6. Relationship Between Mass, Mole, and Volume in Chemical Reactions

$$\text{Mass of } A \times \frac{1 \text{ mol } A}{\text{gfm } A} \rightarrow \text{mol } A \times \frac{b \text{ mol } B}{a \text{ mol } A} \rightarrow \text{mol } B \times \frac{\text{gfm}}{1 \text{ mol } B} \rightarrow \text{mass of } B$$

$$\text{Representative particles of } A \times \frac{1 \text{ mol } A}{6.02 \times 10^{23}} \rightarrow \text{mol } A \times \frac{b \text{ mol } B}{a \text{ mol } A} \rightarrow \text{mol } B \times \frac{6.02 \times 10^{23}}{1 \text{ mol } B} \rightarrow \text{Representative particles of } B$$

$$\text{Volume of } A \text{ (L) at STP} \times \frac{1 \text{ mol } A}{22.4 \text{ L } A} \rightarrow \text{mol } A \times \frac{b \text{ mol } B}{a \text{ mol } A} \rightarrow \text{mol } B \times \frac{22.4 \text{ L } B}{1 \text{ mol } B} \rightarrow \text{volume of } B \text{ (L) at STP}$$

A = given quantity of a reactant or product,
B = wanted quantity of a reactant or product,
a = number of moles of G in the balanced chemical equation,
b = number of moles of W in the balanced chemical equation,
gfm = gram-formula mass.

Example:

1. (a) How many moles of carbon dioxide are produced by burning 1.50 moles ethyl alcohol (C_2H_5OH) in the following reaction?

$$C_2H_5OH(l) + 3O_2(g) \rightarrow 2CO_2(g) + 3H_2O(g)$$

From the equation, the mole relationship between C_2H_5OH and CO_2 is obtained to form a conversion factor:

$$\frac{2 \text{ moles } CO_2}{1 \text{ mole } C_2H_5OH}$$

Multiplying the mole ratio (conversion factor) by the given number of moles of C_2H_5OH yields:

$$1.5 \text{ moles } C_2H_5OH \times \frac{2 \text{ moles } CO_2}{1 \text{ mole } C_2H_5OH} = 3.00 \text{ moles } CO_2$$

(b) Now determine how many grams of CO_2 are produced when 1.50 moles of C_2H_5OH is burned.

Multiply 3.00 moles of CO_2 by a factor that changes moles CO_2 into grams of CO_2. The factor is the gram-molecular mass in units of g/mole derived from the formula CO_2 and the atomic masses of carbon and oxygen.

$$1.50 \text{ moles } C_2H_5OH \times \frac{2.00 \text{ moles } CO_2}{\text{mole } C_2H_5OH} \times \frac{44.0 \text{ g } CO_2}{\text{mole } CO_2} = 132 \text{ g } CO_2$$

(c) How many grams of CO_2 are produced when 23 g C_2H_5OH is burned?

Three steps are needed to determine this:

(1) Convert grams C_2H_5OH into moles C_2H_5OH:

$$23 \text{ g } C_2H_5OH \times \frac{\text{mole } C_2H_5OH}{46 \text{ g } C_2H_5OH} = 0.50 \text{ moles } C_2H_5OH$$

(2) Convert moles C_2H_5OH into moles CO_2:

$$0.50 \text{ moles } C_2H_5OH \times \frac{2.00 \text{ moles } CO_2}{\text{mole } C_2H_5OH} = 1.0 \text{ moles } CO_2$$

(3) Convert moles CO_2 into grams of CO_2:

$$1.0 \text{ moles } CO_2 \times \frac{44 \text{ g } CO_2}{\text{mole } CO_2} = 44 \text{ g } CO_2$$

The complete step for these three conversions is:

$$23 \text{ g } C_2H_5OH \times \frac{\text{mole } C_2H_5OH}{46 \text{ g } C_2H_5OH} \times \frac{2.00 \text{ moles } CO_2}{\text{mole } C_2H_5OH} \times \frac{44 \text{ g } CO_2}{\text{mole } CO_2} = 44 \text{ g } CO_2$$

(d) How many grams of CO_2 are formed when 32 g O_2 reacts with 23 g C_2H_5OH?

This reaction involves determining the amount of the reactants that may be in excess and not completely consumed. The amount of product is determined by the reactant that is not in excess. A preliminary calculation is needed to determine which reactant is in excess.

(1) Calculate the moles of each reactant:

For oxygen:

$$32 \text{ g } O_2 \times \frac{\text{mole } O_2}{32 \text{ g } O_2} = 1.0 \text{ mole } O_2$$

For ethyl alcohol:

$$23 \text{ g } C_2H_5OH \times \frac{\text{mole } C_2H_5OH}{46 \text{ g } C_2H_5OH} = 0.5 \text{ mole } C_2H_5OH$$

It is not apparent which is in excess; therefore, calculate the moles of one reactant needed to react with the given quantity of the second reactant:

(2) Calculate the moles of O_2 required to react with 0.50 mole C_2H_5OH.

$$0.5 \text{ mole } C_2H_5OH \times \frac{3 \text{ mole } O_2}{\text{mole } C_2H_5OH} = 1.5 \text{ mole } O_2$$

Since 1.5 moles of O_2 are required and only 1.0 mole is available, the ethyl alcohol must be in excess and the amount of CO_2 produced will be determined by the O_2 present.

(3) Calculate the moles and grams of CO_2 produced:

$$1.0 \text{ mole } O_2 \times \frac{2.0 \text{ moles } CO_2}{3 \text{ moles } O_2} = 0.66 \text{ moles } CO_2 \text{ produced}$$

$$0.66 \text{ moles } CO_2 \text{ produced} \times \frac{44.0 \text{ g } CO_2}{\text{mole } CO_2} = 29 \text{ g } CO_2$$

(e) How many liters of CO_2 are produced at STP when 23.0 g ethyl alcohol is burned?

The first step is to convert 44.0 g CO_2 into moles and then convert moles into liters at standard conditions, temperature/pressure (abbreviated, STP). The conversion factor for this is 22.4 L/mole, which is the volume of 1 mole of any gas at STP.

(1) Convert gram CO_2 to mole CO_2:

$$44.0 \text{ g } CO_2 \times \frac{1 \text{ mole } CO_2}{44.0 \text{ g } CO_2} = 1.00 \text{ mole } CO_2$$

(2) Convert mole CO_2 to volume (in liters) CO_2 using the 22.4 L/mole conversion:

$$1.00 \text{ mole } CO_2 \times \frac{22.4 \text{ L } CO_2}{\text{mole } CO_2} = 22.4 \text{ L } CO_2$$

The complete step is:

$$23 \text{ g } C_2H_5OH \times \frac{\text{mole } C_2H_5OH}{46 \text{ g } C_2H_5OH} \times \frac{2.00 \text{ moles } CO_2}{\text{mole } C_2H_5OH} \times \frac{22.4 \text{ L } CO_2}{\text{mole } CO_2} = 22.4 \text{ L } CO_2$$

2. From the Haber process, ammonia is formed by reacting hydrogen with nitrogen under heat and pressure as shown:

$$3H_2 + N_2 \rightarrow 2NH_3$$

(a) How many grams of H_2 are needed to react with 168 g of N_2?
(b) How many grams of NH_3 can be produced?

Step 1: below each symbol, write what is given and what must be found:

$$3H_2 + N_2 \rightarrow 2NH_3$$
$$\text{?g} \quad 168 \text{ g} \quad \text{?g}$$

Step 2: change the grams of given N_2 into moles:

$$\text{moles } N_2 = (168 \text{ g}) \times \frac{1 \text{ mole}}{28 \text{ g}} = 6 \text{ moles}$$

Step 3: using the coefficients of the balanced equation, obtain moles of H_2 needed and NH_3 produced:

$$\text{moles } H_2 = (6 \text{ moles } N_2) \times \frac{3 \text{ moles } H_2}{1 \text{ mole } N_2} = 18 \text{ moles}$$

$$\text{moles } NH_3 = (6 \text{ moles } N_2) \times \frac{2 \text{ moles } NH_3}{1 \text{ mole } N_2} = 12 \text{ moles}$$

Step 4: calculate the grams of H_2 needed and NH_3 produced:

$$\text{g } H_2 = (18 \text{ moles}) \times \frac{2 \text{ g}}{1 \text{ mole}} = 36 \text{ g}$$

$$\text{g } NH_3 = (12 \text{ moles}) \times \frac{17 \text{ g}}{1 \text{ mole}} = 204 \text{ g}$$

Therefore, 36 g of H_2 plus 168 g N_2 equal the grams (204 g) of NH_3. This can be summarized as:

$$\text{mass } N_2 \times \frac{\text{mol } N_2}{\text{gfm } N_2} \times \text{mol } N_2 \times \frac{b \text{ mol } NH_3}{a \text{ mol } N_2} \times \text{mol } NH_3 \times \frac{\text{gfm } NH_3}{\text{mol } NH_3} = \text{mass } NH_3$$

$$168 \text{ g } N_2 \times \frac{\text{mol } N_2}{28 \text{ g } N_2} = 6 \text{ mol } N_2$$

$$6 \text{ mol } N_2 \times \frac{2 \text{ mol } NH_3}{1 \text{ mol } N_2} = 12 \text{ mol } NH_3$$

$$12 \text{ mol } NH_3 \times \frac{17 \text{ g } NH_3}{\text{mol } NH_3} = 204 \text{ g } NH_3$$

3. (a) Calculate the weight of iron when 16 g FeO_2 reacts with CO. (b) What weight of CO is required for the reaction? (c) What weight of CO_2 is formed?

$$Fe_2O_3 + 3CO \rightarrow 2Fe + 3CO_2$$

1 mole	3 mole	2 mole	3 mole
16 g	? g	? g	? g

(a) $16 \text{ g } Fe_2O_3 \times \dfrac{\text{mol } Fe_2O_3}{160 \text{ g } Fe_2O_3} = 0.10 \text{ mol } Fe_2O_3$

$$0.10 \text{ mol } Fe_2O_3 \times \frac{2 \text{ mol } Fe}{\text{mol } Fe_2O_3} = 0.20 \text{ mol } Fe$$

$$0.20 \text{ mol } Fe \times \frac{55.8 \text{ g } Fe}{\text{mol } Fe} = 11.2 \text{ g } Fe$$

(b) $0.10 \text{ mol } Fe_2O_3 \times \dfrac{3 \text{ mol } CO}{\text{mol } Fe_2O_3} = 0.30 \text{ mol } CO$

$$0.30 \text{ mol } CO \times \dfrac{28 \text{ g } CO}{\text{mol } CO} = 8.4 \text{ g } CO$$

(c) $0.10 \text{ mol } Fe_2O_3 \times \dfrac{3 \text{ mol } CO_2}{\text{mol } Fe_2O_3} = 0.30 \text{ mol } CO_2$

$$0.30 \text{ mol } CO_2 \times \dfrac{44 \text{ g } CO_2}{\text{mol } CO_2} = 13.2 \text{ g } CO_2$$

Molarity

For counting chemical particles by measuring volumes of solutions, concentrations of a compound and its components are commonly expressed as molarity. **Molarity** (designated as M) is the number of moles of a compound dissolved in 1 liter of solution.

$$\text{Molarity, } M = \frac{\text{moles of solute}}{\text{liter of solution}}$$

A *molar solution* contains 1 mole of solute (or 6.022×10^{23} molecular of a subtance) in one liter of solution. For example, 1 liter of a 1 molar ($1\ M$) solution of glucose ($C_6H_{12}O_6$) is prepared by adding water to 1 mole of glucose (molecular weight: 180 g) until the volume of the solution reaches 1 liter. Half this quantity of glucose (90 g) in 1 liter of solution forms a $0.5\ M$ solution. Twice this quantity (360 g) per liter of solution yields a $2\ M$ solution. Two moles of solute is formed from each of the following: adding $1\ M$ solute concentration in 2 liters or adding $2\ M$ solute in 1 liter or adding $4\ M$ solute in 0.5 liter.

Name	Symbol	Solute Unit	Solution Unit	Dimensions	
Molarity	M	mole	liter solution		
				$\dfrac{\text{mole solute}}{\text{liter solution}} =$	$\dfrac{\text{g of solute}}{\text{g/mole}} \Big/ \dfrac{\text{g/mole}}{\text{liters of solution}}$

The number of moles of reagent in a solution equals the product of the molarity (M) of a solution and the volume (V) of that solution: $M \times V = \text{moles}$. For example, (1) the following will yield exactly 1 mole of ammonium nitrate (NH_4NO_3), while (2) accounts for a volume of a specific molarity.

	NH_3	+	HNO_3	$\rightarrow$	NH_4NO_3
	ammonia		nitric acid		ammonium nitrate
(1)	1 mole (= 17 g)		1 mole (= 63 g)	$\rightarrow$	1 mole (= 80 g)
(2)	1 liter of $1\ M\ NH_3$		1 liter of $1\ M\ NHO_3$	$\rightarrow$	2 liters of $0.5\ M\ NH_4NO_3$

Example:

1. How many moles of household ammonia (NH_3) are in 1.2 liters of a solution that is 0.50 *M* ammonia?

   By using the definition of molarity as the number of moles of solute per liter of solution:

   $$1.2 \text{ liter} \times \frac{0.5 \text{ moles NH}_3}{\text{liter}} = 0.60 \text{ moles NH}_3$$

2. What volume of the 0.5 *M* ammonia solution is needed to obtain 1.8 *M* of ammonia?

   Now the number of moles needed is divided by the molarity:

   $$1.8 \text{ } M \text{ NH}_3 \times \frac{\text{liters}}{0.5 \text{ } M \text{ NH}_3} = 3.6 \text{ liters}$$

3. If the solution runs out in Example 2, what weight of ammonia is needed to prepare an additional 5 liters of 0.50 *M* ammonia?

   Step 1: First convert between moles of ammonia and grams of ammonia using its molecular weight:

   $$
   \begin{array}{lll}
   \text{N:} & 1 \times 14 \text{ g} = & 14 \text{ g} \\
   \text{H:} & 3 \times 1 \text{ g} = & \underline{3 \text{ g}} \\
   & & 17 \text{ g}
   \end{array}
   $$

   Step 2: Now determine the total grams of ammonia needed in 5 liters to obtain a 0.5 *M* solution.

   $$5 \text{ liters} \times \frac{0.5 \text{ } M}{\text{liter}} \times \frac{17 \text{ g NH}_3}{M} = 42 \text{ g NH}_3$$

   The desired solution contains 42 g of ammonia in 5 liters of solution.

4. A bottle of concentrated ammonia contains 28.0% (by mass) NH_3 and has a density of 0.898 g/mL. What is the molarity of the NH_3?

   Step 1: Determine how many moles of ammonia are in 1.0 L by using the density to find the mass of 1 L of concentrated ammonia.

   $$\frac{0.898 \text{ g}}{\text{mL}} \times \frac{1000 \text{ mL}}{\text{liter}} = \frac{898 \text{ g solution}}{\text{liter solution}}$$

   Step 2: The solution only contains 28.0% (by mass) NH_3; thus, find out how many grams of ammonia are in 1 liter.

$$\frac{898 \text{ g}}{\text{liter}} \times \frac{28.0 \text{ g NH}_3}{100 \text{ g}} \times \frac{251 \text{ g NH}_3}{\text{liter}}$$

Step 3: Now convert grams NH_3 to moles NH_3 (the molecular weight of NH_3 is 17 g).

$$\frac{251 \text{ g NH}_3}{\text{liter}} \times \frac{1 \text{ mole NH}_3}{17 \text{ g NH}_3} = \frac{14.8 \text{ mole NH}_3}{\text{liter}} \quad \text{or} \quad 14.8 \text{ } M \text{ NH}_3$$

With practice, these steps can be combined as:

$$\frac{0.898 \text{ g}}{\text{mL}} \times \frac{1000 \text{ mL}}{\text{liter}} \times \frac{28.0 \text{ g NH}_3}{100 \text{ g}} \times \frac{1 \text{ mole NH}_3}{17 \text{ g NH}_3} = \frac{14.8 \text{ mole NH}_3}{\text{liter}} \quad \text{or } 14.8 \text{ } M \text{ NH}_3$$

Examples:

1. What weight of calcium bromide ($CaBr_2$) is needed to prepare 150 mL of a 3.50 *M* solution?

$$\frac{\text{mole solute}}{\text{liter solution}} = \frac{\dfrac{\text{g solute}}{\text{g/mole}}}{\text{liters solution}}$$

$$3.50 \text{ } M = \frac{\dfrac{\text{g CaBr}_2}{200 \text{ g CaBr}_2/\text{mole}}}{150 \text{ mL} \times 1 \text{ liter}/1{,}000 \text{ mL}}$$

This can be rearranged as follows:

$$\text{g CaBr}_2 = \frac{3.50 \text{ moles}}{\text{liter}} \times 150 \text{ mL} \times \frac{1 \text{ liter}}{1{,}000 \text{ mL}} \times \frac{200 \text{ g}}{\text{mole}}$$

$$= 105 \text{ g CaBr}_2$$

2. What is the molarity of a solution containing 17.1 g of granulated sugar ($C_{12}H_{22}O_{11}$) dissolved in 0.5 liter of solution? (The molecular weight of sugar is 342 g.)

Step 1: the moles of solute and liters of solution need to be calculated.

moles solute: $\quad 17.1 \text{ g sugar} \times \dfrac{\text{mole sugar}}{342 \text{ g sugar}} \times 0.0500 \text{ moles sugar}$

Step 2: calculate molarity as mole solute per liter of solution.

molarity: $\quad \dfrac{\text{mole solute}}{\text{liter solution}} = \dfrac{0.0500 \text{ moles sugar}}{0.500 \text{ liters solution}} = \dfrac{0.100 \text{ moles}}{\text{liter}} = 0.100 \text{ } M$

3. How many grams of sucrose ($C_{12}H_{22}O_{11}$) are in 1 liter of 0.25 M solution?

   $C_{12}H_{22}O_{11}$ = 342 g/m and 0.25 M = 0.25 m/L; therefore,
   1 liter contains 342 g/m × 0.25 m/L = 86 g.

4. What is the molarity of a solution of KCl in water if 74 g are dissolved per liter of solution?

   KCl = 39 + 35 g/m = 74 g/m; therefore,
   74 g/L = 1.0 M solution

5. (a) Find the molarity, weight per liter solution, and weight per liter of 88% by weight and 1.802 g/mL density H_2SO_4 (sulfuric acid), (1 mole H_2SO_4 = 98.1 g).

   The density of a solution is a function of the concentration of solute and is commonly shown on a bottle label.

   $$\text{weight of 1 liter} = \frac{1.802 \text{ g solution}}{\text{mL}} \times \frac{1,000 \text{ mL}}{\text{liter}}$$

   $$= 1,802 \text{ g/liter}$$

   $$\text{weight } H_2SO_4 \text{ per liter} = \frac{1,802 \text{ g solution}}{\text{liter}} \times \frac{88 \text{ g } H_2SO_4}{100 \text{ g solution}}$$

   $$= 1,586 \text{ g } H_2SO_4/\text{liter}$$

   $$\text{molarity} = \frac{\text{mole solute}}{\text{liter solution}} = \frac{\dfrac{\text{g solute}}{\text{g/mole}}}{\text{liters solution}}$$

   $$= \frac{1,586 \text{ g } H_2SO_4/\text{liter}}{98.1 \text{ g } H_2SO_4/\text{mole}} = 16.2 \text{ mole } H_2SO_4/\text{liter}$$

   (b) What volume of 16.2 M H_2SO_4 solution is needed to prepare 3 L of 6 M solution?

   $$\text{moles } H_2SO_4 \text{ needed} = V \times M = 3 \text{ liters} \times \frac{6 \text{ moles } H_2SO_4}{\text{liter}} = 18 \text{ moles}$$

   $$\text{volume of 16.2 } M \text{ solution needed} = \frac{18 \text{ moles } H_2SO_4}{16.2 \text{ moles } H_2SO_4/\text{liter}} = 1.11 \text{ liter}$$

6. A label of the herbicide Roundup Pro indicates 41% by weight of the active chemical glyphosate, as an isopropylamine salt, is present. Convert this to grams per liter and pounds active ingredient glyphosate per gallon of solution. Average density is 1.18 gmL, and molecular weight of glyphosate ($C_6H_{17}N_2O_5P$) is 228.19 g.

$$\frac{1.18 \text{ g}}{\text{mL}} \times \frac{1000 \text{ mL}}{\text{liter}} \times \frac{41 \text{ g } C_6H_{17}N_2O_5P}{100 \text{ g}} = \frac{480 \text{ g } C_6H_{17}N_2O_5P}{\text{liter}}$$

to convert to pounds active ingredient (designated as "ai") per gallon:

$$\frac{480 \text{ g}}{\text{liter}} \times \frac{1 \text{ lb}}{454 \text{ g}} \times \frac{3.785 \text{ liter}}{\text{gal}} = \frac{4 \text{ lbs ai}}{\text{gal}}$$

7. What mass of silver nitrate ($AgNO_3$), expressed in grams, is needed to prepare 0.500 liter of a 0.100 M solution?

   Step 1: calculate the moles of solute needed:

   $$\text{moles solute} = \frac{0.100 \text{ moles}}{\text{liter}} \times 0.500 \text{ liter} = 0.0500 \text{ moles}$$

   Step 2: calculate the grams of solute needed:

   $$0.05 \text{ moles } AgNO_3 \times \frac{170 \text{ g } AgNO_3}{\text{mole } AgNO_3} = 8.50 \text{ g } AgNO_3$$

   One step could be used to solve this problems where:

   $$\frac{0.1 \text{ moles } AgNO_3}{\text{liter}} \times 0.500 \text{ liter} \times \frac{170 \text{ g } AgNO_3}{\text{mole } AgNO_3} = 8.50 \text{ g } AgNO_3$$

8. How many grams of HCl are dissolved in 200 mL of a 0.3 M HCl solution?

   $$200 \text{ mL} \times \frac{1 \text{ L}}{1,000 \text{ mL}} = 0.2 \text{ L; therefore,}$$

   $$\frac{0.3 \text{ moles HCl}}{\text{liter}} \times 0.2 \text{ liter} \times \frac{35.5 \text{ g HCl}}{\text{mole HCl}} = 2.2 \text{ g HCl}$$

9. How would one prepare 2 liters of a 3.5 M H_2SO_4 solution?

   $$3.5 \text{ } M \text{ } H_2SO_4 = \frac{3.5 \text{ mole}}{\text{liter}} \times \frac{98 \text{ g}}{\text{mole}} = 343 \text{ g/L; therefore,}$$

   dissolve 646 g H_2SO_4 with enough water to make 2 liters of total solution.

Parts per Million

Another means of expressing exceedingly small concentrations is parts per million (ppm). One expression of ppm is the concentration of one milligram (mg) of one substance distributed through one kilogram (kg) of another. For example, the concentration of potassium iodide, KI, in iodized table salt is about 7.6×10^{-5} g of KI per gram of NaCl. This can be converted into ppm by the following: a million

$\times$ 1,000,000 = 10^6. Since the concentration of KI in table salt is 7.6×10^{-5} g KI per gram NaCl and we want to know how many grams of KI are in 10^6 g of table salt, multiply both the numerator and denominator by 1,000,000:

$$\frac{7.6 \times 10^{-5} \text{ g KI}}{1 \text{ g NaCl}} \times \frac{10^6}{10^6} \times \frac{7.6 \times 10 \text{ g KI}}{10^6 \text{ g NaCl}} = 7.6 \times 10 \text{ ppm KI} = 76 \text{ ppm KI}$$

ppm also represents the concentration of one milligram of one substance dissolved throughout one liter of another (usually water).

Examples:

1. What is the concentration of Cu^{+2} ions, in parts per million, of a 750 mL aqueous solution containing 14.38 mg of Cu^{+2} ions (parts per million = mg/ L)?

$$750 \text{ mL} \times \frac{1 \text{ L}}{1,000 \text{ mL}} = 0.7500 \text{ L, and,}$$

ppm is normally expressed as mg/L; therefore,

$$\frac{14.38 \text{ mg Cu}^{+2}}{0.750 \text{ L}} = 19.2 \text{ ppm Cu}^{+2}$$

2. What is the concentration, in ppm, of a 0.20% volume solution of isopropyl alcohol in water?

$$\text{ppm (vol)} = \frac{\text{volume of solute}}{\text{volume of solution}} \times 10^6$$

$$= \frac{0.2 \text{ mL isopropyl alcohol}}{100 \text{ mL solution}} \times 10^6$$

$$= 2.0 \times 10^3 \text{ (or 2,000) ppm}$$

3. What is the Mn^{+7} concentration, in ppm, of a 3×10^{-7} *M* solution of manganese(VII)? ppm is expressed as mg/L, but the problem lists mole/L; therefore, this must be converted:

$$\frac{3 \times 10^{-7} \text{ mole Mn}^{+7}}{\text{L solution}} \times \frac{54.94 \text{ g Mn}^{+7}}{1 \text{ mole Mn}^{+7}} \times \frac{1,000 \text{ mg}}{1 \text{ g}}$$

$$= \frac{0.0164 \text{ mg Mn}^{+7}}{\text{L solution}} \text{ or 0.02 ppm Mn}^{+7}$$

Millimoles

In many measurements, especially with those dealing with soil, it is convenient to express the volume of a solution in milliliters instead of liters. Since a 1 *M* solution contains one mole of solute per liter of solution, a milliliter of solution contains one-thousandth (1/1,000) of a mole or a millimole (m mol). This is a formula weight of solute expressed in milligrams; therefore,

$$\text{molarity of solution} = \frac{\text{m mol solute}}{\text{mL solution}} \quad \text{and}$$

$$\text{number of m mol of solute} = M \times V \text{ (or volume, mL)}$$

Thus, the weight of solute is: mg solute $= M \times V \text{ (mL)} \times \dfrac{\text{mg}}{\text{m mol}}$

If a measurement involves milliliters, it is often convenient to use m mol, mg, and mL.

Equivalent Weights

Solution concentration can be expressed to allow chemically equivalent quantities of different solutes to be measured simply. **Equivalent weights,** as the name implies, are the amounts of reactants that are equivalent (have the same combining capacity) to each other in chemical reactions. Two methods are used to determine equivalences. The first is the equivalent weight of an acid, which is that weight of the substance that furnishes 1 mole of hydronium (H_3O^+ or hydrogen, H^+) ions, while that of a base is the weight that furnishes 1 mole of hydroxide (OH^-) ions. The equivalent weight of an acid or a base is its molecular weight divided by the number of "equivalents" the compound supplies per mole—that is, the number of moles of hydronium (H_3O^+ or H^+) ions or OH^- ions available. For example, sulfuric acid, H_2SO_4, contains two equivalents of hydronium (H_3O^+ or H^+) ions based on its formula, while sodium hydroxide, NaOH, supplies one equivalent of hydroxide (OH^-) ions.

$$H_2SO_4 \text{ (aq)} \rightarrow 2H^+ \text{ (aq)} + SO_4^{-2} \text{ (aq)}$$

$$NaOH \text{ (aq)} \rightarrow Na^+ \text{ (aq)} + OH^- \text{ (aq)}$$

Thus, the equivalent weight of H_2SO_4 is 98/2 = 49 g, the equivalent weight of NaOH is 40/1 = 40 g, and the equivalent weight of H_3PO_4 is 98/3 = 32.7 g. For complete neutralization, 1 equivalent of a monoprotic (one H^+) acid is the same as 1 mole of the acid; 1 equivalent of a diprotic (2 H^+) acid is the same as one-half mole of the acid; and 1 equivalent of a triprotic ($3H^+$) acid is the same as one-third mole of the acid. Phosphoric acid (H_3PO_4), for example, is triprotic and can furnish 3 moles of H^+ ions per mole of acid, and its equivalent weight is one-third mole.

equivalent weight

$$= \frac{\text{molecular weight}}{\text{number of } H^+ \text{ or } OH^- \text{ per molecule}} \quad \text{or} \quad \frac{\text{molecular weight}}{\text{oxidation number (or valence)}}$$

From the equation $Zn + 2HCl \rightarrow ZnCl_2 + H_2$, one atomic weight of zinc reacts with two formula weights of HCl and replaces two atomic weights of hydrogen. To replace one equivalent weight of hydrogen, only one-half an atomic weight of zinc is needed. In the case of zinc, the equivalent weight is $65.4/2 = 32.7$.

The second measure of equivalents is the *chemical equivalents* of elements. This is the quantity, in grams, that supplies or acquires 1 mole of electrons in a chemical reaction. For example, a mole of sodium atoms (23 g) loses 1 mole of electrons to form 1 mole of Na^+ ions, while a mole of calcium atoms (40 g) supplies 2 moles of electrons when Ca^{+2} ions are formed and a mole of aluminum atoms (27 g) supplies 3 moles of electrons when Al^{+3} ions are formed. Thus, 1 equivalent of calcium is the mass of one-half mole of calcium atoms, 20 g (40 g ÷ 2), and 1 equivalent of aluminum is the mass of one-third mole of aluminum atoms, 9.0 g (27 g ÷ 3). The mass of 1 mole of atoms of the elements is divided by the change in oxidation state these atoms undergo in a chemical reaction. These relationships can be summarized as follows:

$$1 \text{ equivalent } Na^+ = \frac{1 \text{ mole Na}}{1 \text{ mole electron}} \times \frac{23 \text{ g Na}}{\text{mole Na}} = \frac{23 \text{ g Na}}{\text{mole electron (or equivalent)}}$$

$$1 \text{ equivalent } Ca^{+2} = \frac{1 \text{ mole Ca}}{2 \text{ moles electrons}} \times \frac{40 \text{ g Ca}}{\text{mole Ca}} = \frac{20 \text{ g Ca}}{\text{mole electron}}$$

$$1 \text{ equivalent } Al^{+3} = \frac{1 \text{ mole Al}}{3 \text{ moles electrons}} \times \frac{27 \text{ g Al}}{\text{mole Al}} = \frac{9.0 \text{ g Al}}{\text{mole electron}}$$

$$1 \text{ equivalent } Fe^{+3} = \frac{1 \text{ mole Fe}}{3 \text{ moles electrons}} \times \frac{55.8 \text{ g Fe}}{\text{mole Fe}} = \frac{18.6 \text{ g Fe}}{\text{mole electron}}$$

$$1 \text{ equivalent } Fe^{+2} = \frac{1 \text{ mole Fe}}{2 \text{ moles electrons}} \times \frac{55.8 \text{ g Fe}}{\text{mole Fe}} = \frac{27.9 \text{ g Fe}}{\text{mole electron}}$$

Examples of equivalent weights of some common acids and bases are listed in Table 1-7.

TABLE 1-7. Examples of Equivalent Weights of Some Acids and Bases

Substance	Formula	Molecular Weight	Equivalent Weight
Hydrochloric acid	HCl	36.5	36.5
Sulfuric acid	H_2SO_4	98.1	49.05
Phosphoric acid	H_3PO_4	98.0	32.7
Sodium hydroxide	NaOH	40.0	40.0
Calcium hydroxide	$Ca(OH)_2$	74.1	37.5

Examples:

1. How many equivalents are in 16 g of H_3PO_4? $H_3PO_4 \rightarrow PO_4^{-3} + 3H^+$

   Step 1: Determine the gram molecular weight of H_3PO_4: = 98.0 g

   Step 2: set up the equation to determine equivalent:

$$16.0 \text{ g } H_3PO_4 \times \frac{1 \text{ mole } H_3PO_4}{98.0 \text{ g } H_3PO_4} \times \frac{3 \text{ equiv } H_3PO_4}{1 \text{ mole } H_3PO_4} = 0.490 \text{ equivalence } H_3PO_4$$

2. Suppose one wished to neutralize 100 negative charges (CEC, $cmol_c/kg$) in a soil sample using the least amount of material. The cations at your disposal include H^+, K^+, Na^+, Ca^{+2}, Mg^{+2}, and Al^{+3}. Which cation would provide the least weight needed to neutralize these 100 grams of negative charges and which one would require the most weight to neutralize this?

   Step 1: the equivalent weight of each cation first needs to be determined which will satisfy the charges of one negative charge:

$$\text{equivalent weight (g)} = \frac{\text{molecular weight (g)}}{\text{oxidation number (or valence)}}$$

$$1 \text{ eq } H^+ = \frac{1 \text{ g}}{1} = 1 \text{ g } H^+ \qquad 1 \text{ eq } Na^+ = \frac{23 \text{ g}}{1} = 23 \text{ g } Na^+$$

$$1 \text{ eq } K^+ = \frac{39 \text{ g}}{1} = 39 \text{ g } K^+ \qquad 1 \text{ eq } Ca^{+2} = \frac{40 \text{ g}}{2} = 20 \text{ g } Ca^{+2}$$

$$1 \text{ eq } Mg^{+2} = \frac{24 \text{ g}}{2} = 12 \text{ g } Mg^{+2} \qquad 1 \text{ eq } Al^{+3} = \frac{27 \text{ g}}{3} = 9 \text{ g } Al^{+3}$$

   Since:

$$1 \text{ eq } H^+ = 1 \text{ eq } K^+ = 1 \text{ eq } Na^+ = 1 \text{ eq } Ca^{+2} = 1 \text{ eq } Mg^{+2} = 1 \text{ eq } Al^{+3}$$

   On an equivalent basis:

$$1 \text{ g } H^+ = 39 \text{ g } K^+ = 23 \text{ g } Na^+ = 20 \text{ g } Ca^{+2} = 12 \text{ g } Mg^{+2} = 9 \text{ g } Al^{+3}$$

   Step 2: Since 100 grams of negative charges need to be neutralized, these values are multiplied by 100. Therefore, 100 g H^+, 3,900 g K^+, 2,300 g Na^+, 2,000 g Ca^{+2}, 1,200 g Mg^{+2}, and 900 g Al^{+3} are needed to satisfy 100 negative charges. Hydrogen would require the least equivalent weight (100 g) to satisfy the 100 negative charges, while potassium would require the most (3,900 g).

Milliequivalent Weight. In biological sciences the term **milliequivalent** is often used when describing nutrients and their levels in soils. A milliequivalent (meq) is that amount of an ion that will displace (or combine with) 1 milligram (mg) of hydronium (H_3O^+) (or hydrogen, H^+) ion. One mg is 1/1,000 of a gram. In soil science, a milliequivalent is the amount of a cation (positive ion) that will displace 1 mg of hydrogen ions from the active soil solids, which are clay and humus. That amount, expressed in mg, is called the milliequivalent weight (meq-weight). Thus, one meq-weight is that amount (in mg) of a cation that will displace 1 meq-weight (1 mg) of H^+. When dealing with meq, 1 equivalent equals 1,000 meq and 1 equivalent/1,000 equals 1 meq.

Example problem:

What is 1 milliequivalent (meq) of calcium (Ca^{+2})?

Step 1: the equivalence of calcium is determined:

$$1 \text{ equivalent } Ca^{+2} = \frac{40 \text{ g (atomic weight of Ca)}}{2 \text{ (valence charge of } Ca^{+2})} = 20 \text{ grams}$$

Step 2: this has to be converted to meq: therefore if 1 equivalent Ca^{+2} = 20 grams, then this is divided by 1,000 to obtain meq. Thus 1 meq of Ca^{+2} = 0.020 g = 20 mg. This can be rewritten as:

$$20 \text{ g } Ca^{+2} \times \frac{1 \text{ eq}}{1,000 \text{ meq}} \times \frac{1,000 \text{ mg}}{1 \text{ g}} = 20 \text{ mg}$$

CHEMICAL REACTIONS

When two substances capable of reacting with each other are mixed, their atoms, molecules, or ions, being in constant motion, begin to collide with one another. Those that collide with sufficient energy will react and form new substances. **Chemical reactions** involve the exchange of electrons between atoms. This often involves the breaking of bonds and the formation of new bonds. Reactions may be described by **chemical equations.** The participant(s) to the left of the arrow are the starting substances called **reactant(s)**; those to the right are the new substance(s) called **product(s)** formed in the reaction. For example, the balanced equation for the formation of water from oxygen gas and hydrogen gas is:

$$2H_2 + O_2 \rightarrow 2H_2O$$
— reactants —   product

The arrow ($\rightarrow$) in the equation means "forms" and indicates the direction of the chemical change. The number and kind of atoms on the side of the product must equal the number and kind of atoms on the reactant side. The equation above tells us that two moles (molecules) of diatomic hydrogen (H_2) react with one mole (molecule) of diatomic oxygen(O_2) to yield two moles (molecules) of water. Another example involves preparing oxygen by heating mercury(II) oxide. Under the action of heat, mercury(II) oxide is decomposed into its two elements, mercury

(Hg) and oxygen (O_2). This reaction is represented by the following chemical equation:

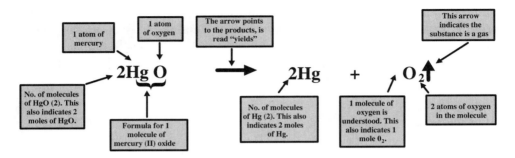

Whole number coefficients, such as two moles of water, are used in the above equation to comply with the *Law of Conservation of Atoms (or Mass)*. This law states that the total number of each atom (or mass) involved in a chemical reaction remains constant. In other words, no new atoms are added or lost. A new species of atom cannot be represented on the product side and no species of atom can disappear from the reactant side. Balancing requirements are met by adjusting the coefficient in front of the reactants and products to the smallest possible whole numbers, ensuring the equation meets the requirements of the law of conservation of atoms. The letters 's,' 'l,' 'g,' and 'aq' are used to indicate where a substance is a solid (s), liquid (l), gas (g), or an aqueous (aq) or water solution.

$$2Na(s) \quad + \quad 2H_2O(l) \rightarrow \quad 2NaOH(aq) \quad + \quad H_2(g)$$

sodium metal   water   sodium hydroxide   hydrogen gas

Balancing Chemical Reactions

To write an equation, the nature of the reactant(s) and product(s) must be known. Usually it is easier to find the composition of and identify the reactants. Balancing chemical equations is necessary to account for all molecules, atoms and/or ions and to ensure the law of conservation of atoms is met, where the total number of atoms on the reactant side of an equation must equal those found on the product side. *The total mass of the products must equal the total mass of the reactants.* Coefficients, therefore, are placed in front of the formulas to bring all elements into balance. However, since the formulas are fixed, balancing cannot be attempted by changing any of the subscripts in the formula. The following equation is not balanced since the total number of oxygen atoms on the left side of the equation does not equal those on the right side.

$$H_2O \rightarrow \quad H_2 \quad + \quad O_2 \qquad \text{(not balanced)}$$

water   diatomic   diatomic
hydrogen   oxygen

How can this equation be balanced? Many equations can be balanced by trial and error. A subscript '$_2$' may not be added to the oxygen (O) of the water molecule (H_2O) since this subscript would change the formula. Coefficients, therefore, are used to balance the total number of each atom in an equation, not subscripts. The first step is to begin with the compound with the most atoms or most kinds of atoms and use one of those atoms as a starting point. Currently, two hydrogen (H) atoms are on each side of the reaction and are balanced; however, only one oxygen atom is on the left side and two oxygen atoms are on the right. If the number of water molecules is increased to 2 to indicate two moles combine:

$$2H_2O \rightarrow H_2 + O_2 \quad \text{(not balanced)}$$

The second step is to balance elements appearing only once on each side of the reaction first. The equation is still not balanced since there are four hydrogen atoms on the left side of the equation but only two hydrogen atoms on the right. To balance the number of hydrogen atoms on the product side, a coefficient of 2 is placed in front of the hydrogen molecule, making it $2H_2$, as shown:

$$2H_2O \rightarrow 2H_2 + O_2 \quad \text{(balanced)}$$

The equation is now balanced since the same number of each atom is found on both sides of the equation. In this case, the same number of hydrogen atoms (4) are on each side of the reaction as are oxygen molecules (2). When dealing with more complicated reactions, balance free elements such as O and H atoms last.

When a whole number coefficient is placed in front of a compound it applies to all atoms in that compound. For example: $2H_2O$ = 4 atoms of H and 2 atoms of O. Similarly, when placed in front of a diatomic molecule, the product of the coefficient and subscript indicates the total number of atoms. The coefficients in an equation are always expressed to the smallest (simplest) whole number ratio. For example:

$$4H_2O \rightarrow 4H_2 + 2O_2 \text{ should be simplified to}$$

$$2H_2O \rightarrow 2H_2 + O_2$$

Summary of Steps for Writing Chemical Equations (Umland and Bellama, 1999).

1. Write a word equation after identifying the reactants and products.
2. Write symbols for elements (formulas for elements existing as polyatomic molecules) and correct formulas for compounds.
3. Balance by changing coefficients in front of symbols and formulas. Do not change formulas or add or remove substances (remember the Law of Conservation of Atoms, or Mass).
4. Check to see if the same number of each kind of atom is shown on both sides. If coefficients have a common divisor, simplify.
5. Add symbols showing whether substances are solids (s), liquids (l), gases (g), or in aqueous solution (aq). If the conditions required for the reaction to take place, such as catalysts, is known, write them over the arrow.

Example:

Balance the following word equation:

sodium chloride (s) → sodium metal (s) + chlorine gas (g)

Step 1: Write the formulas for the reactants and products:

$$NaCl(s) \rightarrow Na \ (s) + Cl_2 \ (g)$$

Step 2: Change coefficients in front of symbols and formulas. There is one chlorine atom on the left side of the equation but two on the right side. These are balanced by placing a 2 in front of the NaCl. To balance the sodium ions, a 2 is also placed in front of the Na.

$$2NaCl(s) \rightarrow 2Na(s) + Cl_2(g) \qquad \text{balanced}$$

Step 3: Subscripts cannot be changed to balance a chemical reaction. For example, the sodium chloride equation cannot be balanced by:

$$NaCl_2(s) \rightarrow Na(s) + Cl_2(g) \qquad \text{balanced, but wrong}$$

Coefficients must be placed in front of the symbol, not as subscripts, as $NaCl_2$ above is the incorrect formula for sodium chloride.

Types of Chemical Reactions

Four common types of reactions typically occur (Table 1-8).

Chemical Equilibrium

Most chemical reactions are reversible. When net change of the chemical concentration ceases, the reaction is said to be at equilibrium. Consider the following imaginary reaction:

$$A + B \rightleftharpoons C + D$$

Equilibrium is reached when as many molecules of C and D are being converted to molecules of A and B as molecules of A and B are being converted to molecules of C and D. At equilibrium, the concentration of reactants does not have to equal the concentration of products. Only the *rates* of the forward and reverse reactions must be the same.

Suppose the reaction is set up so that only A and B molecules are present initially. At first, the reaction goes to the right, with A reacting with B to yield C and D. As C and D accumulate, the rate of the reverse reactions increases. At the same time, the rate of the forward reaction decreases because the concentrations of A and B are decreasing. At some point, the rates of the forward and reverse reactions equalize and no further changes in concentration take place. The propor-

TABLE 1-8. Four Basic Types of Chemical Reactions

1. **Combination (also called direct union composition or synthesis):** two or more substances combine to form (or synthesize) a more complex substance.

$$A + B \;\; \rightarrow AB$$

examples:

$$C + O_2 \;\; \rightarrow CO_2$$

$$2H_2 + O_2 \;\; \rightarrow 2H_2O$$

$$SO_3 + H_2O \rightarrow H_2SO_4$$

$$CaO + H_2O \rightarrow Ca(OH)_2$$

2. **Single replacement:** one substance is replaced in its compound by another substance, setting the replaced element free.

$$AB + C \;\; \rightarrow CB \;\;\; + A$$

examples:

$$H_2O + 2Na \rightarrow 2NaOH + H_2\uparrow$$

$$MgSO_4 + Ca \;\; \rightarrow CaSO_4 \; + Mg$$

$$H_2SO_4 + Zn \;\; \rightarrow ZnSO_4 \; + H_2$$

3. **Double replacement (or ion exchange):** two substances replace (or exchange) their ions with two other substances.

$$A^+B^- + C^+D^- \;\; \rightarrow A^+D^- \;\;\; + C^+B^-$$

examples:

$$NaCl + AgNO_3 \rightarrow NaNO_3 \;\; + AgCl\downarrow \text{ (precipitant)}$$

$$2NaCl + H_2SO_4 \;\; \rightarrow Na_2SO_4 \; + HCl\uparrow \text{ (gas)}$$

$$NaCl + KNO_3 \;\; \rightleftharpoons NaNO_3 \;\; + KCl$$

4. **Decomposition (or analysis):** one substance breaks down to form two or more simpler substances. This is a reversal of the composition reaction. Decomposition reactions are usually endothermic, requiring energy in the form of heat or electricity.

$$AB \rightarrow A \;\;\; + B$$

examples:

$$2H_2O \rightarrow 2H_2\uparrow \; + O_2\uparrow$$

$$2NH_3 \rightarrow N_2 \;\;\; + 3H_2$$

$$CaCO_3 \rightarrow CaO \; + CO_2$$

$$H_2CO_3 \rightarrow H_2O \; + CO_2$$

$$2KClO_3 \rightarrow 2KCl + 3O_2$$

tions of reactants (A + B) and products (C + D) will remain the same. Increasing either the concentration or the temperature increases the rate of reaction. Catalysts can also speed up a reaction by bringing the particles close together on the catalyst surface.

Oxidation-Reduction Reactions

Chemical reactions are essentially energy transformations in which stored energy in chemical bonds are transferred to other, newly formed chemical bonds. In such transfers, electrons shift from one energy level to another and in many reactions, electrons pass from one atom or molecule to another. An oxidation-reduction (also called redox) reaction is one in which electrons are transferred from one group or molecule to another. The charge that a molecule acquires is called its oxidation number or status. A simple reaction involving oxygen (or the oxidation of) in the presence of other elements forms *oxides* which are simple compounds of oxygen plus another element. A positive ion forms when a neutral atom is oxidized, while a negative ion forms when it is reduced. The original meaning of the term *oxidation* was the *addition of oxygen* to a compound, with the compound *losing the oxygen* being *reduced* (oxygen means "acid former"). Today, oxidation, in a chemical context, refers to the loss of electrons (to become more positive; the oxidation number of an element increases), with the molecule or atom which *gains* those electrons (to become more negative; the oxidation number of an element decreases) being reduced. The total oxidation number of all atoms in a formula is always zero. The loss of the electron through loss of a hydrogen atom will accomplish the same purpose; thus if a molecule loses a hydrogen it will be oxidized, if it gains a hydrogen, it is reduced. Oxidation and reduction reactions always occur simultaneously. In the formation of common table salt (NaCl) the equation is written:

Cl gains 1 electron, thus becomes negatively charged, and its oxidation number decreases from 0 to -1 (a.k.a., it is reduced)

$$2Na^0 \quad + \quad Cl_2^0 \quad \rightarrow \quad 2Na^+ \, Cl^-$$

Na loses 1 electron, thus becomes positively charged, and its oxidation number increases from 0 to $+1$ (a.k.a., it is oxidized)

In this equation, both reactants are initially neutral (e.g., $2Na^0$, Cl^0). During the reaction, sodium loses an electron (becomes positively charged) and so is oxidized, while chorine gains that electron and becomes negatively charged and reduced. The oxidation of one substance in a reaction causes the reduction of another, and the number of electrons lost by one equals the number gained by the other. The number of electrons lost by the reducing agent must equal the number of electrons gained by the oxidizing agent. The only way to know if a reaction is redox or not is by assigning oxidation numbers to each element and observing if a change in oxidation number occurs for these elements. When viewed separately, each sodium atom loses an electron and is said to be oxidized and becomes a sodium ion. The oxidation state of sodium has changed from the 0 state of the atom to the more positive $+1$ state of the ion.

$$Na^0 \rightarrow Na^+ + e^-$$

sodium   sodium   electron
atom   ion

Simultaneously, each chlorine atom acquires an electron (becoming negatively charged) and is said to be reduced to a chloride ion.

$$Cl^0 + e^- \rightarrow Cl^-$$

chlorine   electron   chloride
atom   ion

Redox reactions occur simultaneously and the degree of oxidation must be equal to the degree of reduction. When two sodium atoms are oxidized to Na^+ ions, an diatomic chlorine molecule is reduced to two Cl^- ions.

$$2Na^0 \rightarrow 2Na^{+1} + 2e^- \quad \text{(oxidation)}$$
$$\underline{Cl_2^0 + 2e^- \rightarrow 2Cl^{-1} \qquad\quad \text{(reduction)}}$$
$$Cl_2^0 + 2Na^0 \rightarrow 2Na^+Cl^- \quad \text{(combined)}$$

Another example:
$$4Al^0 \rightarrow 4Al^{+3} + 12e \quad \text{(oxidation)}$$
$$\underline{Cl_2^0 + 2e^- \rightarrow 6O^{-2} \qquad\quad \text{(reduction)}}$$
$$4Al^0 + 3O_2^0 \rightarrow 2Al_2O_3 \quad\quad \text{(combined)}$$

During photosynthesis electrons and hydrogen atoms are transferred from water to carbon dioxide, thereby oxidizing the water to oxygen and reducing the carbon dioxide to form a sugar containing six carbon atoms:

$$6CO_2 + 6H_2O + \text{energy} \xrightarrow[\text{photosynthesis}]{\lambda \text{ (light)}} 6O_2 + C_6H_{12}O_6$$

carbon   water   oxygen   sugar
dioxide

In biology and soils, O_2, C, N, S and to a lesser extent, Fe and Mn, are the primary elements that carry out electron transfer (or energy transfer) via redox reactions. Other important redox reactions include the use of batteries, chlorination of drinking water, and corrosion of metals. Rust is the corrosion of iron to various reddish brown oxides when exposed to moisture and air. **Galvanizing,** which is a process of coating metals with zinc, protects them from corrosion.

The Energy Factor in Chemical Reactions

Chemical reactions are either exothermic or **endothermic** processes. During a reaction a definite amount of chemical binding energy is changed into thermal (or internal) energy or vice versa. If a process is exothermic the total heat content of the products is lower than that of the reactants because of the loss of thermal energy.

Most **spontaneous reactions,** those that occur naturally or unassisted, give off energy (heat), thus are exothermic. If energy (heat) is added to the reaction, then it is endothermic. The products of an endothermic reaction must have a higher heat content than the reactants. For example, heat must be added to toast bread (this is endothermic and **nonspontaneous**), while in burning wood heat is given off and the reaction of burning continues by itself, thus is exothermic and spontaneous (once it is initially lit).

Molecules react with each other only when they collide with sufficient energy to (1) overcome the repulsive forces between their negatively charged electron orbitals and (2) break existing chemical bonds. The energy, called the **energy of activation,** is the amount of energy required to loosen bonds in molecules so they can cause a reaction. The energy of activation varies with the nature of the molecules: the more stable the substance, the more forceful the collision must be for a reaction to occur. Each chemical bond has a characteristic energy content, or bond energy. The higher the bond energy, the stronger the chemical bond and the greater the energy required to break it. The total bond energy of any molecule is the amount of energy required to break it into its constituent atoms.

In any given sample of molecules, some are moving with sufficient kinetic energy for a reaction to occur. At normal temperatures and pressures, the proportion of molecules with this energy may be so small that, for all practical purposes, the reaction does not take place. For example, hydrogen and oxygen gases do not combine spontaneously to form water when mixed at room temperature. The bonds of these molecular species must be broken, then new bonds between O and H atoms must be formed. Bond-breaking is an endothermic process and bond-forming is exothermic. The H and O molecules acquire enough energy to break the bonds between their atoms when the molecules collide and water is formed. Conversely, when atoms of H and O unite to form molecules of water, energy is released (exothermic). The amount of energy released is sufficient to provide the necessary activation energy for further H and O collisions to form water, and this "chain reaction" continues until either H or O sources are used up.

Reaction rates can be increased by increasing the likelihood of sufficiently forceful collisions between molecules. It appears that an initial energy "kick" (or activation) is needed to start the reaction. This can be achieved by: **raising the temperature,** thereby increasing the average velocity at which the molecules move, increasing their energy, and increasing the likelihood of their colliding with sufficient force to react. The use of heat to drive a chemical reaction is common in laboratories and in industry. **High pressure** and increasing the concentration of reaction molecules are additional techniques used to increase the rate of reactions. Increasing pressure increases the frequency of collision between reactants, thus increasing the reaction rate. An increase in pressure of a gas is similar to an increase in the concentration of the gas. **Catalysts** (commonly found as enzymes in plants) are used to increase the rates of reactions by lowering the energy of activation necessary to start a reaction and are shown above or below the arrow in chemical equations. For example, the reactions of *A* and *B* to form *AB* may be difficult because of a high energy of activation, but an alternative set of reactions may be possible, such as:

$$A + D \rightarrow AD$$

$$AD + B \rightarrow AB + D$$

The energies of activation for A and D and for AD and B are both low. A substance such as D is a catalyst since it permits a reaction to occur rapidly at low temperature. Catalysts work in various ways but in general they form a weak complex with the reactants and after the energy barrier is passed, the catalyst is regenerated in its original state. A catalyst is not consumed during a reaction, thus only very small amounts are usually required. For example, if potassium chlorate is heated strongly it decomposes into potassium chloride and oxygen. However, if certain catalysts such as manganese dioxide are mixed with potassium chlorate, oxygen is released at a much lower temperature and at a more rapid rate. The manganese dioxide does not furnish the oxygen, it only speeds up the reaction.

$$2KClO_3 \xrightarrow{MnO_2} 2KCl + 3O_2\uparrow$$

Living systems such as plants cannot use extreme temperatures and pressures to increase reaction rates, and the concentrations of reacting substances are often very low. Catalysts called **enzymes** are used by all living organisms to lower activation energies and increase rates.

The energy changes that occur in chemical reactions can be measured, and the relationships among various forms of energy are the bases for the science of **thermodynamics.** Consider a common respiration reaction where glucose is completely oxidized (or combusted to form carbon dioxide and water) represented by the following equation:

$$C_6H_{12}O_6 + 6O_2 \rightarrow 6CO_2 + 6H_2O + \text{energy (heat)}$$

This reaction releases energy in the form of heat to its surroundings. The release of heat can be measured precisely and is expressed:

$$\Delta H = -673 \text{ kilocalories per mole of glucose}$$

where ΔH is the change in heat content. The negative value indicates that heat is released and thus is an exothermic reaction. Endothermic reactions require energy (heat) and have positive ΔH values.

A calorie is defined as the amount of heat necessary to raise the temperature of 1 gram of water by 1°C; (1,000 calories = 1 kilocalorie = 4,184 Joules, another means of expressing energy). A reaction that liberates heat, such as glucose combustion, is *exothermic. Endothermic* reactions require heat (or energy) to occur. In the case of glucose formation via photosynthesis, the energy source is the sun. Heat serves to increase the motion of molecules, which increases the frequency of collisions between reactants. In general, the rate of a reaction doubles for each 10°C (18 F) increase in temperature. Once an exothermic reaction begins, it often becomes self-sustaining by the heat energy it produces, like the burning of a piece of paper once a match starts the flame.

Plants cannot convert a portion of the energy generated by the digestion of food to work. Instead, plants transfer the energy, in each of many discrete steps, in the form of chemical-bond energy. A series of coupled reactions takes place in which, at each stage, a low-energy molecule from the surroundings is converted into a relatively high-energy molecule at the expense of the free energy of the oxidation. Figure 1-8 is an example of this stepwise transfer of energy involved in **photosynthesis** through the **Z-scheme.** Energy is provided by red and orange light from sunlight, followed by a series of coupled reactions where a group of atoms (e.g., the phosphate group associated with adenosine triphosphate [ATP] and adenosine diphosphate [ADP]) are transferred from one molecule to another down the chain, acting as an energy carrier. Not only is the energy transferred efficiently in the oxidation process, new high-energy species (such as ATP and NADP) are formed, and these can enter into other vital reactions elsewhere in the organism (such as the Calvin cycle). Plants appear green because red, orange, and violet light bands in light are absorbed by leaf tissue while green, yellow, and blue light bands are reflected, causing the leaf to appear green to the eyes.

Every spontaneous reaction increases the disorder or randomness (called **entropy**). Generally, entropy increases as a substance changes from solid to liquid to

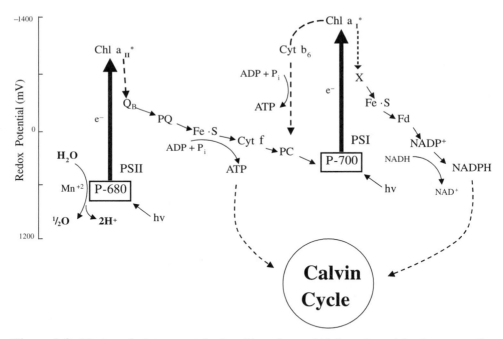

Figure 1-8. Electron (e^-) transport in the chloroplasts of higher plants (also known as the **Z-scheme**). Individual components are positioned according to their redox potential (electron donating or accepting properties). The diagram illustrates the antennae chlorophyll molecules feeding energy from sunlight (hv) into the special chlorophylls (Chl $a_{I \text{ and } II}$) associated with photosystem I (indicated as PSI) and photosystem II (PSII). The broken line indicates a cyclic electron flow in the PSI system allowing electrons to be recycled through a quencher (Q_B), iron-sulfur protein (Fe·S), cytochrome f (Cyt f), cytochrome b_6 (Cyt b_6), plastoquinone (PQ), and ferredoxin (Fd) under special conditions. Almost all of the molecular oxygen in the atmosphere is a product of photosynthesis.

gas. Entropy increases especially from liquid to gas because of the large increase in volume. Entropy also increases downward within a group of the periodic table, as the temperature of the substance increases and as the number of atoms bonded together increases for similar structures.

PRACTICE PROBLEMS

1. What is an *atom*? (*the smallest particle that can exist as an element*).
2. What is a *molecule*? (*the smallest particle of a substance that retains properties of that substance*).
3. What is an *element*? (*a substance that cannot be broken into a simpler substance by chemical change*).
4. How does a *mixture* differ from a *compound*? (*elements in a compound are chemically combined; they cannot be separated by physical means, as the constituents of a mixture can*).
5. Which is the stronger acid, HPO_3 or HPO_4? (*HPO_4*).
6. Determine the oxidation number of the underlined element in each compound.
   a. $\underline{Cu}Cl$ (*$^+1$*)
   b. $\underline{Fe}O$ (*$^+2$*)
   c. $\underline{Fe}_2O_3$ (*$^+3$*)
   d. $\underline{Sn}F_4$ (*$^+4$*)
7. What is 1 meq of aluminum (Al^{+3})? (*9 mg*).
8. What is the number of atoms in 2.25 mole of Cu? (*1.35×10^{24}*).
9. (a) How many grams are in 1.00 mole H_2S? (*34 g*).
   (b) How many atoms and molecules are in 10.3 g H_2S? (*atoms = 5.45×10^{23}; molecules = 1.82×10^{23}*).
10. How many atoms are present in 2 moles of water molecules? (*$2 \times 3 \times [6.02 \times 10^{23}] = 3.612 \times 10^{24}$ atoms*).
11. What is meant by the term *mole*? (*chemical unit to "count" atoms and molecules. There are 6.02×10^{23} particles in a mole*).
12. What is the significance of *Avogadro's Number* (6.02×10^{23})? (*by knowing exactly the number of molecules in one mole, one can calculate relative weights of one molecule of an element*).
13. How many bricks would be found in 2 moles of bricks? (*$2 \times [6.02 \times 10^{23}] = 12.04 \times 10^{23}$ bricks = 1.204×10^{24}*).
14. How many moles are in each: (a) 2,000 g of water, (*111.0 moles*); (b) 14 g of CO_2, (*0.318 mole*). (c) 24 g of O_2, (*0.75 mole*); and, (d) 92 g of ethyl alcohol (C_2H_5OH)? (*2 moles*).
15. What are the number of moles in: (a) 2.53×10^{22} atom of Al? (*0.042*); and (b), 14.3 g of $NaC_{18}H_{35}O_2$ (soap)? (*0.0467*).
16. What information does a formula such as $PbCl_2$ provide? (*two types of atoms are present; Pb and Cl; Pb and Cl atoms are in a 1:2 ratio; there is one mole of $PbCl_2$ molecules, and 278.1 g of $PbCl_2$*).

17. Consider the formula for table sugar (or sucrose), $C_{12}H_{22}O_{11}$. What does it indicate in regard to:
    a. types of atoms present? (*three types—carbon, hydrogen, and oxygen*).
    b. number of each type of atom present? (*12 C atoms; 22 H atoms; 11 O atoms*).
    c. moles of molecules present? (*1 mole of $C_{12}H_{22}O_{11}$ molecules*).
    d. weight (g) of one mole of sugar molecules? (*C = 12 × 12.00 = 144.0; H = 22 × 1.00 = 22.0; O = 11 × 16.00 = 176.0; 144 + 22 + 176 = 342 g*).

18. How many moles of *molecules* and *atoms* are represented in the formula P_4? (*1 mole of P_4 molecules and 4 moles of phosphorus [P] atoms*).

19. What is the percent composition of H and O in H_2O? (*11.1% H, 88.9% O*).

20. What is the percent composition of $Ca(NO_3)_2$? (*24.5% Ca; 17.1% N; 58.5% O*).

21. What is the percent composition of glucose ($C_6H_{12}O_6$)? (*40% C; 6.71% H; 53.29% O*).

22. How many kg of iron can be removed from 639 kg of Fe_2O_3? (*Fe_2O_3 is 70% Fe, therefore, 447 kg Fe*).

23. Determine the empirical formula of the compound with 29.1% Na, 40.5% S, and 30.4% O. (*$Na_2S_2O_3$*).

24. What is meant by *molecular weight*? (*the weight, in grams, of one mole [$6.02 × 10^{23}$ molecules] of a compound*).

25. What is the weight of:
    a. $6.02 × 10^{23}$ atoms of N? (*14.0 g*).
    b. one atom of N? (*$2.33 × 10^{-23}$ g*).

26. What is the weight of:
    a. 1 mole of iron (Fe) atoms? (*1 m × 55.8 g/m = 55.8 g*).
    b. 1 atom of Fe? (*55.8 g/m ÷ $6.02 × 10^{23}$ molecules/m = $9.27 × 10^{-23}$ g*).

27. Calculate the formula weights of:
    a. KNO_3 (potassium nitrate) (*101.8 g*).
    b. $CO(NH_2)_2$ (urea) (*60.04 g*).
    c. NaOCl (bleach) (*74.44 g*).
    d. K_2SO_4 (potassium sulfate) (*174.3 g*).

28. Find molarities of the following:

Solution	Density (g/mL)	Weight Percent	Molarity
KOH	1.344	35	(*8.40*)
HNO_3	1.334	54	(*11.45*)
H_2SO_4	1.834	95	(*17.74*)
$Al_2(SO_4)_3$	1.253	22	(*0.805*)

29. What is the excess reagent when 3.1 mole SO_2 reacts with 2.7 mole O_2? (*1.6 mole O_2 is required, thus, SO_2 is in excess*).

30. (a) How many liters of CO_2 at standard temperature and pressure are consumed by a plant in producing 454 g of glucose by the following photosynthesis reaction, and (b) how many liters of air are needed to supply the required CO_2 in part (a) assuming air is 0.040 percent CO_2 by volume? [(a) *338 liters*, (b) *8.45 × 10^5 liters*].

$$6CO_2 + 6H_2O \rightarrow C_6H_{12}O_6 + 6O_2$$

31. In the production of ammonium sulfate fertilizer, the following reactions occurs. If 22.7 g NH_3 and 54.8 g H_2SO_4 are used: (a) Which reactant is limiting, (b) which reactant will be left over and how much (grams), and (c) how many grams of ammonium sulfate can be formed? [(a) *H_2SO_4* (b) *3.7 g NH_3* (c) *73.8 g*].

$$6NH_3 + H_2SO_4 \rightarrow (NH_4)_2SO_4$$

32. (a) How many moles of H_2SO_4 are needed to completely react with 0.15 mole NaOH, and (b) How many grams of NaOH are needed to react with excess H_2SO_4 to prepare 60 g of Na_2SO_4? [(a) *0.075 mol H_2SO_4*; (b) *33.8 g NaOH*].

33. How many moles of $KClO_3$ are in 500 mL of 0.150 M solution? (*0.075 moles*).

34. How many grams of $BaCl_2$ are needed to prepare 200 mL of a 0.500 M solution? (*20.8 g*).

35. How many grams of NaOH are needed to prepare 1 liter of 0.20 M NaOH? (*8.0 g NaOH*).

36. What is the molar concentration of hydrochloric acid (HCl) with a density of 1.2 g/mL and is 36% HCl by mass? (*12 M*).

37. How much H_2SO_4 with a density of 1,840 g/L is needed to prepare 0.5 liter of 6.0 M solution? (*0.160 liter or 160 mL*).

38. How many grams of sucrose, $C_{12}H_{22}O_{11}$, are needed to make 300 mL of a 0.50 M solution? (*51.3 g*).

39. How many mL of 2.0 M NaBr are needed to prepare 300 mL of 0.75 M NaBr? (*112.5 mL*).

40. What is the molarity of a 200 mL solution prepared by adding water to 10 g of KCl? (*0.670 M*).

41. How many moles of sodium hydroxide (NaOH) are needed to completely neutralize 1 liter of the following?

    a. 1 M hydrochloric acid, HCl (*1*).

    b. 1 M phosphoric acid, H_3PO_4 (*3*).

    c. 1 M sulfuric acid, H_2SO_4 (*2*).

42. Determine the number of equivalents per mole of the following:

a. H_2O (*2*).
b. $HClO_4$ (*1*).
c. K_2SO_4 (*2*).
d. $CaCl_2$ (*2*).
e. HF (*1*).

43. What is the equivalent weight of KOH? (*56.1 g*).
44. How many grams are in 1 equivalent of each of the following?
    a. $Ca(NO_3)_2$ (*82 g*).
    b. Zn (*32.7 g*).
    c. HCO_3^- (*61.0 g*).
    d. KCl (*74.6 g*).
    e. $Al_2(SO_4)_3$ (*57.0 g*).
45. How many equivalents are in 20.5 g of sulfurous acid, H_2SO_3? (*0.50 equivalents*).
46. What is the equivalent weight of HSO_4^-? (*97 g*).
47. Convert 97.5 mg of K^+ to milliequivalent weight. (*2.5 meq K^+*).
48. A soil sample from a coastal golf course fairway was analyzed and found to have a sodium (Na) concentration of 8,000 ppm (mg/kg). How many meq Na^+/100 g does this soil contain? (*34.8 meq/100 g. This would be considered very high and only the most salt tolerant turfgrasses would be expected to survive*).
49. Balance the following equations and tell what type reaction each represents.
    a. zinc + chlorine → zinc chloride (*$Zn + Cl_2 \rightarrow ZnCl_2$; combination*).
    b. mercury(II) oxide → mercury + oxygen (*$2HgO \rightarrow 2Hg + O_2$; decomposition*).
    c. calcium carbonate + sulfuric acid (H_2SO_4) → calcium sulfate + water + carbon dioxide (*$CaCO_3 + H_2SO_4 \rightarrow CaSO_4 + H_2O + CO_3$; double replacement*).
    d. sodium hydrogen carbonate → sodium carbonate + water + carbon dioxide
       (*$2NaHCO_3 + Na_2CO_3 + H_2O + CO_2$; decomposition*).
    e. Al_2O_3 → Al + O_2 (*$2Al_2O_3 \rightarrow 4Al + 3O_2$; decomposition*).
    f. Fe + Br_2 → $FeBr_3$ (*$2Fe + 2Br_3 \rightarrow 2FeBr_3$; combination*).
    g. Zn + HCl → H_2 + $ZnCl_2$ (*$Zn + 2HCl \rightarrow H_2 + ZnCl_2$; single replacement*).
    h. $AgNO_3$ + AlI_3 → AgI + $Al(NO_3)_3$ (*$3AgNO_3 + AlI_3 \rightarrow 3AgI + Al(NO_3)_3$; double replacement*).
    i. NaOH + H_2SO_4 → Na_2SO_4 + H_2O (*$2NaOH + H_2SO_4 \rightarrow Na_2SO_4 + 2H_2O$; double replacement*).
50. Balance the following equations and tell what type reaction each represents.
    a. zinc + chlorine → zinc chloride (*$Zn + Cl_2 \rightarrow ZnCl_2$; combination*).
    b. mercury(II) oxide → mercury + oxygen (*$2HgO \rightarrow 2Hg + O_2$; decomposition*).

c. calcium carbonate + sulfuric acid (H_2SO_4) → calcium sulfate + water + carbon dioxide (*$CaCO_3$ + H_2SO_4 → $CaSO_4$ + H_2O + CO_3; double replacement*).

d. sodium hydrogen carbonate → sodium carbonate + water + carbon dioxide (*$2NaHCO_3$ → Na_2CO_3 + H_2O + CO_2; decomposition*).

e. Al_2O_3 → Al + O_2 (*$2Al_2O_3$ → $4Al$ + $3O_2$; decomposition*).

f. Fe + Br_2 → $FeBr_3$ (*$2Fe$ + $2Br_3$ → $2FeBr_3$; combination*).

g. Zn + HCl → H_2 + $ZnCl_2$ (*Zn + $2HCl$ → H_2 + $ZnCl_2$; single replacement*).

h. $AgNO_3$ + AlI_3 → AgI + $Al(NO_3)_3$ (*$3AgNO_3$ + AlI_3 → $3AgI$ + $Al(NO_3)_3$; double replacement*).

i. sodium oxide + water → sodium hydroxide (*Na_2O + H_2O → $2NaOH$: combination*).

j. NaOH + H_2SO_4 → Na_2SO_4 + H_2O (*$2NaOH$ + H_2SO_4 → Na_2SO_4 + $2H_2O$; double replacement*).

k. sulfurous acid (aq) → water + sulfur dioxide (*H_2SO_4 → H_2O + SO_2: decomposition*).

l. Fe + $CuSO_4$ → $FeSO_4$ + Cu (*balanced; single replacement*).

m. aluminum + hydrochloric acid → aluminum chloride + hydrogen (*$2Al$ + $6HCl$ → $2AlCl_3$ + $3H_2$; single replacement*).

n. hydrochloric acid + magnesium hydroxide → magnesium chloride + water (*$2HCl$ + $Mg(OH)_2$ → $MgCl_2$ + $2H_2O$; double replacement*).

51. For the following reactions, determine which substance is oxidized and which is reduced.

a. Zn + 2HCl → $ZnCl_2$ + H_2 (*zinc is oxidized as its oxidation number changes from 0 to +2; hydrogen is reduced as its oxidation number changes from +1 to 0; chlorine is unchanged*).

b. C + O_2 → CO_2 (*carbon is oxidized; oxygen is reduced*).

c. 2HgO → 2Hg + O_2 (*mercury oxidation changes from +2 to 0, thus, is reduced; the oxygen changes from −2 to 0, thus, is oxidized*).

CHAPTER 2

CHEMICAL PROPERTIES AND ANALYSIS OF WATER

Understanding the basic chemical and physical properties of water is essential when trying to manage turf and agricultural plants with less than ideal quality or adequate amounts. This chapter begins by presenting water, its hydrogen bonding properties, pH, acids and bases, and dissociation constants. The second half of the chapter lists and discusses in sufficient details how to interpret a water analysis report, convert reported values to useable forms, and the most recent guidelines on water quality values.

PROPERTIES OF WATER

Pure water is a odorless, tasteless, and in shallow containers, colorless liquid. Deep bodies of water, such as the ocean, have a blue color due to the blue color of the sky. The odor and taste associated with water humans use are due to various substances dissolved in it, including air.

Physical Properties. Pure water boils at 100°C (212°F) and freezes at 0°C (32°F) when the pressure is 760 mm of mercury. If the pressure is decreased, as at higher elevations, the boiling point also decreases so that boiling water is not as hot at high altitudes compared to sea level. Therefore, a longer time is required to cook foods at high altitudes. Conversely, increasing the pressure above 760 mm, as with pressure cooking, the boiling point of water is raised and food will cook quicker because of the higher temperature attainable.

Chemical Properties. Water is involved with many chemical reactions. Chemical action is promoted by dissolving substances in water. Baking soda, for example, when mixed with acids in milk, eggs, etc., releases carbon dioxide. Moisture in the air promotes rusting of metals such as iron; it combines with metallic oxides to form hydroxides (or bases) or with nonmetallic oxides to form acids.

72

Hydrogen Bonding

Water is an essential component of life. Over 70% of human body weight is water. It has unusual physical properties as a solvent due to its strong intermolecular **hydrogen bonding** (or internal cohesiveness) that occurs among water particles. The H_2O molecule has a bent geometrical shape with an H—O—H bond angle of 104.5° (Figure 2-1). A hydrogen bond forms between the negative "corner" (or δ^-) of one water molecule and the positive "corner" (or δ^+) of another (Figure 2-1). Hydrogen bonds do not involve the sharing of electrons, thus they are not covalent; they do not bind two ions together, so they are not ionic, and they are too electrostatic in nature to be **van der Waals** (e.g., weak intermolecular) forces. The energies of hydrogen bonds are about 10 times those of van der Waals forces and about one-tenth those of ionic or covalent bonds.

In a water molecule, electrons are not shared equally. Electrons spend more time near the oxygen atom, creating a partial negative charge (designated as δ^-) region that attracts the bonding electrons much like a magnet from each of the two hydrogen atoms. A partial positive region (designated as δ^+) is created around each of the two hydrogen nuclei. These partial positive regions and the partial negative regions around the oxygen atom found in water, along with its unsymmetrical shape, create a molecule that is referred to as **polar** in nature (Figure 2-1). These partial attraction charges, called **dipole-dipole** attractions, are not nearly as strong as the attraction between ions with full positive and negative charges. The ionic attraction between Na^+ and Cl^- ions in NaCl is much stronger than the attraction between the polar (dipole) molecules of covalently bonded molecules such as molecules HCl and H_2O.

Hydrogen bonds occur from unusually strong dipole-dipole attraction between molecules in which H is bonded to nitrogen (N), oxygen (O), or fluorine (F). The

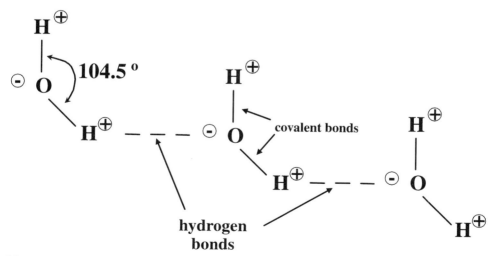

Figure 2-1. Hydrogen bonds are intermolecular forces *between* molecules. Hydrogen bonding in water occurs between the partially positively charged hydrogen nuclei and partially negatively charged oxygen atom between water (H_2O) molecule. Covalent intramolecular bonds connect atoms together *within* molecules; for example, within H and O molecules in water molecules.

TABLE 2-1. Comparison of Melting and Boiling Points of Various Compounds with Water

Substance	Common Use	Melting Point (C)	Boiling Point (C, atmospheric pressure)
Acetic acid	Vinegar	17°	118°
Ammonia	Household cleaner	−78°	−33°
Benzene	Gasoline hydrocarbon	5.5°	80°
Citric acid	Citrus fruit	153°	decomposes
Ethyl alcohol	Beer, wine, liquors	−117°	79°
Gold	Coins, jewelry	1,064°	3,080°
Hydrogen chloride	Muriatic acid	−115°	−85°
Oxygen	Atmosphere	−218°	−183°
Potassium iodide	Iodized salt	681°	1,330°
Propane	Fuel for grills	−190°	−42°
Sodium chloride	Table salt	801°	1,413°
Sodium hydroxide	Lye	318°	1,390°
Sucrose	Table sugar	185°	decomposes
Toluene	Paint remover	−95°	111°
Water	Water	0°	100°

bonding properties where each water molecule can potentially form hydrogen bonds with four other molecules allow water to bind to itself and make water a relatively structured solvent, and account for its strong internal cohesion as a liquid.

The degree of hydrogen bonding varies with water temperature. Energy is required to break hydrogen bonds, causing water to have a relative high boiling point (212°F or 100°C) and low freezing point (32°F or 0°C). Unlike water, **nonpolar substances** do not undergo hydrogen bonding, thus molecules move easily past each other, so they flow with little viscosity. When energy is supplied, there are only negligible forces to hold the molecules in place and slow them, so their speed quickly increases, raising their temperature. Nonpolar substances also boil and turn into a gas even at low temperatures, with little energy needed. Molecules without hydrogen bonding have vastly different boiling and freezing points compared to water (Table 2-1). For example, the boiling point of methane (CH_4) is −328°F (−161°C), ammonia (NH_3) is −91°F (−33°C), and hydrofluoric acid (HF) is 66°F (19°C) while their freezing points are −363°F (−184°C) for methane, −172°F (−78°C) for ammonia, and −198°F (−92°C) for hydrofluoric acid.

Water is also an excellent solvent for many charged (ionic) and neutrally charged (nonionic) molecules due to its polarity and hydrogen-bonding properties. Most solids are more dense than their liquids and the solid sinks in its liquid. Water is only one of a few substances that expands by about 10% when freezing, thus reducing its density, allowing it to float. When ice melts, hydrogen bonds are broken, the open expanded structure is destroyed, and molecules move closer together. Water is therefore denser than ice.

Example:

Calculate the energy released when 8.0 g of oxygen reacts with 1.0 g of hydrogen to form 9.0 g of water if 59.6 kcal of energy are released when 16 g of oxygen reacts with 2.0 g of hydrogen to form 18 g of water vapor.

$$\frac{59.6 \text{ kcal}}{18 \text{ g water}} = \frac{\times}{9.0 \text{ g water}} \quad \times = 29.8 \text{ kcal}$$

Hydrogen bonds are extremely important in biological systems. In proteins, for example, hydrogen bonds form between the H of NH groups and O of CO groups giving the coiled shape of the polypeptide chains, thus directly affecting the properties of proteins.

Hydrogen bonds are also found in the nucleic acids, DNA and RNA. DNA is the substance that makes up genes, which are the hereditary units that control the functions of cells and manufacturing of proteins (see Chapter Four). Hydrogen bonds between N—H $\cdots$ O and N—H $\cdots$ N hold together the double helix structure of DNA and therefore are an important factor in heredity.

Density. The density of any substance is its mass per unit volume.

$$\text{density} = \frac{\text{mass}}{\text{volume}}$$

The units used in science to indicate density are grams per milliliter (g/mL) or grams per cubic centimeter (g/cm³) which are interchangeable as they are equal. The standard for density is water, which has a density of 1.0 g/mL. Anything less dense than water, ice for example, floats; anything more dense, lead for example, sinks (Table 2-2).

Metal and concrete sink because they are more dense than water – they have a greater mass than the volume of water they displace. Fats, oils, and ice are less dense than water – have a smaller mass than its equivalent volume of water – so

TABLE 2-2. Average Densities of Selected Solids. Values >1.0 (for Water) Sink While Those <1.0, Float

Substance	Density (g/mL or g/cm³)
Aluminum	2.7
Cork	0.2
Diamond	3.5
Glass	2.6
Gold	19.3
Ice	0.9
Lead	11.4
Pyrite ("fool's gold")	5.0
Quartz	2.6
Sodium chloride (rock salt)	2.2
Sucrose (sugar)	1.6
Wax	0.9
Wood	
Balsa	0.1
Birch	0.6
Maple	0.7
Oak	0.8

they float. Boats, ducks, and wood float because air trapped next to them provides buoyancy.

Surface Tension, Soaps, and Surfactants. Water surface tension occurs as water molecules exert relatively large forces of attraction on all their neighboring molecules – those to their sides, in front and behind, and above and below. This attraction is dispersed spherically, in all directions. At water surface, the forces of attraction become focused toward the sides and downward. This particular strong attraction of the surface molecules for each other and for the molecules immediately below them results in the cohesion of the surface called **surface tension**. Surface tension keeps certain insects, for example, from sinking as they walk across water. Needles, paper clips, and razor blades do not sink if placed carefully on a smooth water surface, even though the metal they consist of is denser than water. Although the surface of water "stretches" a little when an insect walks on it or a needle is placed on it, the surface would have to break to let the insect's feet or the needle go through it.

Capillary action is another result of surface tension which raises the surface of water slightly in a glass tube. The molecules of a liquid attract each other and are also attracted by the walls of the container. The forces between the molecules of a substance are called **cohesive forces**, and the force between the molecules of different substances are **adhesive forces**. The attraction of glass for water pulls the water that touches the glass up, and surface tension makes the rest of the surface of the water follow. Gravity limits the height water will rise. The smaller the diameter of the capillary, the more surface area that comes in contact with water, thus the higher the water rises.

Capillary action, for example, causes paper towels and cotton to absorb water. Capillary action also influences water movement through the soil and the rise of water from roots to leaves in plants.

Detergent is Latin meaning "to wipe off" or "to clean" and is anything that cleans. *Soaps* are detergents and help clean oily and greasy dirt. Soaps are a very narrow class of detergents composed of sodium (or sometimes potassium) salts of long-chain carboxylic acids ($-COOH$). The anion of the carboxyl group ($-COO^-$) is balanced by a sodium (Na^+) cation and tied by a covalent bond to a long chain of $-CH_2-$ groups and terminated by a methyl ($-CH_3$) group with the general equation:

$$\text{general equation for soap:} \quad CH_3-(CH_2)_n-COO^-Na^+$$

With this structure, a soap molecule possesses two opposing chemical tendencies. The methyl ($-CH_3$) end tends to dissolve in materials that are hydrocarbons, such as gasoline and grease, but not in water. This end is referred to as **hydrophobic** (Greek meaning "water fearing") since it shuns water but mixes easily with oily, greasy substances (Figure 2-2). The other end ($-COO^-Na^+$) of soap is ionic and tends to dissolve in water. This **hydrophilic** (Greek meaning "water loving") end is attached to water but shuns hydrocarbons and other oily and greasy substances. The hydrophobic ends of soaps are attracted to hydrocarbons, such as grease, and tend to surround these. The hydrophilic end allows the soap to remain suspended in water and easily rinses away with the grease particle still attached to it.

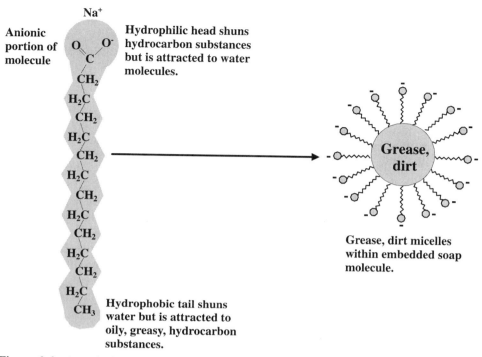

Figure 2-2. A typical soap molecule (left) with a hydrophilic head which shuns hydrocarbons but is attracted to water molecules and a hydrophobic tail which shuns water but is attracted to hydrocarbons such as grease, oil, or dirt. A cross section of a spherical detergent micelle (right) showing the grease micelle with embedded soap molecule.

Soaps, detergents, and other substances that interfere with the strong attractive forces surface water molecules normally exert on each other and so lowers the surface tension to allow water to spread out, are referred to as *surface-active agents* or **surfactants** for short. Surfactants are common additives to pesticide sprays to reduce the surface tension of water, allowing water to better and more evenly disperse or spread along the waxy surface of plants. This waxy surface (cuticle) of plants is present, among other things, to reduce internal water loss. This waxy surface is similar to waxing a car, which repels water, causing it to form beads. Soaps, detergents and surfactants decrease the surface tension of water, allowing the water beads to spread out more evenly, making them a better wetting agent.

Conductivity of Solutions

Naturally occurring water is never chemically pure. It contains dissolved substances, gases, bacteria, fine particles of soil, and other foreign matter. Water-soluble substances may be classified as electrolytes or nonelectrolytes. Substances that conduct electricity (ions or charged particles that have mobility and are free to move through a liquid) when dissolved in water are referred to as **electrolytes**. Examples include solutions of sodium chloride, hydrochloric acid, sodium hydroxide, copper sulfate, and potassium nitrate. **Non-electrolytes** are covalent substances that form molecular solutions that do not conduct electric currents. Examples include pure water and water solutions of covalent substances such as sugar (sucrose), alcohol, and glycerol. **Dissociation** is when certain substances dissolve in solution they break up (or dissociate) into ions. Dissociation is discussed in more detail later in this chapter.

Electrolytes affect the freezing and boiling points of solvents to a greater extent than nonelectrolytes. For example, the electrolytic solution of alcohol or ethylene glycol is used as antifreeze since it lowers the freezing point of the coolant in automobile radiators. The extent of this effect on freezing and boil points depends on the number of solute molecules dissolved in a given number of water molecules. For example, a 0.1 M solution of sodium chloride, an electrolyte, in water lowers the freezing point nearly twice as much as a 0.1 M solution of sugar, a nonelectrolyte. In other words, salt water freezes at a lower temperature than fresh water. This is why salts are applied in winter to lower the freezing points of wet or frozen roads.

In other conditions, the freezing point of water can also be lowered by decreasing the amount of pressure exposed on the solution. The extent of boiling point (bp) elevation and freezing point (fp) depression are proportional to the **molality** (not molarity) of the solution. Specifically, the freezing point depression of water is lowered 1.86°C per kg water by each mole of solute added. This is called the **molal freezing point** depression for water.

$$\Delta \text{fp} = K_{fp}m \text{ and bp} = K_{bp}m$$

Δfp is the overall change in freezing point, K_{fp} is a constant (1.86°C for water) while m is the molality of the solution. In similar fashion, the boiling point of water is raised by the presence of solute molecules. The molal boiling point of water is raised 0.512°C per kg water by each mole of solute added.

Molality is a concentration unit similar to molarity and is the number of moles of solute dissolved in one kilogram of solvent, while molarity is the number of moles of solute per volume of solution in liters. With molality, molal solutions are measured by mass, whereas molar solutions are measured by volume which is generally easier and quicker to perform.

$$m \text{ (molality)} = \frac{\text{moles solute}}{\text{kg of solvent}}$$

$$M \text{ (molarity)} = \frac{\text{moles solute}}{\text{liters of solution}}$$

Molality and molarity can be interconverted if the density of the solution is known.

Example:

What is the molality of the following solution?

1. 0.43 mole NaCl in 2.4 kg H_2O

$$\text{molality} = \frac{\text{moles solute}}{\text{kg solvent}} = \frac{0.43 \text{ moles NaCl}}{2.4 \text{ kg } H_2O} = 0.18 \text{ moles/kg}$$

2. 4.00 g NaCl in 850 g H_2O

Step 1: Convert 4.00 g NaCl to moles solute.

$$4.00 \text{ g} \times \frac{1 \text{ mole NaCl}}{58.5 \text{ g}} = 0.068 \text{ moles NaCl}$$

Step 2: Convert g to kg and incorporate into the molality equation.

8.50 g = 0.850 kg,

$$\text{molality} = \frac{\text{moles solute}}{\text{kg solvent}} = \frac{0.068 \text{ moles}}{0.85 \text{ kg}} = 0.08 \text{ moles/kg}$$

Electrolytes also raise the boiling point of water to a greater extent than non-electrolytes. A 0.1 *M* solution of potassium sulfate, an electrolyte, raises the boiling point nearly three times that of a 0.1 *M* solution of sugar. The raising or lowering of freezing and boiling points by electrolytes is directly proportional to the molecular concentrate of the solute and is independent of the properties of the particles themselves.

$$\text{change boiling point } (\Delta bp) = K_{bp}m$$

K_{bp} is a constant (+0.512 for water) while *m* is the molality of solute particles in the solution.

Example:

1. What effect on freezing point depression of water occurs if 1 mole of NaCl is placed in 1 kg water (assuming 100% ionization or dissociation)?

Step 1: set up the equation.

$$\begin{array}{cccc}
1 \text{ mole} & 1 \text{ mole} & & 1 \text{ mole} \\
NaCl(aq) \rightarrow & Na^+(aq) & + & Cl^-(aq)
\end{array}$$

↑___ 2 moles of ions total __↑

Step 2: insert the values in the freezing point depression equation:

$$\text{freezing point depression} = \frac{(1.86°C)(1 \text{ kg } H_2O)}{\text{mole solute}} \times 2 \text{ moles}$$

$$= 3.72°C$$

therefore, the freezing point of water is 3.72°C lower for each mole of NaCl added per kg water.

2. What effect on freezing point depression of water occurs if 1 mole of $CaCl_2$ is placed in 1 kg water (assuming 100% ionization or dissociation)?

Step 1: set up the equation.

$$
\begin{array}{cccc}
\text{1 mole} & \text{1 mole} & & \text{2 mole} \\
CaCl_2(aq) \rightarrow & Ca^+(aq) & + & 2Cl^-(aq)
\end{array}
$$

↑   3 moles of ions total   ↑

Step 2: insert the values in the freezing point depression equation:

$$\text{freezing point depression} = \frac{(1.86°C)(1 \text{ kg } H_2O)}{\text{mole solute}} \times 3 \text{ moles}$$

$$= 5.58°C$$

therefore, the freezing point of water is lowered 5.58°C for each mole of $CaCl_2$ added per kg water.

3. What effect on freezing point depression of water occurs if 1 mole of glucose ($C_6H_{12}O_6$) is placed in 1 kg water? Since glucose is a nonelectrolyte, thus does not breakdown into individual particles, the freezing point depression of water is only lowered 1.86°C.

4. What is the molality of a solution of 30 g of benzene (C_6H_6) and 65 g of the solvent toluene (C_7H_8)?

Step 1: calculate the number of moles in benzene.

$$30 \text{ g } C_6H_6 \times \frac{1 \text{ mol } C_6H_6}{78.15 \text{ g } C_6H_6} = 0.384 \text{ mol}$$

Step 2: insert the values into the molality formula.

$$\text{molality (m)} = \frac{\text{moles solute}}{\text{kg solvent}} = \frac{0.384 \text{ mole } C_6H_6}{0.0650 \text{ kg } C_7H_8}$$

$$= 5.91 \text{ m}$$

The opposite effect on boiling point elevation occurs as the freezing point depression of water. However, the boiling point elevation of water is raised 0.512°C per kg water by each mole of solute added. For glucose in water containing 1 mole of solute, the boiling point of water would be raised from a normal 100°C to 100.512°C. The NaCl solution would have a boiling point of 101.2°C and the $CaCl_2$ solution's boiling point would be 101.53°C.

Example:

What are the boiling and freezing points for a 0.650 m solution of urea in water (for water, K_{bp}=0.512°C/m and K_{fp} = -1.86°C/m)?

$$fp = \frac{(-1.86°C)(0.650 \text{ m})}{\text{mole solute}} = -1.21°C$$

$$bp = \frac{(0.512°C)(0.650 \text{ m})}{\text{mole solute}} = 0.333°C$$

$$= 100°C + 0.333 \text{ C} = 100.3°C$$

Ionic compounds result from the transfer of electrons from one kind of atom to another. Thus the compounds consist of atoms that have lost or gained electrons. Atoms that gain electrons (are reduced) in forming the compound become ions with a negative charge. Those that lose electrons (are oxidized) become ions with a positive charge. Atoms lose electric neutrality by forming ions and gain chemical stability by associating with other ions of opposite charge. Generally, the smaller an ion and the higher its charges, the stronger its tendency to dissolve (become hydrated).

Heat Capacity of Substances

In certain situations, it is helpful to know the specific heat capacity of a substance such as water or soil. This reflects the number of calories required to raise the temperature of one gram of that substance by 1°C. The number of calories gained or lost by a given mass of substance may be expressed as:

calories gained or lost = grams water present × change in temperature
× specific heat capacity

When comparing two soils, for example, the following equation is used to calculate the weighted average heat capacity of a mixture of substances:

$$\text{heat capacity (or } C) = \frac{C_1 M_1 + C_2 M_2}{M_1 + M_2}$$

where, C_1 and M_2 are the heat capacity and mass of substance 1 (soil in this case), and C_2 and M_2 are heat capacity and mass of substance 2 (water in this case). For example, the following compares the heating capacity of dry versus wet soil:

C_1 = heat capacity of soil, 0.2 calorie/gram of soil

M_1 = mass of soil, in this case, 1 gram of soil

C_2 = heat capacity of water, 1.0 calorie/gram of water

M_2 = mass of water or number of calories needed to raise the temperature

of the water by 1°C. The amount of water present

(grams) is multiplied by 1.0 cal/g

Example:

For two soils, $Soil_1$ is wetter as it contains 35 grams water/100 grams of soil. $Soil_2$ is drier, containing 15 grams water/100 grams of soil. Which soil has the higher heat capacity? For $Soil_1$, there are 35 grams water/100 grams soil (or 0.35 g). This is multiplied by 1.0 cal/g, which is the number of calories needed to raise the temperature of 0.1g of water by 1°C to achieve 0.35.

$$Soil_1 = \frac{C_1 M_1 + C_2 M_2}{M_1 + M_2}$$

$$= \frac{(0.2 \text{ cal/g} \times 1 \text{ g}) + (1 \text{ cal/g} \times 0.35 \text{ g})}{1.0 \text{ g} + 0.35 \text{ g}} = 0.407 \text{ cal/g}$$

For $Soil_2$, 15 grams water/100 grams of soil is multiplied by 1.0 cal/g to achieve 0.15 g.

$$Soil_2 = \frac{C_1 M_1 + C_2 M_2}{M_1 + M_2}$$

$$= \frac{(0.2 \text{ cal/g} \times 1 \text{ g}) + (1 \text{ cal/g} \times 0.15 \text{ g})}{1.0 \text{ g} + 0.15 \text{ g}} = 0.304 \text{ cal/g}$$

The wetter $Soil_1$ has a heat capacity of 0.407 cal/g, where the drier $Soil_2$ has a heat capacity of 0.304 cal/g. The wet soil, therefore, needs an additional 0.103 cal (0.407 to 0.304) of solar radiation for every degree of temperature rise of the dry soil and will warm up and cool down slower than the dry soil.

Another example of the heating capacity of water is the solar energy absorbed by seawater having a direct effect on the climate of adjacent land masses. Usually the winter average temperature of adjacent land to seawater is greater than that of inland locations. This occurs as water absorbs energy slowly and also releases it slowly. Many barrier islands, for example, do not experience the frequency or severity of freezes that inland locations have due to this warming effect of the surrounding ocean. The energy released at night by the surrounding water helps moderate the average nighttime temperature.

Several unusual physical properties of water offer certain biological advantages, especially in the maintenance of constant internal temperatures. One is water's high **heat of vaporization,** which is the number of calories (or heat, 540 cal) absorbed when water is vaporized. The calories removed by evaporation of water provide a mechanism by which organisms can dissipate heat. This heat of vaporization is the method plants and humans use to cool themselves when surface moisture evaporates; it removes surface heat. Heat of vaporization also provides a unique thermostat, ensuring chemical reactions are only slightly changed by external temperature variations.

The other unique property of water is its high **specific heat capacity**. This is the number of calories (heat) required to raise the temperature of one gram of water by 1°C. Water absorbs more heat for a given temperature rise than any other common inorganic substance. As a result, water absorbs heat well without drastic changes in temperature and therefore helps keep an organism's temperature constant. For example, the specific heat of lead is 33 times smaller than that of water, meaning the temperature of one pound of lead would increase 33 degrees with the same heat input required to raise the temperature of one pound of water by 1 degree.

Relative Humidity. The concentration of water vapor in air is usually expressed as relative humidity (RH):

$$RH = \frac{\text{amount of water in the air}}{\text{maximum amount of water the air can hold at same temperature}} \times 100$$

Relative humidity is the percent saturation of the air with water vapor. As the air's temperature increases, the relative humidity of a sample of air decreases. As moist air cools (such as at night), the relative humidity may become greater than 100%, and water as **dew** condenses on plants. If plants are cooler than 0°C (32°F), with dew formation, ice forms as **frost**. Clouds and rainfall form when condensation occurs as warm air comes in contact with cool air.

When water evaporates, thermal energy is absorbed from the surface by the evaporating moisture, thus cooling the surface. Plants absorb water from the soil and lose water to the atmosphere. Most of this water is lost as vapor from the leaves, to the atmosphere, by the process of **transpiration**. Water is also lost by **evaporation** from soil and leaf surfaces. Evaporation is typically much lower than transpirational losses in a mature turf. The combined total of water lost through transpiration and evaporation is termed **evapotranspiration**, abbreviated ET. Evapotranspiration is usually expressed in inches or millimeters per day, week, or month. Since ET is the total water lost from the turf system, it represents the water demand, or that which must be replaced to maintain healthy plants. Environmental parameters largely controlling ET are light intensity and duration, relative humidity, wind velocity, and temperature. Increasing solar radiation, temperature, and wind increases ET while increasing relative humidity decreases ET. Other parameters that affect ET to a lesser extent include soil-water content, turf-root system development, inherent turf water needs and dehydration avoidance mechanisms, and various cultural practices.

Although it might seem like transpiration is just a waste of water, it is in fact critically important because it cools the leaf. If not for transpirational cooling, a leaf could reach 120°F or higher during midsummer, a lethal temperature for most plants. Fortunately, transpiration keeps leaves much cooler, usually below 90°F. This is due to the **latent heat of vaporization** for water, or the large amount of energy it takes to convert one gram of liquid water to one gram of water vapor via evaporation. For example, for every calorie of solar energy absorbed by the plant, one gram of turfgrass tissue (mainly water) will increase by nearly two Fahrenheit degrees. Ten calories of solar energy could warm a gram of turf tissue by about 18°. But it takes a lot of energy, 540 calories, to evaporate one gram of water. By transpiring only one gram of water, a turf plant loses enough energy to cool 540 grams of plant tissue by roughly two degrees. Multiply this by the millions of grams of water that a turfgrass area loses daily and the incredible cooling capacity of transpiration becomes evident. Humans have a similar process where perspiration evaporates, cooling our bodies.

Turf managers often apply a light application of water (a process called **syringing**) in the attempt to cool the plants through evaporation. However, as the atmosphere's relative humidity increases, this water does not evaporate fast enough to keep the plants adequately cooled. This is why high relative humidity areas such as the eastern United States feels "stuffy" in summer and low relative humidity areas such as the desert southwestern United States feels arid (or dry).

Water as a Solvent

Many substances are found in aqueous solution. A **solution** is a uniform mixture of the molecules or ions of two or more substances. The substance present in greatest amounts, usually a liquid, is called the **solvent**, whereas the substances present in lesser amounts are called **solutes**. The number of solute molecules in a given volume of solvent is the **solute concentration**.

Water is often called the "universal solvent." The polarity of water molecules tends to separate substances into their constituent ions (Figure 2-3). The separation of ions during the solution process is called **dissociation**. Molecules are said to dissociate when they dissolve in water. For example, salt (NaCl) is a substance which water molecules cluster around and segregate the sodium and chloride ions.

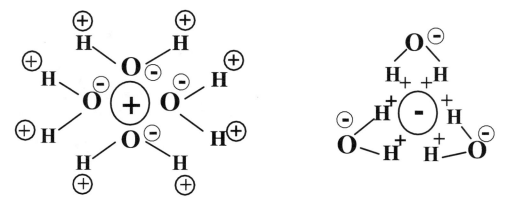

Figure 2-3. Water is the universal solvent because the negatively charged oxygen molecules are attracted to and surround positive ions, such as Na^+, while the partially positive charge hydrogen ions are attracted to negative ions, such as Cl^-.

Many molecules are polar (electrically charged) or have polar regions, and thus attract water molecules. Small polar molecules such as the sugars glucose and sucrose readily dissolve in water. Larger molecules with polar regions interact with water at these regions and are referred to as **hydrophilic** ("water loving").

Hydrophobic ("water fearing or hating") molecules are those that lack polar regions, thus cannot form hydrogen bonds, and tend to be very insoluble in water. As a result, nonpolar molecules, such as oil or fat, tend to cluster together as droplets in water since there is very little (or van der Waal) interaction between the two types of molecules. In turf, organic acids originating from the breakdown of organic matter in soil can coat soil and the roots, rhizomes, and stolons of plants causing a hydrophobic condition, known as **localized dry spots**.

pH

Water (H_2O) contributes hydrogen ions to biological systems because it ionizes (or separates) to a very slight extent to yield a hydrated hydrogen ion (H^+) known as a hydronium ion (H_3O^+) and a hydroxyl ions (OH^-) as shown:

Dissociation of Water

$$\underset{\text{water}}{2H_2O} \rightleftharpoons \underset{\text{hydronium ion}}{H_3O^+} + \underset{\text{hydroxyl ion}}{OH^-}$$

or

$$\underset{\text{water}}{H_2O(aq)} \rightleftharpoons \underset{\text{hydrogen ion}}{H^+(aq)} + \underset{\text{hydroxyl ion}}{OH^-(aq)}$$

Technically, the proper name of the hydrated hydrogen ion (H^+) is hydronium ion (H_3O^+), which corresponds to the polar nature of water where the hydrogen atoms ionize and combine to form:

$$H_2 + O_2 \rightarrow H^+(aq) \text{ or } H^+ \cdot H_2O \text{ or } H_3O^+$$

Although the hydronium ion (H_3O^+) best represents this reaction, the hydrogen ion (H^+) is often listed for clarity and brevity.

The hydrogen ion concentrations (symbolized as $[H^+]$) are often expressed as pH values. The values of $[H^+]$ for most solutions are inconveniently small and difficult to compare. Therefore, a more practical quantity, pH, is used. The term pH expresses the concentration (in terms of molarity) of hydrogen ions as a logarithmic function and is defined as the negative logarithm of the hydrogen (or hydronium) ion concentration. A logarithm to the base 10 is the power to which 10 must be raised to give the number. For example, $\log(100) = 2$ because $10^2 = 100$. If the number is less than 1, the value becomes negative. For example, $\log(0.01) = -2$ because 10^{-2} is the same as 0.01 (see Appendix D)

$$pH = -\log[H^+]$$

A relationship exists between hydrogen and hydroxyl ion concentrations, such as that in water at 25°C:

Relationship Between Hydrogen and Hydroxyl Ion Concentrations

$$\underset{\substack{[H^+] \\ \text{hydrogen ion}}}{10^{-7}} \times \underset{\substack{[OH^-] \\ \text{hydroxyl ion}}}{10^{-7}} = 10^{-14}$$

For example, at a pH of 5.0 the hydrogen ion concentration is 10^{-5} (or 0.00001 or 1/100,000) mole/liter and the hydroxyl concentration is 10^{-9} (or 0.000000001) mole/liter since these values must total 10^{-14}.

$$\log 1.0 \times 10^5 = \log 1.0 + \log 10^5 = 0 + 5 = 5$$

Remember that for negative powers of 10, the greater the numerical values of the exponent, the smaller the value. For example, 10^{-9} (or 1/1,000,000,000) is a much smaller value than 10^{-5} (or 1/100,000). Table 2-3 lists several common substances to illustrate the range of the pH scale.

Pure water ionizes slightly and the number of H^+ ions equals the number of OH^- ions. The concentration of H^+ and OH^- ions in pure water is 10^{-7} mole per liter, respectively.

TABLE 2-3. Range of pH Values for Several Common Substances

H^+ Concentration (moles per liter)	pH	OH^- Concentration (moles per liter)	Examples	pH	Description
1×10^{-14}	14	1.0	Lye (bleach)	13.0	Strong alkaline
1×10^{-13}	13	1×10^{-1}	Household ammonia	12.0	$\wedge$
1×10^{-12}	12	1×10^{-2}	Milk of magnesia	10.5	
1×10^{-11}	11	1×10^{-3}	Soap	9.3	
1×10^{-10}	10	1×10^{-4}	Antacid tablets	9.4	
1×10^{-9}	9	1×10^{-5}	Baking soda	8.0	
1×10^{-8}	8	1×10^{-6}	Seawater	7.9	$\vee$
			Human blood	7.3	Weak alkaline
1×10^{-7}	7	1×10^{-7}	Pure water	7.0	Neutral
1×10^{-6}	6	1×10^{-8}	Fresh milk	6.7	Weak acids
1×10^{-5}	5	1×10^{-9}	Rain	5.6	$\wedge$
1×10^{-4}	4	1×10^{-10}	Sour milk	4.7	
1×10^{-3}	3	1×10^{-11}	Beer	4.4	
1×10^{-2}	2	1×10^{-12}	Coffee & Tomato juice	4.2	
1×10^{-1}	1	1×10^{-13}	Orange juice	3.7	
1.0	0	1×10^{-14}	Wine	3.5	
			Vinegar	2.9	
			Classic Coke	2.5	
			Lemon juice	2.4	
			Gastric juice	2.0	$\vee$
			Battery acid	0.5	Strong acids

$$pH < 7.00 - \text{acidic}$$
$$pH = 7.00 - \text{neutral}$$
$$pH > 7.00 - \text{basic (alkaline)}$$

Example Problems:

1. In a solution with pH = 9.3, what is $[H^+]$?
   Because pH = $-\log [H^+]$ and can be rearranged as $\log [H^+] = -pH$, and furthermore, $[H^+] = $ antilog $(-pH)$, then antilog $(-9.3) = 5.0 \times 10^{-10}$
2. If the $[H^+]$ of a solution $= 4 \times 10^{-3}$, what is the resulting pH?
   If $[H^+] = 4.0 \times 10^{-3}$ M, then $\log [H^+] = -2.40$ and pH $= -(-2.40) = 2.40$
3. Find the pH of a 0.02 *M* HCl solution (assuming 100% ionization).
   Since the $[H^+] = 0.02 \ M = 2 \times 10^{-2} \ M$

$$pH = -\log [H^+] = \log 2 + \log 10^{-2} = 0.30 - 2 = -1.70$$
$$pH = 1.70$$

4. What is the $[H^+]$ and pH of a 0.080 *M* HNO_3 solution (assuming 100% ionization)?

$$HNO_3 \rightarrow H^+ + NO_3^-$$

   0.080 *M* HNO_3 will ionize completely into 0.080 *M* H^+ and 0.080 *M* NO_3^-. Therefore, $[H^+] = [NO_3^-] = 0.080 \ M$. pH can be found from using 0.08 = $8.0 \times 10^{-2} \ M$:

$$pH = -\log[H^+] = -\log 8 + \log 10^{-2}$$
$$= 1.10$$

It is important to remember that on a logarithmic scale the decrease or increase of one pH unit represents a tenfold difference in hydrogen ion concentration. For example, a solution with a pH of 5 is ten times more acidic (in other words, contains more hydrogen ions) than a solution with a pH of 6.

The pH scale of 0 to 14 is used to indicate the strength (or amount) of hydrogen ions present (Table 2-3). At pH of 0, 1 *M* (moles/liter) of hydrogen ions are present and this represents acid very strongly. A pH value of 7 is a neutral pH with a hydrogen ion concentration of 1×10^{-7}. Values larger than 7 are basic (or alkaline) with the highest being 1×10^{-14}.

Examples:

1. A solution has hydrogen ion concentration (indicated by $[H^+]$) of 6.0×10^{-3}.
   (a) What is the $[OH^-]$?
   (b) Is the solution acidic, neutral, or basic?

Remember, in any dilute solution: $[H^+] [OH^-] = 1.0 \times 10^{-14}$, therefore rearrange this as follows:

(a) $[OH^-] = \dfrac{1.0 \times 10^{-14}}{[H^+]} = \dfrac{1.0 \times 10^{-14}}{6.0 \times 10^{-3}} = 2.0 \times 10^{-12}$

(b) The $[H^+] = 6.0 \times 10^{-3}$, which is greater than neutral pH (or 1.0×10^{-7}), therefore it is acidic.

2. If 25 mL of 0.16 M NaOH is added to 50 mL of 0.1 M HCl, what is the pH?

Step 1: find the moles of acid and base in the solution:

moles HCl = V (volume) $\times$ M = 0.05 L (or 50 ml) $\times$ 0.1 mole/liter
= 0.005 mole

moles NaOH = V $\times$ M = 0.025 L $\times$ 0.16 mole/L = 0.004 mole

Step 2: Since the acid (HCl) is in excess (0.005 M HCl − 0.004 NaOH = 0.001 HCl), all the base (NaOH) is used up. The concentration of the HCl remaining after NaOH is added is:

$$\text{concentration } (M) = \frac{\text{number of moles}}{\text{volume}}$$

$$= \frac{0.001 \text{ g HCl}}{0.05 \text{ L HCl} + 0.025 \text{ L NaOH}} = \frac{0.001 \text{ g}}{0.075 \text{ L}}$$

$$= [H^+] = 0.0133 \ M = 1.33 \times 10^{-2} \text{ moles/liter}$$

$$\text{pH} = -\log (1.33 \times 10^{-2}) = -(0.12 - 2) = -(-1.88) = 1.88$$

Acids. The term "acid" is from the Latin word *acidus* which means "sour" or "having a sharp taste." Acids are very important in modern living. Common foods and fruits contain acids. For example, citrus fruits contain citric acid; vinegar, acetic acid; and sour milk, lactic acid. Sulfuric acid is used in manufacturing fertilizer and explosives. Hydrochloric acid is found in gastric juices of the stomach and is also used to clean metals, prepare sugar from starch, and in making metal chlorides, dyes, glue, and many other chemicals. Additionally, many other important uses of acids also exist.

Several definitions of an acid exist: (1) the **Classical acid definition** is a substance that increases the concentration of hydrogen ions (H^+). However, since much chemistry takes place without water, this definition is too limited for widespread use. (2) The **Brønsted-Lowry acid definition** is any species that can donate a proton (H^+ ion). The Brønsted-Lowry definition is needed for reactions occurring in the gas phase or in solvents other than water. (3) A broader definition of an acid is one called a **Lewis acid,** which is a species that accepts an electron pair to form a covalent bond; thus, a Lewis acid must have an empty valence orbital available to accept the electron pair from a Lewis base. The Lewis definition works best for reactions that do not include proton transfer and thus limits the Brønsted-Lowry definitions. Appendix E details the particular acid and base definitions. The Brønsted-Lowry definition of acids offers a compromise of simplicity and generality.

Summary of definitions of acids and bases

Definition	Acid	Bases
Classical	Increases $[H^+]$	Increases $[OH^-]$
Brønsted-Lowry	Proton donor	Proton acceptor
Lewis	Electron pair acceptor	Electron pair donor

For example, the reaction between ammonia (NH_3) and hydrogen chloride (HCl) in the gas phase is an acid-base reaction.

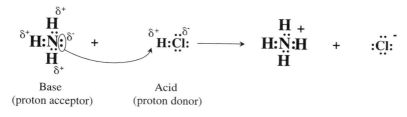

Base	Acid
(proton acceptor)	(proton donor)

The unshared pair of partially negatively charged (δ^-) electrons on the nitrogen of ammonia is attracted by the partial positive (δ^+) charge on the hydrogen in the polar chloride molecule. A proton is transferred from chlorine to nitrogen.

Water can act as an acid or a base (this is termed **amphoteric**). When combined with acids, such as hydrochloric acid (HCl) and hydrofluoric acid (HF), water reacts as a base as it accepts a H^+ ion:

$$H_2O + \underset{acid}{HCl} \rightarrow H_3O^+ + Cl^-$$
$$\underset{base}{}$$

$$\underset{base}{H_2O} + \underset{acid}{HF} \rightarrow H_3O^+ + F^-$$

However, when water is mixed with a base, such as ammonia (NH_3), water reacts as an acid since it donates a H^+ ion:

$$\underset{base_1}{NH_3(aq)} + \underset{acid_2}{H_2O(l)} \rightarrow \underset{acid_1}{NH_4^+(aq)} + \underset{base_2}{OH^-(aq)}$$

When a substance is dissolved in water it may change the relative numbers of H^+ (also represented by $H^+ \cdot H_2O$ or H_3O^+) and OH^- such that the concentration of H^+ no longer equals $[OH^-]$. In chemical reactions, an **acid** is a substance that increases (or releases or donates) the relative number of hydrogen ions (also called protons) to another substance when dissolved in water. Many acids contain hydrogen; for example, HCl, H_2SO_4, HNO_3. Other substances react with water to produce acids; these are called **acid anhydrides**.

Acids are solutions that:

1. Liberate H_2 gas when they react with certain metals.
2. Neutralize basic (hydroxide) solutions due to their hydrogen (H) ions.
3. Cause blue litmus paper to turn red.
4. Taste sour, like vinegar (acetic acid), lemon juice (citric acid), and sour milk (lactic acid). Strong acids also taste sour, but must be sufficiently diluted before tasting or burning, as corrosive actions occur.

Bases are solutions that:

1. React with salts of heavy metals to form insoluble hydroxides (OH^-).
2. Neutralize acid solutions.
3. Turn red litmus paper to blue.
4. Taste bitter, like soap.
5. Feel slippery to the touch.
6. Emulsify and disperse fats and oils and thus are often used to make soap and other cleansing agents.

The *extent* to which an acid dissociates (converts to a hydrogen ion and an accompanying anion) and not the *amount* of hydrogen in the molecule determines its strength. For example, when hydrochloric acid (HCl) dissolves in water, it is almost completely ionized (separated) into H^+ and Cl^- ions. As a result, $[H^+]$ exceeds $[OH^-]$ and this is considered a strong acid. The general reaction of an acid and base is:

$$HA \rightleftharpoons H^+ + A^-$$
$$\text{acid} \qquad \text{proton} \quad \text{ion}$$

for example,
$$HCl \rightleftharpoons H^+ + Cl^-$$
$$\text{hydrochloric acid} \quad \text{proton} \quad \text{chloride (ion)}$$

Hydrochloric, sulfuric, and nitric acid are 'strong' acids, because they dissociate completely, meaning they readily release all of their hydrogen ions into solution, thus reducing the pH of the solution dramatically. Weak acids such as carbonic, boric, and acetic acids dissociate (that is, produce H^+ and A^-) but only partially when placed in solution (reacts only very slightly with water); therefore, they do not reduce the pH as much as strong acids (Table 2-4). Acetic acid is the acid found in vinegar.

Neutralization of an acid occurs when it reacts with a base (a source of hydroxyl or OH^- ions) to form a salt and water.

TABLE 2-4. Some Common Acids and Bases and Their Dissociation Products

Monoprotic Acids (*only has one ionizable hydrogen ion*)

dissociation example: $HCl(aq) \rightarrow H^+(aq) + Cl^-(aq)$

Examples of Monoprotic Acids:

HF	Hydrofluoric acid	$HClO_3$	Chloric acid
HCl	Hydrochloric acid	HNO_3	Nitric acid
HBr	Hydrobromic acid	HNO_2	Nitrous acid
HOCl	Hypochlorous acid	$HC_2H_3O_2$	Acetic acid

Diprotic Acids (*has two ionizable hydrogen ions*)

dissociation example:
1. $H_2SO_4 \rightarrow H^+ + HSO_4^-$
2. $HSO_4^- \rightarrow H^+ + SO_4^{-2}$

summary: $H_2SO_4 \rightarrow 2H^+ + SO_4^-$

Diprotic Acid examples:

H_2SO_4	Sulfuric acid	$H_2C_2O_4$	Oxalic acid
H_2SO_3	Sulfurous acid	H_2S	Hydrosulfuric acid
H_2CO_3	Carbonic acid	H_3PO_3	Phosphorous acid (only $2H^+$ can be removed)

Triportic Acids (*has three ionizable hydrogen ions*)

dissociation example:
1. $H_3PO_4 \rightarrow H^+ + H_2PO_4^-$
2. $H_2PO_4^- \rightarrow H^+ + HPO_4^{-2}$
3. $HPO_4^{-2} \rightarrow H^+ + PO_4^{-3}$

summary: $H_3PO_4 \rightarrow 3H^+ + PO_4^-$

Triportic Acid examples:

H_3PO_4	Phosphoric acid	H_3BO_3	Boric acid

Bases examples:

$Ca(OH)_2$	Calcium hydroxide	$(Ca(OH)_2$	$\rightleftharpoons$	Ca^+	+	$OH^-)$
$Zn(OH)_2$	Zinc hydroxide	$(Zn(OH)_2$	$\rightleftharpoons$	$ZnOH^+$	+	$OH^-)$
NH_3	Ammonia	$(NH_3 + H_2O$	$\rightleftharpoons$	NH_4^+	+	$OH^-)$
N_2H_4	Hydrazine	$(N_2H_4 + H_2O$	$\rightleftharpoons$	N_2H_5	+	$OH^-)$

Neutralization

$$acid + base \rightleftharpoons salt + water$$

for example,

$$\underset{\text{hydrochloric acid}}{HCl} + \underset{\text{sodium hydroxide}}{NaOH} \rightleftharpoons \underset{\text{sodium chloride}}{NaCl} + \underset{\text{water}}{H_2O}$$

$$\underset{\text{sulfuric acid}}{H_2SO_4} + \underset{\text{sodium hydroxide}}{2NaOH} \rightleftharpoons \underset{\text{sodium sulfate}}{Na_2SO_4} + \underset{\text{water}}{2H_2O}$$

In agriculture, acid neutralization is often achieved by using lime as the base as discussed in **Chapter 5** on Soil Chemistry.

Monoprotic acids have only one ionizable hydrogen (e.g., HCl, HNO_3, $HClO_4$, etc.). **Polyprotic acids** have more than one ionizable hydrogen (e.g., H_2SO_4, H_2CO_3, H_3PO_4, etc.). Polyprotic acids ionize stepwise with an equilibrium constant for each step. For example, oxalic acid ($H_2C_2O_4$) is polyprotic with ionization reactions and equilibrium constants of:

$$H_2C_2O_4 \rightleftharpoons H^+ + HC_2O_4^- \qquad K_{a1} = 5.9 \times 10^{-2}$$

$$HC_2O_4^- \rightleftharpoons H^+ + C_2O_4^{-2} \qquad K_{a2} = 6.5 \times 10^{-5}$$

Carbonic acid is a weak acid found in most soft drinks, some groundwater, and in some rainwater that forms as water in the atmosphere or root zone reacts with carbon dioxide. Being a weak acid, carbonic acid can eventually dissolve sedimentary limestone to form sinkholes and caves.

$$\underset{\text{carbon dioxide}}{CO_2} + \underset{\text{water}}{H_2O} \rightarrow \underset{\text{carbonic acid}}{H_2CO_3}$$

Predicting Acid Strengths. The strength of an acid can be predicted from the strength and polarity of the bond between H^+ and the nonmetal; the longer and/or more polar this bond becomes, the stronger the acid. For binary acids (acids consisting of H^+ plus a nonmetal) the strength of the acid increases as one goes down a group in the periodic table (for example, in Group VIIA or 17, HI>HBr>HCl>HF). Acids also increase as one goes across a row from left to right (for example, in Period 2, HF>H_2O>NH_3), just as electronegativities of the elements also increase from left to right.

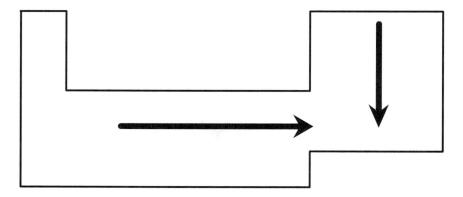

The strength of binary acids increase from top to bottom in Groups and from left to right across periods in the periodic table.

For oxygen containing acids (called **oxo acids**), the strength of the acid is predicted from the polarity of the O-H bond. The stronger the attraction of the central atom in an oxo acid for electrons, the more polar the O-H bonds, and the more acidic the oxo acid. For oxo acids with similar structures, the acid strength increases as the electronegativity of the central atom increases. For example, HOCl>HOBr>HOI.

For oxo acids with differing numbers of extra oxygen (those not part of the —OH group), acid strength increases as the number of extra oxygen increases. For example, $HClO_4$>$HClO_3$>$HClO_2$>HOCl. Like oxo acids, the strengths of organic acids are related to the polarity of the O—H. For example, chloroacetic acid ($ClCH_2COOH$) is a stronger acid than acetic acid (CH_3COOH). Substitution of the more electronegative Cl atom for a H close to the O—H group makes the O-H more polar.

Examples:

Which member of each of the following pairs is the stronger acid?

1. CH_3CH_2OH or CH_3CH_2SH. These two acids differ only by the O and S. O and S are both in Group VIA (16) of the periodic table. S is larger than O and the H—S bond is longer and weaker than the H—O and thus will ionize more easily; thus, CH_3CH_2SH is the stronger acid.
2. $HBrO_2$ or HOBr. These two oxo acids contain the same nonmetal Br and differ only in the number of oxygen atoms. $HBrO_2$ is the stronger acid since it contains more oxygen atoms.
3. H_2S or HCl. These two binary acids contain S and Cl in the same row (Period 3) of the periodic table. Acid strength of binary acids increases as one goes from left to right in a row; thus HCl is the stronger acid.
4. $HClO_2$ or HNO_2. These two oxo acids contain the same number of oxygen atoms and differ only in the central atom (Cl vs. N). The more electronegative the central atom, the more polar the O-H bond and the stronger the acid. Cl is closer to the upper right corner of the periodic table; thus it is more electronegative than N and $HClO_2$ is the stronger acid.
5. CH_3CH_2OH or CH_3CH_2COOH. These acids differ only in their number of oxygen atoms. Higher oxygen atom numbers mean stronger acids; thus CH_3CH_2COOH is the stronger acid.

Dissociation Constant (also called the ionization constant). To measure the relative strength of an acid, its dissociation constant (or its ability to dissolve in solution, indicated as K_a) is obtained by: $HA \rightleftharpoons H^+ + A^-$

$$K_a = \frac{[H^+] [A^-]}{[HA]}$$

The brackets indicate the concentration of the general acid (HA), protons (H^+), and base (A^-). The higher the K_a value, the greater the number of hydrogen (or hydronium) ions liberated (or ionized) per mole of acid in solution, hence, the stronger the acid. Strong acids like HCl, HNO_3, $HClO_4$, and H_2SO_4 completely dissociate into H^+ and an anion. Weak acids deprotonate less readily. Examples include HF, and organic acids such as acetic acid, CH_3COOH. Their more tightly bound protons dissociate at higher pH than strong acids.

Example:

Calculate the dissociation constant, K_a, in 1.00 *M* solution of acid, HA, which has a pH of 2.0.

$$HA \rightleftharpoons H^+ + A^-$$

Step 1: find the $[H^+]$ in a pH solution of 2.0: $[H^+] = [A^-] = -\log [H^+] = -\log 2.0 = 1.00 \times 10^{-2}$

Step 2: determine the concentration of HA: $1.00 \ M - (1.00 \times 10^{-2}) = 0.990$ moles/L

$$K_a = \frac{[H^+][A^-]}{[HA]} = \frac{(1.00 \times 10^{-2}) \times (1.00 \times 10^{-2})}{0.990 \text{ mole/L}} = 1.01 \times 10^{-4} \text{ moles/L}$$

Ranges for describing K_a values include:

Relative acid strength	K_a values
very strong	$>1 \times 10^3$
strong	1×10^3 to 1×10^{-2}
weak	1×10^{-2} to 1×10^{-7}
very weak	$<1 \times 10^{-7}$

Table 2-5 shows the K_a values of some common weak acids. The stronger an acid, the weaker its conjugate base; therefore, the acids in Table 2-5 become stronger going down the left-hand column and bases become weaker going down the right-hand column.

To avoid small numerical numbers associated with K_a values, pK_a values are often calculated to represent a logarithmic scale much like pH. Values for pK_a and K_a are converted to each other in the same way as pH and $[H^+]$. The relationship is mathematically described as:

$$pK_a = -\log K_a$$

pK_a example:

The K_a value for acetic acid is 1.7×10^{-5}. What is the pK_a value?

TABLE 2-5. Ionization Constants of Some Common Weak Acids at 25°C

Relative Strength	Acid				Conjugate Base		Relative Strength
	Name	Formula	K_a	pK_a	Name	Formula	
weak acids	Water	H_2O	2×10^{-16}	15.70	Hydroxide ion	OH^-	strong base
	Bicarbonate	HCO_3^-	5.6×10^{-11}	10.26	Carbonate ion	CO_3^{-2}	
	Ammonium ion	NH_4^+	5.6×10^{-10}	9.25	Ammonia	NH_3	
	Propionic acid	CH_3CH_2COOH	1.4×10^{-5}	4.85	Propionate ion	$CH_3CH_2COO^-$	
	Acetic acid	CH_3COOH	1.8×10^{-5}	4.77	Acetate ion	CH_3COO^-	
	Benzoic acid	C_6H_5COOH	6.5×10^{-5}	4.19	Benzoate ion	$C_6H_5COO^-$	
	Nitrous acid	HNO_2	5.6×10^{-4}	3.25	Nitrite ion	NO_2^-	
strong acids	Hydrogen sulfate ion	HSO_4^-	1.2×10^{-2}	1.92	Sulfate ion	SO_4^{-2}	weak base

Using the above formula: $pK_a = -\log K_a$
$$-\log (1.7 \times 10^{-5}) = 4.77$$

Table 2-6 lists pK_a values for several common acids. Note that the stronger the acid, the lower its pK_a.

Bases. Several common bases are household products including ammonia water, lye, and milk of magnesia. Bases are also used in industry in the refining of petroleum and in the manufacturing of paper, soap, etc.

Bases are defined in several ways: (1) the classical definition of a base is a species which increases the concentration of hydroxyl (OH^-) ions. (2) A Brønsted-Lowry base is a proton (H^+) acceptor, while (3) a Lewis base is an electron pair donor.

A solution is basic or alkaline when $[OH^-]$ is greater than $[H^+]$. For example, when sodium hydroxide (NaOH) dissolves in water, it ionizes into Na^+ and OH^- ions, and $[OH^-]$ exceeds $[H^+]$ in the sodium hydroxide solution. The pH is alkaline (or basic). A **base** is a substance that causes a decrease in the relative number of H^+ ions—that is, an increase in the relative number of OH^- ions—in a solution. Sodium hydroxide, or lye, (NaOH), calcium oxide (CaO), potassium oxide (K_2O), potassium hydroxide (KOH), magnesium hydroxide (or milk of magnesia) [$Mg(OH)_2$], calcium hydroxide [$Ca(OH)_2$], aluminum hydroxide [$Al(OH)_3$], ammonium hydroxide (NH_4OH), lithium hydroxide (LiOH), iron(III) hydroxide [$Fe(OH)_3$], and ammonia (NH_3) are common bases which neutralize an acid when their solutions are mixed. Concentrated solutions of strong bases often feel slippery. Also, the OH^- ion always appears on the product side for every reactant acting as a base, just as the H^+ ion must appear on the product side for every reactant acting as an acid.

Base Reaction

KOH	$\rightarrow$	K^+	+	OH^-
potassium hydroxide		potassium ion		hydroxyl ion

NaOH	$\rightarrow$	Na^+	+	OH^-
sodium hydroxide		sodium ion		hydroxyl ion

Ammonia, NH_3, is also a base because it reacts with water to produce hydroxide (OH^-) ions. However, ammonium-water solutions are weakly basic because they have a low concentration of OH^- ions. Ammonia, NH_3, is not a strong base and thus does not acquire very many protons from water molecules when in solution and thus is a very poor conductor of electricity. Relatively few NH_4^+ ions and OH^- ions are present. Ammonia is very soluble in water where about 2,000 volumes of granular ammonia will dissolve in one equal volume of water.

NH_3	+	H_2O	$\rightarrow$	NH_4^+	+	OH^-
ammonia		water		ammonium ion		hydroxyl ion
(H^+ acceptor, base)		(H^+ donor, acid)		(H^+ donor, acid)		(H^+ acceptor, base)

Another common basic anhydride (or dry substance) used to raise soil pH is cal-

TABLE 2-6. Dissociation Properties of Some Polyprotic Acids at 25°C

Acid	Dissociation Steps	Dissociation Constant for Each Step	pK_a
Phosphoric	$H_3PO_4 \rightleftharpoons H^+ + H_2PO_4^-$	$K_{a1} = 7.5 \times 10^{-3}$	2.13
	$H_2PO_4^- \rightleftharpoons H^+ + HPO_4^{-2}$	$K_{a2} = 6.2 \times 10^{-8}$	7.21
	$HPO_4^{-2} \rightleftharpoons H^+ + PO_4^{-3}$	$K_{a3} = 2.2 \times 10^{-12}$	11.66
Sulfuric	$H_2SO_4 \rightleftharpoons H^+ + HSO_4^-$	$K_{a1} =$ very large	<0
	$HSO_4^- \rightleftharpoons H^+ + SO_4^{-2}$	$K_{a2} = 1.2 \times 10^{-2}$	1.92
Sulfurous	$SO_2 + H_2O \rightleftharpoons H^+ + HSO_3^-$	$K_{a1} = 1.5 \times 10^{-2}$	1.82
	$HSO_3^- \rightleftharpoons H^+ + SO_3^{-2}$	$K_{a2} = 1.0 \times 10^{-7}$	7.00
Hydrogen sulfide	$H_2S \rightleftharpoons H^+ + HS^-$	$K_{a1} = 1.1 \times 10^{-7}$	6.96
	$HS^- \rightleftharpoons H^+ + S^{-2}$	$K_{a2} = 1.0 \times 10^{-14}$	14.00
Carbonic	$CO_2 + H_2O \rightleftharpoons H^+ + HCO_3^-$	$K_{a1} = 4.3 \times 10^{-7}$	6.37
	$HCO_3^- \rightleftharpoons H^+ + CO_3^{-2}$	$K_{a2} = 5.6 \times 10^{-11}$	10.26

cium oxide (CaO). When it reacts with water in the soil, calcium hydroxide is formed.

$$CaO + H_2O \rightarrow Ca(OH)_2$$
calcium oxide　　water　　calcium hydroxide (or slaked lime)

When the calcium hydroxide dissolves, it dissociates (separates) into calcium (Ca^{+2}) and hydroxide ions (OH^-).

$$Ca(OH)_2 \rightarrow Ca^+ + 2OH^-$$
calcium hydroxide　　calcium　　hydroxyl ion

Acids and bases are important due to their contributions of protons (H^+) and hydroxyl (OH^-) ions, which can move onto and off of other compounds present in a solution. If a nonpolar, water-insoluble molecule picks up a proton because an acid is present, the nonpolar molecule becomes positively charged and water soluble.

The strength of the base depends on the *concentration* of OH^- (hydroxyl) ions in solution and does not depend on the number of hydroxide ions per mole of the solution. Strong bases include sodium hydroxide (NaOH) and potassium hydroxide (KOH). Weak bases include ammonia water (NH_3) and dimethylamine [$(CH_3)_2NH$].

Salts. Salts are crystalline compounds of metallic cations of a base (such as an ammonium ion, NH_4^+) and nonmetallic anions of an acid (such as nitrate ion, NO_3^-). Many salts are found as minerals on earth or dissolved in seawater. Sodium chloride (NaCl) and magnesium nitrate [$Mg(NO_3)_2$] are typical salts. Salts are formed when acids and bases react in a neutralization reaction [acid + base → salt + water]. For example, hydrochloric acid, a strong cleaning product, and sodium hydroxide (a base), lye, used to clear clogged drains, react to form the salt, sodium chloride, and water:

Neutralization / Salt Formation

$$\underset{\substack{\text{hydrochloric} \\ \text{acid}}}{\text{HCl}} \quad + \quad \underset{\substack{\text{sodium hydroxide} \\ \text{(base)}}}{\text{NaOH}} \quad \longrightarrow \quad \underset{\text{sodium chloride (salt)}}{\text{NaCl}} \quad + \underset{\text{water}}{H_2O}$$

$$\underset{\text{sulfuric acid}}{H_2SO_4} \quad + \quad \underset{\substack{\text{potassium hydroxide} \\ \text{(base)}}}{\text{2KOH}} \quad \longrightarrow \quad \underset{\substack{\text{potassium sulfate} \\ \text{(salt)}}}{K_2SO_4} \quad + \underset{\text{water}}{2H_2O}$$

Example:

Which of the following compounds is the acid, which is the base, and which is the salt?

$$\underset{\text{lithium hydroxide}}{\text{LiOH}} \quad + \quad \underset{\text{hydrogen iodide}}{\text{HI}} \quad \longrightarrow \quad \underset{\text{lithium iodide}}{\text{LiI}} \quad + \underset{\text{water}}{H_2O}$$

Since an acid is a proton donor, the H from HI leaves and moves to the LiOH to form water, thus HI is the acid. The LiOH is the base since it donates an OH^- ion. When this occurs, the Li^+ cation combines with the anion, I^- to form the salt, LiI or lithium iodide.

The reaction of an acid with a base to form a salt and water is called **neutralization**. In these reactions where a salt and water are products, heat is always released. When a salt is formed by the neutralization of an acid with a base, the cation comes from the base and the anion from the acid. In the solid state, the salt ions are held by their strong opposite charges. When a salt is dissolved in water, the ions become free to move and carry an electric current. The reaction is referred to as **hydrolysis** (Greek meaning "water" and "loosening"). Hydrolysis reactions split one part of a water molecule from the other. For example, the hydrolysis of ammonia with water involves:

$$\underset{\text{ammonia}}{NH_3} \; + \underset{\text{water}}{H_2O} \rightleftharpoons \underset{\text{ammonium}}{NH_4^+} \; + \quad \underset{\text{hydroxyl ion}}{OH^-}$$

The N atom pulls an H^+ ion away from a water molecule, leaving an OH^- ion as one of the products. This same reaction is typical of many compounds which contain the element nitrogen, N, and function as bases. Some common salts include sodium chloride, or table salt (NaCl), sodium nitrate, or Chile saltpeter ($NaNO_3$), sodium bicarbonate, or baking soda ($NaHCO_3$), potassium carbonate, or potash (K_2CO_3), potassium iodide (KI), which provides the iodide of iodized salt, magnesium sulfate ($MgSO_4$), better known as *epsom salt*, calcium carbonate ($CaCO_3$), or common chalk, ammonium chloride (NH_4Cl), copper(I and II) chloride (CuCl and $CuCl_2$), iron(II) oxide (FeO), manganese chloride ($MnCl_2$), and copper(I and II) sulfate (Cu_2SO_4 and $CuSO_4$), aluminum chloride ($AlCl_3$), barium sulfate ($BaSO_4$), calcium chloride ($CaCl_2$), iron(II) sulfate ($FeSO_4$), potassium chloride (KCl) and silver sulfate (Ag_2SO_4).

Buffered Solutions. A **buffer** is a mixture of a weak acid and a weak base. This can be obtained by mixing a weak acid plus one of its salts, or a weak base plus one of its salts. This name is given because of the regulating action a buffer mixture has on the pH of the solution. Small additions of either strong acids or strong bases produce little change in the pH of a **buffered solution**. For example, ammonium ions (an acid) react with the addition of hydroxide ions to form ammonia, but with little change of pH.

$$\underset{\text{ammonium}}{NH_4^+} + \underset{\text{base}}{OH^-} \rightleftharpoons \underset{\text{ammonia}}{NH_3} + \underset{\text{water}}{H_2O}$$

Similarly, a buffering effect occurs when a solution contains carbonic acid and bicarbonate ions as shown:

when an acid is added,

$$\underset{\text{bicarbonate}}{HCO_3^-} + \underset{\text{acid}}{H^+} \rightarrow \underset{\text{carbonic acid}}{H_2CO_3}$$

when a base is added,

$$\underset{\text{carbonic acid}}{H_2CO_3} + \underset{\text{base}}{OH^-} \rightarrow \underset{\text{water}}{H_2O} + \underset{\text{bicarbonate}}{HCO_3^-}$$

The bicarbonate ions combine with the excess H^+ ions to form carbonic acid (a very weak acid); carbonic acid combines with the excess OH^- ions to form bicarbonate ions (a weak base). With either reaction, both solutions are considered buffered since little change in pH occurs with small additions of either an acid or base. Seawater and blood are naturally buffered solutions.

Example problems:

1. Find the pH of a buffer solution containing 1 mole/liter each of acetic acid and sodium acetate.
   From Table 2-5, the K_a value of acetic acid is 1.8×10^{-5}. Since the solution contains 1 mole/liter each of acetic acid and sodium acetate, the $[H^+]$ is first found to eventually find pH.

$$[H^+] = K_a \times \frac{[\text{acid}]}{[\text{salt}]} = [1.8 \times 10^{-5}] \times \frac{1 \text{ mole/L}}{1 \text{ mole/L}} = 1.8 \times 10^{-5} \, M$$

$$pH = -\log (1.8 \times 10^{-5}) = -(0.26 - 5) = 4.74$$

2. How many moles of sodium acetate must be added to 1 liter 0.2 M HOAc (acetic acid) solution to make a buffer of pH 5?

$$[H^+] = K_a \times \frac{[acid]}{[salt]} = [1.8 \times 10^{-5}] \times \frac{[acid]}{[salt]}$$

Since a pH of 5 is specified, $[H^+] = 10^{-5}\ M$

$$10^{-5}\ M = 1.8 \times 10^{-5} \times \frac{[0.2\ M]}{[salt]},\ \text{rearranging this, we find}$$

$$[salt] = \frac{1.8 \times 10^{-5}}{1.0 \times 10^{-5}} \times 0.2\ M = 0.36\ M$$

3. Which of the following combination of solutions could be buffers? Remember, a buffer must contain a weak acid and a salt of the weak acid or a weak base plus a salt of the weak base.
   a. HNO_3 and $NaNO_3$ − since HNO_3 is a strong acid, this cannot be a buffer solution.
   b. NH_4Cl and NH_3 − NH_3 is a weak base ($NH_3 + H_2O \rightleftharpoons NH_4^+ + OH^-$), while NH_4^+ is the common ion and NH_4Cl contains a salt of the weak base. This is a buffer solution.
   c. H_2SO_4 and H_2SO_3 − H_2SO_4 is a strong acid, not a salt of H_2SO_3, and thus this cannot be a buffer solution.
   d. $HC_2H_3O_2$ and $Cu(C_2H_3O_2)_2$ − $HC_2H_3O_2$ is a weak acid and a salt of it must contain the common ion, $C_2H_3O_2^-$ which $Cu(C_2H_3O_2)_2$ does; thus this is a buffer solution.
   e. $HOCl$ and KBr − $HOCl$ is a weak acid and a salt of $HOCl$ must contain the common ion, OCl^- which KBr does not; thus this is not a buffer solution.

In commercial turfgrass and agriculture applications, buffer or acidifying agents are often used to modify the pH of a spray mixture. The water pH greatly affects the breakdown (or hydrolysis) of pesticides. In general, high pH water conditions cause a shorter half-life (or more rapid breakdown) of the pesticide. At high pH, alkaline hydrolysis can occur where a chemical is altered to lower its effectiveness or make it completely inactive. The addition of hydrogen can break double bonds in a molecule, replace other atoms, or alter the chemical structure. Most tank mixtures should be near neutral (pH=7) or slightly acidic (pH 4 to 7). Insecticides are especially sensitive to spray-tank water pH. For example, acephate (Orthene) has a half-life of 65 days at a pH of 3 (acidic), and a half-life of 16 days at pH 9 (basic). Carbaryl (Sevin) has a half-life of 100 to 150 days at pH 6, but only 24 hours at pH 9. The **half-life** of a substance is the time required for half of it to be inactivated.

The pH of spray-tank water should be adjusted with buffers or acidifiers to within a certain range for adequate usage:

Spray-Tank pH Levels and Precautionary Statements

pH Range	Comments
3.5 to 6.0	Satisfactory for spraying and short-term storage of most spray mixtures in the spray tank.
6.1 to 7.0	Adequate for immediate spraying of most pesticides. Do not allow mixture to sit over 1 to 2 hours to prevent loss of effectiveness.
≥ 7.1	Should add buffer or acidifier to adjust.

To test and adjust the pH of water to be used for mixing pesticides, do the following:

1. Test the water by using a clean container to obtain a 1 pint sample of water to be used. Check the pH using a pH meter, test kit, or test paper and determine if the pH needs to be adjusted.
2. Adjust the pH by using a standard eyedropper to add 3 drops of buffer or acidifier to the measured pint of water. Stir well with a clean glass rod or clean, nonporous utensil. Check pH as above and if further adjustments are needed, repeat the previous steps until proper pH is obtained. Record the number of times 3 drops of buffer or acidifier were added.
3. Correct pH in spray tank by filling the tank with water. Add 2 ounces of buffer or acidifier for each 3 drops used in the jar test above per 100 gallons of water in the spray tank. Recheck the pH of water in the tank and adjust if necessary. Specific product labels should always be consulted on use rates as these vary according to the gallons of spray solution and initial spray solution pH. Often a 1% solution (e.g., 1 gal/100 gal) is initially used.

Most commercial buffering or acidifying agents are proprietary blends of various alcohols, paraffin oil, fatty acid esters, methylated seed oils, silicones, phosphoric acid and other ingredients. Most products suggest the following sequence when mixing fertilizers and/or pesticides and buffers/acidifiers.

1. micronutrients and fertilizers
2. dry flowables or water dispersible granules
3. wettable powders
4. flowables
5. water soluble products
6. emulsifiable concentrates

The buffering/acidifying agent is added last while the tank agitator is running.

Spray solutions should be checked periodically with a pH meter following mixing to ensure the desired pH range is reached and the mixture should be applied as soon as possible to minimize hydrolysis. Spray solutions should also be kept from exposure to sunlight as this also hastens chemical breakdown.

IRRIGATION WATER QUALITY

One of the most important tasks turf managers face is being able to interpret a water analysis report. Unfortunately, many reports are presented in confusing formats or terms, with little guidelines on their meanings. The following will aid superintendents in understanding the numbers generated by a water analysis report and how to interpret them.

SALINITY

With an ever-increasing demand on potable (drinking) supplies, turf managers will probably be using increasing amounts of poorer quality water. Problem levels of salinity (primarily sodium), pH and bicarbonate can occur with any of these sources, especially when located near the coast or in arid regions. Salt affected plants must expend large amounts of energy to absorb water from the soil solution, energy that would otherwise be used for plant growth. One of the first processes from which this energy is diverted is cell elongation. Leaf cells continue to divide but do not elongate. More cells per unit leaf area then occurs and accounts for the typically dark green color of osmotically (salt) stressed plants. Turfgrasses continually irrigated with water containing salts often become weak, eventually declining to a point of no longer being acceptable. Salinity problems in turf usually occur when insufficient rainfall and irrigation are available to leach excess salts, soils have poor drainage, saline irrigation water is used, upward movement of leached salt from parched water tables occurs, and/or when saltwater intrusion occurs.

The following tests provide information concerning soil and water quality:

- Total salt content, measured as electrical conductivity (EC)
- Sodium level (SAR or ESP)
- Toxic ion levels, especially boron, chloride, and fluoride
- Bicarbonates measured as Residual Sodium Carbonate (RSC)
- pH

Principal Soluble Salts

Soluble salts are those inorganic chemicals more soluble than gypsum ($CaSO_4$), which has a solubility of 2.4 g/L of water. For example, table salt (NaCl) has a solubility almost 150 times greater (357 g/L) than that of gypsum. Principal soluble salts found in water are chloride and sulfate salts of sodium, calcium (Ca^{+2}), potassium (K^+), and magnesium (Mg^{+2}). Table salt (sodium chloride) is also found in some soils. Insoluble salts occur (e.g., gypsum and lime) but excessive soluble salts are the primary ones which may impede plant growth. As a comparison, Table 2-7 lists the most common solutes (dissolved substances) in seawater.

Formation of a white crust on the soil surface indicates salt accumulation, as does shoot browning. Salts accumulate when insufficient rainfall occurs to leach them from the soil. This generally is a problem in low humidity and low rainfall

TABLE 2-7. Most Common Solutes in Seawater

Solute	%	Solute	%
Chlorine (Cl^-)	55.05	Potassium (K^+)	1.10
Sodium (Na^+)	30.61	Bicarbonate (HCO_3^-)	0.41
Sulfate (SO_4^{-2})	7.68	Bromine (Br^-)	0.19
Magnesium (Mg^{+2})	3.69	Boric acid (H_3BO_3)	0.07
Calcium (Ca^{+2})	1.16	Strontium (Sr^{+2})	0.03

areas such as arid western states, unless extended droughts occur elsewhere such as coastal areas.

Reclaiming saline soils requires leaching of soluble salts out of the soil. This requires: (1) internal soil drainage; (2) replacement of excess sodium in sodic soils usually with calcium (Ca^{+2}) ; and (3) leaching out of soluble salts.

Measuring and Classifying Irrigation Salinity

Salinity is determined by measuring the ability of water to conduct an electrical current. The amount of current that can flow through a solution is proportional to the concentration of dissolved salts (or ions). Salty water is a good conductor of electrical current, whereas chemically pure water is a relatively poor conductor. Salinity is expressed in two different ways, either as **electrical conductivity** (ECw) or **total dissolved solids (or salts)** (TDS). There are several units commonly used to express ECw: deciSiemens per meter (dS/m), millimhos per centimeter (mmhos/cm), or micromhos per centimeter (micromhos/cm). The relationship between these units is:

$$1 \text{ deciSiemens per meter (dS/m)} = 0.1 \text{ Siemens/meter} = 1 \text{ mmhos/cm}$$

$$= 1000 \text{ micromhos/cm}$$

Total dissolved salts are expressed in parts per million (ppm) or milligrams per liter (mg/L) and are generally not measured directly, but calculated from an ECw measurement.

$$1 \text{ milligram/liter (mg/L)} = 1 \text{ part per million (ppm)}$$

$$\text{electrical conductivity, } EC_w \text{ (mmhos/cm or dS/m)} \times 640$$

$$= \text{total dissolved salts (TDS) (mg/L or ppm)}$$

The ratio of total dissolved salt to electrical conductivity (ECw) of various salt solutions ranges from 550 to 700 ppm per dS/m. The most common salt in saline water has a total dissolved salts (TDS) of 640 ppm at an electrical conductivity (ECw) of 1 dS/m. Most laboratories use this relationship to calculate total dissolved salts (TDS) from electrical conductivity (ECw), but some multiply by 700. In general, fresh water has less than 1,500 mg/L (or ppm) of total dissolved salts

(TDS), brackish water between 1,500 and 5,000 mg/L, and saline water above 5,000 mg/L. Water sample salinities are often compared to those of seawater which has an average electrical conductivity (ECw) of 43 dS/m or about 32,000 ppm dissolved salts. Individual salts are also reported in milliequivalents per liter (meq/L).

Irrigation water is classified into four categories based on salinity hazard, which considers the potential for damaging plants and the level of management needed for utilization as an irrigation source (Table 2-8). Water with electrical conductivity (ECw) readings of less than 0.75 dS/m is suitable for irrigation without problems. Successful use of water with electrical conductivity (ECw) values above 0.75 dS/m depends upon soil conditions and plant tolerance to salinity. Generally, higher salinity levels can be used on sandy soils where salts can be flushed (leached) compared to similar values on poorly draining clay soils which may hold salts in the root zone. Under typical summer stress, electrical conductivity (ECw) of turfgrass irrigation should ideally not exceed 1.25 dS/m soluble salts. Salinity levels above 3.0 dS/m are unsuitable for any length as an irrigation source. Salinity levels of 3.0 dS/m contribute almost 3 tons of salts per acre foot of irrigation water applied.

Assessing Irrigation Water for Infiltration Problems

In addition to direct salinity hazard of water to plants, tests are performed to help indicate the potential of irrigation water to cause poor soil infiltration properties.

TABLE 2-8. USDA Salinity Laboratory's Classification of Saline Irrigation Water Based on Salinity Level, Potential Injury to Plants, and Management Necessary for Satisfactory Utilization

Salinity Class	Electrical Conductivity (dS/m)	Total Dissolved Salts (ppm)	Potential Injury and Necessary Management for Use as Irrigation Water
Low	<0.25	<150	Low salinity hazard; generally not a problem; additional management is not needed.
Medium	0.25 to 0.75	150–500	Damage to salt-sensitive plants may occur. Occasional flushing with low salinity water may be necessary.
High	0.75 to 2.25	500–1500	Damage to plants with low tolerance to salinity will likely occur. Plant growth and quality will be improved with excess irrigation for leaching, and/or periodic use of low salinity water and good drainage provided.
Very High	>2.25	>1500	Damage to plants with high tolerance to salinity may occur. Successful use as an irrigation source requires salt-tolerant plants, good soil drainage, excess irrigation for leaching, and/or periodic utilization of low salinity water.

The potential for irrigation water to have poor infiltration properties is assessed by determining the **sodium adsorption ratio** (SAR) and the electrical conductivity (EC) of the water. The sodium adsorption ratio relates the concentration of sodium to the concentration of calcium and magnesium. The higher the sodium concentration relative to calcium and magnesium (higher SAR), the poorer the water infiltration, and increased problems with soil deflocculation (infiltration) result. Such soils crust badly, swell, and disperse, greatly reducing the soil's infiltration. SAR is defined as:

$$SAR = \frac{Na^+}{\sqrt{\dfrac{Ca^{+2} + Mg^{+2}}{2}}} \qquad SAR = \frac{Na^+}{\sqrt{Ca^{+2} + Mg^{+2}}}$$

Ion concentrations in the above left equation are expressed in milliequivalents per liter (meq/L), while the equation on the right is expressed in millimoles per liter (mmoles/L). Milliequivalent describes the molecular weight adjusted for the valence number (number of positive charges) of the ion. The SAR determines the number of milligrams per liter (or ppm) of Na^+, Ca^{+2}, and Mg^{+2} in a water sample. To convert parts per million (or mg/L) to meq/L use the following equation and equivalent weights for Na^+, Ca^{+2}, and Mg^{+2} of 23, 20, and 12.2 mg/meq, respectively (Table 2-9).

$$\text{meq/L} = \frac{\text{ppm (or mg/L)}}{\text{equivalent weight (in mg/meq)}}$$

Example:

A water sample test reports 1,000 mg/L Na^+, 200 mg/L Ca^{+2}, and 100 mg/L Mg^{+2}. Determine its SAR value.

Step 1: First, calculate the number of milliequivalents per liter for each ion (or refer to Table 2-9):

Na^+ = 1000 mg/L ÷ 23 mg/meq = 44 meq/L; Ca^{+2} = 200 mg/L ÷ 20 mg/meq = 10 meq/L; Mg^{+2} = 100 mg/L ÷ 12.2 mg/meq = 8.20 meq/L

Step 2: These values are then placed into the sodium adsorption ratio (SAR) equation as:

$$SAR = \frac{Na^+}{\sqrt{\dfrac{Ca^{+2} + Mg^{+2}}{2}}} = \frac{44}{\sqrt{\dfrac{10 + 8.2}{2}}} = 20.6 meq/L$$

The effects of high sodium adsorption ratio (SAR) on irrigation water infiltration are dependent on the electrical conductivity of the water. For a given sodium adsorption ratio (SAR), the lower the electrical conductivity (ECw) the poorer the infiltration properties, the higher the ECw the better the infiltration. For example, irrigation water with a sodium adsorption ratio (SAR)=15 has poor infiltration properties if the electrical conductivity (ECw)=0.5 dS/m, but good infiltration

TABLE 2-9. Laboratory Analysis to Determine Water Quality and Factors for Converting Ion Concentration Reported in Parts per Million (ppm) or Milligrams per Liter (mg/L) to Moles per Liter (mol/L) or Milliequivalents per Liter (meq/L) (McCarty, 2001)

ppm (or mg/L) ÷ molecular weight (g) = moles per liter (mol/L)
ppm (or mg/L) ÷ milliequivalent weight (mg/meq) = milliequivalents per liter (meq/L)
milliequivalents per liter (meq/L) = molecular weight ÷ total valence number

Analysis	Reporting Symbol	Reporting Unit	Molecular Weight (g)	Milliequivalent Weight (mg/meq)
electrical conductivity	EC_w	mmhos/cm	—	—
Calcium	Ca^{+2}	meq/L	40	20
Magnesium	Mg^{+2}	meq/L	24.3	12.2
Sodium	Na^{+1}	meq/L	23	23
Carbonate	CO_3^{-2}	meq/L	60	30
Bicarbonate	HCO_3^{-1}	meq/L	61	61
Chloride	Cl^{-1}	meq/L	35.4	35.4
Sulfate	SO_4^{-2}	meq/L	96	48
Boron	B	mg/L	10.8	10.8
Nitrate-nitrogen	NO_3-N	mg/L	14	14
Acidity	pH	pH	—	—
SAR	—	meq/L	—	—
Potassium	K^{+1}	meq/L	39.1	39.1
Lithium	Li^{+1}	mg/L	7	7
Iron	$Fe^{+2 \text{ or } +3}$	mg/L	55.8	27.9 or 18.6
Ammonium-nitrogen	NH_4-N	mg/L	14	14
Phosphate phosphorus	PO_4-P	mg/L	31	varies

Conversion Values Between mg/L and meq/L for Most Water Constituents

Constituents	Multiply by the Following Value to Convert mg/L to meq/L	Multiply by the Following Value to Convert meq/L to mg/L
Sodium (Na^{+1})	0.043	23
Magnesium (Mg^{+2})	0.083	12
Calcium (Ca^{+2})	0.05	20
Chloride (Cl^{-1})	0.028	36
Sulfate (SO_4^{-2})	0.021	48
Bicarbonate (HCO_3^{-1})	0.016	61
(CO_3^{-2})	0.033	30

properties with an electrical conductivity (ECw)=2.0 dS/m. A good rule of thumb is if the sodium adsorption ratio (SAR) is more than 10 times greater than the ECw, then poor water infiltration is likely to occur.

General guidelines for precautions and management of irrigation water with various SAR values and an electrical conductivity (ECw) =1.0 dS/m are provided in Table 2-10. Fine-textured soils such as clay can have permeability problems if a water sodium adsorption ratio (SAR) >9 is used over an extended period. In our

TABLE 2-10. Sodium Adsorption Ratio (SAR) Values, Categories, and Precautions for Irrigation Sources with $EC_w \geq 1.0$ dS/m

SAR (meq/L)	Category	Precaution
0–10	1 (low Na water)	Little danger
10–18	2 (medium Na water)	Problems on fine textured soils and sodium-sensitive plants, especially under low-leaching conditions. Soils should have good permeability.
18–24	3 (high Na water)	Problems on most soils. Good salt-tolerant plants are required along with special management such as the use of gypsum.
>24	4 (very high Na water)	Unsatisfactory except with high salinity (>2.0 dS/m), high calcium levels, and the use of gypsum.

Note: some labs report adjusted sodium adsorption ratio (SAR) values instead of sodium adsorption ratio (SAR). The adjusted sodium adsorption ratio (SAR) includes the added effects of the precipitation or ionization of calcium in soils as related to carbonate and bicarbonate concentrations. Bicarbonates can interact with Ca and Mg in soil to precipitate out lime ($CaCO_3$) or magnesium carbonate ($MgCO_3$), causing an increase in sodium hazard.

earlier example where the water sample had a sodium adsorption ratio (SAR) of 20.6 meq/L, problems could occur if this water source is used long-term on finer texture (e.g., clay) soils.

Exchangeable sodium percentage (ESP) is another means of measuring the soil sodium status and is still used by many laboratories, where:

$$ESP = \frac{\text{exchangeable Na} \times 100}{\text{cation exchange capacity (CEC)}}$$

Exchangeable Na is the amount of sodium on the CEC in units of cmol kg^{-1} or meq $100g^{-1}$. Soil salinity is categorized as one of three classes: saline, sodic, or saline-sodic (Table 2-11) based on soil conditions near the surface. Measuring ESP, however, is tedious and subject to error and since a generally good relationship exists between SAR of the soil solution and ESP of the soil, the SAR is normally used.

ESP indicates the probability a soil is or will disperse, thereby reducing the permeability of soil to water and air. In the environment, salts and sodium do not act independently. For example, high soluble salt concentration can negate the soil particle dispersal (thus, impermeability) from the effects of sodium. Table 2-11 lists the combined effects of salinity (EC) and soluble salt contents (ESP). Usually little or only minor problems occur when ESP values are less than 13 to 15%.

Salt-affected soil comprises about 10% of the total arable lands in the world and occurs in over 100 countries. These affected soils occur most often in arid and semiarid climates but can also be found where the climate and mobility of salts cause saline water and soils, especially along seacoasts or river delta regions where seawater has inundated the soil.

Salt-affected soil can be classified as **saline, sodic**, and **saline-sodic** soils. **Saline soils** are plagued by high levels of soluble salts, primarily Cl^-, SO_4^{-2}, and some-

TABLE 2-11. U.S. Salinity Laboratory Classification of Salt-Affected Soils

Class (previous name)	Total Salt Levels EC ds/m	Sodium Levels ESP (%)	SAR	Soil pH	Comments
Normal soil (proposed revision)	<4.0 (<2.0)	<15	5.5 to 7.5 (<15)		—
Saline (white alkali) (proposed revision)	≥4.0 (>2.0)	<15 (—)	<12 (—)	<8.5	The exchange complex is usually dominated by Ca^+ and Mg^+, thus the soil pH is usually below 8.5. A white salt crust, referred to as 'white alkali,' forms on the soil surface as the soil dries. Soil permeability or hydraulic conductivity is not adversely affected by adsorbed sodium.
Sodic (black alkali) (proposed revision)	<4.0 (—)	≥15 (—)	≥12 (>15)	>8.5	Sodic soils are nonsaline and soil pH is generally 8.5 to 10 due to the hydrolysis of sodium carbonate. Referred to as 'black alkali' due to black puddles of water, like oil, from dispersed soil humus that crusts after drying ('slick spots'). Sodic soils do not form a white salt crust on the soil surface but clay particles are dispersed in these soils due to high levels of Na and low levels of Ca and Mg. Structureless soils result with low water infiltration and air permeability which few plants can tolerate.
Saline-sodic (none) (proposed revision)	≥4.0 (<2)	≥15 (—)	≥12 (15)	≤8.5	These soils have characteristics intermediate between those of saline and sodic soils. They contain both high soluble salt and high exchangeable sodium levels. Like sodic soil, soil pH is usually below 8.5. The soils resemble saline soils if the soluble salts are not leached. Saline-sodic soils reduce plant growth from their high soluble salt content. With leaching these soils can become sodic, as leaching removes salts faster than it removes exchangeable sodium, unless calcium and magnesium are applied.

times NO_3^-. Salts of low solubility, such as $CaSO_4$ and $CaSO_3$, may also be present. Because exchangeable sodium is not a problem, saline soils are usually flocculated with good water permeability (Table 2-11).

An ESP >15% or a soil SAR >13 indicates a **sodic soil** where sodium causes soil colloids to disperse and plug the soil's drainage pores which reduces the permeability of the soil to water and air. Sodic soils become saturated with sodium ions compared to calcium and magnesium ions, especially if bicarbonate ions are present. Symptoms of reduced permeability include waterlogging, reduced infiltration rates, crusting, compaction, disease occurrence, weed invasion, and poor aeration. Sodic soils often have considerable clay which is sticky due to the sodium. Sodic soils have high levels of exchangeable sodium and along with low EC, these soils tend to disperse, reducing water infiltration. Sodic soils also have a pH between 8.5 and 10 and are often called **black alkali soils** because the humus in the soil tends to disperse. Calcium and magnesium ions in sodic soils tend to form lime, leaving soluble Ca and Mg levels low, allowing the sodium problems. **Saline-sodic soils** have both high contents of soluble salts and exchangeable sodium.

BICARBONATES AND CARBONATES

Bicarbonate ions (HCO_3^-) and to a lesser extent, **carbonate** ions (CO_3^{-2}), are found in water with a high pH. The primary source of carbonates and bicarbonates in soils is carbonic acid (H_2CO_3) that forms when carbon dioxide from microbial and root respiration reacts with water.

$$\underset{\text{carbon dioxide}}{CO_2} + \underset{\text{water}}{H_2O} \rightleftharpoons \underset{\text{carbonic acid}}{H_2CO_3}$$

Carbonic acid is a very weak acid ($pK_{a1} = 6.37$; $pK_{a2} = 10.26$) that is noncorrosive, and is a chief ingredient in soft drinks. In higher pH soils, the abundance of hydroxyl (OH^-) ions react with the carbonic acid to form first bicarbonate ions (HCO_3^-) and then, carbonate (CO_3^{-2}) ions.

Step 1:

$$\underset{\text{carbonic acid}}{H_2CO_3} + \underset{\text{hydroxyl ion (pH 6-9)}}{OH^-} \rightleftharpoons \underset{\text{bicarbonate}}{HCO_3^-} + \underset{\text{water}}{H_2O}$$

Step 2:

$$\underset{\text{bicarbonate}}{HCO_3^-} + \underset{\text{hydroxyl ion (pH >9)}}{OH^-} \rightleftharpoons \underset{\text{carbonate}}{CO_3^{-2}} + \underset{\text{water}}{H_2O}$$

As the concentrations of bicarbonates and carbonates increase, more hydroxyl ions are formed with a corresponding reduction of hydrogen ions (H^+), causing an increase in pH.

When water containing HCO_3^- dries at the soil surface, Ca and Mg carbonates (calcitic lime) are formed.

$$Ca^{+2} + 2HCO_3^- \rightleftharpoons CaCO_3 + H_2O + CO_2$$

Since Ca and Mg are no longer dissolved, they do not counteract the effects of Na, and problems related to high exchangeable sodium percentage (ESP) may occur. This results in an increase in soil pH and a corresponding decrease in water quality and soil infiltration. White lime deposits may also become visible on turf leaves during hot, dry periods as bicarbonates are deposited during evaporation.

There are two measurements used for assessing the carbonate level of irrigation water, the direct measurement of carbonate and bicarbonate and the **residual sodium carbonate** equation (RSC).

Residual sodium carbonate (RSC) equation reflects alkalinity of water by indicating this potential precipitation of Ca and Mg and resulting increases of effective sodium percentage of water. Residual sodium carbonate (RSC) specifically measures presence of excess carbonates (CO_3^{-2}) and bicarbonate (HCO_3^-) content over calcium (Ca^{+2}) and magnesium (Mg^{+2}) ions expressed each as meq/L (or millimoles/L):

Residual Sodium Carbonate (RSC) Equation

$$RSC = (CO_3^{-2} + HCO_3^-) - (Ca^{+2} + Mg^{+2})$$

Assessment for poor water infiltration due to high carbonates and low calcium and magnesium as determined by the residual sodium carbonate (RSC) equation is listed in Table 2-12.

If hazardous residual sodium carbonate (RSC) water is repeatedly used, the soil becomes alkaline and is likely to become sodic over time. Values greater than 1.5 meq/L may justify irrigation acid injection. Acid injection changes the carbonates and bicarbonates to carbon dioxide and water but does not affect the calcium or magnesium. Normally, if irrigation residual sodium carbonate (RSC) values are high but sodium adsorption ratio (SAR) values are low, acid injection is unnecessary since insufficient sodium is present to cause a problem. This also is true in areas of high rainfall where sodium is readily leached out of the soil profile.

Bicarbonate levels alone are sometimes used to assess potential limitations of an irrigation water source (Table 2-13). Water containing 2 to 4 meq/L of bicarbonates can be managed by applying ammoniacal fertilizer as part of a regular fertilizer program to help reduce soil pH. Water with greater than 4 meq/L bicarbonates may need to be acidified with sulfuric or phosphoric acid. Blending poor

TABLE 2-12. Potential for Precipitation of Calcium and Magnesium at the Soil Surface by High Carbonate and Bicarbonate in the Irrigation Water as Determined by Residual Sodium Carbonate (RSC) Equation

RSC Value (meq/L)	Potential Use
≤1.25	Generally safe for irrigation
1.25 to 2.5	Potentially hazardous
>2.5	Usually unsuitable for irrigation (hazardous)

TABLE 2-13. Potential Limitation of Irrigation Water Due to Bicarbonate (HCO$_3^-$) Level

HCO$_3^-$		
(meq/L)	(ppm or mg/L)	Potential Limitation
<1.5	0–120	Generally safe for irrigation
1.5–8.5	120–180	Increasing problem
>8.5	180–600	Severe problem

quality water with better quality water and applying soil amendments such as gypsum or sulfur also are means to help manage bicarbonate problems. The negative effects on soil infiltration of bicarbonate and carbonate are negated by high levels of Ca and Mg. Bicarbonate and carbonate are good indicators of hazard when irrigation water calcium and magnesium concentrations are low, but the RSC equation should be utilized when water calcium and magnesium are high. High HCO$_3^-$ and CO$_3^{-2}$ water can have good infiltration properties if Ca and Mg levels are also high.

Nutrient Loads. To determine the amount (lb/acre) of calcium and magnesium supplied in an acre-foot of irrigation water, multiply each element (in mg/L or ppm) by 2.72. For example, an irrigation source containing 75 mg/L calcium and 30 mg/L magnesium would supply the following:

$$Ca^{+2} = 75 \text{ mg/L} \times 2.72 = 204 \text{ lb calcium supplied per acre-foot irrigation water.}$$

$$Mg^{+2} = 30 \text{ mg/L} \times 2.72 = 82 \text{ lb magnesium per acre-foot irrigation water.}$$

pH

Continued use of high bicarbonate and carbonate water also leads to a high soil pH. When sodium (Na$^+$) is the predominant cation in the soil, sodium bicarbonate and sodium carbonate form, causing the pH to be as high as 10 since these ions are water soluble and tend to ionize, which keeps high levels of bicarbonate and carbonate. However, when Ca predominates, usually insoluble calcium carbonate forms which, unlike sodium carbonate, does not ionize to form more carbonate ions and thus the soil pH generally stabilizes around 8.0. High pH can induce iron, manganese, and to a lesser extent zinc deficiencies by rendering these micronutrients unavailable to turfgrass roots. Unfortunately, simply adding these micronutrients in granular fertilizers is sometimes ineffective since these elements quickly become unavailable in high pH soils. Using chelates and foliar applications help avoid interactions between micronutrients and high pH soils.

With moderate levels of HCO3- and CO$_3^{-2}$ acidifying amendments can be soil-, rather than irrigation-applied to reduce soil pH. Acidifying N fertilizers or elemental S are generally employed. Although N fertilizers containing or generating ammonium (NH$_4^+$) reduce soil pH, it is important to note that nitrate (NO$_3^-$) fertilizers increase soil pH. Usually, irrigating with water sources containing low bicarbonate concentrations can be managed by using acidifying fertilizers (e.g., ammonium sulfate) or application of granular elemental sulfur.

Acidification of the irrigation water converts bicarbonate and carbonate to carbon dioxide and water, but does not affect its sodium, calcium, or magnesium content. However, acidification allows calcium and magnesium to remain soluble so they could displace sodium from the soil cation exchange sites.

Irrigation water high in bicarbonate/carbonate and high in calcium and/or magnesium react to form insoluble lime ($CaCO_3$ or $MgCO_3$) in the upper centimeter of soil as shown:

Step 1:

$$\underset{\text{carbon dioxide}}{CO_2} + \underset{\text{water}}{H_2O} \rightleftharpoons \underset{\text{carbonic acid}}{H_2CO_3} \rightleftharpoons \underset{\text{hydrogen}}{2H^+} + \underset{\text{carbonate}}{CO_3^{-2}}$$

Step 2:

$$\underset{\text{calcium}}{Ca^{+2}} + \underset{\text{carbonate}}{CO_3^{-2}} \rightarrow \underset{\text{calcite (insoluble)}}{CaCO_3\downarrow}$$

This insoluble lime, called **calcite**, can eventually coat soil and sand particles, reducing water infiltration. Concentrations of these in irrigation water which can cause reduced water infiltration are shown in Table 2-14.

Ways to disrupt the calcite layer include physically breaking it up by periodic cultivation or dissolving it into more mobile forms such as gypsum ($CaSO_4$) and magnesium sulfate ($MgSO_4$). This is performed by using acidifying fertilizers such as ammonium sulfate or by applying elemental sulfur to the turfgrass surface. Acidification of irrigation water is also helpful but is expensive, may not be needed on all areas of the golf course, and may not completely dissolve this layer, thus supplemental measures are required.

Irrigation Acid Injection. Water with high bicarbonate levels may require acidification (via injection into the irrigation system) with acids such as sulfuric or phosphoric acids to correct the problem. The general reaction with an acid is shown below. The second two-step process shown forms carbon dioxide (CO_2) and water (H_2O) forming from the reaction with an acid, such as sulfuric acid (H_2SO_4), with bicarbonate (HCO_3^-):

TABLE 2-14. Amounts of Bicarbonate, Carbonate, Calcium, and Magnesium in Irrigation Which Can Cause Soil Deflocculation, Reducing Soil Water Infiltration

Element	Levels in Irrigation Water Which May Reduce Soil Water Infiltration, mg/L (or ppm)
Bicarbonate (HCO_3^-)	100 to 400
Carbonate (CO_3^-)	0 to 5
Calcium (Ca)	25 to 200
Magnesium (Mg)	20 to 40

General Reactions of Neutralizing Carbonate and Bicarbonate with an Acid:

$$\underset{\text{carbonate}}{CO_3^{-2}} + \underset{\text{acid source}}{H^+} \rightarrow \underset{\text{bicarbonate}}{HCO_3^-}$$

$$\underset{\text{bicarbonate}}{HCO_3^-} + \underset{\text{acid source}}{H^+} \rightarrow \underset{\text{carbonic acid}}{H_2CO_3} \rightarrow \underset{\text{carbon dioxide}}{CO_2\uparrow} + \underset{\text{water}}{H_2O}$$

Bicarbonates Neutralization with Sulfuric Acid:

Step 1:

$$\underset{\text{sulfuric acid}}{H_2SO_4} + \underset{\text{bicarbonate}}{HCO_3^-} \rightleftharpoons \underset{\text{bisulfate}}{HSO_4^-} + \underset{\text{carbonic acid}}{H_2CO_3}$$

Step 2:

$$\underset{\text{carbonic acid}}{H_2CO_3} \rightleftharpoons \underset{\text{water}}{H_2O} + \underset{\text{carbon dioxide gas}}{CO_2\uparrow}$$

Other acidifying units (often called sulfur generators) dissolve sulfur chips or flakes into stored irrigation water to form sulfites (SO_3^{-2}) and then sulfur dioxide gas (SO_2). The sulfur dioxide then reacts to form sulfurous acid (H_2SO_3) and sulfuric acid (H_2SO_4) which then has the same effect as acid injection. The generator consists of a sulfur chip storage hopper, oxidizing chamber, blower, and absorption tower. Pure elemental sulfur chips or flakes are combusted (burned) in the oxidizing chamber to form sulfur dioxide gas as shown:

$$\underset{\substack{\text{sulfur} \\ \text{(from chips)}}}{S} + \underset{\substack{\text{oxygen} \\ \text{(from air)}}}{O_2} \rightleftharpoons \underset{\text{sulfur dioxide gas}}{SO_2\uparrow}$$

When sulfur dioxide gas mixes with water, sulfurous acid is formed:

$$\underset{\text{sulfur dioxide gas}}{SO_2\uparrow} + \underset{\text{water}}{H_2O} \rightleftharpoons \underset{\text{sulfurous acid}}{H_2SO_3}$$

Sulfurous acid is a weak acid that is only slightly corrosive and easy to handle. In comparison, sulfuric acid (H_2SO_4) which is also used as battery acid, is a extremely strong and corrosive acid and difficult to handle. Sulfurous acid improves water quality by lowering water pH and neutralizing bicarbonates and carbonates. Sulfurous acid reduces pH by dissociating into hydrogen and sulfite ions:

$$\underset{\text{sulfurous acid}}{H_2SO_3} \rightleftharpoons \underset{\substack{\text{hydrogen ions} \\ \text{(pH}\downarrow)}}{2H^+} + \underset{\text{sulfite ions}}{SO_3^{-2}}$$

The hydrogen ions reduce water pH.

Bicarbonates and carbonates often form lime (calcium or magnesium carbonate), thus increase soil pH, and tend to reduce soil percolation and drainage. These are neutralized by the sulfurous acid to form sulfite, carbon dioxide, and water.

Bicarbonate Neutralization with Sulfurous Acid:

$$\underset{\text{sulfurous acid}}{H_2SO_3} + \underset{\text{bicarbonates}}{2HCO_3^-} \rightarrow \underset{\text{sulfite}}{SO_3^{-2}} + \underset{\text{carbon dioxide}}{2CO_2\uparrow} + \underset{\text{water}}{2H_2O}$$

Carbonate Neutralization with Sulfurous Acid:

$$\underset{\text{sulfurous acid}}{H_2SO_3} + \underset{\text{carbonates ions}}{CO_3^-} \rightarrow \underset{\text{sulfite ions}}{SO_3^{-2}} + \underset{\text{carbon dioxide}}{CO_2\uparrow} + \underset{\text{water}}{H_2O}$$

The carbon dioxide gas escapes to the air. This reaction is similar to mixing baking soda (sodium bicarbonate) and vinegar (acetic acid) in the kitchen. The resulting "fizz" is escaping carbon dioxide.

Sulfur treatment will reduce water pH, bicarbonates, and carbonates. This treatment, however, will not in itself correct water sodium problems. Sodium-rich water is usually injected with soluble gypsum and/or gypsum is added to the soil surface. Sulfur treated water, however, helps maintain soluble calcium and magnesium ions, reducing sodium adsorption ratio (SAR) values, and thus helping to counter the detrimental effects of sodium ions in the water.

General rates of amendments used are based on neutralizing only 75% of the HCO_3^- and CO_3^{-2} in the irrigation water. This precaution is taken because once the HCO_3^- and CO_3^{-2} are neutralized, the pH of the water decreases precipitously with further additions of acid. This process requires specialized equipment and constant monitoring to ensure successful acidification of water without phytotoxic effects occurring to turf. Normally, a desirable soil pH range for turfgrasses is 5.5 to 7.0 and for irrigation water, 6.0 to 8.0. Values within the optimum range for turfgrass growth allow the plant to expend less energy to obtain the necessary nutrients from the soil.

Other Acidifying Methods. Phosphoric acid is also used to lower the pH of irrigation water. In most areas, when using phosphoric acid, the pH of the irrigation water must be lowered below 6.0 to prevent formation of insoluble phosphates in the irrigation lines. At higher than 6.0 pH, phosphorus may combine with calcium and magnesium ions in the water to form insoluble calcium or magnesium phosphate deposits which then clog irrigation orifices. This problem is most severe in areas where hard water, water high in concentration of calcium and magnesium ions, occurs.

Another acidifying solution that is injected directly into irrigation lines is mono-ocarbamide dihydrogensulfate (trade name: *pHairway*). This compound is formed from the reaction of urea and sulfuric acid. As always, careful records should be kept with the use of this solution as the addition of urea to the soil may further reduce soil pH from the conversion to nitrate. Additional nitrogen also will be added to the turf from the urea; thus, total nitrogen added by fertilizer and this acidifying source should be monitored.

Amending Irrigation Water High in Sodium

Mixing high sodium adsorption ratio (SAR) water with water low in both calcium and electrical conductivity (ECw) does not reduce the sodium hazard of the mixture, because the sodium adsorption ratio (SAR) is generally not changed appreciably but the electrical conductivity (ECw) is reduced. Recall that high SAR water with low ECw has worse infiltration properties than high SAR water with high electrical conductivity (ECw).

Adding gypsum (calcium sulfate) to water with high sodium adsorption ratio (SAR) is one method of increasing the suitability of the water. Gypsum decreases the SAR and increases the electrical conductivity (ECw), which increases the infiltration properties of the water. The impacts of gypsum on calcium and electrical conductivity (ECw) are listed in Table 2-15. Sodium adsorption ratio and electrical conductivity (ECw) for the water sample should be recalculated using the changes indicated. Adjust the electrical conductivity (ECw) and SAR of the water with gypsum to produce a water that has sufficient electrical conductivity (ECw) and SAR to be considered acceptable as assessed by the criteria in Table 2-9.

Several forms of gypsum are available including natural dihydrate gypsum and the natural anhydrite form. The dihydrate form dissolves quicker because of attached water molecules. The finest grade available should be used because it contains fewer contaminates.

A gypsum machine with agitators and mixing tanks injects a slurry of suspended (not dissolved) particles into the water. Near 100% dissolution of the gypsum should occur within a few minutes. If not, the hard particles could be abrasive to the irrigation emitters.

An injection gypsum rate between 2 and 2.5 meq/L is a suggested range. This must be continuously used if salinity levels are excessive in the irrigation water source.

TOXIC IONS

Irrigation water quality is also influenced by other specific ions. Most irrigation water sources contain low levels of a variety of elements. Normally these pose minimum problems but can increase under conditions of inadequate leaching with

TABLE 2-15. Changes in Water Calcium and Electrical Conductivity Due to Gypsum Addition

Gypsum rate, lb/1000 gal	Gypsum added in acre-foot of water (lb/acre)	Ca^{+2} added, meq/L	Increase in ECw, dS/m
0.72	234	1.0	0.1
1.44	468	2.0	0.2
2.16	702	3.0	0.3
2.88	936	4.0	0.4
3.60	1170	5.0	0.5
4.32	1404	6.0	0.6
5.04	1638	7.0	0.7

quality water, poor soil permeability and during periods of high evaporation (Tables 2-16 and 2-17).

Sodium. Sodium (Na^+) is of prime concern because it is often found in the largest amount. Sodium is also an antagonistic ion which displaces potassium and can limit availability of iron and manganese in soils. Sodium toxicity appears as marginal scorch of older leaves. A water sodium content of 3 meq/L (70 ppm) can damage the foliage of sensitive ornamental plants.

Boron. Boron (B) in irrigation water is rarely a problem with turfgrasses because boron accumulates in leaf tips which are removed by regular mowing. However, other landscape plants may be more sensitive to boron levels. Boron toxicity symptoms typically show first on older leaf tips and edges either as yellowing, spotting, or drying of leaf tissue. The yellowing or spotting is sometimes followed by drying which progresses from near the tip along the leaf edges and toward the center between the veins (interveinal chlorosis). Landscape plants may be damaged if irrigation water has B contents above 0.75 meq/L or if leaf B contents exceed 250 to 300 ppm (dry weight). Turfgrasses generally will grow in soils with B levels as high as 10 ppm.

Chloride. High concentration of chloride, sulfate, and bicarbonate ions also can cause specific ornamental plant injury under certain soil conditions. Chloride (Cl^-) is not adsorbed by soils but moves readily with the water in soil. It is absorbed by plant roots and accumulates in the leaves. Chloride toxicity symptoms are a leaf burn or drying which typically occurs initially at the leaf tip of older leaves and progresses back along the edges as severity increases. Leaf drop and defoliation also occurs with excessive leaf burn. Tables 2-16 and 2-17 offer general ranges of elements and some expected results at various concentrations. A water chloride content of 10 meq/L (355 ppm) can damage the foliage of sensitive ornamental plants.

Chlorine. Chlorine toxicity normally occurs if reclaim sewage water containing excessive disinfectants is used for irrigation. If stored between treatment and application in a holding pond, much of the free chlorine in water will dissipate into the atmosphere since it is very unstable.

Fluoride. Fluoride (F^-) may also be another ion of concern to ornamental plants. Severe leaf tip burn and scorch can occur on ornamental plants exposed to high fluoride-containing (>1 mg/L) water.

Heavy metals. Heavy metals such as copper, nickel, zinc, and cadmium may be contained by reclaimed water. The National Academy of Science recommends irrigation water should contain no more than 0.01 mg/L of cadmium, 0.2 mg/L of copper, 0.2 mg/L of nickel, and 2.0 mg/L of zinc.

TABLE 2-16. Potential Trace Element Tolerances for Irrigation Water (Modified from Westcot and Ayers, 1984)

Element	Continuous Use (ppm)	Short-Term Use on Fine-Textured Soils (ppm)	Comment
Aluminum (Al)	1.0–5.0	20	Can cause nonproductivity in acid soils (pH <5.5), but most alkaline soils (pH > 7.0) will precipitate the ion and eliminate any toxicity.
Arsenic (As)	0.1	10	Toxicity to plants varies widely, ranging from 12 mg/L (or ppm) for Sudangrass to less than 0.05 mg/L for rice.
Beryllium (Be)	0.1	1.0	Toxicity to plants varies widely, ranging from 5 mg/L for kale to 0.5 mg/L for bush beans.
Boron (B)	0.75	2.0	Accumulates in leaf tips. Sensitive landscape plants can be damaged if >2 mg/L B is present in irrigation water.
Cadmium (Cd)	0.01	0.05	Toxic to beans, beets, and turnips at concentrations as low as 0.1 mg/L in nutrient solutions.
Chlorine (Cl)	10	—	Accumulates in leaf tips. Landscape plants can be especially sensitive.
Chromium (Cr)	0.1	20	Not generally recognized as an essential growth element.
Cobalt (Co)	0.05	10	Toxic to tomato plants at 0.1 mg/L in nutrient solutions. Tends to be inactivated by neutral and alkaline soils.
Copper (Cu)	0.2	5	Toxic to a number of plants at 0.1 to 1.0 mg/L in nutrient solutions.
Iron (Fe)	5.0	?	Not toxic to plants in aerated soils, but can add to soil acidification and to the loss in availability of P and Mo. Overhead irrigation may discolor plants, equipment, and buildings.
Lead (Pb)	5.0	20	Can inhibit plant cell growth at very high concentrations.
Lithium (Li)	2.5	5.0	Tolerated by most crops up to 5 mg/L; mobile in soil. Acts similarly to B.

TABLE 2-16. Potential Trace Element Tolerances for Irrigation Water (Modified from Westcot and Ayers, 1984) (Continued)

Element	Continuous Use (ppm)	Short-Term Use on Fine-Textured Soils (ppm)	Comment
Manganese (Mn)	0.2	20	Toxic to a number of crops, but usually only in acid soils.
Molybdenum (Mo)	0.01	0.05	Not toxic to plants at normal concentrations. Can be toxic to livestock if forage has high concentrations.
Selenium (Se)	0.02	0.05	Toxic to plants at concentration as low as 0.025 mg/L.
Tin (Sn)	?	?	Effectively excluded by plants; specific tolerance is unknown.
Tungsten (W)	?	?	See remarks for tin.
Vanadium (V)	0.1	10	Toxic to many plants at relatively low concentrations.
Zinc (Zn)	2.0	10	Toxic to many plants in widely varying concentrations; reduce toxicity at pH >6.0 and in fine textured or organic soils.

Managing Toxic Elements. Managing toxic ions is difficult in established landscapes. If a problem develops, replacing plants sensitive to particular elements is probably the easiest and cheapest means of overcoming it. Blending better-quality water with that containing the toxic ions and applying additional water to leach the ions are additional means of managing toxic elements.

Water Hardness

Natural water, passing through rocks and soil, dissolves small quantities of chlorides, sulfates, and bicarbonates of calcium (Ca^{+2}), magnesium (Mg^{+2}), and iron (Fe^{+2}). Water containing such compounds is called **hard water** because of its action on soap. Ordinary soap is a sodium or potassium salt of certain high-molecular-weight acids. When soap is added to hard water, the calcium, magnesium, and ferrous, Fe(II), salts of these acids reacts. This leads to the formation of insoluble metallic soaps, which precipitate as a greasy scum on tubs or clothes of lathering. Until all of these calcium and magnesium ions from the water are used up, additional soap will be needed to form lather.

$$Ca^{+2} + CH_3(CH_2)_{10}COO^- \rightleftharpoons [CH_3(CH_2)_{10}COO^-]_2Ca^{+2}9$$

hardness ion   soap   soap scum (insoluble precipitate)

Hard water is undesirable due to the stains on clothes, leather, and paper products it causes during the manufacturing process. When exposed to heat, as in pipes and

TABLE 2-17. General Guidelines for Toxicities of Sodium, Chloride, Boron, and Bicarbonate by Root Absorption and Foliar Contact (Modified from Westcot and Ayers, 1984; Farnham, et al, 1985)

Item		Minor Problems	Increasing Problems	Severe Problems
Soil Permeability/Infiltration				
Electrical conductivity (ECw)	(mmhos/cm or ds/m)	<0.75	0.75–3	>3
Sodium adsorption ratio	(SAR)	<6	6–9	>9
Total dissolved salts (TDS)	(mg/L or ppm)	<450	450–2,000	>2,000
Residual Sodium Carbonate	(meq/L)	≤1.25	1.25–2.5	>2.5
Toxicity by ROOT absorption				
Sodium	(SAR)	<3	3–9	>9
Chloride	(meq/L)	<2	2–10	>10
	(mg/L)	<70	70–355	>355
Boron	(mg/L)	<1.0	1.0–2	>2
Toxicity by Foliar contact				
Sodium	(meq/L)	<3	>3–9	>9
	(mg/L)	<70	>70	—
Chloride	(meq/L)	<3	3–10	>10
	(mg/L)	<100	100–350	>350
Boron	(meq/L)	<0.75	0.75–3.0	>3.0
Miscellaneous Effects (for sensitive plants)				
NH_4–N (ammonium-N)	(mg/L)	<5	5–30	>30
NO_3–N (nitrate-N)	(mg/L)	<5	5–30	>30
Bicarbonate HCO_3^-	(meq/L)	<1.5	1.5–8.5	>8.5
Unsightly foliar deposits	(mg/L)	<90	90–520	>520
Residual chlorine	(mg/L)	<1.0	1–5	>5
pH			Normal range is 6.0 to 8.0	

TABLE 2-17. General Guidelines for Toxicities of Sodium, Chloride, Boron, and Bicarbonate by Root Absorption and Foliar Contact (Modified from Westcot and Ayers, 1984; Farnham, et al., 1985) (Continued)

Item	Minor Problems						Increasing Problems						Severe Problems		

Irrigation Water Analysis Report

Sample No.	Phosphate (PO$_4$-P)	K	Ca	Mg	Fe	Na	Cl	B	Sulfate (SO$_4$-S)	Nitrate (NO$_3$-N)	TDS	EC mmhos/cm	pH	HCO$_3$ meq/L	CO$_3$ meq/L
	ppm														
10	0.0	3.1	9.6	2.1	6.0	13	12.8	0.1	2	0	70	0.11	7.3	0.8	0.0
11	0.1	35.9	14.2	19.8	0.0	896	1276.2	3.5	81	0	3347	5.23	8.5	12.4	0.0

Example:
Find SAR and RSC for each water sample.

Sample 10: first the values used in SAR need to be converted from ppm (or mg/L) to meq/L.

$$RSC = (CO_3^{-2} + HCO_3^{-}) - (Ca^{+2} + Mg^{+2}) = (0.0 + 0.8) - (0.48 + 0.17) = 0.15 \text{ meq/L}$$

Na: $\dfrac{13 \text{ ppm}}{23 \text{ mg/meq}} = 0.57 \text{ meq/L}$

Ca: $\dfrac{9.6 \text{ ppm}}{20 \text{ mg/meq}} = 0.48 \text{ meq/L}$

$$SAR = \frac{Na^{0}}{\sqrt{\dfrac{Ca^{+2} + Mg^{+2}}{2}}} = \frac{0.57}{\sqrt{\dfrac{0.48 + 0.17}{2}}} = 1 \text{ meq/L}$$

Mg: $\dfrac{2.1 \text{ ppm}}{12.2 \text{ mg/meq}} = 0.17 \text{ meq/L}$

Sample 11: $RSC = (CO_3^{-2} + HCO_3^{-}) - (Ca^{+2} + Mg^{+2}) = (0.0 + 12.4) - (0.71 + 1.62) = 10.1 \text{ meq/L}$

Na: $\dfrac{896 \text{ ppm}}{23 \text{ mg/meq}} = 39 \text{ meq/L}$

Ca: $\dfrac{14.2 \text{ ppm}}{20 \text{ mg/meq}} = 0.71 \text{ meq/L}$

$$SAR = \frac{Na^{+}}{\sqrt{\dfrac{Ca^{+2} + Mg^{+2}}{2}}} = \frac{39}{\sqrt{\dfrac{0.71 + 0.62}{2}}} = 33.5 \text{ meq/L}$$

Mg: $\dfrac{19.8 \text{ ppm}}{12.2 \text{ mg/meq}} = 1.62 \text{ meq/L}$

boilers, the bicarbonates decompose, forming carbonate precipitates. These precipitates build up, preventing good contact between the water and pipes. Additional deposits of slightly soluble salts, such as calcium sulfate ($CaSO_4$), occur when the water is evaporated. Therefore, the boiler pipes may overheat and fail under pressure.

Softening Hard Water. Hardness of water is classified as (1) *temporary*, or *bicarbonate*, and (2) *permanent*, or *noncarbonate*. Temporary hard water is fresh water containing Ca^{+2} and bicarbonate (HCO_3^-), and can be softened by boiling the water.

$$Ca^{+2} + 2HCO_3^- \overset{heat}{\rightleftharpoons} CaCO_3{\downarrow} + H_2O + CO_2{\uparrow}$$

In the boiling of temporary hard water, calcium, magnesium, or ferrous ions are precipitated as carbonates. Carbon dioxide is lost because it is less soluble in hot water than in cold water. However, in industry, temporary hard water is not softened by boiling due to the cost of fuel required. Chemical methods are used instead, such as the addition of ammonia (NH_3) or slaked lime [$Ca(OH)_2$]:

$$Ca^{+2} + 2HCO_3^- + 2NH_3 \rightleftharpoons CaCO_3{\downarrow} + 2NH_4^+ + CO_3^{-2}$$

$$Ca^{+2} + 2HCO_3^- + Ca(OH)_2 \rightleftharpoons 2CaCO_3{\downarrow} + 2H_2O$$

The permanent type of hardness involves other anions, particularly chloride (Cl^-) and sulfates (SO_4^{-2}). This harness is responsible for the scale that deposits in boilers, hot-water heaters, and teakettles, and is not affected by boiling. The calcium carbonate ($CaCO_3$) deposit is a poor conductor of heat and hinders the transfer of heat to water. In addition, it clogs pipes and contributes to corrosion problems. In general, softening of hard water requires the removal from solution of the metallic ions causing the hardness. These ions may be removed as precipitates or by ion-exchange methods using sodium carbonate.

$$Ca^{+2} + SO_4^{-2} + 2Na^+ + CO_3^{-2} \rightleftharpoons CaCO_3{\downarrow} + 2Na^+ + SO_4^{-2}$$

When washing clothes, detergents made from sulfonating higher alcohols, such as lauryl alcohol ($C_{12}H_{25}OH$), with sodium hydroxide are used. Calcium and magnesium salts of sodium lauryl sulfate are soluble, so these detergents may be used efficiently with hard water without forming precipitates with calcium and magnesium.

In wastewater treatment, the use of both lime and sodium carbonate for treating both kinds (Ca and Mg carbonates) of hard water simultaneously is called the lime-soda ash treatment. Two reactors, two flocculators, two sedimentation tanks, and a filter operate in series to remove calcium and magnesium carbonates using lime [$Ca(OH)_2$] and soda ash (Na_2CO_3). Alkaline substances such as borax and trisodium phosphate (TSP) are also used in water softening. This method is used for large volumes of water, such as for municipalities or factories.

Zeolites, synthetic sodium aluminosilicate minerals, are used in industry by "ion or cation exchange." The process is a cation exchange in which as water passes through the softener, calcium and magnesium are exchanged for sodium.

$$Na_2(zeolite) + Ca^{+2}(aq) \rightleftharpoons Ca(zeolite)_2 + 2Na^+(aq)$$

Zeolites are called ion exchangers, because the essential process involves the exchange of calcium ions for sodium ions. The zeolite must be reactivated after it becomes saturated by calcium and magnesium by treatment with concentrated sodium chloride (rock salt or brine) solution. This reverses the reaction in the equation above, thus regenerating the initial Na(zeolite), which can be reused in a water-softening tank. The use of an ion-exchange softening unit does not require careful and frequent chemical control, and is often used in homes, beauty parlors, and hospitals.

Classifying Water Hardness. Water hardness is measured as parts per million (ppm) or meq/L of $CaCO_3$ regardless of what other minerals are present. Water having a hardness of <50 ppm is considered "soft"; 50 to 150 ppm, "medium hard"; and 100 to 300 ppm, "hard" (see Table 2-18).

It is not always desirable that water be completely free from minerals that make it hard, because very soft water is likely to be corrosive, especially if the pH value is very low. Highly alkaline water usually will leave a rustation on well screens and pipes. Acid water will be corrosive. Carbonic acid is a major source of low pH. Good water should be nearly neutral in pH.

TABLE 2-18. Relative Classification of Water Hardness

$CaCO_3$		
ppm	meq/L	Classification
<50	<1	Soft water
50 to 150	1–3	Medium hard
150 to 300	3–6	Hard water
>300	>6	Very hard

PRACTICE PROBLEMS (answers in parentheses)

(1) In a solution that has $[H^+] = 7 \times 10^{-9}$
  (a) What is the $[OH^-]$? (*1.43 × 10⁻⁶*)
  (b) Is the solution acidic, neutral, or basic? (*acidic*)
(2) In a solution that has $[OH^-] = 9.0 \times 10^{-4}$
  (a) What is the $[H^+]$? (*1.11 × 10⁻¹¹*)
  (b) Is the solution acidic, neutral, or basic? (*basic*)
(3) Calculate the $[H^+]$ of
  (a) solution with pH = 8.90. (*1.26 × 10⁻⁹*)

(b) cow's milk, pH = 6.6. *(2.0 × 10⁻⁷ M)*

(c) tomato juice, pH = 4.3. *(5.0 × 10⁻⁵ M)*

(d) lemon juice, pH = 2.3. *(5.01 × 10⁻³ M)*

(e) blood plasma, pH = 7.4. *(3.98 × 10⁻⁸ M)*

(4) What is the pH of a solution that has

    (a) $[H^+]$ = 1.1 × 10⁻⁶? *(5.96)*

    (b) $[H^+]$ = 8.4 × 10⁻³? *(2.08)*

    (c) $[H^+]$ = 4.0 × 10⁻²? *(1.40)*

    (d) $[H^+]$ = 4.0 × 10⁻⁸? *(7.40)*

(5) Calculate the pH and pOH for the following:

    (a) 1.00 × 10⁻⁴ *M* HCl. *(pH=4, pOH=10)*

    (b) 2.00 × 10⁻³ *M* NaOH. *(pH=11.3, pOH=2.7)*

    (c) 1.00 × 10⁻³ *M* $HClO_4$. *(pH=3, pOH=11)*

    (d) 0.10 *M* H_2S. *(pH=4, pOH=10)*

    (e) 3.00 *M* NaOH. *(pH~0; pOH~14)*

    (f) 1.00 × 10⁻⁶ *M* HCl. *(pH=6, pOH=8)*

(6) Find the pH following 26 mL of 0.2 *M* NaOH being added to 50 mL of 0.1 *M* HCl. *(11.42)*

(7) Which member of the following pairs is the stronger acid and why?

    a. H_2S or PH_3 *(H_2S: S is more electronegative than P)*

    b. CH_3OH or CH_3SH *(CH_3SH: S-H bond is longer and weaker than the O-H bond)*

    c. H_2SO_3 or H_2PO_4 *(H_2SO_3: same number of extra oxygens; however, S is more electronegative than P)*

    d. H_2SO_3 or H_2SO_4 *(H_2SO_4: has an extra oxygen)*

    e. CH_3OH or CH_3COOH *(CH_3COOH; has an extra oxygen)*

(8) Convert the following from an Irrigation Water Analysis report (answers in italics).

Measurement	ppm	mg/L	meq/L	lb Nutrient in an Acre-Foot of Irrigation Water
Ca^{+2}	**131**	*(131)*	*(6.6)*	*(356)*
Mg^{+2}	*(190)*	**190**	*(15.57)*	*(517)*
HCO_3^- (bicarbonates)	*(488)*	*(488)*	**8.0**	—
Nitrate-nitrogen (NO_3-N)	**13**	*(13)*	*(0.93)*	*(35)*

	mmhos/cm	dS/m	S/m	micromhos/cm	TDS (ppm)
EC (electrical (conductivity)	**1.10**	*(1.10)*	*(0.11)*	*(1100)*	*(704)*

(9) What is the K_a for a 0.35 *M* of the acid HX where $[H^+]$ = 4.1 × 10⁻²? *(5.4 × 10⁻³)*

(10) Fill in the following information.

Sample	pH	pOH	[H$^+$]	[OH$^-$]	acid, base, or neutral?
1	6.88	(7.11)	(1.3 × 10^{-7})	(7.7 × 10^{-8})	(acid)
2	(0.92)	13.08	(0.12)	(8.4 × 10^{-14})	(acid)
3	(10.89)	(3.11)	1.3 × 10^{-11}	(7.8 × 10^{-4})	(base)
4	(7.00)	(7.00)	(1.0 × 10^{-7})	1.0 × 10^{-7}	(neutral)

(11)

Irrigation Water Analysis Report

Sample No.	Sodium (Na)	Calcium (Ca)	Magnesium (Mg)	Carbonate (CO_3^-)	Bicarbonate (HCO_3)	Chloride (Cl)	Phosphorus (P)	Potassium (K)	Nitrate (NO_3-N)	Sulfate (SO_4-S)	Boron (B)	Iron (Fe)
						ppm						
12	2600	121	300	1	670	5800	0.88	150	4	130	1.4	0.03
13	1240	90	140	0	580	2000	0.48	38	3	276	0.24	0.02
14	90	81	58	0	188	150	0.38	12	11	37	0.20	0.01

Sample No.	EC (mmhos/cm)	pH
12	11.0	8.2
13	7.94	6.9
14	1.40	8.0

For each sample, find:

(1) total dissolved salts (TDS) (ppm),
(2) SAR (meq/L),
(3) RSC (meq/L),
(4) how much Ca and Mg is added to an acre of turf irrigated with 6 inches of water,
(5) which source, if any, is most acceptable as an irrigation source.

Answer

	12	13	14
Total dissolved salts (TDS) (ppm)	7040	5082	896
SAR (meq/L)	29	19	1.86
RSC (meq/L)	640	564	179
Ca (lb/a)	165	122	110
Mg (lb/a)	408	190	79

Sample 14 is the most acceptable of the 3 as an irrigation source.

CHAPTER 3

ORGANIC COMPOUNDS AND
THEIR CHEMISTRY

Organic chemistry is the study of compounds containing carbon. The name *organic* was given to carbon-containing compounds before synthetic ones were made, as all organic compounds were originally thought to come from plants and animal. This branch of chemistry now deals with synthetic carbon-containing substances such as plastics, drugs, pesticides, fertilizers, and soaps. Organic chemistry began in 1828 when the first organic compound, urea $(NH_2)_2CO$, was synthesized by heating the inorganic compound ammonium cyanate (NH_4NCO). Over 18 million compounds are currently known with over 90% of these being organic (containing carbon). However, not all carbon-containing compounds are considered organic. Carbonate compounds, such as calcium and sodium carbonates ($CaCO_3$ and Na_2CO_3), and the oxides of carbon, carbon monoxide and dioxide (CO and CO_2) are considered inorganic compounds.

Carbon is a small atom (atomic number 6, atomic mass 12) and is a group IVA (14) element, thus has four electrons in its outermost energy level (shell). The carbon atom can use its four electrons to form covalent bonds with other carbon atoms or other elements such as nitrogen (N), oxygen (O), hydrogen (H), and sulfur (S). The key feature of the chemistry of carbon is it is the only element capable of forming long chains from atoms of the same type or molecules in the form of rings (cyclic compounds). There does not appear to be a limit to the number of carbon chains that can join together as over 7,000 carbons are linked in polyethylene, for example. In addition to single bonds, carbon forms double bonds with other C, N, O and S, as well as triple bonds with C and H (Figure 3-1 and Table 3-1). These diverse properties of carbon enable the chemical flexibility to produce a vast array of different biomolecules. The principal organic compounds in plants are carbohydrates, lipids, proteins, enzymes, nucleic acids, pigments, and growth hormones. Most of these will be discussed in the Plant Biochemistry chapter of this publication. Unfortunately, until one becomes familiar with organic compounds and their components, a certain amount of memorization will be required.

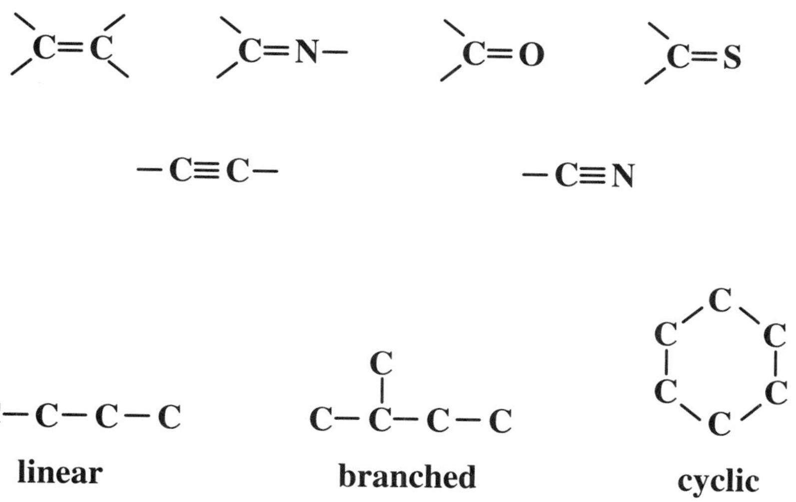

$$\diagup C=C \diagdown \qquad \diagup C=N- \qquad \diagup C=O \qquad \diagup C=S$$

$$-C\equiv C- \qquad\qquad -C\equiv N$$

$$C-C-C-C$$
linear

$$C-\overset{\displaystyle C}{\underset{\displaystyle |}{C}}-C-C$$
branched

cyclic

Figure 3-1. Examples of double and triple bonds formed by carbon with its ability to form linear, branched chain or cyclic arrangements.

Carbon Bond Stability. So many carbon-containing compounds exist due to the unusual strength of carbon-carbon (C—C) bonds, whereas the bonds of many other compounds, such as B—B, N—N, P—P, O—O, and S—S are unstable and very reactive and thus do not last long.

Carbon atoms have relatively small electron clouds, thus the atoms become closer together and the C—C bonds become shorter and stronger (harder to break). Carbon is in the second row of the periodic table with eight valence electrons in its second shell. Since only eight electrons can occupy the valence shell of second period elements, a new bond to carbon cannot form until an old bond breaks. Energy, therefore, must be supplied to break the old bond before new ones can form. This high requirement of activation energy to cause carbon reactions results in no low-energy pathway for reaction of most carbon compounds and thus they are stable. Carbon compounds also are composed mostly of uncharged molecules and not ions. Molecules do not attract each other the way oppositely charged ions do; thus are less reactive.

Functional Groups. One distinguishing biochemical feature of carbon is its ability to bond with as many as four other carbon atoms. This four bonding capacity is referred to as *tetravalent*. This allows different forms of linked carbon atoms, in linear or branched chain or cyclic arrangements, to serve as a backbone structure for biomolecules. Clusters of other atoms, such as N, H, O, S, and the halogens can covalent bond with carbon to incorporate *functional groups* into additional biomolecules (Figure 3-2). A functional group is an atom or group of atoms in a molecule that accounts for the characteristic properties of the molecule. The —COOH group in acetic acid (CH_3COOH), the —OH group in ethyl alcohol (CH_3CH_2OH), and the C=C in ethylene ($H_2C=CH_2$) are examples of functional groups. In general, the functional groups often determine the properties of the

TABLE 3-1. Bonding Possibilities for Elements Commonly Found in Organic Compounds

Element	Number of Bonds	Number of Unshared Pairs	Bonding Possibilities
C	4	0	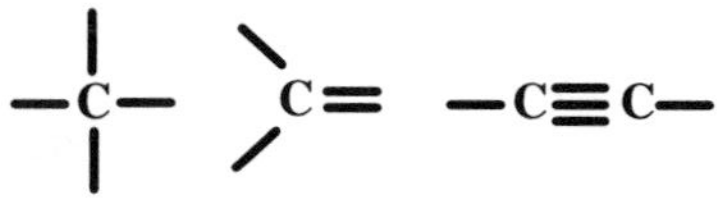 (structures shown)
H	1	0	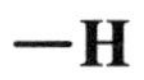 —H
Halogens (Cl, Br, F, and I)	1	3	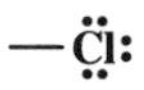 —C̈l:
N	3	1	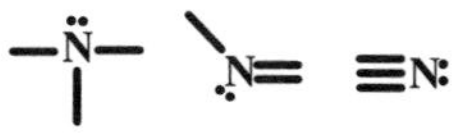 (structures shown)
O	2	2	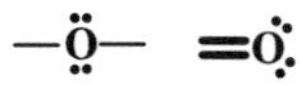 (structures shown)

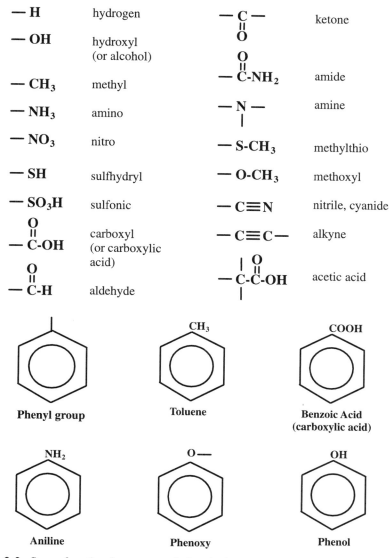

Figure 3-2. Some functional groups and chemical groups associated with biomolecules.

compound more so than the carbon chain itself. For example, when '—OH' takes the place of an 'H' molecule in methane, it becomes methanol. Methanol is a simple alcohol that has different characteristics than methane. Molecules having the same functional group function or react similarly. Functional groups play an important role in pesticides. For example, functional groups can be slightly charged so that they bind to objects such as insects and soil. Organic compounds such as the insecticide Dursban (chlorpyrifos) have functional groups that help it to absorb onto the surface of soil particles. Pesticides are also classified or grouped into families according to the functional groups they possess or are composed of. Ex-

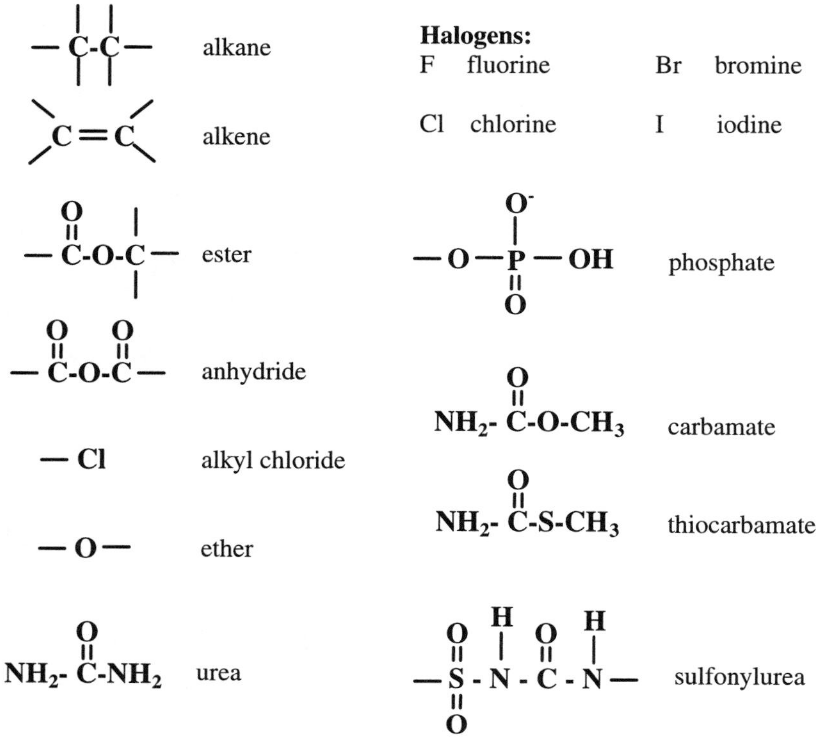

$$-\overset{|}{\underset{|}{C}}\text{-}\overset{|}{\underset{|}{C}}-$$ alkane

$$\overset{\diagdown}{\diagup}C=C\overset{\diagup}{\diagdown}$$ alkene

$$-\overset{O}{\overset{||}{C}}\text{-O-}\overset{|}{\underset{|}{C}}-$$ ester

$$-\overset{O}{\overset{||}{C}}\text{-O-}\overset{O}{\overset{||}{C}}-$$ anhydride

$$-\text{Cl}$$ alkyl chloride

$$-\text{O}-$$ ether

$$NH_2\text{-}\overset{O}{\overset{||}{C}}\text{-}NH_2$$ urea

Halogens:

F fluorine   Br   bromine

Cl chlorine   I   iodine

$$-\text{O}-\overset{O^-}{\underset{\underset{O}{||}}{P}}-\text{OH}$$ phosphate

$$NH_2\text{-}\overset{O}{\overset{||}{C}}\text{-O-}CH_3$$ carbamate

$$NH_2\text{-}\overset{O}{\overset{||}{C}}\text{-S-}CH_3$$ thiocarbamate

$$-\overset{O}{\underset{\underset{O}{||}}{\overset{||}{S}}}\text{-}\overset{H}{\overset{|}{N}}\text{-}\overset{O}{\overset{||}{C}}\text{-}\overset{H}{\overset{|}{N}}-$$ sulfonylurea

Figure 3-2. (*Continued*).

amples include the herbicide families: the phenoxies, carbamates, thiocarbamates, ureas, sulfonylureas, benzoic acids, and anilines.

Within the functional groups, a common function group constituent, C=O, is called a **carbonyl group**. Any compound containing a benzene ring is an **aromatic compound**.

Example:

Identify the functional groups in the following compound.

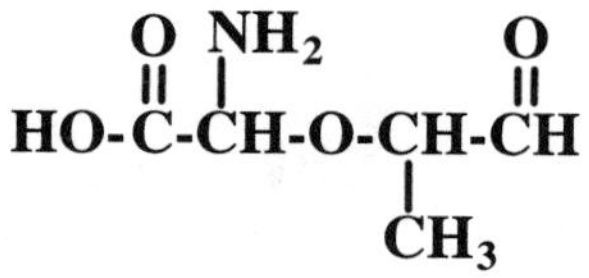

$$\text{HO-}\overset{O}{\overset{||}{C}}\text{-}\overset{NH_2}{\overset{|}{C}H}\text{-O-}\underset{\underset{CH_3}{\overset{|}{}}}{C}H\text{-}\overset{O}{\overset{||}{C}}H$$

From Figure 3-2, start from the left-hand end of the compound,

$$\begin{array}{c} O \\ \parallel \\ HO\text{-}C\text{-} \end{array}$$

is a carboxylic acid (not aldehyde, ketone, or alcohol)

$$\begin{array}{c} NH_2 \\ \mid \\ \text{-CH-OH}_2 \end{array}$$

is an amine (not amide)

C-O-C

is an ether

$$\begin{array}{c} O \\ \parallel \\ \text{-CH} \end{array}$$

is an aldehyde (not carboxylic acid or ketone)

Solubility. An important concept to consider when dealing with organic chemicals is that "like dissolves like." Chemicals that are polar such as water (H_2O) and hydrogen peroxide (H_2O_2) will dissolve (or dissociate) into each other. Likewise, chemicals that are nonpolar such as octane (C_8H_{18}) and hexane (C_6H_{14}) will dissolve (or dissociate) into each other. Since the chemicals are composed of like molecules and atoms, they will mix with one another. However, octane and water will not mix because the molecules are different. This is why oil and water will not mix.

Organic compounds with a low molecular weight, such as simple alcohols and carboxylic acids, are soluble in water. However, as the hydrocarbon chain gets larger, thus increasing its molecular weight, its ability to dissolve in water decreases.

Leaching Capabilities. Water solubility affects leaching capabilities. An organic compound that is not soluble in water will not leach well in a soil profile. Several pesticides used today may or may not be water-soluble. Water insoluble compounds such as Prodiamine (N,N-dipropyl-4-(triflouromethyl)-5-amino-2,6-dinitroaniline), which is a preemergence herbicide for crabgrass control, has the ability to stay in the soil profile for an extended period of time. Another preemergence herbicide, Atrazine (2-chloro-4 ethylamino-6 isopropylamino-1,3,5 triazine), is a water-soluble compound that will combine with water and possibly leach through the soil profile.

CLASSIFYING ORGANIC COMPOUNDS

Hydrocarbons

Because so many organic compounds exist, these are grouped into **families** that have similar structures and properties. **Hydrocarbons** are compounds containing only carbon and hydrogen. They are found primarily in natural gas, petroleum, and coal with only small amounts distributed in plants and animals. All hydrocarbons react (combust) with oxygen at high temperature to yield carbon dioxide and water with a release of heat. Two main categories of hydrocarbons exist: (1) **aliphatic hydrocarbons**, which are straight-chain, branched-chain, and cyclic compounds;

and (2) **aromatic hydrocarbons**, which are the benzene (C_6H_6)-like compounds. For example, the base structure for most pesticides are aliphatic carbon chains and aromatic rings. The aliphatic hydrocarbons can be further subdivided into two groups: (a) **saturated hydrocarbons**, which contain only carbon-carbon single bonds; and (b) **unsaturated hydrocarbons**, which possess carbon-carbon double bonds or triple bonds.

I. **Aliphatic hydrocarbons**—straight-chain, branched-chain, and cyclic compounds
   1. *Saturated hydrocarbons*—compounds with only carbon-carbon single bonds
      a. Alkanes—compounds related to methane, CH_4.
   2. *Unsaturated hydrocarbons*—compounds with carbon-carbon double or triple bonds
      a. Alkenes—compounds related to ethylene, $CH_2=CH_2$.
      b. Alkynes—compounds related to acetylene, $CH\equiv CH$.

II. **Aromatic hydrocarbons**—compounds related to benzene, C_6H_6.

Saturated Hydrocarbons. Compounds which are saturated hydrocarbons (containing a single chain of carbon-carbon single bonded CH_2 groups capped at each end by a hydrogen atom) are called the **alkanes** (or paraffins). The alkanes are the simplest family of organic compounds. The names of each alkane member are composed of two parts. The first part, *meth, eth, prop*, and so on (Table 3-2) reflects the number of carbon atoms in the chain. The second part, which is the same for all members, is "ane" after the parent name alk*ane*. Methane, a gas, is the simplest aliphatic compound and consists of one carbon, ethane has two, propane consists of three carbons, and so on. The general formula for all alkanes is C_nH_{2n+2}, where *n* is the number of carbons in the molecular chain (Figure 3-3). Since all bonds are single in the alkane series, thus fully used, these compounds are not very reactive. For this reason, the alkane series is also known as the paraffin series, from the Latin *parum affinis* meaning "having little affinity." Paraffin wax is a member of this series. The only reaction of real significance of hydrocarbons is that they burn, thus provide a large portion of the energy used for heating, cooling, etc. Natural gas and petroleum are the most important sources of alkanes.

When forming larger members of the alkanes from methane, a hydrogen atom is removed to produce a methyl **free radical** (CH_3), which contains an unpaired electron.

$$\begin{array}{ccc} & \text{H} & & \text{H} \\ & \overset{\displaystyle\cdot\cdot}{\text{H:C:H}} & \longrightarrow & \overset{\displaystyle\cdot\cdot}{\text{H:C}}\cdot & + & \cdot\text{H} \\ & \text{H} & & \text{H} \end{array}$$

$$CH_4 \longrightarrow CH_3\cdot + \cdot H$$
$$\text{methane} \quad\quad \text{methyl} \quad \text{hydrogen}$$
$$\text{radical} \quad\quad \text{atom}$$

Free radicals are usually reactive and often react to pair up their odd electrons

TABLE 3-2. First 10 Members of the Straight-chain Alkanes and Their Corresponding Alkyl Side Chains or Groups. Note that as the number of carbons increase, so do their density and melting and boiling points.

Name	No. of Carbons	Molecular Formula	Alkyl Group	Formula	Density (g/mL)	Melting Point °(C)	Boiling Point °(C)
Methane	1	C_1H_4 or CH_4	methyl	$-CH_3$	0.000667	$-182°$	$-164°$
Ethane	2	C_2H_6 or CH_3-CH_3	ethyl	$-C_2H_5$	0.00125	$-183°$	$-89°$
Propane	3	C_3H_8 or $CH_3-CH_2-CH_3$	propyl	$-C_3H_7$	0.00183	$-190°$	$-42°$
Butane	4	C_4H_{10} or $CH_3-CH_2-CH_2-CH_3$	butyl	$-C_4H_9$	0.00242	$-138°$	$-0.5°$
Pentane	5	C_5H_{12} or $CH_3-CH_2-CH_2-CH_2-CH_3$	pentyl	$-C_5H_{11}$	0.626	$-130°$	$36°$
Hexane	6	C_6H_{14} or $CH_3-CH_2-CH_2-CH_2-CH_2-CH_3$	hexyl	$-C_6H_{13}$	0.660	$-95°$	$69°$
Heptane	7	C_7H_{16} or $CH_3-CH_2-CH_2-CH_2-CH_2-CH_2-CH_3$	heptyl	$-C_7H_{15}$	0.684	$-91°$	$98°$
Octane	8	C_8H_{18} or $CH_3-CH_2-CH_2-CH_2-CH_2-CH_2-CH_2-CH_3$	octyl	$-C_8H_{17}$	0.702	$-57°$	$126°$
Nonane	9	C_9H_{20} or $CH_3-CH_2-CH_2-CH_2-CH_2-CH_2-CH_2-CH_2-CH_3$	nonyl	$-C_9H_{19}$	0.718	$-51°$	$151°$
Decane	10	$C_{10}H_{22}$ or $CH_3-CH_2-CH_2-CH_2-CH_2-CH_2-CH_2-CH_2-CH_2-CH_3$	decyl	$-C_{10}H_{21}$	0.730	$-30°$	$174°$

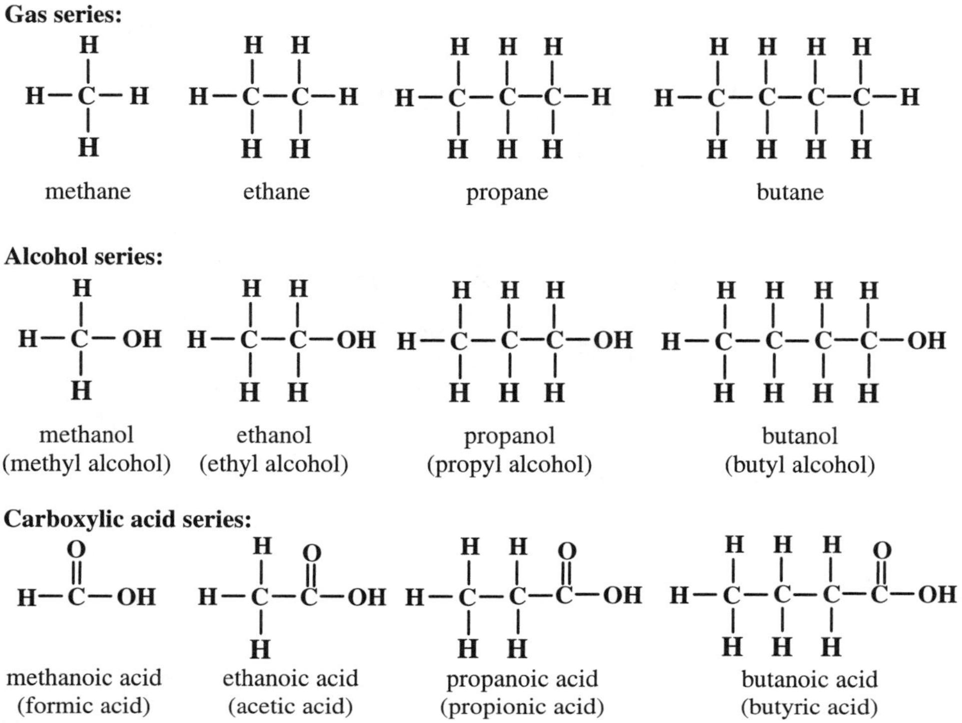

Gas series:

methane   ethane   propane   butane

Alcohol series:

methanol   ethanol   propanol   butanol
(methyl alcohol)   (ethyl alcohol)   (propyl alcohol)   (butyl alcohol)

Carboxylic acid series:

methanoic acid   ethanoic acid   propanoic acid   butanoic acid
(formic acid)   (acetic acid)   (propionic acid)   (butyric acid)

Figure 3-3. Alkanes composed of one to four carbon atoms (top) with nomenclature of alcohol (middle) and carboxylic acid (bottom) series.

with another electron, from another chemical species. The pairing of electrons leads to the formation of covalent bonds. It results in the formation of diatomic molecules of hydrogen and other elements such as the halogens (F, Cl, Br, and I).

Like other radicals, the methyl radical is also highly reactive. When two of these methyl radicals meet, they join together to pair their odd electrons into a covalent bond and form the next larger member of the alkane, ethane (C_2H_6).

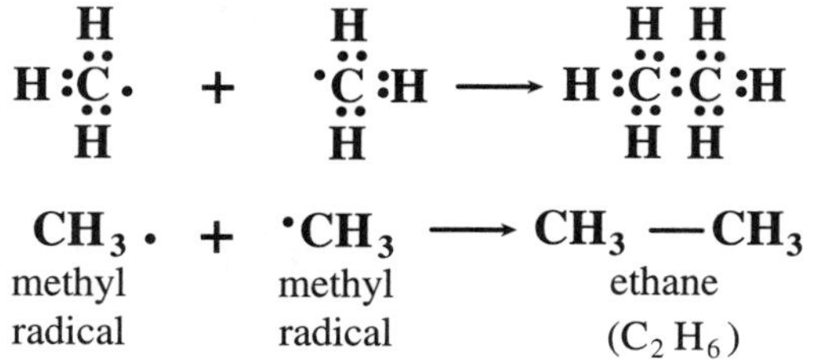

$CH_3 \cdot$ + $\cdot CH_3$ ⟶ $CH_3 - CH_3$
methyl   methyl   ethane
radical   radical   (C_2H_6)

Continuing this addition of CH_2 gives the molecular formulas of the entire alkane series: C_4H_{10}, C_5H_{12}, C_6H_{14}, and so on.

To denote the location of substituents on aliphatic hydrocarbons, the carbon atoms of the base carbon chain are numbered consecutively from the end of the chain that results in the use of the smallest numbers to indicate their respective positions. The location of substituents on alkanoic (open carbon-chain acid) compounds are denoted by numbering consecutively the carbon atoms of the carbon chain, beginning with the carbon atom of the carboxyl (COOH) group (Figure 3-4). An aliphatic group with a carboxyl group (—COOH) at the end of the chain is called a **carboxylic acid** (Figure 3-3). A carboxylic acid with two carbons in the chain is called **acetic acid** (CH_3COOH), which is found in vinegar.

Alkanes as a class are compounds of very low toxicity, they are colorless and odorless. The first three members of the alkanes—methane, ethane, and propane— are all gases under ordinary temperatures and are ignited easily when mixed with air. Methane is the major component of natural gas used for heating and cooking while propane is used as the commercial field, LP gas. Larger members are liquids and are major components of gasoline, candle wax, mineral oil, and petroleum jelly.

Alcohols. A carbon chain in which one or more of the hydrogens is replaced by a –OH functional group is called an **alcohol** (Figure 3-3). A functional group is any hydrocarbon fragment, such as a –OH or —NH_2 group, which is not in, but is attached to, the longest unbroken chain of carbon atoms (Figure 3-2). Hundreds of alcohols derived from hydrocarbons are known. The simplest ones from the alkanes have the general formula R-OH where R has the composition —C_nH_{2n+1}. The first few members of this series are:

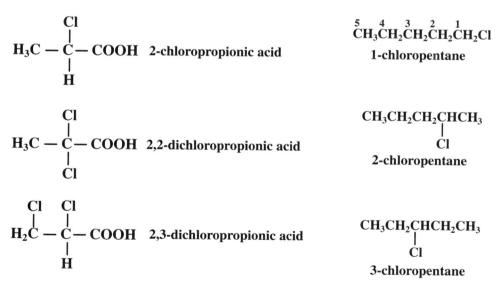

Figure 3-4. Using the numbering system to denote location of substituents on alkanoic compounds.

CH_3OH methanol (methyl alcohol) or wood alcohol—previously prepared by the destructive distillation of wood, hence the common name, wood alcohol. This alcohol is poisonous.

C_2H_5OH ethanol (ethyl alcohol) or grain alcohol, the alcohol in distilled spirits

$C_3H_5(OH)_3$ glycerol (glycerine)—a by-product of the soap industry

C_3H_7OH propanols (isopropyl alcohol) or rubbing alcohol, is used to give sponge baths to reduce fevers

C_4H_9OH butanols

C_6H_5OH phenol (carbolic acid)

The name of alcohols is obtained from the name of the parent alkane by re-placing the *e* with *ol*. Also, when necessary, the position of the —OH group is identified by number. The hydroxy derivatives of benzene are usually referred to as *phenols*. Carbolic acid (C_6H_5OH) is the simplest phenol.

Glycols are alcohol molecules with two hydroxyl (—OH) groups attached to the carbon skeleton (also called *dihydroxyl alcohol*) while *trihydroxyl alcohol* contains three —OH groups. Examples of a dihydroxy alcohol is ethylene glycol (CH_2OHCH_2OH), a commonly used antifreeze, and the simplest trihydroxyl alcohol is glycerol [$C_3H_5(OH)_3$].

OH OH

H—C—C—H
H H

ethylene glycol
(a dihydroxyl alcohol)

OH OH OH

H—C—C—C—H
H H H

glycerol
(a trihydroxyl alcohol)

Alkyls. The general term **alkyl group** refers to an alkane hydrocarbon with the removal of a hydrogen (Table 3-2). With the removal of one hydrogen atom from one alkane, the name of the respective is changed by replacing the suffix *-ane* with the suffix *-yl*; the respective prefix remains the same (Figure 3-5). For example, methyl (—CH_3) is derived from methane (CH_4) and ethyl (—CH_2CH_3) is derived from ethane (CH_3CH_3).

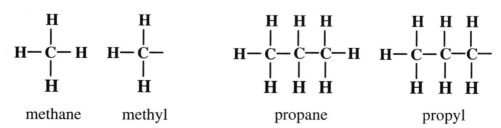

Figure 3-5. Alkanes with the removal of a hydrogen atom form a group with the suffix designation *-yl*.

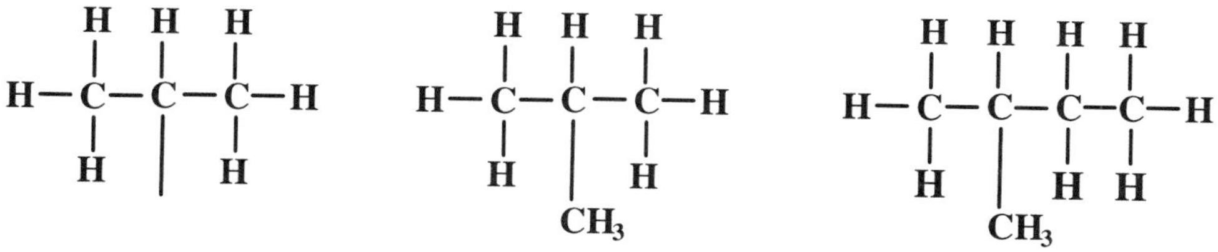

Figure 3-6. Isopropyl (3 carbon atom), isobutane (4 carbon atoms), and isopentane (five carbon atoms) are examples of *iso* hydrocarbons.

Two possible alkyl groups can be derived from propane ($CH_3CH_2CH_3$). Its alkyl group is obtained by removal of a hydrogen from either terminal carbon atom to obtain the normal (or *n*) propyl or *n*-propyl group (Figure 3-5). However, if a hydrogen is removed from the central atom, an isomeric propyl group called *iso-propyl* is formed (Figure 3-6). An *iso* hydrocarbon has a methyl ($-CH_3$) group substituted for a hydrogen on the next-to-last carbon of a carbon chain consisting of three or more carbon atoms (Figure 3-6).

Isomers are different compounds that share the same molecular formula. Isomers is a word derived from the Greek words *isos*, meaning "equal," and *meros*, meaning "a share." Butane and isobutane are examples of isomers. They share the same molecular formula, C_4H_{10}, but have different molecular structures and different properties.

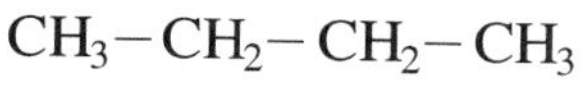

$$CH_3-CH_2-CH_2-CH_3$$
butane

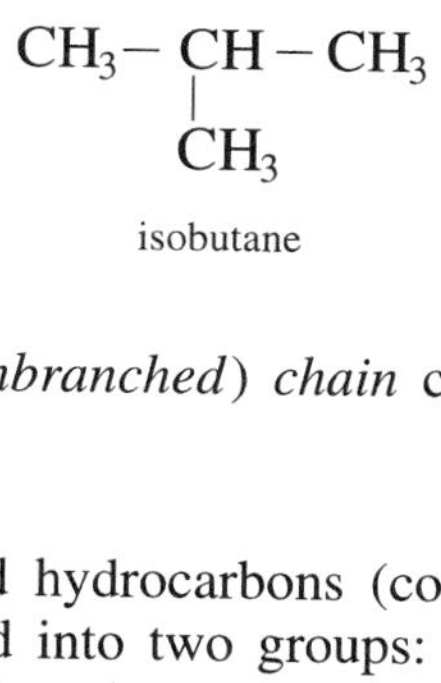

$$CH_3-CH-CH_3$$
$$\overset{|}{CH_3}$$
isobutane

Butane is also an example of a *straight (unbranched) chain* compound while isobutane is a *branched chain* compound.

Unsaturated Hydrocarbons.

The unsaturated hydrocarbons (containing double or triple carbon-carbon bonds) are also divided into two groups: (1) **alkenes** (or olefins), which contain at least one carbon-carbon double bond; and (2) **alkynes**, which contain a carbon-carbon triple bond. Because of their double and triple bonds, alkenes and alkynes have a much more rigid structure than alkanes.

Like the alkanes, the alkenes consist of a series of compounds with an increasing number of carbon atoms in a chain. The simplest alkene contains two carbons (C_2H_4), the three-carbon alkene (C_3H_6), followed by the formulas C_4H_8, C_5H_{10}, C_6H_{12}, and so on. The general formula for all alkenes is C_nH_{2n}, where n is the number of carbons in the molecule. Other members of the series are formed by the addition of CH_2 groups, just as in the case of the alkanes. The difference is that *one* pair of carbon atoms shares a double bond in the alkene series.

Alkene molecules (C_nH_{2n}) have two hydrogen atoms less than the corresponding alkane molecules (C_nH_{2n+2}). Ethene or ethylene (C_2H_4), the simplest alkene, arises from ethane (C_2H_6) by the loss of two hydrogen atoms. The two odd electrons on the carbons then form a two-electron bond:

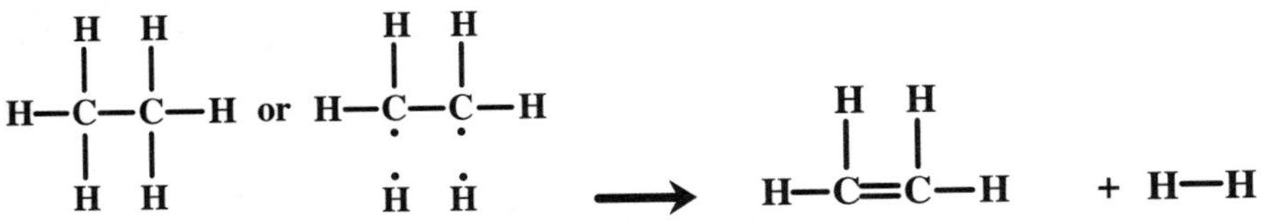

$$
\begin{array}{ccc}
\text{H--C--C--H or H--C--C--H} & \longrightarrow & \text{H--C=C--H} \quad + \quad \text{H--H} \\
C_2H_6 & \rightarrow & H_2C{=}CH_2 \quad + \quad H_2 \\
\text{ethane} & & \text{ethene (or ethylene)} \qquad \text{hydrogen}
\end{array}
$$

Ethylene (or ethene) is a gaseous growth hormone which is used to artificially ripen fruit and as a growth inhibitor in certain ornamental and turfgrass species.

The names of straight-chain alkenes also consist of two parts. The first, which is the same used for the alkanes, indicates the number of carbons in the chain: *eth-*, (two); *prop-*, (three); *but-*, (four); and so on. To this stem, "ene" is added to indicate a carbon-carbon double bond is present. The first few members of this group would be called ethene (C_2H_4), propene (C_3H_6), butene (C_4H_8), etc. These compounds also are commonly known as ethylene, propylene, and butylene, respectively.

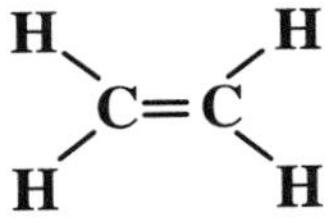

$$
\begin{array}{c}
\text{H} \diagdown \qquad \diagup \text{H} \\
\text{C=C} \qquad (C_2H_4) \\
\text{H} \diagup \qquad \diagdown \text{H}
\end{array}
$$

ethylene (or ethene)

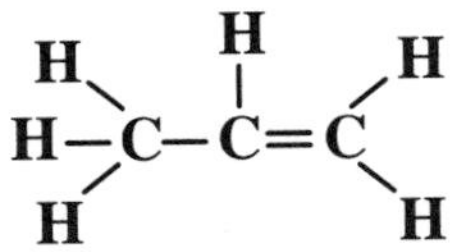

$$
\begin{array}{c}
\text{H} \qquad \text{H} \\
\diagdown \quad | \quad \diagup \text{H} \\
\text{H--C--C=C} \qquad (C_3H_6) \\
\diagup \qquad \diagdown \text{H} \\
\text{H} \qquad \text{H}
\end{array}
$$

propylene (or butene)

A common alkene in plants is *carotene*. Carotene is responsible for various colors such as for tomatoes, carrots, and autumn leaves. It is also involved in photosynthesis.

The rigid structure associated with double bonds gives rise to *cis* and *trans* isomerism. These two molecules have the same set of atoms and the same bonds among those atoms. The difference between the two compounds lies in the spatial orientation of the bonds. For example, 1,2-dichloroethene can exist as *cis* and *trans* geometrical isomers. The *cis* isomer is polar, but the *trans* isomer is not.

cis-dichloroethene   *trans*-dichloroethene

Alkenes are often used as intermediates in producing other chemicals. For example, many alcohols and chlorinated hydrocarbons are made from the appropriate alkene. Alkenes are also intermediates in the manufacturing of polymers. *Polymers are large molecular compounds, made by a repetitive connection of many small molecular units called monomers.* For example, by connecting thousands of ethene (ethylene) molecules ($CH_2=CH_2$), the polymer polyethylene is formed ($-CH_2-CH_2-CH_2-CH_2-CH_2-)_n$.

The second type of unsaturated hydrocarbons are the **alkynes,** a series of compounds containing a carbon-carbon triple bond. The simplest, but very important alkyne member is $HC\equiv CH$, which is called *ethyne* or more commonly *acetylene*, a common fuel in welding torches. When combusted (or oxidized) acetylene produces a highly exothermic reaction, yielding high temperatures of the oxyacetylene flame (2,700°C) used in welding.

$$C_2H_2 + O_2 \rightarrow 2CO_2 + H_2O + 300 \text{ kcal/mole energy}$$
acetylene

The next three members of the alkynes are propyne, $CH_3-C\equiv CH$; butyne, $CH_3-CH_2-C\equiv CH$; and pentyne, $CH_3-CH_2-CH_2;-C\equiv CH$. In naming these compounds, the stems *eth-*, *prop-*, *but-*, and *pen-*, again are used to indicate 2, 3, 4, and 5 carbons, respectively, while *-yne* is now the suffix used instead of *-ene* for alkenes or *-ane* for alkanes.

The naming of alkene and alkyne groups (formed by the removal of one hydrogen atom from the respective compound) is similar to that for groups of corresponding alkanes, but for alkenes, the double bond is indicated by adding *-ene* as the suffix to the name of the corresponding alkane group (e.g., propylene), while with alkynes, the triple bond is indicated by adding *-yne* as the suffix (e.g., propylyne).

A carbon atom bonded to another carbon atom is called *primary* (often designated as 1°) and each of the hydrogens bonded to it is called a *primary hydrogen;* bonded to two other carbon atoms, it is called *secondary* (abbreviated *sec* or its designation, 2°) and its hydrogens are called *secondary hydrogens;* bonded to three other carbon atoms, it is called *tertiary* (abbreviated *tert* or its designation, 3°) and its hydrogens are called *tertiary hydrogens.*

Rules for Naming Organic Compounds:

1. The *longest unbroken chain* of carbon atoms in a molecule serves as the parent name for any hydrocarbon or its derivative. Refer to Table 3-2 for these names. With the alkenes this longest chain must contain the double bond, while in the alkynes, the triple bond must be included.

2. The stem of the parent name indicates the number of carbon atoms in the chain and has the following suffixes:

   a. *-ane* when there is a carbon-carbon single bond

   b. *-ene* when there is a carbon-carbon double bond

   c. *-yne* when there is a triple bond

   d. *-diene* when there are two double bonds present

   e. *-triene* when there are three double bonds present

3. Branched isomers are named as derivatives of straight-chain hydrocarbons in which one or more hydrogen atoms are replaced by hydrocarbon fragments.

4. Number the main chain to denote the positions of the groups attached to the parent chain as well as the double and triple bonds present. Start from the end with the *lower number* to the carbon where the first branch (side chain) is attached. Identify and name each side chain in the compound. If more than one group is present on the chain, indicate each individual group location number. The position of attachment of the side chain and the number of carbons in it are shown as a prefix to the name of the longest continuous chain.

5. In compounds with more than one side group, then: (a) the *prefixes* di (2), tri (3), tetra (4), etc., immediately precede its name when the groups are identical; for example, use dimethyl for two methyl groups, trimethyl for three methyl groups, and so on; and (b) if they are different, they are listed in alphabetical order along with their respective locations.

   Separate numbers from each other by *commas*, and separate numbers from letters by a *hyphen*. For example, $(CH_3)_3CCH_2CH_2CH_3$ is shown as:

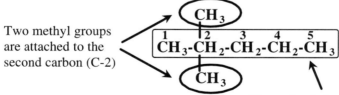

Two methyl groups are attached to the second carbon (C-2)

The main chain consists of 5 carbons. This compound, therefore, is named as a derivative of pentane.

2,2-dimethylpentane

Examples:

Name the following alkanes:

1.

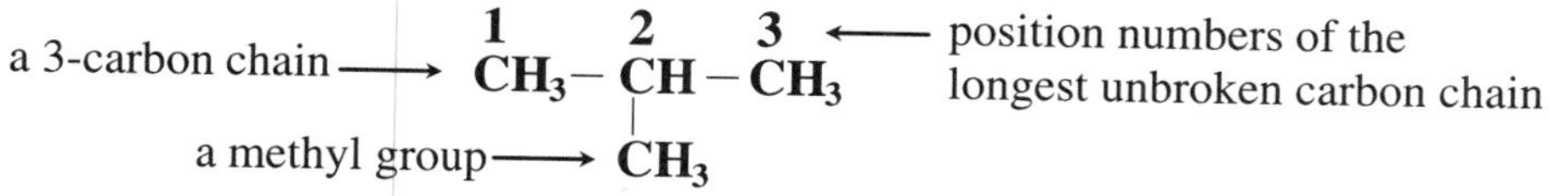

$$\text{a 3-carbon chain} \longrightarrow \overset{1}{CH_3} - \overset{2}{CH} - \overset{3}{CH_3} \longleftarrow \text{position numbers of the longest unbroken carbon chain}$$

$$\text{a methyl group} \longrightarrow CH_3$$

   a. From Table 3-2, the longest continuous chain of carbon is three and has no double bonds, thus the compound is a propane.

   b. The number of carbons until the first (and only one in this example) branch is two.

   c. Locate and name each side chain. The side chain in this example is a methyl. Therefore, this compound is named 2-methyl propane (also known as isobutane).

2.

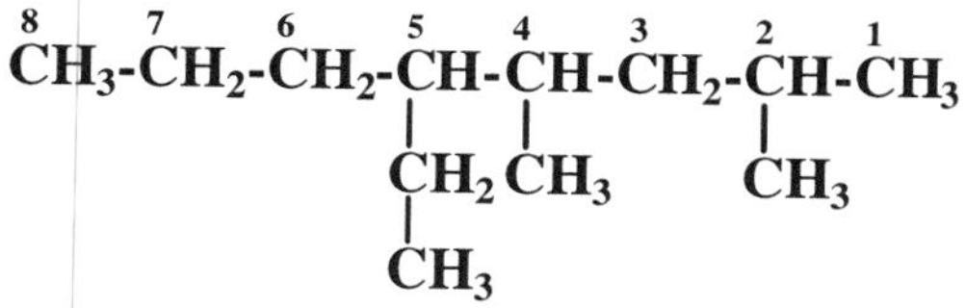

$$\overset{8}{CH_3}-\overset{7}{CH_2}-\overset{6}{CH_2}-\overset{5}{CH}-\overset{4}{CH}-\overset{3}{CH_2}-\overset{2}{CH}-\overset{1}{CH_3}$$
$$CH_2\ CH_3 \qquad CH_3$$
$$CH_3$$

   a. From Table 3-2, the longest continuous chain has eight carbon, thus the compound is a octane.

   b. Number the main chain starting at the end with the lower number to the carbon where the first branch is attached (right to left in this example). The number 2 and 4 carbons have a methyl side chain attached. This is named dimethyl. The number 5 carbon has a ethyl (3 carbon) side chain. Thus, the compound is called either 2,4-dimethyl-5-ethyloctane or 5-ethyl-2,4-dimethyloctane.

   c. Since the side chains are different, they are arranged in alphabetical order according to the name of the side chain. Numerical prefixes (e.g., di-, tri-, etc.) are not included in this alphabetizing. Therefore, the correct name is 5-ethyl-2,4-dimethyloctane.

3.

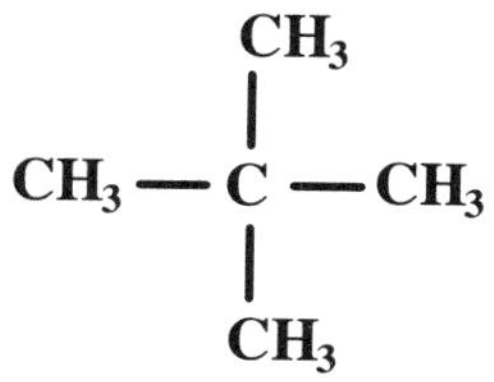

$$CH_3$$
$$|$$
$$CH_3 - C - CH_3$$
$$|$$
$$CH_3$$

2,2-dimethylpropane

4. Write the structure for *3-ethylhexane.*

The last part of the compound's name indicates 6 carbons (hexane) form the longest continuous chain. The rest of the name indicates an ethyl group (2 carbon) is attached to carbon 3 of the longest continuous chain. Therefore, this is drawn as:

$$\overset{6}{C}H_3\text{-}\overset{5}{C}H_2\text{-}\overset{4}{C}H_2\text{-}\overset{3}{C}H\text{-}\overset{2}{C}H_2\text{-}\overset{1}{C}H_3$$
$$|$$
$$CH_2CH_3$$

5. Write the structure *3-methyl-1-hexene.*

$$CH_2\text{=}CH\text{-}CH\text{-}CH_2\text{-}CH_2\text{-}CH_3$$
$$|$$
$$CH_3$$

6. Name the following:

$$\overset{7}{C}H_3\text{-}\overset{6}{C}H_2\text{-}\overset{5}{C}H_2\text{-}\overset{4}{C}H_2\text{-}\overset{3}{C}H_2\text{-}\overset{2}{C}\text{=}\overset{1}{C}H_2$$
$$|$$
$$CH_3$$

The longest chain is a heptene. The double bond is in the 1 position while the methyl group is in the 2 position, therefore, *2 methyl-1-heptene.*

Aromatic Hydrocarbons. Benzene and benzene-ring-containing compounds are collectively known as the aromatic hydrocarbons. In general, these compounds have a pleasant odor (except benzene), hence the name aromatic, but many of them are extremely harmful. Plants have the ability to synthesize some necessary aromatics that are essential to our diets.

Benzene. The benzene (C_6H_6) ring is a common constituent of many plant protection products including fungicides and herbicides. Each benzene hydrocarbon molecule contains six carbon atoms linked together to form a hexagonal ring. It is a common practice to simplify the benzene structure by omitting the individual carbon and hydrogen atoms as in Figure 3-7. The benzene structure with one hydrogen atom removed is called a **phenyl ring** or **phenyl group** and in this form can accept an appropriate substitution. For example, the replacement of the hydrogen atom with a hydroxy (OH^-) group forms **phenol.**

Other substituted ring structures include benzoic acid, toluene, and aniline (Figure 3-2). The terms **benzene** and **phenyl** are often used interchangeably when referring to this six-carbon hexagon ring structure as a component of the molecule.

For convenience in identifying the positions (location) of possible substitutions on the benzene ring, the carbon atoms of the ring structure are numbered from 1 to 6 as shown in Figure 3-8. Positions 2 and 6 are the ortho positions; 3 and 5, the meta positions; and 4, the para position. Figures 3-9 and 3-10 show examples of benzene isomers and other common benzene (aromatic) compounds.

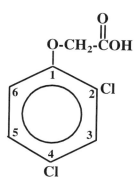

Figure 3-7. The chemical structure of benzene and the various ways (termed *resonance hybrids*) this is expressed to represent the same molecule.

The following example of 2,4-dichlorophenoxyacetic acid (or 2,4-D, a herbicide) illustrates the general makeup of a chemical name as each component of the respective names denotes some part or location of a part in the molecule.

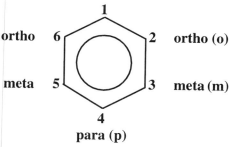

2,4-dichlorophenoxyacetic acid

1. *2,4-* preceding dichloro denotes that one chlorine atom is bonded to the phenyl ring at the number 2-position and the other at the number 4-position.
2. *dichloro* denotes two chlorine atoms (di = two; chloro = chlorine atom).
3. *phen* denotes the phenyl ring.

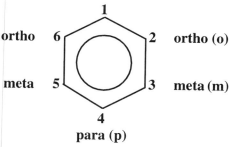

Figure 3-8. Numbering of carbon atoms of the benzene ring as means of designating location of substituents on the ring.

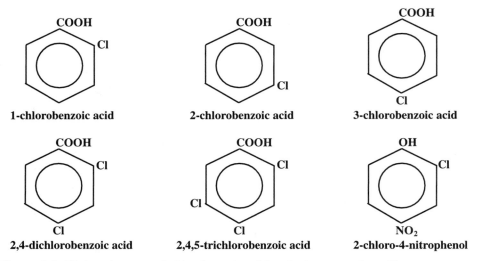

Figure 3-9. Various isomers of chlorobenzoic acid and other examples of benzene nomenclature.

Benzene Derivatives:

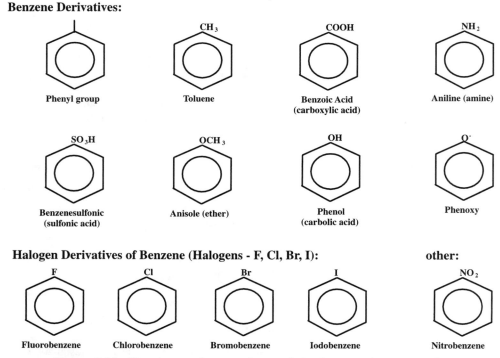

Figure 3-10. Chemistry and nomenclature of simple aromatic compounds.

4. *oxy* denotes the oxygen atom bonded to the phenyl ring.
5. *acetic acid* denotes the acetic acid side chain (—CH$_2$COOH) bonded to the oxygen atom.

Example:

1. Name the following compounds:
   (a)

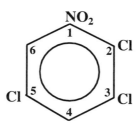

   (*1-nitro-2,3,5-trichlorobenzene*)

   (b)

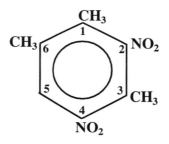

   (*1,3,6-trimethyl-2,4-dinitrobenzene*)

   (c)

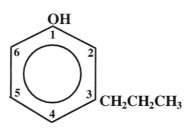

   (*3-propylphenol*)

2. Draw the following compounds:
   (a) 3-chloroaniline

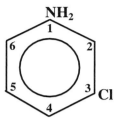

(b)   1-nitro-2,3,5-triiodobenzene

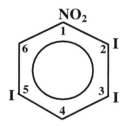

Additional Important Functional Groups

Aldehydes and Ketones. Aldehyde and ketone molecules (Figure 3-2) are characterized by the presence of a carbonyl (—CHO) group. A *carbonyl group* consists of an oxygen atom doubly bonded to a carbon atom (C=O). The general formulas for aldehydes and ketones are shown with *R* representing an alkyl or aryl group.

$$
\begin{array}{cc}
\text{H} & \text{R} \\
| & | \\
\text{R—C=O} & \text{R—C=O} \\
\text{aldehyde} & \text{ketone}
\end{array}
$$

Examples of aldehyde include formaldehyde (HCHO) and acetaldehyde (CH_3CHO). A common ketone is acetone (CH_3COCH_3).

Organic Acids (Carboxylic Acids). Organic acids contain the carboxyl group. A *carboxyl group* consists of a carbonyl group (—COOH) with a hydroxyl group attached to the carbon atom. Carboxylic acids are represented by the general formula R—COOH. In water solution, the carboxyl group dissociates so that such acids behave as weak acids and react with bases to form salts. Examples of organic acids include formic acid (HCOOH), an acid first obtained by the distillation of ants. Acetic acid (CH_3COOH) is found in vinegar, while butyric acid ($CH_3CH_2CH_2COOH$) is present in rancid butter. Many fruits and vegetables contain organic acids. Lemons and other citrus fruits contain citric acid ($C_6H_8O_7$). Oxalic acid ($H_2C_2O_4$) is found in the wood-sorrel (*Oxalis* spp.) plant family, a common weed, while tartaric acid ($H_2C_4H_4O_6$) is found in grapes.

$$\begin{array}{c} O \\ \| \\ R-C\text{-OH} \end{array}$$

carboxylic acid

Esters. Organic acids react with alcohols to form esters and water, a process called **esterification**. The overall net reaction involves the elimination of the elements of water from the reactant molecules. For example, ethyl alcohol reacts with acetic acid to form ethyl acetate, a common ingredient in nail polish remover. Nitroglycerine, an explosive ester, is formed when the alcohol glycerine reacts completely with nitric acid. Dynamite is made by absorbing nitroglycerine with wood pulp or porous earth.

Esters are often volatile liquids with pleasant odors. Ethyl butyrate has a pineapple odor, amyl acetate a banana odor, and methyl salicylate is wintergreen oil.

$$\begin{array}{c} O \\ \| \\ -C\text{-O-C}- \\ | \end{array}$$

ester

Fats and Fatty Acids. Fats and oils (liquid fats) are usually esters of long-chain fatty acids such as oleic, palmitic, or stearic acids and glycerol, a trihydroxy alcohol. Solid fats are generally derivatives of saturated fatty acids—fatty acids with no double bonds. Examples of saturated fatty acids are stearic acid [$CH_3(CH_2)_{16}COOH$ or $C_{17}H_{35}COOH$] whose glycerol ester is present in butter and lard, and palmitic acid [$CH_3(CH_2)_{14}COOH$ or $C_{15}H_{31}COOH$] whose ester is present in palm oil, butter, and lard. Unsaturated fatty acids contain double bonds and include oleic acid [$CH_3(CH_2)_7CH=CH(CH_2)_7COOH$ or $C_{17}H_{33}COOH$] whose glyceryl ester is in olive oil, and linoleic acid [$CH_3(CH_2)_4CH=CHCH_2CH(CH_2)_7COOH$ or $C_{16}H_{30}COOH$] whose ester is present in sunflower-seed and soybean oils. Peanut oil, cottonseed oil, soybean oil, coconut oil, and castor oil are other common oils and fats produced in plants while cod liver, lard, butter, suet, and whale oil are animal-produced oils and fats. Waxes are often esters of long-chain (>20°C atoms) alcohols and fatty acids. Additional information on fatty acids and waxes is in the chapter on Plant Biochemistry.

Soap is formed when esters react with OH^- ions in a reaction called *saponification* or hydrolysis. Sodium hydroxide or potassium hydroxide are most often used as base sources of OH^- ions. During saponification, the ester is converted to an alcohol and the salt of fatty acid. These reactions are the reverse of esterification where organic acids react with alcohols to form esters and water.

$$(C_{17}H_{35}COO)_3C_3H_5 + \quad 3NaOH \quad \rightarrow C_3H_5(OH)_3 + 3C_{17}H_{35}COONa$$

| stearin | sodium hydroxide | glycerine | sodium soap |

Soaps contain a polar group which is hydrophilic (water-loving), and a nonpolar chain which is hydrophobic (water-fearing). Detergent action takes place at the interface or surface between oil droplets and water. The detergent anions orient themselves at this interface with their nonpolar ends binding with the dirt-containing oil phase via weak, intermolecular **van der Waals forces**, while their polar ends are attached to water molecules. Thus, the covalent nonpolar oil and grease become dispersed in the water and can be washed away.

Insoluble metallic soap forms when sodium soap is used in hard water, water with calcium, magnesium, or other metallic ions. A greasy scum precipitates on bathtubs, washing machines, dishwashers, or clothes. Suds will not form until enough soap has been used to remove all the Ca and Mg ions from the water. Detergents are organic compounds made from higher alcohols such as sodium lauryl sulfate which cause Ca and Mg salts to become soluble and thus can be used efficiently with hard water.

Amines. Amines are nitrogen-containing organic derivatives of ammonia (NH_3). They are classified as primary, secondary, or tertiary depending on the number of alkyl or aryl groups attached to the nitrogen atom. The simplest aromatic amine is aniline ($C_6H_5NH_2$), a commonly used raw material in the synthesis of many dyes and drugs.

primary amine   secondary amine   tertiary amine

Amino Acids. Amino acids contain both the amine and carboxyl group with the general formula:

general formula for amino acids

Because the amine group has basic characteristics and the carboxyl group has acid characteristics, amino acids have the characteristics of both, thus are *amphoteric* substances; that is, they react with either an acid or a base.

Amino acids are the building blocks of proteins but not all of them are found in any single protein. Twenty amino acids exist and are covered in more detail in the Plant Biochemistry chapter.

Amides. Amides are derivatives of either ammonia and amines or of carboxylic acids. The general formula for a primary amide is shown:

$$\underset{\text{general formula for amides}}{R-\overset{\overset{\displaystyle O}{\|}}{C}\text{-}NH_2}$$

A special type of amide known as a *peptide* is formed during the bonding of two amino acids. During this process a water molecule is eliminated between the amino group of one amino acid and the carboxyl group of another amino-acid molecule. The amino acids are joined by *peptide bonds* and the linking together of many amino acids produces a *polypeptide*. Proteins are examples of complex polypeptides.

Carbohydrates

Carbohydrates represent a large group of organic compounds that play various roles in plant function. Carbohydrates are primary products produced by the process of photosynthesis where CO_2 from air and water from soil are used to form starch and sugar. They are found as (a) structural components in cell walls, (b) integral parts of the cytoplasm, (c) food storage products, (d) compounds which provide energy, and (e) raw materials for the synthesis of various other organic compounds.

Carbohydrates such as sugars, starches, and cellulose all contain C, H, and O. Typically a 2:1 ratio exists between the H and O atoms in most carbohydrates. The molecular formula for carbohydrates is $(CH_2O)_n$, where n represents a number.

Monosaccharides. The basic building blocks of carbohydrates are simple sugars called **monosaccharides** represented by the formula $(CH_2O)_n$. The root "*-sacchar-*" is Latin for "sugar." Monosaccharides, therefore, means "one sugar." Monosaccharides cannot be converted by hydrolysis into simpler sugars. Monosaccharide carbohydrates contain three, four, five, six, or seven carbon atoms, with those containing either five or six carbon atoms being the most important. The names of monosaccharides end in *-ose* (signifying a sugar), and the prefix designates the number of carbon atoms present (Table 3-3). Common monosaccharides include the sugar sources glucose (dextrose, grape sugar, blood sugar) and fructose (levulose, fruit sugar).

TABLE 3-3. Number of Carbon Atoms and Molecular Formulas for Monosaccharides

Sugar	Number of Carbon Atoms	Molecular Formula $(CH_2O)_n$	Value for n
Triose	3	$C_3H_6O_3$	3
Tetrose	4	$C_4H_8O_4$	4
Pentose	5	$C_5H_{10}O_5$	5
Hexose	6	$C_6H_{12}O_6$	6
Heptose	7	$C_7H_{14}O_7$	7

Monosaccharides are often artificially produced by heating starch with a dilute solution of hydrochloric acid, under pressure. The starch is hydrolyzed, and the acid acts as a catalyst:

$$(C_6H_{10}O_5)_n + XH_2O \rightarrow XC_6H_{12}O_6$$
$$\text{starch} \qquad\qquad\qquad \text{glucose}$$

Chemical compounds are often designated by their structural formula—the arrangement of atoms within the molecule. Within the structural formula, the carbon atoms are numbered. The structural formulas for the monosaccharides ribose (a pentose monosaccharide), glucose (a hexose), and fructose (a hexose) are shown in Figure 3-11. Both glucose and fructose contain 6 carbon atoms, 12 hydrogen atoms, and 6 oxygen atoms. However, their chemical properties are different. Molecules with similar chemical compositions but with different arrangements of the same atoms, and therefore different chemical properties, are referred to as **isomers**.

Some monosaccharides, such as glucose and fructose, often assume a molecular configuration resembling a ring-shaped arrangement of atoms. An oxygen bridge joins specific carbon atoms to form this ring configuration. By comparison, the straight-chain, or linear, arrangement of glucose and fructose are shown along with the ring configuration in Figure 3-12. Table 3-4 lists some of the most common carbohydrates.

Disaccharides. A second class of carbohydrates, called **disaccharide**, forms when two monosaccharides combine with each other, having the common formula

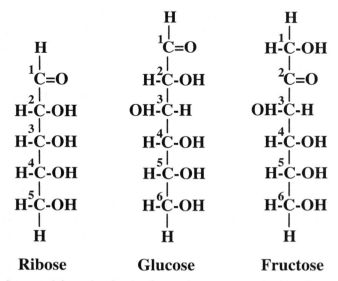

Ribose   **Glucose**   **Fructose**

Figure 3-11. Structural formulas for the five carbon monosaccharide ribose and six carbon monosaccharides glucose and fructose. Glucose and fructose are **isomers** in that they have the same chemical composition but with different arrangements.

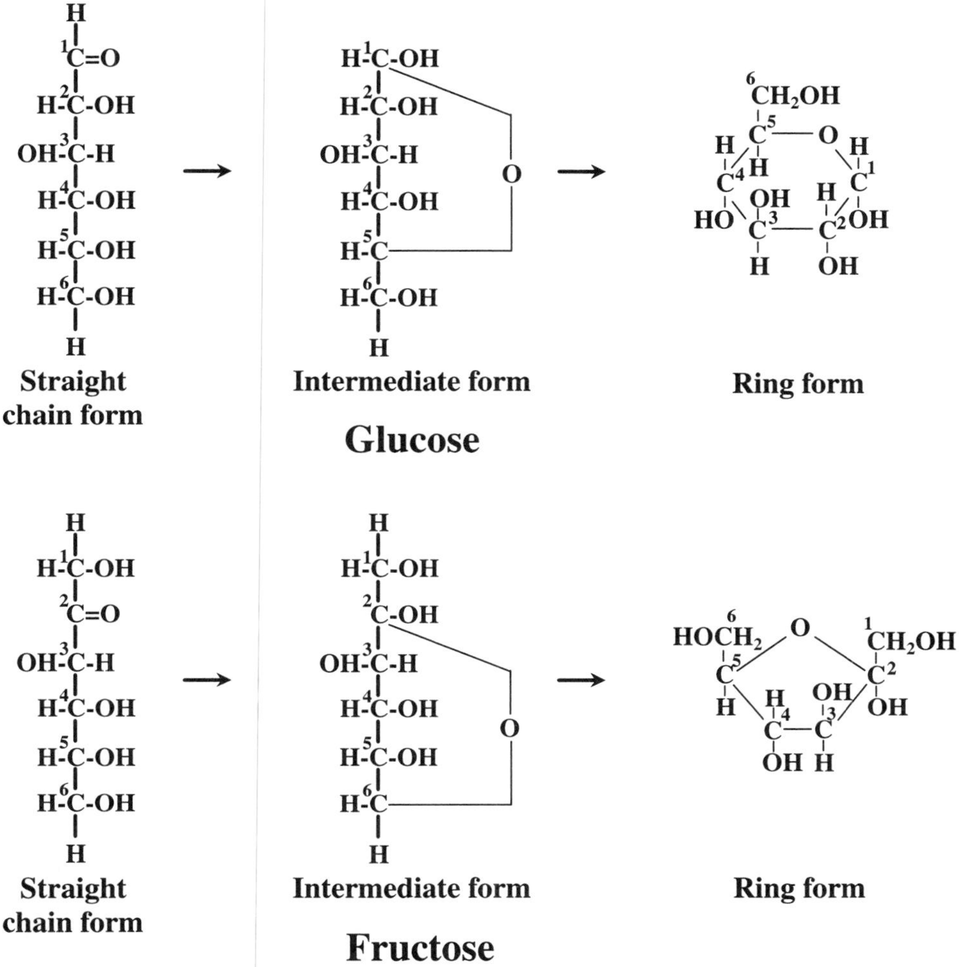

Figure 3-12. Straight chain, intermediate, and ring forms for glucose and fructose. Note the relative positions of the numbered carbon atoms as each molecule assumes a ring configuration as well as the oxygen bridge between carbon atoms.

$C_{12}H_{22}O_{11}$. In this process a molecule of water is lost and the reaction is termed *dehydration synthesis*. A common example of a disaccharide is sucrose (or common table sugar) where molecules of glucose and fructose combine through dehydration synthesis. In the process the smaller molecules (glucose and fructose in this case) join with the loss of water (termed *dehydration synthesis*), to form larger, more complex molecules (sucrose in this case). Caramel is a brown, viscous liquid formed when some water is removed from sucrose, and is used as a coloring and flavoring material in the food industry.

The reverse reaction of dehydration synthesis is *hydrolysis* (or digestion) where larger molecules are broken down into smaller, simpler ones with the addition of

TABLE 3-4. Some Common Carbohydrates

Carbohydrate	Common Name(s)	Molecular Formula	Source
Monosaccharide		$C_6H_{12}O_6$	
Glucose	blood sugar, grape sugar, dextrose		blood, plant sap, fruit, honey
Fructose	levulose		plants, fruits, honey
Galactose	—		hydrolysis of lactose
Disaccharide		$C_{12}H_{12}O_{11}$	
Sucrose	table sugar, beet sugar, cane sugar		sugar cane; sugar beets; maple sugar; various fruits and vegetables
Maltose	malt sugar		partial hydrolysis of starch
Cellobiose	—		partial hydrolysis of cellulose
Lactose	milk sugar		makes up about 5% of milk
Polysaccharide		$[C_6H_{10}O_5]_n$	
Starch	—		potatoes, corn, grains
Cellulose	—		cell walls of plants

water. For example, sucrose can be hydrolyzed into glucose and fructose, or a molecule of maltose may be hydrolyzed into two glucose molecules (Figure 3-13). Other examples of disaccharides include galactose and lactose (milk sugar). Table 3-5 lists the relative degree of sweetness among carbohydrates. The monosaccharide fructose is the sweetest sugar and thus is often used in the manufacturing of many candies.

Polysaccharides. A third class of carbohydrates, **polysaccharides**, forms from the dehydration synthesis of three or more monosaccharides. Polysaccharides have the molecular formula $(C_6H_{10}O_5)_n$. Like disaccharides, polysaccharides can be broken down by hydrolysis into their constituent sugars. However, unlike monosaccharides or disaccharides, polysaccharides are not usually soluble in water and they lack the characteristic sweetness of sugars. Among the most important plant polysaccharides are **starches** and **cellulose** (Figure 3-14).

Starch composes the reserve food supply of plants, especially in seed. Starch serves as a macronutrient in potatoes, corn, and rice, while cellulose provides mammals with dietary fiber, sometimes called roughage. The difference between the two polysaccharides originates in their molecular structures. Starch is made exclusively of rings of straight chains of glucose (called alpha (α) − glucose) while cellulose is composed of alternating molecules of glucose called beta (β) − glucose, which gives cellulose its cellular strength and lack of digestibility by humans. **Chitin** is another important polysaccharide and forms the outer covering of many insects and the shells of lobsters, crabs, shrimp, and barnacles. In addition, the cell walls of most fungi are composed of chitin.

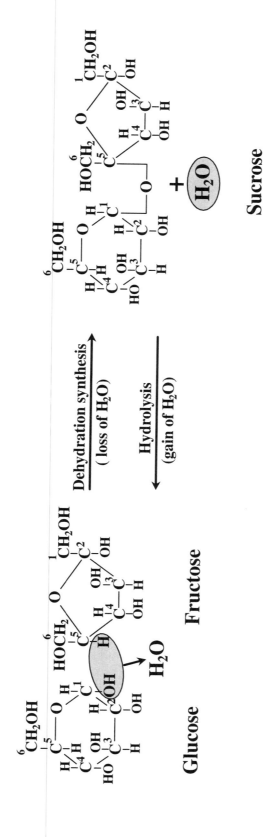

Figure 3-13. Formation of the disaccharide carbohydrate, sucrose, from the combination of a molecule of glucose and fructose by dehydration synthesis (removal of water). The reverse reaction, hydrolysis (addition of water), transforms sucrose into glucose and fructose.

TABLE 3-5. Relative Sweetness of Selected Sugars

Sugar	Relative Sweetness to Sucrose
Sucrose	100
Fructose	173
Invert sugar (equal mixture of glucose and fructose)	130
Glucose	74
Galactose	32
Maltose	32
Lactose	16

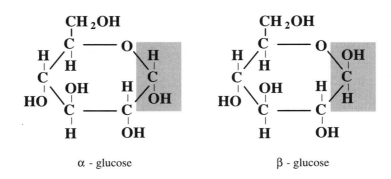

α - glucose   β - glucose

Starches are the principal food reserve or storage products in most green plants such as wheat, corn, and potatoes. Typically, they are stored in seeds, stems, leaves, and roots. Starches consist of a long series of glucose molecules bonded to each other. Within the starch molecules two distinguishable components exist—*amylose* and *amylopectin*. Amylose consists of unbranched coiled chains of glucose molecules, while amylopectin are branched chains of glucose molecules.

Cellulose is an important structural component of cell walls of higher plants. Cellulose makes up the more fibrous structures of bran; seed husks of oats, rye, and wheat; celery stalks; and lettuce leaves. Cellulose is a polymer (large, chainlike molecules) of 1,000 or more glucose molecules. These are like amylose in that it is unbranched but, unlike, amylose, cellulose is not coiled. The amount and arrangement of the cellulose molecules determine the basic physical properties of cell walls—tensile strength, elasticity, and plasticity. Cellulose and starch have the same molecular formula $(C_6H_{10}O_5)_n$ but have different molecular weights. Cellulose, unlike starch, cannot be made digestible by cooking. Humans lack the enzyme *cellobiase* which is needed to digest cellulose. Ruminants such as cow, goats, and sheep as well as termites contain microorganisms that produce the needed cellobiase to digest cellulose.

Carbohydrate Metabolism. Energy is liberated when carbohydrates are oxidized. These reactions proceed through a series of steps and require the presence of enzymes. For example, the overall equation of the oxidation of glucose is:

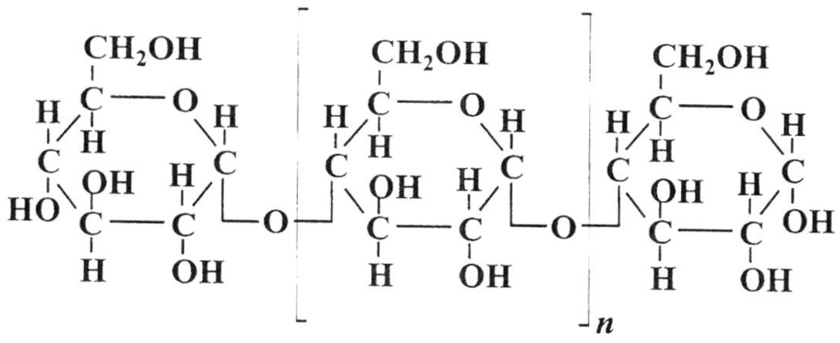

Starch

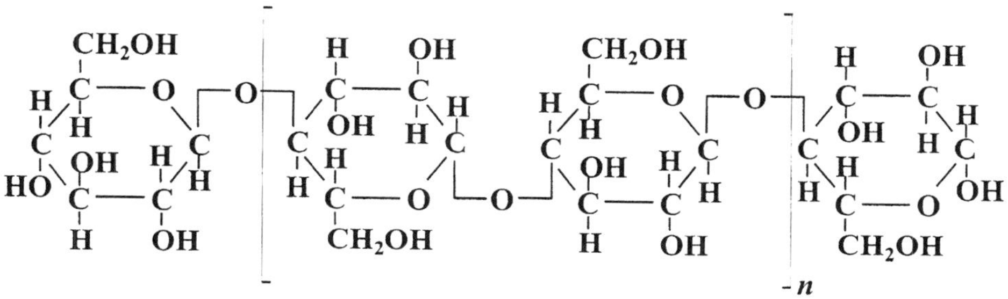

Cellulose

Figure 3-14. Starch and cellulose, two important plant polysaccharides, composed of long-chain glucose units as indicated by *n*. The glucose units in cellulose have an alternating orientation.

$$C_6H_{12}O_6 + 6O_2 \rightarrow 6CO_2 + 6H_2O + \text{energy}$$
glucose   oxygen   carbon dioxide   water

The energy is used to synthesize more complex molecules such as proteins and to support the activities of the organism.

The large amount of energy produced by the oxidation of simple carbohydrates is often stored in compounds which have very high-energy phosphate bonds. The most important of these is ATP (adenosine triphosphate). Energy is supplied by the hydrolysis of ATP to ADP (adenosine diphosphate). The energy released is used to "drive" biochemical reactions which require energy. This is covered in greater detail in the Plant Biochemistry chapter.

PRACTICE PROBLEMS

1. What distinguishing feature characterizes chemicals as organic rather than inorganic? (*organic compounds contain carbon atoms while inorganic ones do not*).

2. How are carbon atoms unique? (*it is the only element capable of forming long chains from atoms of the same type*).

3. What shapes may chains of carbon atoms form? (*straight-chain, branched-chain, and cyclic compounds*).

4. How many bonds does the carbon atom have to share with other atoms? (*four*).

5. Name the three elements that occur most frequently in organic chemicals. (*carbon, hydrogen, and oxygen followed by nitrogen and sulfur*).

6. What general term is used to denote organic chemicals that contain only carbon and hydrogen atoms in their structures? (*hydrocarbons*).

7. What is an *isohydrocarbon*? (*a 3 or more carbon-containing atom with a methyl (—CH$_3$) group substituted for a hydrogen on the next to last carbon of the chain*).

8. Distinguish between saturated and unsaturated hydrocarbons. (*saturated—contain only carbon-carbon single bonds; unsaturated—contain carbon-carbon double or triple bonds*).

9. What feature characterizes an aliphatic hydrocarbon? (*compounds which are straight-chain, branched-chain, or cyclic*).

10. What feature characterizes an aromatic hydrocarbon? (*these are benzene (C$_6$H$_6$)-like compounds*).

11. Draw three ways the benzene ring structure is commonly presented.

12. What distinguishes a benzene from a phenyl structure? (*a phenyl structure is a benzene structure with one hydrogen atom removed, and often replaced with OH$^-$*).

13. Define isomer. (*compounds having the same percentage composition or molecular formula but different structural formulas, e.g., glucose and fructose*).

14. Define what is meant by saponification. (*hydrolysis where an ester is converted to an alcohol and the salt of fatty acid*).

15. Define carbohydrates, distinguishing between monosaccharides and disaccharides. (*organic compounds produced by photosynthesis which provide energy, food storage, raw materials for synthesis of other compounds and integral parts of the cytoplasm. Monosaccharides—simple sugars containing 3, 4, 5, 6, or 7 carbon atoms; disaccharides—complex carbohydrate that forms when two monosaccharides combine*).

16. Define polysaccharides and distinguish between starches and cellulose. (*polysaccharides—insoluble carbohydrate chains that form from the dehydration synthesis of three or more monosaccharides; starches consist of a*

series of glucose molecules bonded together, cellulose is a polymer component of cell walls of 1,000 or more glucose molecules).

17. Define and contrast *dehydration synthesis* and *hydrolysis.* (*dehydration synthesis is a chemical reaction where two molecules combine with the resulting lost of water; hydrolysis is when larger molecules are broken down into smaller, simpler ones with a resulting net gain in water).*

18. Why do chemicals such as oil and water not mix? (*the polarity of water tends to interact with larger molecules to make them dissolve while oil lacks polar regions and thus cannot form hydrogen bonds, and tends to be very insoluble in water or simply, oil and water do not mix because they are not like molecules).*

19. Why are functional groups important? (*functional groups are important because they are combined with existing molecules to yield another molecule with different properties).*

20. What are aldehydes and ketones? (*molecules characterized by the presence of a carbonyl group which consists of an oxygen atom doubly bonded to a carbon atom).*

21. Identify the functional groups in each of the following.

$$\underset{\text{HO-}\overset{\displaystyle O}{\overset{\|}{C}}\text{-CH}_3}{} \qquad \textit{-carboxylic acid}$$

$$\text{H}_2\text{C=CH}_2 \qquad \textit{-alkene}$$

$$\text{CH}_3\text{-O-CH}_3 \qquad \textit{-ether}$$

$$\underset{\text{CH}_3\text{-}\overset{\displaystyle O}{\overset{\|}{C}}\text{-CH}_3}{} \qquad \textit{-ketone}$$

$$\underset{\text{CH}_3\text{-CH}}{\overset{\displaystyle O}{\overset{\|}{}}} \qquad \textit{-aldehyde}$$

22. Name the following alkane. (*4-ethyl-2,3-dimethylhexane*)

$$\underset{\overset{|}{\text{CH}_3}\ \overset{|}{\text{CH}_3}\ \overset{|}{\text{CH}_2\text{CH}_3}}{\text{CH}_3\text{-CH-CH-CH-CH}_2\text{-CH}_3}$$

23. Write the structure for:
    (a) 2,3,5-trimethylheptane

$$\underset{\overset{|}{\text{CH}_3}\qquad\ \overset{|}{\text{CH}_3}\ \overset{|}{\text{CH}_3}}{\text{CH}_3\text{-CH}_2\text{-CH-CH}_2\text{-CH-CH-CH}_3}$$

(b) -chloro-4-ethyl-3-hexene

$$\underset{\underset{\textstyle Cl}{|}}{CH_2}-CH_2-CH=\underset{\underset{\textstyle C_2H_5}{|}}{C}CH_2-CH_3$$

24. Name at least five nitrogen-containing functional groups. (*amino, nitro, amide, amine, nitrile or cyanide, aniline, urea, carbamate, thiocarbamate, sulfonylurea*).

25. Why would the herbicide Prodiamine not leach as quickly through the soil as Atrazine? (*Prodiamine will leach more slowly than Atrazine because it is not water soluble*).

CHAPTER 4

PLANT BIOCHEMISTRY

Biochemistry is the chemistry of living matter based largely on the carbon structures of organic chemistry. The term **biochemistry** encompasses the pathways involved bridging the chemistry of plants with the biology of plants. Relationships develop between plant cell formation and function important in metabolic and mechanical activities. Table 4-1 lists important biochemical compounds synthesized by plants necessary for life. Energy to drive the biochemical reactions in plants is derived from sunlight through photosynthesis. The energy stored by plants in terms of proteins, carbohydrates, and fats are later utilized by plants or are consumed by mammals to provide themselves with energy. Throughout this chapter we will investigate the biochemistry of plants and its importance to growth, development, repair, and reproduction.

Cells

All living organisms consist of one or more cells (Figure 4-1). It is in living cells where the processes of life are carried out. Cells differ in the relative proportion and specific nature of the compounds they use and produce. It is these differences that result in different kinds of cells, performing different functions, in the more highly developed organisms. Most of the organic compounds in cells are **proteins, carbohydrates,** or **fats** (*lipids* and *oils*) (Table 4-1). In addition, there are small amounts of hormones and a class of substances called **nucleic acids** which control the characteristics of cells and carry coded hereditary "instructions" to the next generation. Inorganic substances such as nutrients are also essential to life and are present in most cells.

AMINO ACIDS

Amino acids are compounds carrying both a carboxyl group (—COOH) and an amino group (—NH$_2$). Amino acids have properties of both acids and bases. Amino

TABLE 4-1. Biologically Important Organic Molecules (Modified from Raven, et al. 1999)

Molecule Class	Types	Subunits	Primary Functions	Other Features
Carbohydrates	Monosaccharides (e.g., glucose)	Monosaccharide	Ready available energy source	Carbohydrates are sugars and polymers of sugars. Carbohydrates are identified as compounds of monomers with numerous hydroxyl groups (—OH) and usually one carbonyl (—C=O) group attached to the carbon skeleton. The carbonyl group, however, is usually not evident if the sugars are in the ring form.
	Disaccharides (e.g., sucrose)	Two monosaccharides	Transport form in plants	
	Polysaccharides	Many monosaccharides	Energy storage or structural components	
	Starch		Major energy storage in plants	
	Glycogen		Major energy storage in fungi and animals	
	Cellulose		Component of plant cell walls	
	Lignin		A secondary phenolic metabolite responsible for cell wall strength and stiffness	
	Chitin		Component of fungal cell walls and insect exoskeletons	

160

Category	Type	Building blocks	Function	Description
Lipids	Triglycerides	3 fatty acids + 1 glycerol	Energy storage	Lipids are nonpolar molecules, and thus do not dissolve in polar solvents such as water. They can be stored for long periods in cells and will not dissolve in the watery environment.
	Oils		Energy storage in seeds and fruits	
	Fats		Energy storage in animals	
	Phospholipids	2 fatty acids + 1 glycerol + 1 phosphate group	Major component of all cell membranes	Phospholipids and glycolipids are modified triglycerides with a polar group at one end. Its polar head is hydrophilic (water loving) and thus dissolves in water; the nonpolar tail is hydrophobic (water-hating), thus is insoluble in water. Lipids are the basis in cell membrane formation, where they are arranged tail to tail.
	Cutin, suberin, and waxes	Vary; complex lipid structures	Protection	These provide waterproofing for stems, leaves, and fruits.
	Steroids	Four-linked hydrocarbon rings	Component of cell membranes; hormones	A sterol is a steroid with a hydroxyl group at the three-carbon position.
Proteins (polypeptides)	Many different types	Amino acids	Includes structural and catalytic (as enzymes)	Primary, secondary, tertiary, and quaternary structures.
Nucleic acids	DNA	Nucleotides	Carrier of genetic information	Each nucleotide is composed of a sugar, a nitrogenous base, and a phosphate group. ATP is a nucleotide that is the principal energy carrier for cells.
	RNA		Involved in protein synthesis	

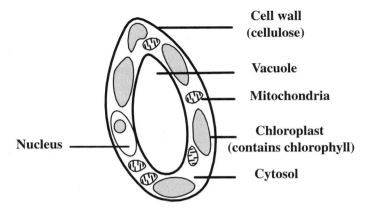

Figure 4-1. Simplified drawing of a plant cell containing the numerous organelles. The nucleus is where DNA is contained. Chloroplasts are surrounded by an envelope consisting of two membranes and is the site of photosynthesis. The mitochondria provides energy for cellular functions. The vacuole is a fluid-filled region enclosed by a membrane, and the cell wall is characteristic of plant cells.

acids play several roles in plants, the most obvious and important being protein synthesis as they are the building blocks to all proteins. Additional functions include the assimilation and transport of nitrogen throughout plants, and evolution of hormones and plant defense mechanisms.

There are 20 amino acids found in plants with these derived from intermediates involved in the Calvin Cycle, glycolysis, and/or the Kreb's Cycle (Figure 4-2). The intermediates include: oxaloacetate (OAA), 3-phosphoglyceraldehyde (3-PGA), phosphophenol-pyruvate (PEP), pyruvate, and α-ketoglutarate. Amino acids are recognized by their structure surrounding a carbon. The carbon to which both —NH_2 and —COOH groups are attached is called the **alpha carbon** (alpha is the first letter of the Greek alphabet). Four different side groups include: (1) the basic —NH_2 or amino group; (2) the acidic —COOH or carboxyl group; (3) —H or hydrogen; and (4) —"R" or carbon-containing molecule. Amino acids are represented by the general formula, $H_2NCH(R)COOH$ or $H_3N^+CH(R)COO^-$.

The "R" group defines the properties of the amino acids, as well as the proteins they create. Differences in overall structure, and chemical and biological makeup allow amino acids to react and interact differently. Some amino acids are nonpolar and hydrophobic (water-repelling), such as alanine and proline, therefore allowing them to react with nonpolar molecules such as fats and lipids. Others are polar (dissolvable) and hydrophilic (water soluble), such as serine and glutamine and therefore only interact with other polar molecules.

Another active role of amino acids is the dispersal of nitrogen throughout the plant. Plant roots absorb nitrogen in the inorganic (nitrate, NO_2^-, or ammonium, NH_4^+) form. Once in the plant, nitrogen is assimilated to useable and transportable amino acids, which can then be used for the production of other amino acids, nucleic acids, and other N-containing compounds. These include glutamate, glutamine, aspartate, and asparagine that translocate throughout plants through the phloem. **Essential amino acids** are those not synthesized by the human body; thus

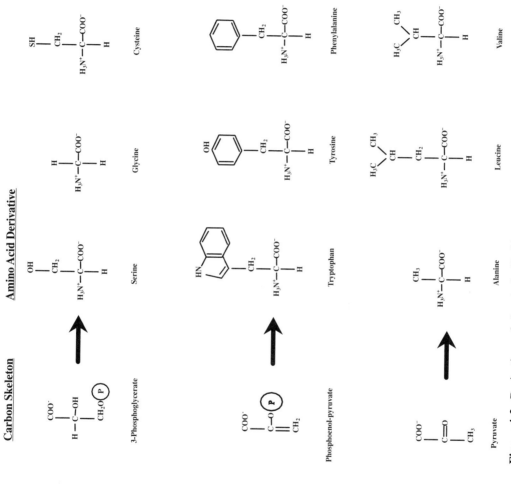

Figure 4-2. Derivatives of glycolysis, Kreb's cycle, and Calvin cycle (left) provide carbon skeletons for the production and transport of amino acids (right) which are later used to form proteins.

163

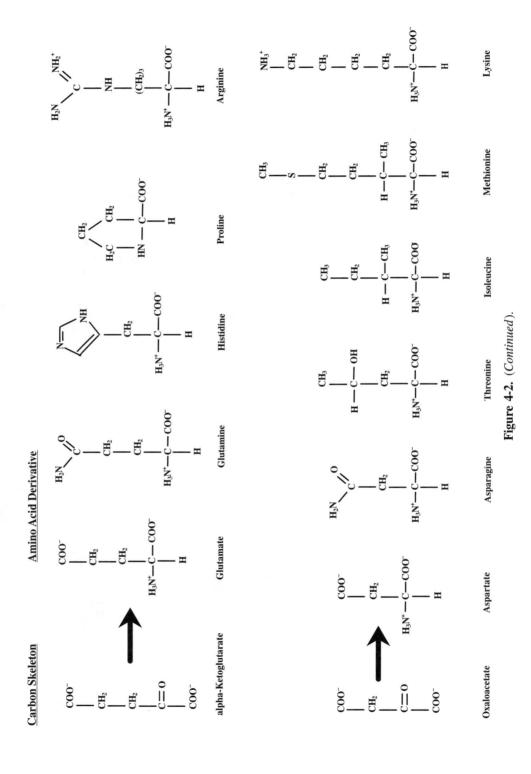

Figure 4-2. (*Continued*).

must be obtained from diet and include lysine, tryptophan, phenylalanine, methionine, threonine, leucine, isoleucine, and valine.

PROTEINS

Proteins are important in plant cell functions, especially cell growth, differentiation, and reproduction. Proteins are synthesized in three different locations; cytoplasm, mitochondria, and chloroplast, with about 75% produced in cytoplasm, 20% in chloroplast, and 5% in mitochondria. All proteins contain carbon, hydrogen, oxygen, and nitrogen while some also contain phosphorus and sulfur. Proteins are composed of unbranched polymers of amino acids, sometimes 100 to 1,000 residues long.

Proteins form one of the three classes of macronutrients. Like the polysaccharides starch and cellulose, proteins exist as long, threadlike molecules formed by linked sequences of smaller units. While each unit of starch and cellulose is a cyclic glucose molecule, protein molecules consist of long sequences of nitrogen containing amino acids units.

Proteins are produced by the various 20 different amino acids reacting together to form polymers. When these amino acids react, they produce a *peptide bond.* A peptide bond is formed when the —H from the amino group (NH$_2$) reacts with the —OH from the carboxyl group (COOH) producing water, freeing a bond to link the two amino acids together (Figure 4-3). Peptide bonds require enzyme activation and are mediated in the ribosome. Molecules containing 1 to 50 peptide links are called **peptides.** Proteins have more than 50 peptide linkages, usually from 100 to 8,000 linkages. In protein synthesis, amino acids are linked together by numerous peptide bonds, and are called **polypeptide chains.**

An important aspect of proteins is the transfer of hereditary characteristics. Genetic information concerning the form and function of proteins is passed along during synthesis. Protein synthesis begins with DNA transferring genetic information to mRNA (messenger RNA) (Figure 4-4). Translation of the mRNA produces a protein. During the translation phase, the mRNA is matched with a corresponding amino acid sequence.

Structurally, proteins are diverse molecules with four levels of organization: primary; secondary; tertiary; and quaternary. The **primary structure** refers to the

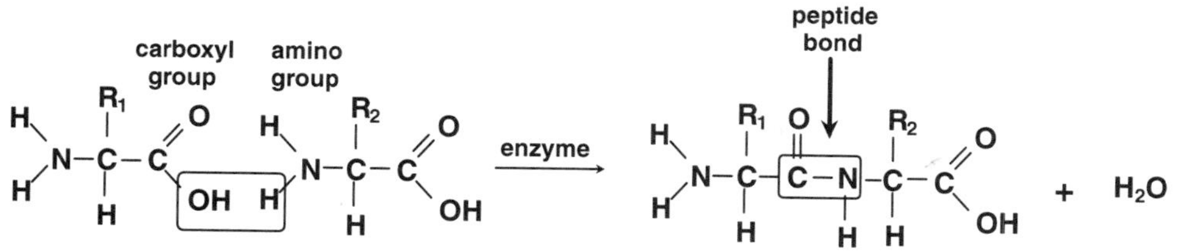

Figure 4-3. Peptide bond formation during the linking of amino acids (left) to form proteins (right). Peptide bonds form by a reaction between the amino group (—NH$_3^+$) of one amino acid with the carboxyl group (—COO$^-$) group of another. Polypeptides are molecules composed of numerous sequential peptide bonds.

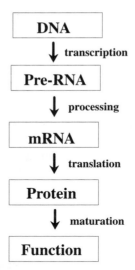

Figure 4-4. Sequential steps in the formation of proteins in plants. Messenger RNA (mRNA) serve as the cytoplasmic messengers of genes and carry genetic information (genetic code) for the subsequent synthesis of polypeptides such as proteins. Ribosomal RNA (rRNA) are structural components of ribosomes, the organelles where synthesis of polypeptides occur while transfer RNA (tRNA) transport amino acids to ribosomes for the subsequent incorporation into polypeptides. DNA serves as the genetic information (or code) for protein synthesis.

number and sequence of amino acids in a protein. This structure is very seldom straight and generally is coiled and/or twisted and held together by peptide linkages. A good example is the double helix of nucleic acids produced through weak hydrogen bonds connecting amino acid chains. This coiling is three-dimensional twisting and turning, which represents the **secondary structure** of proteins. An alpha helix turns in the right-hand direction. Hydrogen bonding between —NH and C=O in the same chain form the alpha helix. The **tertiary structure** refers to the way alpha helixes, folded sheets, and random coils further fold and coil. The chemical differences in the "R" group allow numerous bonding opportunities creating folding and bending throughout the amino acid chain to produce a complex, globular molecular shape. The final structure is the **quaternary structure** which illustrates individual interactions between polypeptide chains to form biologically active proteins and the pockets and grooves in tertiary structures which provide the active sites of enzymes.

Enzymes. Another function of proteins is enzymatic activity in metabolic reactions. **Enzymes** are catalytic proteins that reduce activation energy and time required for a metabolic reaction to occur (Figure 4-5). For example, the hydrolysis of sucrose to glucose and fructose is catalyzed by the enzyme *sucrase.* The activation energy is the energy level required for a reaction to occur. Generally, a single enzyme will be selective to a single substrate giving enzymes a high degree of specificity.

The lock and key theory explains how enzymes and **substrates** (substance on which the enzyme acts) react. The enzyme is like a lock that has a special structure,

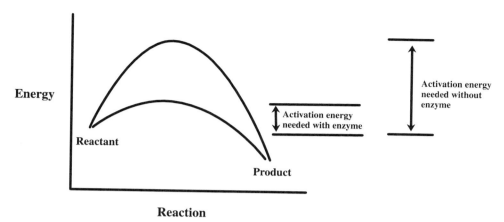

Figure 4-5. Enzymes are catalysts that accelerate reactions by lowering the energy of activation required for a reaction to occur.

while the substrate is like a key that will fit the lock. First, the enzyme (E) and substrate (S) combine to form an enzyme-substrate complex (ES):

$$EP + S \rightleftharpoons ES$$

The active site portion of the enzyme is where the reactants are converted to the products (EP):

$$ES \rightleftharpoons EP$$

The products (P) are released from the surface of the enzyme and the enzyme is now free to catalyze another molecule:

$$EP \rightleftharpoons E + P$$

Almost 2,000 different enzymes exist with Table 4-2 listing the major classes, their subclasses, and their general reactions.

Enzymes act on specific molecules. For example, a *carbohydrase* is an enzyme that acts on a carbohydrate molecule and breaks it down into smaller units. *Amylases* break down starches into smaller molecules.

The numerous different chemical reactions occurring in living systems can be classified into a few general types, each catalyzed by different classes of biological enzymes. Some reactions common in biology include: *condensation* or *dehydration reactions; hydrolysis reactions; oxidation-reduction reactions; phosphorylation reactions; rearrangements* (or **isomerization**) or the internal reorganization of molecules; *carboxylation reactions,* such as the photosynthesis reaction; *addition reactions* where two molecules join to form a larger molecule; and the most common reaction, the *transfer,* where two molecules meet and exchange or transfer parts to form two new molecules (Figure 4-6).

TABLE 4-2. The Major Enzyme Classes and Subclasses and Their General Reactions

Enzyme Class and Subclass	General Reactions
Oxidoreductases Oxidases Reductases Dehydrogenases	Enzymes which remove and add electrons and hydrogen via oxidation-reduction reactions. Oxidases transfer electrons or hydrogen to oxygen only. Examples include alcohol dehydrogenase where alcohol is converted to aldehyde, succinate dehydrogenase where double bonds are formed, and amino acid oxidase.
Transferases Kinases	Enzymes which catalyze transfer of functional groups from one molecule to another. Kinases transfer phosphate groups, especially from ATP. Examples include phosphotransferase which transfer phosphoryl, and aminotransferase which transfer amino groups.
Hydrolases Proteinases Ribonucleases Deoxyribonucleases Lipases	Enzymes which break chemical bonds (e.g., amides, esters, glycosides) by adding water (hydrolysis). Proteinases hydrolyze RNA (or phosphate esters); Ribonucleases hydrolyze DNA (or phosphate esters); Lipases hydrolyze fats (esters). Examples include peptidase which hydrolyze peptide bonds, and phosphatase which hydrolyze monophosphate ester bonds.
Lyases	Breaks bonds by electronic rearrangements and/or addition to double bonds with subsequent removal of a chemical group. For example, carbon dioxide is removed with decarboxylase, while ammonia is removed with deaminase.
Isomerases	Rearranges atoms or a molecule to form a structural isomer (termed isomerization) and does not involve the addition or removal of groups. Examples include epimerase which isomerize C-3 of a 5-C sugar, and racemase which isomerize α-carbon substituents.
Ligases or Synthetases *Polymerases*	Reactions joining two molecules coupled with energy input from the utilization (hydrolysis) of ATP or other nucleoside triphosphate high energy bonds. Polymerases link subunits (monomers) into a polymer such as RNA or DNA. Examples include acetyl-CoA synthetase which form covalent carbon-sulfur bonds, and pyruvate carboxylase which forms covalent carbon to carbon bonds.

Another group of coenzymes important in energy and proton transfer are various forms of nicotinamide—*nicotinamide adenine dinucleotide* (*NAD+*) and *nicotinamide adenine dinucleotide phosphate* (*NADP+*). $NADP^+$ has a phosphate group bonded to the C-2 of the ribose attached to adenine, while NAD^+ does not (Figure 4-7). NAD^+ and $NADP^+$ serve as coenzymes for a class of dehydrogenase enzymes that catalyze oxidation-reduction reactions where two hydrogen (H^+) atoms are generally removed from (or oxidized) or added to (reduced) a substrate. The nicotinamide moiety of NAD^+ and $NADP^+$ serve as the hydrogen atom (electron) carrier by accepting or donating a hydride ion (Figure 4-7). The general reaction catalyzed by an NAD^+- or $NADP^+$-linked dehydrogenase enzyme is:

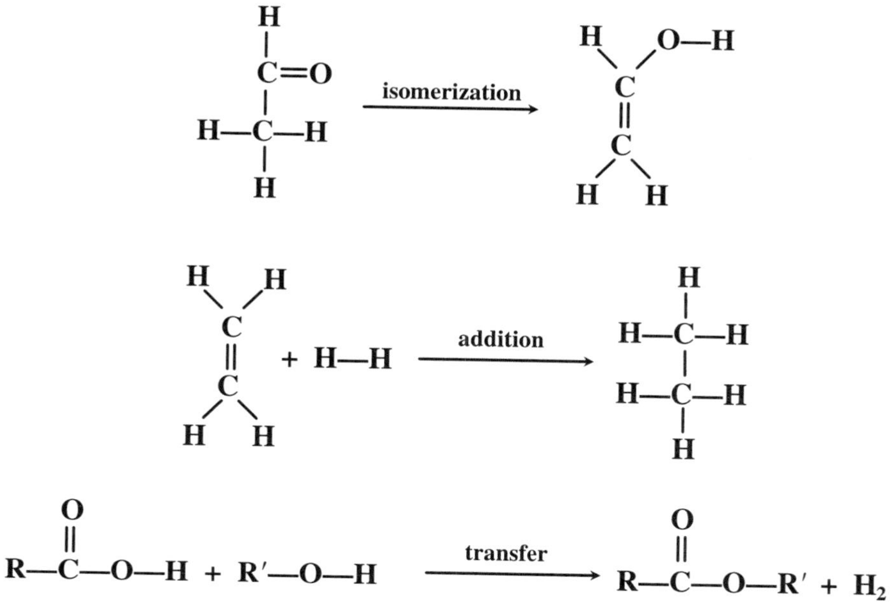

$$
\begin{array}{c}
H \\
| \\
C=O \\
| \\
H-C-H \\
| \\
H
\end{array}
\quad \xrightarrow{\text{isomerization}} \quad
\begin{array}{c}
H \quad O-H \\
\diagdown \diagup \\
C \\
\| \\
C \\
\diagup \diagdown \\
H \quad H
\end{array}
$$

$$
\begin{array}{c}
H \quad H \\
\diagdown \diagup \\
C \\
\| \\
C \\
\diagup \diagdown \\
H \quad H
\end{array}
+ \; H-H \quad \xrightarrow{\text{addition}} \quad
\begin{array}{c}
H \\
| \\
H-C-H \\
| \\
H-C-H \\
| \\
H
\end{array}
$$

$$
\begin{array}{c}
O \\
\| \\
R-C-O-H
\end{array}
+ \; R'-O-H \quad \xrightarrow{\text{transfer}} \quad
\begin{array}{c}
O \\
\| \\
R-C-O-R'
\end{array}
+ \; H_2
$$

Figure 4-6. Examples of three general types of chemical reactions: *isomerization,* which is the rearrangement of internal organization of the molecule; *addition,* where two molecules join to form a larger molecule; and *transfer,* where two molecules meet and exchange or transfer parts to form two new molecules.

General Reaction of Electron Transfer by NAD⁺ or NADP⁺

$$
\text{substrate-H}_2 + \underset{\text{(or NADP}^+)}{\text{NAD}^+} \;\leftrightarrow\; \text{substrate} + \underset{\text{(or NADPH)}}{\text{NADH}} + \text{H}^+
$$

Conversely, when hydrogen atoms are donated to a substrate by NADH or NADPH, it is absorbed from the environment.

PHOTOSYNTHESIS

Photosynthesis is the conversion of light energy (sunlight), carbon dioxide (CO_2), and water (H_2O) to useable chemical plant energy such as glucose. It is the process that serves as the ultimate source of food and oxygen needed to sustain life. Chlorophyll in plants absorbs the energy from sunlight, and this energy is then used to produce carbohydrates from carbon dioxide and water. The process involves a series of chemical reactions in the chloroplasts of plant cells (Figure 4-8) where the transfer of chemical energy occurs when electrons are lost or gained. In photosynthesis, carbon dioxide is reduced (in other words, gains electrons) and water is oxidized (or loses electrons) to produce oxygen and organic compounds in light and dark reactions. Light from the sun provides the energy for electron transfer while the actual steps of carbohydrate formation occur in the dark.

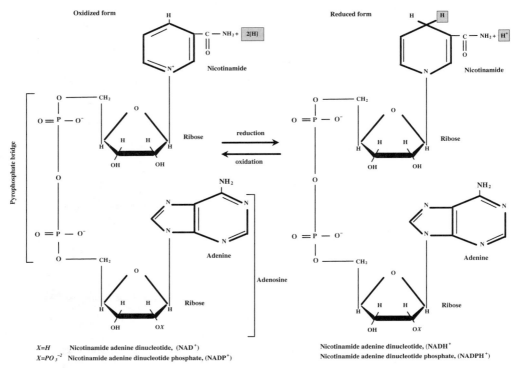

Oxidized form

Reduced form

X=H   Nicotinamide adenine dinucleotide, (NAD⁺)
X=PO₃⁻²   Nicotinamide adenine dinucleotide phosphate, (NADP⁺)

Nicotinamide adenine dinucleotide, (NADH⁺)
Nicotinamide adenine dinucleotide phosphate, (NADPH⁺)

Figure 4-7. Nicotinamide adenine dinucleotide (NAD^+) and nicotinamide adenine dinucleotide phosphate ($NADP^+$), in their oxidized forms (left). These gain two electrons and a proton (H^+) to produce the reduced forms, $NADH^+$ and $NADPH^+$ (right). Similar electron transfer reactions occur with flavin adenine dinucleotide, or FAD^+ (oxidized form) and $FADH_2$ (reduced form) during the electron transport system.

General Photosynthesis Reaction

$$6CO_2 + 6H_2O \xrightarrow[\text{photosynthesis}]{\lambda \text{ (light)}} 6O_2 + C_6H_{12}O_6$$

carbon dioxide   water   oxygen   organic compounds
(e.g., glucose)

I. Light Reactions. The energy obtained from light is used to split water into hydrogen and oxygen to eventually generate ATP and other organic compounds. The light reactions of photosynthesis are in two stages, photosystem I (abbreviated PSI) and photsystem II (PSII) (Figure 4-9). Each photosystem harvests light to provide energy for the transfer of electrons in the process known as the "Z-scheme." This absorbed light provides the energy necessary for water oxidation which produces O_2, H^+ and electrons. These electrons result in the production of energized chlorophyll designated as $P680^+$. This process is the sole source of oxygen for aerobic respiration by all animals and plants.

Energized $P680^+$ initiates the downhill flow of electrons to PSI (Figure 4-9). During this downhill flow, an electrochemical gradient is formed, producing ATP synthesis from ADP plus phosphate (Pi). Electron transfer continues down the chain

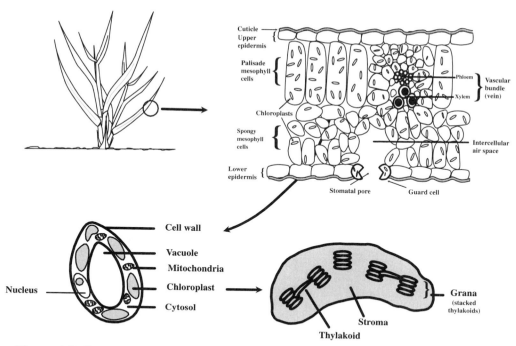

Figure 4-8. From a grass leaf (upper left), the inner tissue of the leaf, called mesophyll (upper right), is specialized for photosynthesis. The mesophyll consists of elongated and irregularly shaped cells which contain numerous chloroplasts. Oxygen, carbon dioxide, and water vapor enter the leaf by stomates while minerals are taken up by the roots and transported via the xylem tissue. Sugars produced by photosynthesis move from the leaf by phloem tissue, traveling to nonphotosynthetic parts of the plant. Photosynthesis occurs primarily in chloroplasts (lower left and right) in leaf cells which surround large vacuole areas. Light reactions (Z-scheme) occur in the thylakoid membranes with the Calvin cycle in the disk-like thylakoids called grana. The thylakoids of the various grana are interconnected by other thylakoids, commonly called stroma thylakoids.

to a chlorophyll P700 in PSI. Excitation energy from additional light absorption produces a strong reductant, P700$^+$. Another series of reductions follows involving chlorophyll, quinones, and iron-sulfur proteins. An electrochemical gradient is again produced reducing NADP$^+$ to NADPH, which along with ATP produced, are required for carbon dioxide fixation into sugars in the Calvin Cycle.

Pigments. Pigments in plants are responsible for the capture of light required for photosynthesis. Pigments are contained in the thylakoid membranes of chloroplasts. Pigments found in plants include: the green colored **chlorophylls *a* and *b*;** orange to yellow colored **carotenoids and xanthophylls;** and blue colored **anthocyanins.** The structures of chlorophyll and a carotenoid are in Figure 4-10.

Chlorophyll is the most abundant of the plant pigments and is a tetrapyrrole compound with a magnesium (Mg) molecule in the center of the ring. Attached to the tetrapyrrole ring is a phytol tail containing 20 carbon molecules. Chlorophylls, as mentioned previously, are important in the absorption of light and transfer of

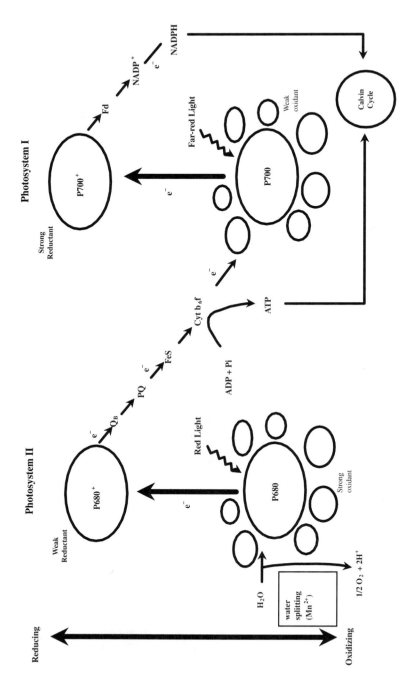

Figure 4-9. Light harvesting complex or 'Z' scheme for light reactions of photosynthesis located in the thylakoid membrane of chloroplasts. The downhill flow of electrons shows a transfer of energy: quencher (Q); plastoquinone (PQ); iron-sulfur protein (FeS); a cytochrome (Cyt b_6f); and, ferredoxin (Fd). ATP and NADPH produced in the Z-scheme are used to make sugars and starches in the Calvin cycle.

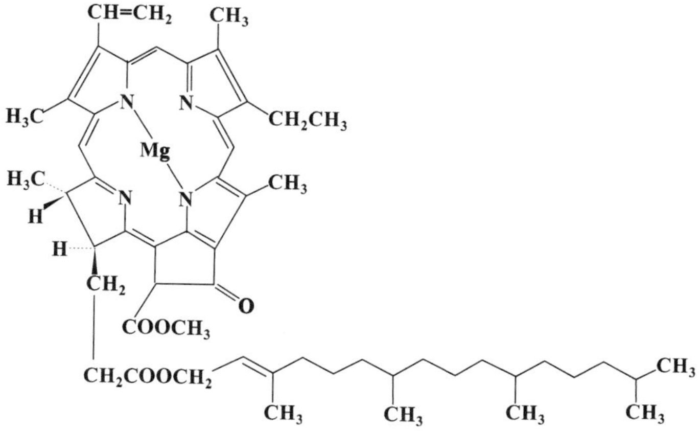

Chlorophyll

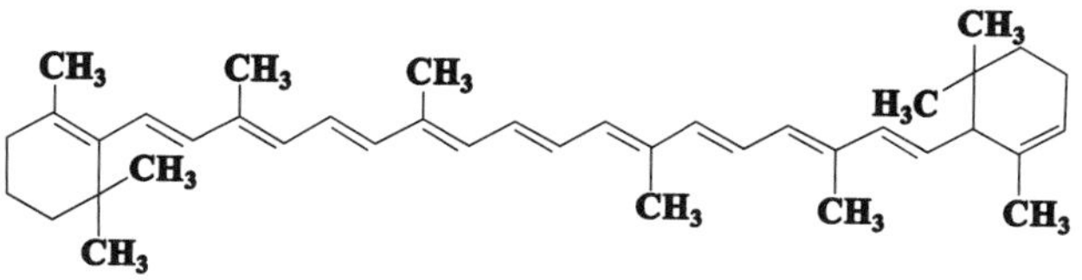

Carotene

Figure 4-10. Basic structure of chlorophyll and carotene (a carotenoid), two pigments involved in the light harvesting scheme of photosynthesis.

energy in the light harvesting complex of photosynthesis. Chlorophylls absorb light in the 430 to 680 nm spectrum, which is blue and red light, respectively. Green light is not absorbed, but rather reflected, giving plants their green color.

Carotenoids and xanthophylls also contribute to absorption of light and transfer of energy. They generally absorb light beyond the blue spectrum, which is the limit of chlorophyll absorption. Another important function of carotenoids is the protection of chlorophyll and the photosynthetic apparatus. Carotenoids prevent photooxidation which occurs when extreme quantities of light (UV) are absorbed so that free radicals of oxygen are produced. A consequence of these free radicals includes potential bleaching (or oxidation) of chlorophyll and destruction of membranes within the chlorophyll. Carotenoids quench or absorb the oxygen-free radicals, thus protecting the chlorophyll and membranes from light damage.

Other pigments in plants are anthocyanins. Anthocyanins absorb red to blue light and are generally responsible for coloring of flowers, fruits, and other plant parts. Anthocyanins also aid in plant defense and reproduction.

II. Dark Reactions. Products of the light reactions (or Z-scheme) of photosynthesis are ATP and NADPH (Figure 4-9). These products are used in a series of reactions known as dark reactions to produce carbohydrates (glucose). It involves the following reactions:

phosphoglyceraldehyde → fructose diphosphate → fructose phosphate → glucose phosphate → glucose

There are two basic reactions in which plants fix CO_2 into carbohydrates: (1) Calvin-Benson Cycle (or C_3 Cycle); and (2) Hatch and Slack (or C_4 Cycle).

A. Calvin-Benson Cycle (C_3 Cycle). The Calvin Cycle is the utilization of CO_2 to produce useable plant carbohydrates, such as sucrose and starch (Figure 4-11). It occurs in the mesophyll cells of the chloroplast and is composed of 13 reactions and 11 enzymes. Initial reactions involve the carboxylation of ribulose-1,5-bis phosphate (RuBP) and the addition of CO_2 to yield a three-carbon compound, 3-phosphoglyceraldehyde (3-PGA), hence the name, C_3 Cycle. After the production of the 3-carbon molecule, a series of reactions occurs producing 6-carbon containing sugars such as glucose and fructose. A summary reaction involves:

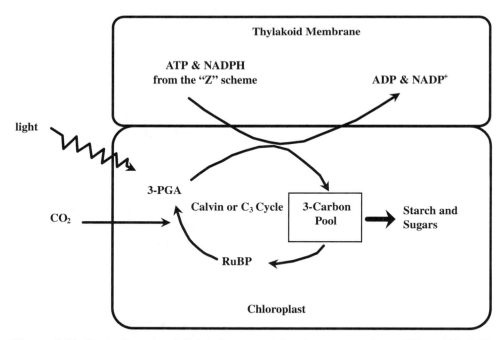

Figure 4-11. Basic diagram of Calvin-Benson cycle where energy from ATP and NADPH drives the reaction of carbon dioxide (CO_2) being combined with ribulose-bisphosphate (RuBP) to form the carbon sugar, 3-phosphoglyceric acid (or 3-PGA). The production of sugars such as glucose and fructose are used to synthesize large carbohydrate molecules such as sucrose, starch, cellulose, and others. This cycle is characteristic of cool-season turfgrasses.

General Reactions in the Calvin (or C₃) Cycle

$$6CO_2 + 12NADPH + 12H^+ + 18ATP + 12H_2O \rightarrow$$
$$C_6H_{12}O_6 + 18P_i + 18ADP + 12NADP^+$$

Cool-season turf species, such as creeping bentgrass, bluegrass, fescue, and rye-grass, use the Calvin Cycle for CO_2 fixation. C_3 plants have mesophyll cells which have low CO_2 concentration, therefore are not as efficient in the production of sugars and starches as warm-season grasses. Cool-season grasses, however, do not require full sunlight or as high a temperature for ATP and NADPH synthesis as warm-season grasses.

B. Hatch and Slack (C₄ Cycle). The Hatch and Slack cycle is another method used by warm-season plants to fix CO_2 and produce useable organic compounds (Figure 4-12). Carbon dioxide fixation begins in the mesophyll cells where it combines with 3-carbon containing phosphoenolpyruvate (PEP) to produce a 4-carbon compound called oxaloacetic acid (OAA), hence the C_4 Cycle name. As mentioned, C_3 plants, in contrast, initially produce a 3-carbon compound (3-PGA). Following OAA formation in C_4 plants, a quick conversion to either malic or aspartic acid occurs, followed by the transport across the membrane to bundle sheath cells. In the bundle sheath, a decarboxylation of the CO_2 occurs leaving a 3-carbon pyruvate molecule. The CO_2 is then refixed within the bundle sheath via the Calvin Cycle. C_4 plants shuttle CO_2 to bundle sheath cells out of mesophyll cells. Mesophyll cells of C_4 plants contain larger quantities of chloroplast, and therefore contain greater

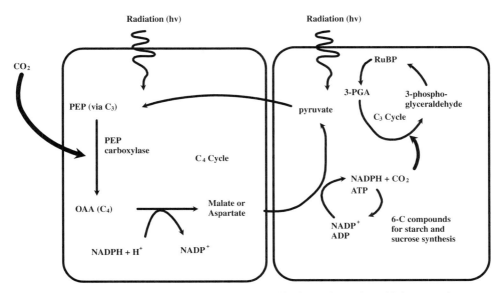

Figure 4-12. Basic diagram pathway of the Hatch-Slack (or C_4 cycle) which occurs in warm-season grasses. Phosphophenylpyruvate (PEP) and oxaloacetic acid (OAA) are involved in carbohydrate synthesis and are considered more efficient in carbohydrate synthesis and ATP production than cool-season grasses.

concentrations of CO_2. This allows C_4 plants to be much more efficient than C_3 plants in fixation of CO_2 and tolerate greater light intensity as well as temperature. C_4 plants are also much more water and nitrogen efficient because they require less of each per unit CO_2 fixed.

Carbohydrate Synthesis

There are two types of carbohydrates manufactured by C_3 or C_4 cycles, **starch** and **sucrose.** Starch is a **polysaccharide** (carbohydrate composed of many sugar molecules) and is the long-term food storage form in all major plant organs. It is mostly found in storage areas such as seeds and tubers, and can also be found in chloroplast, the site of its synthesis. Sucrose is the translocatable form and is a disaccharide (contains two sugar molecules). Sucrose is readily available for carbohydrate metabolism, and is readily transported throughout the plant through the phloem. The basic chemical properties and structures of carbohydrates are covered in **Chapter 3.** Cellulose, chitin, and starch represent the most important polysaccharides.

Synthesis. The ATP molecules originating from the Calvin Cycle begin the synthesis of starch and sucrose. Starch synthesis occurs in the chloroplast, whereas sucrose synthesis occurs in the cytosol. The production of sucrose and starch is a competing pathway determined by the phosphate (P_i) concentration in both the cytosol and chloroplast. When cystolic P_i is high, chloroplast triose-P molecules are transported to the cytosol in exchange for P_i where sucrose is produced. During respiration, ATP is reformed from ADP when glucose is oxidized to carbon dioxide and water. Synthesis and hydrolysis of ATP are as follows:

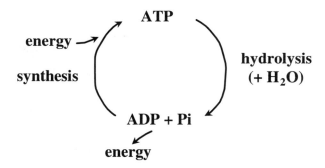

ATP is not used for long-term storage of energy. It is continuously being formed and used. Energy is stored in plants as starch and oils, and as fats and glycogen in animals.

RESPIRATORY METABOLISM

Respiratory metabolism is the utilization of sucrose and starch produced via C_3 and C_4 cycles. It is an aerobic process occurring in the mitochondria where the sugar molecules are split apart and the hydrogen atoms (that is, electrons plus their accompanying H^+) are removed from the carbon atoms and combine with oxygen, which is reduced to form water. The electrons go from a higher energy level to a lower one and thus energy is released. The entire process includes three main pathways: (1) glycolysis; (2) the Krebs Cycle (also called the citric acid or TCA cycle); and (3) oxidative phosphorylation (Figure 4-13).

Glycolysis

Glycolysis (meaning "sugar splitting") is the reversal of photosynthesis where sugar and starch molecules produced via photosynthesis are broken down, producing energy for plants in the form of ATP. Specifically, glycolysis is the conversion of glucose to a pair of 3-carbon molecules of pyruvic acid, and occurs in the cytoplasm of cells (Figure 4-13). Since glycolysis occurs in the cytoplasm, it is anaerobic; therefore, no oxygen is used and no CO_2 is released. Energy for the process is from the reduction of 2 NAD^+ to 2 NADH.

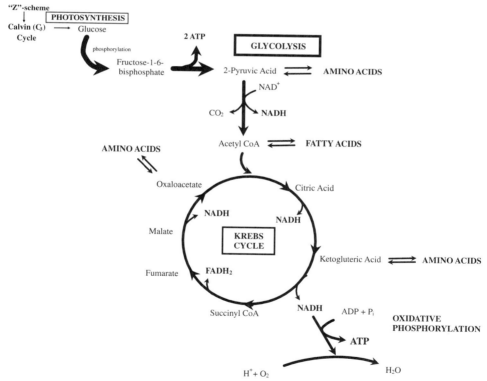

Figure 4-13. Mitochondrial located respiratory pathway of glycolysis, Kreb's cycle, and oxidative phosphorylation to produce ATP, NADH, and FADH. The end result is a release of stored energy from glucose, starch (fatty acids), and carbohydrates for plant use in the form of ATP and formation of water (H_2O).

General Reaction of Glycolysis

Glucose + 2NAD$^+$ + 2ADP^{-2} + 2H$_2$PO^{-4} →

2 pyruvic acid + 2NADH + 2H$^+$ + 2ATP^{-3} + 2H$_2$O

Glycolysis eventually yields 2 pyruvic acid and 4 molecules of ATP, although some is used during the process. Two molecules of ATP are used during the reaction, therefore only two ATP are gained. The pyruvic acid produced will be oxidized in the mitochondria in the next step of respiration, the Krebs Cycle (Figure 4-13).

Krebs Cycle

The Krebs Cycle describes the oxidation of pyruvic acid from glycolysis to produce inorganic compounds of ATP, NADH, and FADH as well as carbon skeletons used further for other plant functions such as amino acids, chlorophyll, and hormones (Figure 4-13). The resulting electrons are passed to the electron transport system. The pathway was discovered by English biochemist Hans A. Kreb in 1937. He named it the citric acid cycle, an important precursor in the pathway. Pyruvic acid produced during glycolysis is channeled to the mitochondria followed by a series of oxidation reactions to produce ATP and NADH.

The first step in the Krebs cycle is the oxidation (loss of CO_2) from the pyruvic acid and the synthesis with a sulfur-containing compound to produce acetyl CoA. Acetyl CoA combines with oxaloacetic acid (OAA) to produce citric acid. The pathway continues the oxidative decarboxylation of acetyl CoA to eventually produce CO_2 and H_2O. The two pyruvic acids synthesized in glycolysis produce two ATP. The production of NADH requires the removal and transfer of electrons from the organic acid intermediates to NAD$^+$ or ubiquinone to produce ubiquinol (FADH$_2$). The remaining carbon skeletons are important in the synthesis of other amino acids.

Krebs Cycle Reactions

2 pyruvic acid + 8NAD$^+$ + 2 ubiquinone + 2ADP + 2H$_2$PO^{-4} + 4H$_2$O →

2CO$_2$ + 2ATP + 2NADH + 2H$^+$ + 2 ubiquinol

Electron Transport and Oxidative Phosphorylation. The final step in respiration is the production of ATP. Electron transport consists of five complexes, which transfer electrons from NADH and/or FADH$_2$ (produced from Kreb's Cycle and Glycolysis) to O$_2$. Water eventually is formed and translocates protons, producing a proton gradient which is important for ATP production (Figure 4-13). Through the electron transport chain and oxidative phosphorylation, three ATP are produced for every molecule of NADH oxidized to NAD$^+$ and 2 ATP produced for every FADH$_2$ oxidized to FAD$^+$.

Photorespiration

The enzyme responsible for CO_2 fixation in the Calvin Cycle (C_3) is Ribulose bisphosphate carboxylase/oxygenase (designated as **RuBP carboxylase**). RuBP carboxylase can react with O_2 as well as with CO_2. High levels of O_2 favor the oxygenase activity whereas high levels of CO_2 favor the carboxylase activity. The oxygenase activity converts RuBP to phosphoglycolic acid and 3-phosphoglyceric acid instead of two molecules of 3-PGA (the normal carboxylase activity of RuBP carboxylase/oxygenase). This oxygenase activity is termed **photorespiration** (Figure 4-14). It is not true respiration as in Glycolysis or the Krebs Cycle where carbon compounds are converted to CO_2, ATP, and carbon compounds with evolution of O_2. Photorespiration, therefore, in C_3 plants is considered wasteful and reduces photosynthetic efficiency and plant productivity. In C_4 plants, PEP carboxylase is not affected by O_2 as RuBP carboxylase is in C_3 plants; thus, in C_4 plants, photorespiration is not significant.

Because C_3 plants cannot concentrate CO_2 as C_4 plants do, their stomates must stay open longer to capture necessary CO_2 levels to incorporate into carbohydrates. However, the more stomates stay open, the larger the amount of water lost via transpiration. Thus C_4 plants lose less water per unit of CO_2 fixed compared to C_3

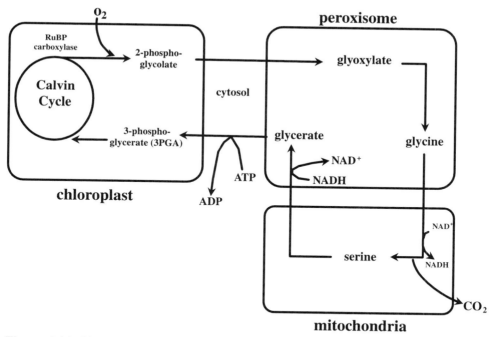

Figure 4-14. Photorespiration pathway in C_3 plants where normal carbon dioxide (CO_2) levels are depleted due to closed stomates to reduce transpiration. This favors oxygen (O_2) uptake and utilization and seemingly wasteful carbon dioxide loss through sugar and carbohydrate utlization with neither ATP or NADH production as with regular respiration. Photorespiration is a key reason C_3 grasses grow poorly outside their naturally adapted cooler regions.

plants and are more efficient at utilizing water and in photosynthesis. Photorespiration and prolonged transpiration during summer months typically weaken C_3 plants.

Overall, energy in the form of ATP required to fix CO_2 into carbohydrates is initially higher in C_4 plants. Five molecules of ATP are required per CO_2 fixed in C_4 plants while only three molecules of ATP per CO_2 fixed are required in C_3 plants. However, additional ATPs are consumed in photorespiration in C_3 plants.

Phosphate Bonds—Energy Providers of ATP

Adenosine triphosphate (ATP) provides energy for all cells including their biosynthesis (Figure 4-15). The hydrolysis of ATP into ADP releases energy that is subsequently used in cellular processes. As shown earlier, the hydrolysis of ATP involves the following reaction:

ATP Hydrolysis Reaction

$$ATP + H_2O \leftrightarrow ADP + Pi + H^+ + energy$$

When combined with water, ATP provides the energy to couple a reaction where there is an overall decrease in free energy. Bonds are considered "high energy" bonds when there is a release of greater than -25 kJ/mole. Hydrolysis of ATP releases about -30 kJ/mole (or -7.3 kcal/mole) of energy, therefore it is a "high energy" bond. The high energy is caused from the attachment of the phosphoryl groups, referred to as *phosphoanhydride bonds*. These single bonds are highly unstable because of the high competition between phosphoryl groups for the two pairs of oxygen electrons (Figure 4-16). Additional instability is from electrostatic repulsion between the two O^- within the phosphoryl groups, creating additional energy.

LIPIDS

Lipids are usually nonpolar organic compounds that are insoluble in water, but soluble in nonpolar organic solvents such as diethyl ether and chloroform. As a result of being insoluble in water, lipids can be stored in plants for long periods

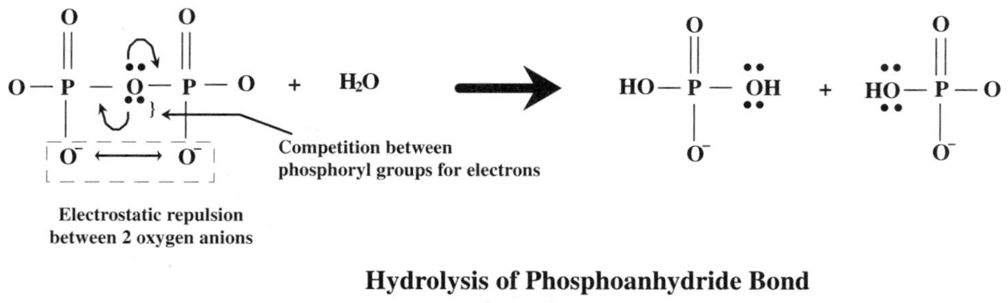

Hydrolysis of Phosphoanhydride Bond

Figure 4-15. Hydrolysis of phosphate bonds of ATP showing competition between phosphoryl groups of ATP for electrons and electrostatic repulsion of oxygen anions creating -30 kj/mole (or -7.3 kcal/mole) of energy per ATP.

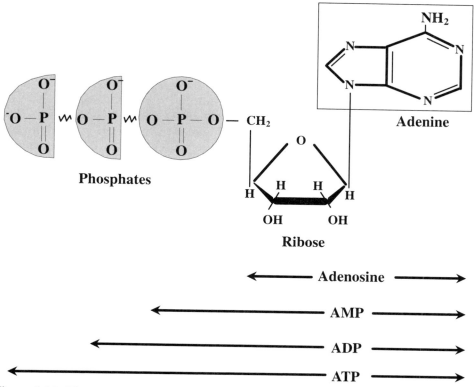

Figure 4-16. The structure of adenosine triphosphate (ATP), diphosphate (ADP), and monophosphate (AMP). A phosphoester bond links the first phosphate group to the ribose of adenosine, whereas phosphoanhydride bonds, designated by squiggly lines, link the second and third phosphate groups to the molecule.

without washing out. Lipids can be classified into an enormous group of compounds with diverse and complex chemical structure and function (Table 4-1). They are highly involved in seed germination and storage of carbohydrates for seedling growth prior to photosynthesis developing. Carbon in lipids is the most reduced form of carbon in plants; therefore, when metabolized, lipids produce the highest quantity of carbohydrates. The majority of all lipids are derivatives of fatty acids. The most common lipids are **triglycerols,** which are esters of long-chain carboxylic acids and glycerol. They have the general formula:

$$CH_2OOCR'$$
$$|$$
$$CHOOCR''$$
$$|$$
$$CH_2OOCR'''$$

where R', R'', and R''' are usually different organic (alkyl) groups.

Lipids are similar to carbohydrates in plants because they lack nitrogen and sulfur and contain mostly carbon, hydrogen, and oxygen. Their chemical structure produces fatty and oily substances containing hydrophobic and water insoluble properties. Lipids are classified into three main classes: (1) fats and oils; (2) waxes; and (3) lipids containing phosphorus (referred to as *phospholipids*).

Fats and Oils. Fats and oils are found throughout plants in globules. **Fats** are solid triglycerides while **oils** are liquid triglycerides. A molecule of fat is composed of two components: (1) glycerol, a 3-carbon molecule; and, (2) a fatty acid. Fatty acids are carboxylic acids (COOH) with a carbon chain attached containing 12 to 24 carbons (Table 4-3). Fatty acids are either *saturated* or *unsaturated*. **Saturated fatty acids** have the maximum number of hydrogen ions bonded to them (referred to as being saturated) and thus do not contain any double bonds and therefore cannot bond to additional hydrogen atoms. **Unsaturated fatty acids,** meanwhile, have one or more double bonds since not all of the exchange sites are bonded to hydrogen atoms; thus, double bonds can form. Fatty acids have many functions in plants including food reserves especially in seed germination, protectants such as waxes and oils, and structural components (Table 4-1). Fats and oils are concentrated foods because their oxidation yields much more energy per gram than proteins and carbohydrates.

Unsaturated fatty acids have substantially lower melting points than saturated fatty acids, and therefore tend to be a liquid rather than a solid. For example, stearic acid (a 18-carbon fatty acid) has a melting point of 70°C; whereas oleic acid (18:1) melts at 13°C; while linolenic acid (18:2) melts at −5°C and linolenic acid (18:3) melts at −11°C. Plant oils (fatty acids) are liquid at room temperature due to their larger proportion of unsaturated fatty acids than animal oils such as lard, which are solid or semisolid at the same temperature. The double bonds associated with unsaturated fatty acids increase the space occupied by fatty acid side chains,

TABLE 4-3. Common Fatty Acids in Plants

Fatty Acid	Symbol[a]	Structure
Saturated fatty acids (contain no double bonds)		
Lauric acid	12:0	$CH_3(CH_2)_{10}COOH$
Myristic acid	14:0	$CH_3(CH_2)_{12}COOH$
Palmitic acid	16:0	$CH_3(CH_2)_{14}COOH$
Stearic acid	18:0	$CH_3(CH_2)_{16}COOH$
Arachidic acid	20:0	$CH_3(CH_2)_{18}COOH$
Behenic acid	22:0	$CH_3(CH_2)_{20}COOH$
Lignoceric acid	24:0	$CH_3(CH_2)_{22}COOH$
Unsaturated fatty acids (contain double bonds)		
Oleic acid	18:1	$CH_3(CH_2)_7CH{=}CH(CH_2)_7COOH$
Linoleic acid	18:2	$CH_3(CH_2)_4(CH{=}CHCH_2)(CH{=}CH(CH_2)_7COOH$
Linolenic acid	18:3	$CH_3(CH_2)_4(CH{=}CHCH_2)(CH{=}CHCH_2)(CH{=}CH(CH_2)_4COOH$
Roughanic acid	16:3	$CH_3(CH_2)(CH{=}CHCH_2)(CH{=}CHCH_2)(CH{=}CH(CH_2)_5COOH$
Erucic acid	22:1	$CH_3(CH_2)_7CH{=}CH(CH_2)_{11}COOH$
Arachidonic acid	20:4	—

[a](No. of carbon atoms: no. of double bonds).

causing unsaturated triglyceride molecules to lie farther from each other. This increased distance of separation decreases the attractive forces the unsaturated molecules exert on each other, lowering the melting points and promoting liquids for unsaturated fatty acids.

Waxes and Cutins. Waxes and cutins are fatty acids combined with long chains of alcohols. The length of the fatty acid chain determines a wax or cutin, with waxes containing longer fatty acid chains. Plant waxes are an integral ingredient in cell walls, while cutin covers the epidermis of stems, leaves, and fruits. Both waxes and cutins are important in water conservation and plant protection.

Phospholipids. *Phospholipids* are lipids containing a phosphate group giving them a hydrophilic (water soluble) characteristic, unlike the hydrophobic (water insoluble) nature of fats (Figure 4-17). The structure of phospholipids produces both a hydrophilic (phosphate group) head and a hydrophobic side (or tail). This property provides an excellent ingredient to building cellular membranes. The hydrophilic outer layer creates external water pressure on the membrane, producing stability (Figure 4-18). Various sterol structures also are found in cell walls (Figure 4-19). Sterols are lipids with ring structure and are a constituent of certain hor-

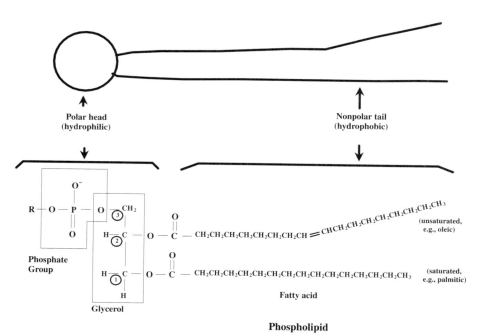

Figure 4-17. A phospholipid molecule consists of two fatty acid molecules linked to a glycerol molecule, as in a triglyceride, while the third carbon of glycerol is linked to the phosphate group of a phosphate-containing molecule. The phospholipid tail is nonpolar and uncharged and is therefore hydrophobic (water-hating or insoluble); the polar head containing the phosphate and R groups is hydrophilic (water-loving or soluble).

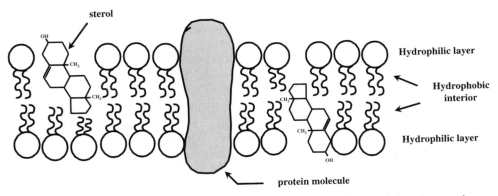

Figure 4-18. Lipid bilayer of cell membranes showing the two layers giving the membrane stability with protein molecules randomly interspersed and used for solute movement. The outer layer contains phospholipids, which are hydrophilic by extending outward into the water with their hydrophobic tails inward away from the water. Sterols also have a relatively small hydrophilic head (made of one hydroxyl group) and a longer hydrophobic portion.

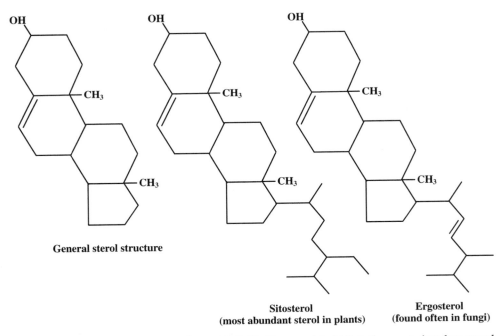

Figure 4-19. General structure of a sterol (left); Sitosterol (middle), the most abundant sterol in green plants; and Ergosterol (right), a sterol found frequently in fungi. Another sterol, cholesterol (not shown), is common in animals.

mones. All steroids have three six-membered rings and one five-membered ring. Certain fungicides called sterol inhibitors (or SIs) control fungi by inhibiting sterol production and formation in their cell walls.

Cell membranes provide cellular structure and integrity by policing the transport system in and out of cells. Membranes also maintain integrity of cellular organelles. Lipid structure, consisting of a polar bi-layer (Figure 4-18), prevents the free diffusion of hydrophilic molecules in and out of cells and organelles. Contained within the bi-layer are protein pumps and channels regulating the influx and outflow of ions. Some of these channels require ATP, such as proton pumps, because ions are being moved against an electrochemical gradient. Other channels move ions by diffusion.

NUCLEIC ACIDS

The characteristics of organisms that are transmitted to subsequent generations are located in the **chromosomes** present in cell nucleus. Chromosomes are long molecules of DNA with bases held together, in sequence. Modern genetics originated when chemical analysis revealed that chromosomes contain two classes of molecules: proteins and nucleic acids. **Nucleic acids** are acidic substances in the nuclei of cells that store genetic information and that direct the synthesis of proteins. The nucleic acids occur in the cell in two forms: **ribonucleic acid (RNA)** and **deoxyribonucleic acid (DNA).** The inheritance message is coded in the structure of DNA. Chromosomes (46 in humans) are nuclear structures containing long, tightly coiled strands of DNA. The **gene** is the segment of DNA within the chromosome that contains the code which controls a single trait or a single reaction in cellular metabolism. Genes direct the synthesis of the polypeptide and proteins that serve as enzymes and hormones.

RNA differs chemically from DNA in that: (1) the sugar molecule it has is ribose as its 5-carbon pentose sugar while DNA has 2-deoxyribose as the sugar subunit in the nucleotides. DNA is missing an oxygen in its heterocyclic ring in each sugar group which is what **deoxy** means, "without oxygen." (2) RNA also has the nitrogenous base, uracil; whereas DNA has thymine, a methylated derivative of uracil. (3) RNA also consists of a single helical chain very similar to half of a double helix DNA molecule and occurs principally outside the nucleus in the cytoplasm. DNA stores and transmits genetic information, while RNA is involved in protein synthesis where it takes the DNA's genetic information to another part of the cell, called the **ribosomes,** the site of protein synthesis.

Nucleic acids (DNA and RNA) act as the memory storage in plants and consist of long chains of nucleotides just as proteins consist of long chains of amino acids. A *nucleoside* is a nitrogenous base (adenine, thymine, cytosine, uracil, or guanine) plus a deoxyribose sugar while a *nucleotide* is a nucleoside plus a phosphate group. Nucleotides are the monomeric units of a nucleic acid and are the repeating units or building blocks of nucleic acids consisting of two classes of nitrogenous bases, *purine* or *pyrimidine* (complex ring molecule containing nitrogen), plus a pentose (5-carbon) sugar, and a phosphate group (Figure 4-20). Pyrimidines contain a single ring and examples include cytosine, uracil, and thymine. Purines are double-ringed molecules, and examples include adenine and guanine. In nucleotide synthesis,

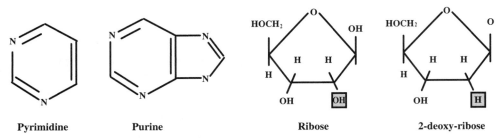

Figure 4-20. Basic nucleic acids in plants. Pyrimidine and purine represent the nitrogenous base. Ribose and deoxyribose are pentose sugars responsible for the polymerization of nucleotides.

pyrimidines and purines act as nitrogenous bases and they are connected by the five carbon sugars, either deoxyribose or ribose, which attach to the phosphate groups as phosphodiester bonds (Figure 4-21).

Nucleotides are joined around a common axis as a single strand of nucleotides as with RNA or produce two strands of nucleotides wound together (a double helix) about a common axis resembling a spiral ladder or coiled phone cord as with DNA (Figure 4-22). Strands of nucleotides on each side represent the uprights of the ladder, which are held together by alternating phosphate and pentose sugar molecules. The rungs of the ladder are paired purine or pyrimidine molecules held weakly by hydrogen bonding occurring between **complementary** adenine (A) and thymine (T) nucleotides and complementary guanine (G) and cytosine (C) nucleotides in the two antiparallel helix strands. The ladder as a whole is twisted to form a double helix. This double helix structure allows DNA to produce complementary strands.

DNA is found in the nucleus of all plant cells as well as chromosomes and plastids in mitochondria (Figure 4-23). The sequencing of DNA determines not only the genetic information of plants, but the primary structure of amino acid polymerization into proteins. The particular sequence of purines and pyrimidines along one side of the double helix may vary without limit, but once the sequence along one side is given, the sequence along the other side is fixed by the pairing rule. Cytosine is always paired with guanine (designated C—G) or thymine is paired with adenine (T—A). It is this fixed pattern of pairing that makes it possible for DNA to duplicate itself exactly during cell division and to serve as a pattern or code for transmitting "instruction" to the rest of the cell.

Polyploidy refers to the number of chromosomes sets in a cell. Haploid (1n) is one set; diploid (2n), two sets. A **polyploid** is any number more than the diploid. A triploid (3n) has three sets of chromosomes while a tetraploid (4n) has four. Polyploid plants are usually more vigorous than diploids, but some are sterile. Most bermudagrasses, for example, used for golf greens are sterile triploids (3n), and thus must be vegetatively reproduced (or planted).

DNA Replication and Mutations. DNA has the ability to split into two and make exact copies of itself. This process is vital to all living organisms. If DNA duplication did not occur, cells could not divide into new cells and still retain the full

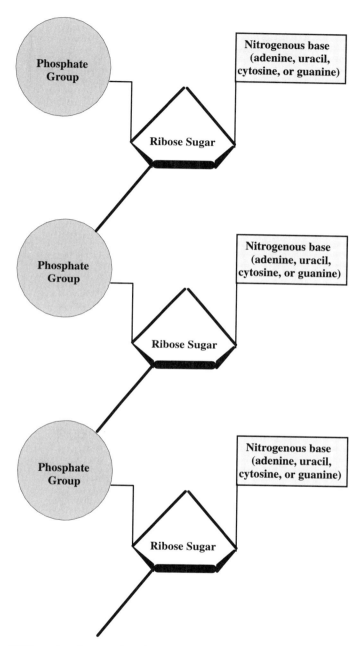

Figure 4-21. RNA molecules consist of a single chain of nucleotides (shown) in which the sugar subunit of one nucleotide is linked to the phosphate group of the next nucleotide. DNA molecules, in contrast, consist of two chains of nucleotides coiled around each other in a double helix. A nucleoside is a dexoyribose sugar unit plus a nitrogenous base of either adenine, thymine, cytosine, or guanine.

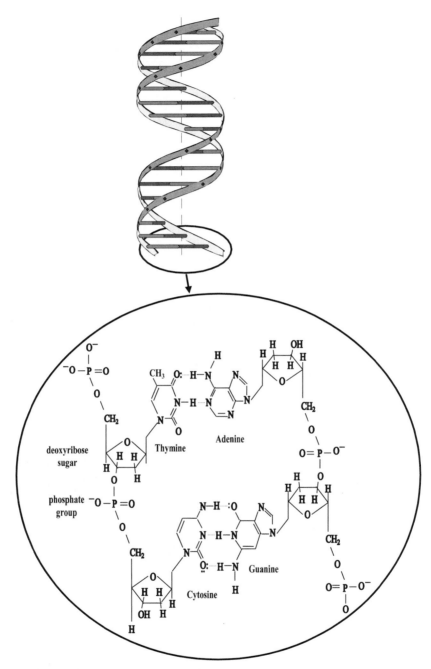

Figure 4-22. DNA consists of two strands of nucleotides wound together in a double helix arrangement about a common axis resembling a spiral ladder or coiled phone cord. Strands of nucleotides on each side represent the uprights of the ladder, which are held together by alternating phosphate and pentose sugar molecules. The rungs of the ladder are paired purine or pyrimidine molecules held weakly by hydrogen bonding occurring between complementary adenine (A) and thymine (T) nucleotides, and complementary guanine (G) and cytosine (C) nucleotides in the two antiparallel helix strands.

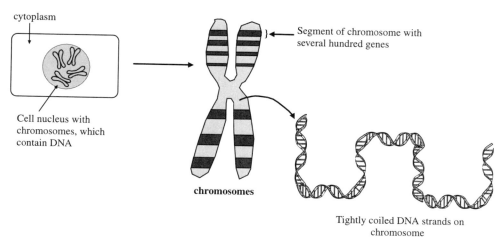

cytoplasm

Segment of chromosome with
several hundred genes

Cell nucleus with
chromosomes, which
contain DNA

chromosomes

Tightly coiled DNA strands on
chromosome

Figure 4-23. Chromosomes located in the nucleus of cells carries genes composed of tightly coiled DNA strands on chromosomes.

store of genetic information. In the process of DNA replication (or duplication), purine-pyrimidine pairs in the "rungs" of the "ladder" draw apart, a process that resembles the opening of a zipper. This leaves unpaired purine or pyrimidine bases attached to the rest of the nucleotide units on the separate chains. As the chains separate, however, single chemical nucleotides, derived from food and always present in the nucleus, attach themselves to appropriate unpaired purine or pyrimidine units. A thymine nucleotide will attach itself to an unpaired adenine unit, and a guanine nucleotide will attach itself to an unpaired cytosine unit. In this process, the same purine-pyrimidine pairs are formed as were originally present.

In this process of replication, an occasional change or "error" does occur in the formation of the nucleotide chains. In such a case, the altered copy is called a **mutation** and it can lead to offspring with altered traits. Mutations are abrupt inheritable changes brought about by alternations in a gene or a chromosome or by an increase in chromosome number. Plants showing these changes are called **mutants.**

Mutations are produced by internal disorders, such as inaccurate gene duplication, and by natural external forces, such as severe temperature changes and radiation. They are induced experimentally by use of atomic radiation, X-rays, chemicals (such as **colchicine**), and sudden temperature changes. In laboratories, plants are exposed with gamma or X-ray radiation to produce mutations. Researchers check the results for new types of plants with desirable features. Thousands of plants may be treated before a desirable trait is obtained.

Most gene mutations are harmful to those when they are transmitted. Such mutations often are eliminated by their failure to be able to reproduce. However, some gene mutations are favorable, and such mutations tend to remain in the species and gradually become more common than the genes they replaced. Over a long period, the accumulation of favorable mutations can lead to the appearance of a new species, better equipped to survive in the natural environment. Plant breeders, for example, are always searching for mutations called somatic variation where they explore populations of plants trying to identify new and, hopefully, better adapted plants which are able to survive harsher environments. Oftentimes, when vegetatively reproduced plants are used, such as sterile hybrid bermudagrasses on golf greens, breeders search existing greens for patches of denser, pest-free turf that appears to better survive the harsh environments often experienced on golf greens. Breeders also introduce mutations, most often by exposing plant to radiation. Although most of the irradiated plants eventually die, some produce plants that possess the characteristics the breeders are searching for. Many of the new "ultradwarf" bermudagrasses used on greens are believed to be natural chance mutations and result from selecting plants apparently better able to survive. 'TifEagle' bermudagrass is an example of irradiating a parent sterile bermudagrass ('Tifway II', in this case) to produce a new species with desired characteristics.

Protein Synthesis. Based on the genetic information provided by DNA, RNA is involved in protein synthesis as demonstrated in Figure 4-4 and consists of three molecular species: *messenger RNA* (or mRNA); *ribosomal RNA* (or rRNA); and *transfer RNA* (or tRNA). Protein synthesis takes place at the *ribosomes,* which are small structures rich in RNA that are present in the cytoplasm. The DNA directs the synthesis of RNA in the nucleus by lining up the necessary sequence of RNA bases along its own spiral chain. Some of this RNA functions as messenger RNA and some as transfer RNA. Messenger RNA carries the information stored on DNA (the "message) to the cell's cytoplasm where protein synthesis occurs. Transfer RNA finds and transports (or "transfers") each amino acid to the site where the peptide bonds are formed as instructed by the mRNA. A specific protein is formed from a specific sequence of amino acids from the line-up transfer RNA molecules as determined by the sequence of the messenger RNA bases. After a protein is formed, it becomes detached from the RNA and begins to perform its functions in the cell. The transfer RNA and messenger RNA now separate and begin to repeat the process.

A **codon** consists of three bases and codes for a specific amino acid. An **anticodon** is part of transfer RNA that decodes the "genetic message" from messenger RNA.

PLANT HORMONES

Plant growth and development is dictated by chemical substances produced by the plant called hormones. Plants, unlike mammals, lack a central nervous system, therefore rely on chemical messengers (hormones) for specific growth responses to environmental stimuli. Hormones operate in plants at very low concentrations and are often triggered by environmental factors. There are five main hormones in plants, three growth promoters and two growth inhibitors (Figure 4-24).

Growth Promoters

Auxins. Auxins were discovered by Charles Darwin around the 1880s when he observed a phototrophic leaning response of grass seedlings toward a light source. Auxin is a growth promoter by increasing cell elongation. There are several auxins

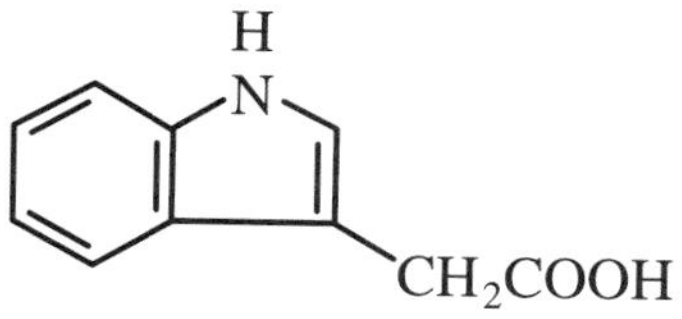

Indole-3-acetic Acid

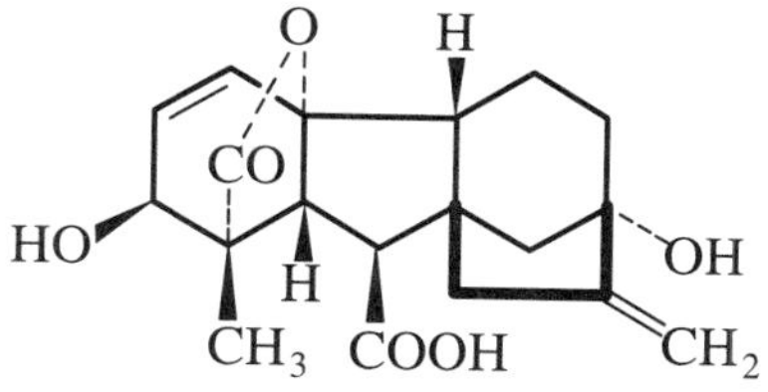

Gibberellic Acid

$CH_2{=}CH_2$

Ethylene

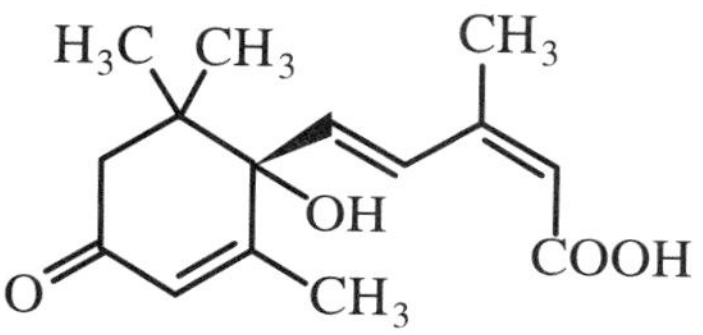

Abscisic Acid

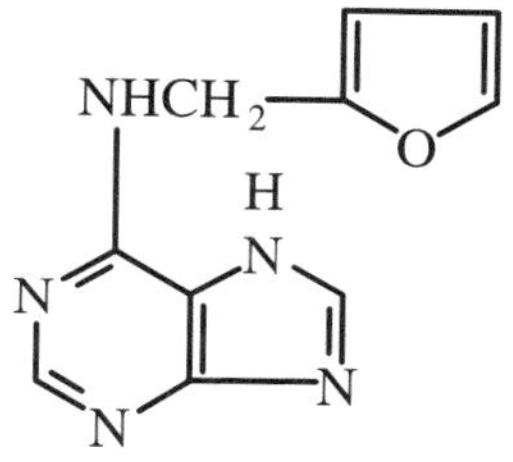

Kinetin

Figure 4-24. Chemical structures of the five major hormones in plants: Indole-3-acetic acid (IAA); Gibberellic acid; Ethylene; Abscisic acid (IAA); and, Kinetin (cytokinin).

found in plants, however indole-3-acetic acid (IAA) is the most prevalent. Other auxins include phenylacetic acid, naphthalene acetic acid (NAA), and 2,4-dichlorophenoxy acid (2,4-D). Auxins are produced in meristematic (actively growing regions of plants) areas and can be translocated throughout the plant. This is most obvious in phototrophic responses similar to Darwin's observations. Phototropism is the plant response to light by bending toward the light source to maximize light absorption. Auxins promote cell elongation of cells opposite the light source inducing light-induced bending. In addition to cell elongation, auxins also influence cell division, cell differentiation, and apical dominance. Apical dominance inhibits lateral bud development, delays leaf senescence and fruit ripening. In turf, apical dominance is eliminated when mowed, therefore stolon and lateral growth is increased when their vertical growth is lost. Auxins also have been found to promote flowering, fruit set, and root development at low concentrations.

Auxin-related growth response requires very low concentrations. At times, auxin levels may exceed the required amounts and inhibit growth and at times be lethal. A good example is the herbicide 2,4-D, which is an auxin-like herbicide that can stimulate growth at low concentrations but inhibit growth at higher levels.

Gibberellins. Gibberellins were discovered by Japanese scientists in the 1950s after observing the excessive growth of rice plants after fungal invasion of *Gib-*

berella fujikuroi. Gibberellins are very similar to auxins in their function and site of production. There are over 80 gibberellins in plants; however, the most important are in GA_3, GA_4, and GA_7. Gibberellins influence cell elongation and division (like auxins). In addition, they also promote growth of dwarf plants, stimulate flowering during cold temperatures (termed *vernalization*), break seed dormancy, and promote germination and seed production without pollination (termed *parenthogenesis*). Important in turf, gibberellins are commercially available and aid grass color following cold-stress or to reverse the effects of gibberellin-inhibiting plant growth regulators.

The chemistry of gibberellins is also important in many plant growth regulators in turf. Interference with gibberellin biosynthesis by these regulators can inhibit or slow cell elongation. Examples of commercial gibberellin plant growth inhibitors include trinexapac-ethyl, paclobutrazol, flurprimidol, and fenarimol. Several specific sites during GA synthesis are interfered with or altered by these PGRs (Figure 4-25).

Cytokinins. The primary function of cytokinins is promoting *cytokinesis,* or cell division. Cytokinins are derivatives of adenine (purine), which as mentioned previously, is important in production of nucleic acids. Kinetin is an adenine-derived cytokinin produced when DNA is broken down. Cytokinin synthesis occurs mainly in root tips and can be transported freely throughout the vascular system. Additional synthesis occurs in meristematic regions such as cambium, vegetative apices, and younger leaves. The main functions of cytokinins involve cell division and cell enlargement, delaying plant aging and leaf senescence through delaying chlorophyll

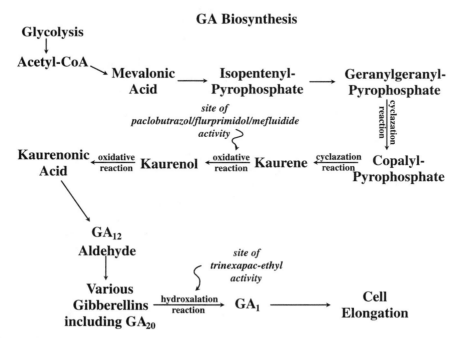

Figure 4-25. Site of action of several commercial plant growth regulators which disrupt gibberellic acid (GA) production in plants.

breakdown, and replacing light requirements for seed germination, pigment synthesis, and chloroplast development.

Growth Inhibitors

Ethylene. Ethylene is a gas in plants that is largely responsible for promoting plant aging, senescence, and fruit ripening in fleshy fruits. Ethylene also inhibits root growth, lateral bud development, increases membrane permeability, and causes epinastic (downward curving) of leaves. Ethylene production coincides with high auxin production. Primary synthesis of ethylene occurs in the shoots when methionine (a sulfur-containing amino acid) is degraded, releasing ethylene gas. A commercial plant growth regulator, ethephon, causes ethylene production in plants which then restricts certain growth parameters such as sucker production in tobacco and vegetative growth in certain turfgrasses.

Abscisic Acid (ABA). ABA was discovered in 1965 when scientists observed that two physiological functions of abscission and dormancy in plants were caused by the same compound. ABA is present in all plants, inhibiting coleoptile growth and promoting senescence and abscission by blocking DNA and protein syntheses. ABA is produced in green tissues, predominately in chloroplasts. ABA levels increase with stress factors including flooding, drought, salinity, injury, and starvation.

PRACTICE PROBLEMS

1. Define biochemistry and how it relates to the growth and development of plants. (*Biochemistry defines the pathways between the chemical and biology aspects of plants. It explains relationships between plant cell formation and function important in metabolic and mechanical activities.*)

2. The light reactions of photosynthesis, or the "Z-scheme," convert light energy to produce what important molecules? Identify these molecules and discuss their use in plant metabolism. (ATP *and* NADPH *are both used for carbon dioxide fixation, or the dark reactions of the* C_3 *and* C_4 *Cycle.*)

3. Explain why C_4 (warm-season) turfgrasses can tolerate higher temperatures than C_3 (cool-season) turfgrasses. (C_4 *plants shuttle* CO_2 *to bundle sheath cells out of mesophyll cells. Mesophyll cells contain larger quantities of chloroplast, therefore contain greater concentrations of* O_2, *which would decrease the efficacy of rubisco (acceptor molecule of* CO_2 *fixation). This allows* C_4 *plants to be much more efficient than* C_3 *plants in fixation of* CO_2 *and tolerate greater light intensity as well as temperature.* C_4 *plants are also much more water efficient because they require less water to fix* CO_2 *than* C_3 *plants.*)

4. Identify the products of the dark reactions of photosynthesis and their usage in plant reactions. (*Sucrose and starch are produced from* C_3 *and* C_4 *reactions and then are used in respiratory metabolism to produce ATP, NADH, and FADH.*)

5. Pyruvic acid, produced from glycolysis, is channeled to the mitochondria where a series of reactions occur to produce what important structures? (*ATP, NADH, FADH, and carbon skeletons used in amino acid biosynthesis.*)

6. How do proteins differ from carbohydrates and lipids? (*Proteins, unlike carbohydrates and lipids, have nitrogen in their structure.*)

7. Identify 3 locations of protein synthesis and define a protein. (*Cytoplasm, chloroplast, and mitochondria. Proteins are unbranched polymer chains of amino acids, sometimes 100 to 1,000 chains long, responsible for cell growth, differentiation, and reproduction.*)

8. List the characteristics of the following three groups of lipids: fats, phospholipids, sterols. (*Fats—glycerol esters of fatty acids, oxidized to produce energy; phospholipids—fat-containing phosphate group and nitrogenous base, found in cell membranes; sterols—lipids with ring structure, often a component of cell membranes, constituent of certain hormones.*)

9. How does an enzyme function as a biological catalyst? (*Enzymes are protein molecules that reduce the activation energy and time needed for a reaction to occur by forming an intermediate complex with a particular substrate.*)

10. Explain the structure of phospholipids and their importance in cellular membrane integrity. (*Phospholipids produce a hydrophilic (phosphate group) and hydrophobic (lipid) side. The hydrophilic outer layer creates external water pressure on the membrane, producing stability. Phospholipids are also important in the passage of nutrients in and out of cells.*)

11. Briefly discuss the energy release during the hydrolysis of ATP. (*ATP is the energy source for many of the biosynthesis reactions in plants. During hydrolysis (reaction with water) of ATP, the phosphoryl groups are broken and ADP is produced. This process is known as phosphorylation. The phosphoryl groups are highly unstable because of the high competition between phosphoryl groups for the two pairs of oxygen electrons. During hydrolysis, these "high energy" bonds are broken creating −30 kJ/mole ATP.*)

12. What is the importance of nucleic acids? (*These control biochemical synthesis of protein and the transfer of genetic material during cell reproduction.*)

13. What are the components of DNA and RNA? (*DNA—a nucleotide with the bases adenine, thymine, guanine, and cytosine; RNA—a nucleotide with the bases adenine, uracil, guanine, and cytosine.*)

14. List the complementary strand for the following DNA strand: (*Since adenine (A) and thymine (T) form complementary pairs, as do cytosine (C) and guanine (G), the complementary strand would be*):

$$A - A - G - T - T - G - C - C - A - T$$
$$(T - T - C - A - A - C - G - G - T - A)$$

15. What function does messenger and transfer RNA perform? (*Messenger RNA transcribes the genetic code from DNA molecules into the ribosomes where amino-acid-bearing transfer RNA molecules "read" and translate the transcribed code to form protein.*)

16. Identify the 5 major plant hormones and indicate if they are a growth promoter or inhibitor. (*Growth promoters: auxins, gibberellins, and cytokinins; Growth inhibitors: abscisic acid and ethylene.*)

17. Many plant growth regulars (PGRs) in turf inhibit vertical growth. Name a PGR currently used and identify how it interferes with plant hormones. (*Trinexapac-ethyl, paclobutrazol, flurprimidol, and fenarimol interfere with gibberellin biosynthesis, therefore slowing or inhibiting cell elongation. 2,4-D is an auxin-like herbicide producing toxic levels of auxins, inhibiting growth.*)

CHAPTER 5

SOIL CHEMICAL PROPERTIES

INTRODUCTION

Plants and soil exist in an integral relationship. Along with sunlight, turfgrass plants require air, water, and nutrients, which soil provides. The physical characteristics of soil influence aeration, water retention, and drainage. The chemical reactions between plants and soil affect the root-zone environment and nutrient availability. Some of these reactions include influences on soil pH and salinity, organic matter decomposition, and retention of nutrients. These properties not only directly influence the grass stand but also indirectly influence other soil characteristics such as soil aggregation, pesticide leaching, and disease activity. Therefore an appreciation of soil chemical properties will improve a manager's ability to grow healthy plants.

Soil pH

Possibly the most important chemical property in soil is **acidity.** Soil acidity can have a pronounced effect on plant nutrient availability, plant rooting and health, pesticide effectiveness, and microbial activity. Acidity is a measurement of the hydrogen ion (H^+) concentration, referred to as pH. As discussed in **Chapter 2,** pH is defined mathematically as the negative logarithm of the hydrogen ion concentration ($-\log [H^+]$) and is a measurement of the relative acidity or basicity of a substance.

Soil pH has many effects on plants, with the greatest being the effect on nutrient availability. For example, when the soil pH value is less than 5, aluminum (Al), iron (Fe), and manganese (Mn) become highly soluble and may be in high enough concentrations to be toxic to plants, causing stunting and nutritional imbalances (Figure 5-1). Also, low pH increases the solubility of heavy metals which can be toxic to plants. Conversely, at higher pH values (>7.0), nutrients such as phosphorus (P), iron, manganese, copper (Cu), boron (B), and zinc (Zn) are less soluble

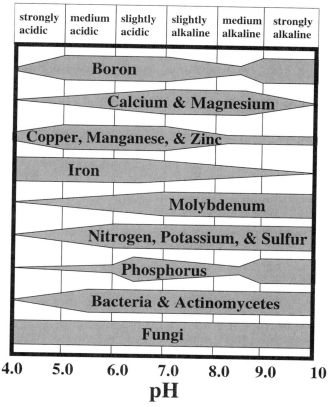

Figure 5-1. Effects of soil pH on soil nutrient availability and soil microbial populations. The relative availability of each element at a specific soil pH is indicated by the width of the bar.

and therefore become increasingly unavailable for plant uptake and cause reduced growth and chlorosis. Molybdenum (Mo) availability actually increases at high pH. Therefore, a pH range exists for each nutrient that is most beneficial for plant growth and development (Figure 5-1).

Also essential for plant growth and development are soil microorganism populations and diversity, which are also influenced by soil pH. Bacteria naturally present for thatch decomposition will decline as soil pH is reduced. Soil pH values lower than 5.0 do not favor microorganisms associated with organic matter decomposition; under these conditions thatch can become a problem. Likewise, algae problems tend to be associated with low soil pH (<5.0).

The recommended soil pH range for optimum turf growth is 5.5 to 6.5. When grown outside this range, possible toxicity, exclusions, or deficiencies of one or more macronutrients (e.g., P, Ca, and Mg) could occur. Growing turf on soils with too low or too high pH values could reduce root growth, cause leaf chlorosis (yellowing), and decrease plant vigor or recuperative potential. Diminished growth reduces the ability of turfgrass to withstand adverse environmental and biotic conditions, such as drought, pest, and heat stress.

SOIL ACIDITY

Soil acidity (pH <7.0) is largely determined by the availability of two elements, Al and H. These can be measured as two types of acidity, **active** and **potential.** The **active acidity** is a measurement of the free hydrogen ions (H^+) in the soil that are easily removed from the binding sites on the soil colloid. In a routine pH determination, as reported by soil test laboratories, it is the active acidity that is measured and does not include the other major pH contributor, Al^{+3} ion, in soil sample solution. For measuring active acidity, usually an equal amount (1:1) of soil and deionized (DI) water (e.g., 10 g of soil and 10 mL of deionized water) are mixed and the solution is measured with an indicator solution or an electronic pH meter. Most laboratory reported soil pH recommendations are based on the active acidity.

Potential acidity (also referred to as *reserve* (or *residual*) *acidity, exchange acidity,* or *buffer acidity*) measures the exchangeable H^+ *and* aluminum (Al^{+3}) ions retained (or fixed) on the soil colloids after the active acidity is measured. In soil, more potential acidity exists than active acidity. When H^+ and Al^{+3} ions move from fixed (or potential) to active acidity, they are replaced by other cations on those particles (colloids) to which they had been affixed by the process *cationic exchange.*

The potential acidity is more difficult to measure and procedures vary across the country depending on soil types. Soil test laboratories often list the measurement of potential acidity as **buffer pH** on soil test reports. Soils containing appreciable amounts of clay, organic matter, and humus tend to have high potential acidity or high buffering capacity because of increased number of exchange sites for Al^{+3} or H^+ to adsorb and be retained. Soils with increased CEC generally have increased base saturation. As a result, these soils resist rapid changes in pH and are considered buffered and thus require more lime or sulfur to adjust their pH values. It is a measurement of the potential acidity that determines the amount of lime or sulfur needed to alter soil pH.

As discussed in Chapter 2, the hydrogen ion concentration in an acid solution increases by a factor of 10 times for each whole number decrease in pH; similarly, the hydroxyl (OH^-) ion concentration decreases by a tenfold factor. Thus, a change in pH from 4 to 3 has a tenfold increase in H^+ ions present, and a similar concentration decrease in OH^- ions.

A soil solution with a H^+ ion concentration of 0.001 *M* (molar) will have a pH value of 3.0; one with a H^+ ion concentration of 0.0001 *M* will have a pH value of 4.0, and so on. A *mole* is the number of grams of a chemical equal to its molecular weight. A *molar solution* contains one mole of a chemical dissolved in 1 liter of water. The molarity (*M*) of a solution denotes the moles of solute per liter of solution. A 1 molar solution contains 6.02×10^{23} atoms, ions, or molecules of the solute. Thus, the number of H^+ ions in a 1 molar acid solution with a pH value of 3.0 is equal to 6.02×10^{23} times 0.001, or 6.02×10^{20} H^+ ions.

Origin of Acidity

To maintain proper soil pH, it is recommended soil test be taken every year or two. Therefore, one might ask why and how does the soil pH change, and where does soil acidity come from? Soil acidity is the natural consequence of weathering and is a dynamic (ever-changing) property of soil. The origin of soil acidity is from the two adsorbed cations—aluminum (Al^{+3}) and hydrogen (H^+). Aluminum is the third most abundant element in the earth's crust, with many parent minerals and clay minerals being **aluminosilicates** (mineral containing aluminum, silicon, and oxygen). Although aluminum is a constant element in the soil mineralogy, hydrogen ions can arise from several sources. Soils containing high organic matter, such as peat and muck, also contain reactive carboxylic (R—COOH) and phenolic (R—OH) groups, which can dissociate, releasing hydrogen ions and leaving negative charges on the remaining groups (R—COOH → R—COO$^-$ + H$^+$; R—OH → R—O$^-$ + H$^+$). The charge on organic colloids is pH dependent—low negative charge at relatively low pH as indicated in the following steps.

Soil pH Reduction When Organic Matter Is Decomposed

Step 1

$$C_2H_4ONS + 5O_2 + H_2O \rightarrow H_2CO_3 + RCOOH + H_2SO_4 + HNO_3$$

organic matter   carbonic acid   strong organic acid from humus   strong inorganic acids (sulfuric + nitric acids)

Step 2

$$RCOOH \rightarrow RCOO^- + H^+ \;\&\; ROH \rightarrow RO^- + H^+$$

carboxyl group of humus (organic matter)   ($\downarrow$pH)   hydroxyl group   ($\downarrow$pH)

The cations of fertilizers can also react with soils to displace adsorbed aluminum, causing a temporary reduction in pH. In this instance, the concentration of Al^{+3} and H^+ are increased or when acidic cations are more available in the soil solution, the pH values will decrease. Soil pH changes naturally with time, and plants influence soil pH as well as cultural practices associated with a healthy turf stand.

Water. Rainfall and irrigation influence the soil acidity, as leaching tends to decrease the pH in most soils. Through the leaching process, the basic cations (e.g., Ca^{+2}, Mg^{+2}, K^+, and Na^+) on the soil colloids are washed away (displaced) and Al^{+3} or H^+ will then occupy the exposed sites on the soil exchange complex. As mentioned, increasing Al^{+3} and H^+ ions lowers soil pH. Leaching occurs when more soil water is present than can be evaporated or used by the plants. It then moves downward through the soil profile, attracting calcium and magnesium ions (the dominant cations on soil exchange sites). Anions such as nitrate (NO_3^-), chloride (Cl^-), or sulfate (SO_4^{-2}) are also effected by leaching of water through the soil profile. In arid regions (areas receiving less than 20 inches, 51 cm, of rain yearly), rainfall is not heavy enough to leach the basic cations; thus, these soils tend to be alkaline and oftentimes salty (saline).

As discussed, the principal component of potential acidity in most soils is *exchangeable aluminum* (Al^{+3}). Hydrogen ions are generated from the hydrolysis (reaction with water) of soluble aluminum, resulting in a decrease in pH. The following three reactions demonstrate aluminum hydrolysis; H^+ is produced (on the right-hand side of each equation), thus, reducing soil pH.

Aluminum Hydrolysis at Various Soil pH (see Figure 5-2)

pH 4.0

$$Al^{+3} + H_2O \rightarrow Al(OH)^{+2} + H^+$$

aluminum   water   hydroxy-Al   hydrogen (↓pH)

$$Al(OH)^{+2} + H_2O \rightarrow Al(OH)_2^+ + H^+$$

hydrogen (↓pH)

pH 6.5

$$Al(OH)_2^+ + H_2O \rightarrow Al(OH)_3 + H^+$$

Gibbsite (insoluble)   hydrogen (↓pH)

Along with reducing soil pH, when soils are strongly acidic due to the presence of aluminum, plant uptake of essential elements like phosphorus, calcium, magnesium, and iron is impeded. Meanwhile, manganese (Mn) is more soluble at lower pH and can lead to toxicity in some plants. Root systems with limited depths, less branching, and brown in color often develop in highly acidic soils (pH < 5.0). The turf then becomes increasingly susceptible to various environmental stresses (heat and moisture).

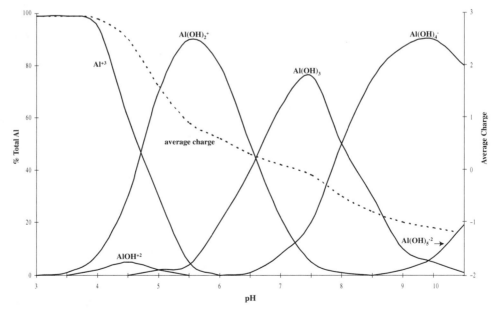

Figure 5-2. Aluminum forms an average charge as a function of pH. (Adapted from G. Marion et al. 1976. *Soil Sci.*, vol. 121, pp. 76–82).

In addition to high amounts of rainfall promoting aluminum hydrolysis, carbonic acid (H_2CO_3), a weak acid, is formed when rainfall reacts with atmospheric carbon dioxide (CO_2) and the soil pH is lowered, as shown:

Formation of Carbonic Acid from Carbon Dioxide and Water

$$CO_2 + H_2O \leftrightarrow H_2CO_3$$

Caves and sinkholes often develop in soils high in limestone because over many years, carbonic acid from rainfall dissolves the limestone.

Other Soil Acidity Origins

Plant Growth. Plants can contribute to soil acidity by removing basic cations such as Ca^{+2}, Mg^{+2}, K^+, and Fe^{+3}, from the soil exchange sites during normal growth processes. Unless an ample soil supply of basic cations is readily available to replace those removed by plants, acidic cations (H^+ and Al^{+3}) will occupy the soil's electrical charge, thus decreasing the pH. Also, in order to absorb cations, plant roots excrete H^+ in the form of organic acids, like humic and fulvic acids, which contribute to lower pH values.

Soil Organisms. While the benefits for organic matter are well accepted, soil acidity can be affected by the breakdown of organic matter. Through the decomposition process, carbonic acid and organic acids are released into the soil solution, thus reducing pH.

Assisting in the decomposition of organic matter, soil microbes also influence soil acidity. Through a process called **nitrification** (oxidation of ammonium to nitrite or nitrate, usually mediated by soil organisms), microbial degradation of urea, ammonium, and organic fertilizers produces hydrogen ions. *Nitrosomonas* soil microorganisms are responsible for the conversion of ammonium to nitrite (NO_2^-), while *nitrobacter* organisms convert nitrite to nitrate.

Microorganism Mediated Nitrification

$$\underset{\substack{\text{ammonium} \\ \text{ion}}}{NH_4^+} + 2O_2 \xrightarrow[\text{soil water \& microorganisms}]{\text{proper temperature, aeration,}} \underset{\text{nitrate}}{NO_3^-} + \underset{(\downarrow pH)}{2H^+} + \underset{\text{water}}{H_2O}$$

Certain microbes also oxidize sulfur, liberating H^+ and reducing pH.

Microbial Conversion of Elemental Sulfur to Sulfuric Acid

$$\underset{\substack{\text{elemental} \\ \text{sulfur}}}{S} + \underset{\text{oxygen}}{{}^3\!/_2 O_2} + \underset{\text{water}}{H_2O} \xrightarrow[\text{(\textit{Thiobacillus} spp.)}]{\text{microorganisms}} \underset{\text{sulfuric acid}}{H_2SO_4}$$

Fertilization. Cultural practices required to maintain turf also influence soil pH. For example, the continued use of certain fertilizers can lower the soil pH. Ammoniacal (NH_4^+) or urea ($(H_2N)_2CO$) based fertilizers, and sulfur-coated urea, are highly effective at acidifying soils, while nitrate (NO_3^-) based fertilizers have less of an effect on soil acidity. The hydrogen ions associated with the chemical formulas of the nitrogen sources, e.g., ammonia (NH_4^+) and urea ($(H_2N)_2CO$) fertilizers, has the potential to influence acidity greatly. The hydrogen ions released as the nitrogen is used or converted by soil microbes help lower soil pH. Less acidity is generated from ammonium nitrate per unit of applied nitrogen than from ammonium sulfate, because only half of the nitrogen in ammonium nitrate can be further oxidized.

Nitrification of Ammonium-Based Fertilizer to Reduce Soil pH

$$NH_4^+ + 2O_2 \rightarrow 2H^+ + NO_3^- + H_2O$$

ammonium $\quad\quad\quad$ (↓pH) $\quad$ nitrate

Meanwhile, nitrate-nitrogen (NO_3^-) has no associated H^+ in its chemical formula and thus, no effect on H^+ concentration occurs in the soil. Furthermore, when soils are saturated for long periods, the process of **denitrification** may occur. Denitrification is a microbial mediated process that converts nitrate-nitrogen to a gaseous (g) form of nitrogen (N_2) which is then easily volatilized. Water is formed and 6 atoms of H^+ are neutralized for each NO_3^-—N converted to $N_2(g)$, resulting in an increase of soil pH.

Denitrification

$$2NO_3^- + 5H_2 + 2H^+ \rightarrow N_2(\uparrow) + 6H_2O$$

nitrate $\quad\quad\quad\quad\quad\quad$ nitrogen
$\quad\quad\quad\quad\quad\quad\quad\quad$ gas

Industrial. Other man-made influences on soil acidity include the production of industrial by-products. When nitrogen dioxide (NO_2) and sulfur trioxide (SO_3) combine with atmospheric water, nitric (HNO_3) and sulfuric (H_2SO_4) acids are produced.

Nitric and Sulfuric Acid Formation

$$2NO_2(g) + H_2O \rightarrow HNO_2(aq) + HNO_2(aq)$$

nitrogen dioxide $\quad\quad\quad$ nitric acid $\quad$ nitrous acid

$$SO_3^{-2}(g) + H_2O \rightarrow + H_2SO_4(aq)$$

sulfur trioxide (or sulfite) $\quad\quad$ sulfuric acid

These acids eventually fall to the earth in the form of acid rain and can alter soil pH. However, it is speculated the effects of acid rain on agricultural soils are minimal compared to the amount of natural soil acidification or through agronomic practices (e.g., fertilization).

Increasing Soil pH

Soil pH can be altered to bring it within the range of optimum growth. Since most turfgrass species prefer a soil pH less than neutral (<7.0), it is common to increase the pH just to the point Al^{+3} and aluminum hydroxides $(Al(OH)_x^{+y})$ are neutralized. The neutralization of Al^{+3} occurs when it reacts with a base (a source of hydroxyl or OH^- ions). Most common acid neutralization is achieved by using lime as a base.

Two-Step Process When Soil Is Limed with Calcium Carbonate

Step 1

$$Al^{+3} + CaCO_3 + OH^- \rightarrow Ca^{+2} + Al(OH)_3\downarrow + OH^- + CO_2\uparrow$$

aluminum   lime   calcium   aluminum hydroxide   carbon
             (calcium   or Gibbsite   dioxide
             carbonate)   (precipitates out)

Step 2

$$H^+ + OH^- \rightarrow H_2O$$

hydrogen ion   hydroxyl ion   ($\uparrow$pH)

A liming material by definition contains calcium (Ca) and neutralizes acidity. All liming materials, whether it is the oxide (CaO), hydroxide $[Ca(OH)_2]$, carbonate $(CaCO_3)$, or dolomitic $[CaMg(CO_3)_2]$ form of calcium, react with carbon dioxide and water to yield the bicarbonate form $[Ca(HCO_3)_2]$ when applied to an acid soil. The calcium (or magnesium in the case of dolomite) of the liming material displaces the acid producing ions, H^+ and Al^{+3}, from the soil exchange complex and places them in solution. This replacement of ions increases base saturation. Hydrogen ions in the soil solution combine with the OH^- to form water. Each Ca^{+2} ion replaces two H^+ ions while three Ca^{+2} ions are required to replace two Al^{+3} ions. The Al^{+3} ions then react with soil water to form insoluble hydroxides and oxides. This neutralization of the hydrogen and aluminum ions results in an increased soil pH.

Generalized Process When Soil Is Limed with Calcium Hydroxide or Calcium Bicarbonate

$$Al^{+3}, H^+ + 2Ca(OH)_2 \rightarrow Ca^{+2} + Al(OH)_3 + H_2O$$

               calcium   aluminum   (or Gibbsite)
               hydroxide   hydroxide

$$Al^{+3}, H^+ + 2Ca(HCO_3)_2 \rightarrow Ca^{+2} + Al(OH)_3 + H_2O + 4CO_2\uparrow$$

                calcium bicarbonate

In addition to raising the pH of acidic soils, liming materials can contribute to the plant nutrients calcium and/or magnesium, increase phosphorus availability, improve microbial activity, and increase potassium efficiency in plant nutrition.

Liming materials most commonly consist of calcium and calcium-magnesium carbonates (including ground, pelletized, and flowable limestone), calcium hydroxide, calcium oxide, marl, and slags (Table 5-1). Ground limestone is the most inexpensive source but is dusty and not as easily spread as the pelletized form. Pelletized limestone is ground limestone (either calcitic or dolomitic) aggregated

TABLE 5-1. Characteristics of Commonly Used Liming Materials (Adapted from McCarty, 2001)

Source	Alternative Name(s)	Chemical Symbol	Characteristics
Calcium carbonates	calcite calcitic limestone aglime marl chalk	$CaCO_3$	Contains approximately 40% Ca when pure. Often used when Mg is not needed. Marl is lime from deposits in the bottom of small freshwater ponds, while chalk is soft limestone deposits in oceans.
Calcium-magnesium carbonates	dolomite	$CaMg(CO_3)_2$	Generally has about 50% calcium carbonate, 35% magnesium carbonate, and 15% soil and other impurities. Used when Mg is needed. Often pelletized to increase ease of application.
	dolomitic limestone	$CaMg(CO_3)_2$	Has unequal proportions of Ca and Mg with 21 to 30% Ca and 6 to 11% Mg. Used when Mg is needed.
Calcium oxide and/or Magnesium oxide	unslaked lime burned lime quicklime	CaO or $CaO + MgO$	White powdery substance, which is the most effective and quickest reacting liming material. However, these have high burn potential, are caustic to handle, and difficult to soil mix.
Calcium hydroxide	slaked lime hydrated lime builder's lime	$Ca(OH)_2$	White powdery substance similar to calcium oxide except moisture has been added. Second most effective and quickest reacting material; however, like calcium oxide, calcium hydroxide has a high burn potential, is caustic to handle, and difficult to soil mix. Also used to make mortar.
Slags	blast-furnace slag basic slag electric-furnace slags	mostly by calcium silicate ($CaSiO_3$)	By-product of iron manufacturing that is ground and screened. Effective if locally available and economically priced. Basic slag often contains phosphorus (2 to 17%), magnesium (about 3%), and iron.

into larger particles to aid in spreading and reduce dust. These pellets disintegrate when they become wet.

Flowable or liquid limestone also is available. These are dust-free and are uniformly applied with a spray unit, but due to potential plant burn, only small amounts can be applied at one time and the spray suspension may be abrasive to sprayer parts. In addition, localized sources of other materials containing calcium and/or magnesium are used as liming agents, including fly ash from coal-burning electrical power plants, ash from hardwoods, sludge from water treatment plants, pulp mill lime, flue dust from cement manufacturing, and carbide lime.

Neutralizing Capacity of Liming Materials. The acid neutralizing capacity of a liming material is based on the relative purity of the material and is measured as the **calcium carbonate equivalent (CCE)**. The CCE of a liming material is expressed as percent by weight of pure calcium carbonate ($CaCO_3$) which has a CCE value of 100 (Table 5-2). For example, pure $CaCO_3$ has a molecular weight of 100 grams per mole (sum of the molecular weights of each element; Ca = 40 g/mole, C = 12 g/mole, O = 16 g/mole × 3 = 40 + 12 + 48 = 100 g/mole of $CaCO_3$). Meanwhile, $MgCO_3$ has a molecular weight of 84 g/mole and when compared to $CaCO_3$ (e.g., 100/84 = 1.19) is 1.19 times more reactive than pure calcium carbonate. Thus, materials with CCE values greater than 100 are usually high in magnesium carbonate, calcium hydroxide, calcium oxide, or magnesium oxide and require less material on a per area basis to achieve the same effects as calcium carbonate.

The higher the neutralizing value, the less lime required to effect a change in pH. In the example above, $MgCO_3$ had a neutralizing value of 119, therefore 84 pounds of this material would produce the same effect on pH as 100 pounds of calcium carbonate. In practice, however, $MgCO_3$ is seldom applied, rather dolomitic lime [$CaMg(CO_3)_2$] with an average CCE of 108 is used more often.

Application rates are adjusted depending on the liming source, as impurities lower the neutralizing values of many limestone sources. An acceptable lime source should have a CCE of 70 or higher; however, each state has its own lime laws and

TABLE 5-2. Relative Neutralizing Values or Calcium Carbonate Equivalent (CCE) of Common Liming Materials Compared to Calcium Carbonate

Material	Relative Neutralizing Value (CCE)
Calcium carbonate ($CaCO_3$)	100
Calcitic lime	85–100
Dolomitic lime	95–108
Magnesium carbonate ($MgCO_3$)	119
Burned lime (CaO or calcium oxide)	150–175
Hydrated lime	120–135
Baked oyster shells	80–90
Burned oyster shells	90–110
Marl	50–90
Basic slag	50–70
Gypsum ($CaSO_4$)	0

regulations regarding the use of alternative liming materials and should be consulted prior to use.

The fineness of a liming material will determine how fast it reacts with a soil to neutralize acidity. The finer the limestone, the more soil surface it contacts and the quicker it reacts. However, the cost of limestone increases with its fineness and powder-like limestone also is difficult to handle and uniformly apply. Although faster acting, the effects of fine limestone are not as long-lasting as for coarser materials since the coarser material dissolves more slowly. Finer limestone sources also increase the probability of leaf tissue burn. Therefore, most agricultural limestone contains both coarse and fine materials.

Sizes are graded by passing a sample through a series of standard sieves with results expressed as a percentage of material passing or retained on the various-sized screens. Screens vary by the number of openings per linear inch. For example, a 60-mesh screen has 60 openings per linear inch or 3,600 openings per square inch. The diameter of particles passing through a 60-mesh sieve would be 0.0098 inches (<0.25 mm), about the same particle size as flour. In general, pelletized limestone (ground limestone which is aggregated into larger particles to aid in spreading and reduce dust), which will pass a 10-mesh screen, should provide desirable results, yet be economical. Coarse particles, those unable to pass through an 8-mesh screen, have almost no effect on soil pH.

Limestone Quality. Most commercially available limestone sources contain impurities, reducing their overall effectiveness and ability to be active in the soil. Limestone quality is determined by two factors: (1) fineness and (2) purity or calcium carbonate equivalent (CCE). These two factors combine to produce the **effective calcium carbonate (ECC)** rating.

$$\underset{\text{(Effective Calcium Carbonate)}}{\textbf{ECC}} = \underset{\text{(Calcium Carbonate Equivalent)}}{\textbf{CCE}} \times \textbf{Fineness Factor}$$

The **fineness factor** determines the activity and speed of reaction to neutralize acidity. Most states have laws requiring percentages of lime that must pass through a 20 mesh sieve (0.84 mm opening). Activity factor of limestone sizes is based on a fraction of the material effective over a 2–3 year period. Activity factors can be found on Table 5-3.

According to Table 5-3, 60% of limestone passing through a 40-mesh sieve but not through a 60-mesh would be active in increasing pH over 2 to 3 years.

The **CCE** measures the ability to neutralize acid relative to an identical weight of pure $CaCO_3$. In most cases, natural limestone has CCE values less than 100%

TABLE 5-3. Determining Limestone Activity Based on Its Particle Size

Sieve Size	Particle Size (mm)	Activity Factor
Coarser than 8-mesh	>2.36	0
8- to 40-mesh	0.425–2.36	25
40- to 60-mesh	0.250–0.425	60
Finer than 60-mesh	<0.250	100

because of impurities. CCE is determined in laboratories by combining $CaCO_3$ with hydrochloric acid (HCl). The solution is then titrated with a base, sodium hydroxide (NaOH), to determine the CCE. Liming materials can have CCE ranging from 50 to 150. A liming material with a CCE of 50% would have only one-half (0.5) of the neutralizing value of pure $CaCO_3$. In contrast, a liming material with a CCE of 150% would have 1.5 the neutralizing value of pure $CaCO_3$.

Example:

A 100 g sample of limestone was shaken through a set of sieves. Five grams were retained on the 8-mesh sieve, 15 g were retained on the 40-mesh, 40 g were retained on the 60-mesh, and 20 g passed the 60-mesh. The limestone has a CCE of 95%. Find the effective calcium carbonate (ECC) and lime required to satisfy a recommendation of 5,000 lb lime/A.

Step 1: Determine the fineness factor:

Sieve Size	Retained (g)	×	Activity Factor	=	Percent Available for Reaction
Coarser than 8-mesh	5 g		0		0
8- to 40-mesh	5 g		0.25		1.25
40- to 60-mesh	20 g		0.60		12
Finer than 60-mesh	70 g		1.00		70
					SUM = 83.25

In 2–3 years approximately 83% of the liming material will be active.

Step 2: Find ECC
Since the CCE was given, multiply the CCE and fineness factor to determine the ECC.

$$\textbf{\% CCE} \times \textbf{\% Fineness Factor} = \textbf{ECC}$$
$$95 \quad \times \quad 83.25 \quad = 79.1$$

Step 3: Limestone recommendation
The ECC was found to be 79.1%, therefore about 80% of the applied limestone will be active in neutralizing acidity. The limestone recommendation was 5,000 lb/A of pure $CaCO_3$.

$$\frac{5,000 \text{ lb}}{\text{acre}} \times \frac{1}{80\%} = 6,320$$

You would need to apply **6,320 lb/A** of the tested limestone to properly apply 5,000 lb of pure $CaCO_3$.

Incorporation and Mixing. Since limestone is relatively insoluble (only one pound will dissolve in 500 gallons of water), the extent of contact between the soil and the limestone is important in determining how fast the limestone will react to increase soil pH. The best time to adjust soil pH is during construction. Uniformly mixed limestone maximizes the neutralization of soil acidity, whereas clumps of limestone react slowly. Limestone should be thoroughly mixed into the upper 6 to 8 inches of soil based on soil analysis of the same soil depth or added during off-site soil mix blending.

Once plants are established, lime application rates should be based on the soil analysis of the upper 4 inches of soil with subsequent limestone applied to the soil surface. Surface applied limestone is in contact with very little soil and therefore reacts extremely slowly and moves minimally downward. With established turf, soil pH should be monitored and adjusted (if necessary) annually, since correction with lime will be slow. Liming after core aerification is a way to more uniformly mix limestone into the soil on established turfgrass and increase the amount of neutralization occurring beyond the upper inch of soil.

Selecting a Liming Material. When choosing a liming material, the degree of fineness, neutralizing value, magnesium content, plant-tissue burn potential, and moisture content should each be considered. In most areas, materials with the least cost per unit of neutralizing value should be considered, assuming that there is the same degree for fineness of all materials. However, many soils are deficient in magnesium, thus dolomitic lime is often used. Turf managers also must carefully consider the burn potential of available materials, especially when irrigation is not readily available and/or temperatures are hot $\geq 80°F(26.7°C)$. In these cases, a more slowly reacting (e.g., pelletized) dolomitic limestone may be the best choice.

Most lime sources contain a certain degree of moisture to minimize dust. In many states, a maximum moisture content of 10% is allowed to prevent consumers paying for more moisture than needed to reduce dust.

It should be noted that limestone crushed for road construction is generally too coarse to be effective in lowering agricultural soil pH. Even if this material is applied in excessive amounts, it usually is inferior to a finer ground source in raising soil pH.

Liming Rates. Rates of lime required to neutralize excessive acidity vary with the degree of soil weathering and soil texture. Lime rate requirements depend on:

(1) the change of soil pH desired,
(2) the potential acidity of the soil, and
(3) the chemical composition and fineness of the liming material to be used.

Cation exchange capacity and potential acidity also influence lime requirements. Soils with high cation exchange and potential acidity, such as clay or muck soils, may require up to twice the amount of lime as soils with a low CEC, such as sands (Table 5-4). However, since these soils have an ability to retain cations on exchange sites, basic cations are not as easily leached and therefore do not need liming as frequently as sandy soils. In general, a clay loam soil with a greater CEC and potential acidity than a sandy soil, will require more lime to achieve a desired pH. Once the pH is achieved, the clay loam soil is more likely to maintain the desired pH for a longer period of time.

TABLE 5-4. Characteristics and Cation Exchange Capacities (CEC) of Various Clay Minerals and Humus (McCarty, 2001)

Material	Structural	Permanent Charge	Expands in Water	Surface area (m^2/g)	CEC at pH 7 (meq/100 g)
Kaolinite	1:1	Very low	No	7–30 (Extremely low)	4–6
Chlorite	2:1:1 (2:2)	Medium	No	25–40 (Low)	20–30
Mica (Illite)	2:1	High	Slightly	65–100 (Low)	20–40
Montmorillonite	2:1	Medium	Yes	600–800 (High)	60–100
Vermiculite	2:1	High	Limited	600–800 (Medium)	100–150
Humic acid	Organic	High	Slightly	500–800 (High)	150–350

Intensively weathered soils generally are highly aluminum dominated with low calcium and magnesium and thus have low pH. Recommended lime rates should be determined by a soil testing lab, and generally do not exceed 50 to 100 pounds per 1,000 ft² per application. If hydrated or burned lime is used, rates over 25 pounds per 1,000 ft² should be avoided in one application. Rates exceeding this, or applications during periods of hot temperatures, can injure (e.g., burn) plants. Plants should be dry at the time of application and should be immediately irrigated to wash lime off the leaves. If over 100 pounds per 1,000 ft² are needed, splitting applications several months apart will improve the efficacy of lime use. Soil analysis will usually indicate the specific amount and type of lime needed to raise the pH of a specific soil type. As mentioned, aerifying prior to lime application aids in placing the material into the root zone.

Example:

If a soil test report indicates a soil contains 4 meq of exchangeable Al^{+3} per 100 g of soil, how much Ca^{+2} would be needed to displace the Al^{+3} in 1 acre of soil?

Step 1: Determine the equivalent weights of Al^{+3} and Ca^{+2}.

$$Al^{+3} = \frac{27\ g}{3} = 9\ g \qquad Ca^{+2} = \frac{40\ g}{2} = 20\ g$$

This indicates 20 g of calcium are needed to displace 9 g of aluminum.

Step 2: Convert this to a per-acre basis (an acre-furrow slice of soil weighs approximately 2,000,000 lb).

$$\frac{4\ meq\ Al^{+3}}{100\ g\ soil} \times \frac{1\ eq}{1,000\ meq} \times \frac{9\ g\ Al^{+3}}{1\ eq\ Al^{+3}} \times \frac{2,000,000\ lb\ soil}{acre}$$

$$= 720\ lb\ Al^{+3}\ per\ acre\ to\ displace$$

Step 3: Determine the amount of Ca^{+2} needed to displace 720 lb of Al^{+3}.

$$\frac{720\ lb\ Al^{+3}}{acre} \times \frac{20\ lb\ Ca^{+2}}{9\ lb\ Al^{+3}} = \begin{array}{l}1,600\ lb\ Ca^{+2}\ needed\ to\ displace\ 720\ lb \\ Al^{+3}\ per\ acre\end{array}$$

The amount of lime needed for a particular soil is determined in the laboratory by mixing the soil with a buffer solution. The buffer solution alone has a high pH (usually around 8.0). The decrease in pH of the buffer/soil mix is an indication of the potential acidity of the soil. If the potential acidity of the soil is low, the resulting pH of the buffer/soil mix will be close to that of the original pH of the added buffer. If the potential acidity of the soil is high, the pH of the buffer/soil mix will be much lower than the initial pH of the buffer. Methods employed differ among soil test laboratories, with certain methods being more applicable to particular regions and soil types. Comparisons of buffer pH readings among laboratories, therefore, may not be valid unless the same procedure to measure buffer capacity is used.

The purpose for applying the lime will also influence the application rate used. As noted, relatively large amounts are needed if the desire is to increase soil pH. One ton or more may be needed per acre for this purpose. If the purpose of liming is to supply calcium or magnesium to the soil as a nutrient, the amount applied is greatly reduced. If the desire is to supply these nutrients and not raise soil pH, then another source of calcium or magnesium should be used. For example, gypsum (calcium sulfate) and magnesium sulfate supply calcium and magnesium, respectively, without significantly affecting soil pH.

Acidic Irrigation Water. With the increase in acid rain (primarily sulfuric and nitric acids from atmospheric sulfur dioxide and nitric oxide reactions) and acidic lakes, problems with excessively low (<5.6) pH irrigation water have also increased. This is most notable around heavy industrial areas, presumably due to industrial air and water pollution problems. Acidic irrigation water not only may create problems for plants, it also causes considerable corrosion to irrigation pumping and piping systems. When needed, a quality, powdered carbonate containing material such as dolomitic lime is the one most often injected into an irrigation system to raise the pH of the irrigation water.

SOIL ALKALINITY

Soil alkalinity occurs when there is an excess of calcium (Ca^{+2}), magnesium (Mg^{+2}), or sodium (Na^+) ions on the soils' exchange sites. Moderate alkalinity occurs in the pH range of 7.5 to 8.5, with excessive alkalinity above these figures. A 2 to 3% by weight calcium carbonate content usually results in a soil pH range between 7.5 and 8.5. In the United States, soil alkalinity is generally of greatest concern in arid (dry) or semiarid western regions, where rainfall is minimal or along some coastal areas. Due to less annual rainfall, leaching of Ca^{+2}, Mg^{+2}, and Na^+ ions does not readily occur in these areas (many of these soils are classified as calcareous soils). Also, native soils with deposits of calcium carbonates in the form of shell, marl, and/or underlying limestone will have high innate pH values. Excessive use can lead to undesirable soil pH values, as is the case when a soil is overlimed or irrigated with water containing high concentrations of bicarbonates (e.g., water from limestone aquifers).

Deficiencies of several plant micronutrients may occur as a result of excessive soil alkalinity. Iron, manganese, zinc, boron, and copper tend to be less available to plants under high soil pH conditions (Figure 5-1). Chlorotic, unhealthy-appearing plants, often resembling nitrogen deficiency, may result. Superintendents not experienced in managing grass grown under alkaline conditions may be confused by these symptoms. The pathogenicity of several diseases (e.g., take-all patch and spring dead spot) is also promoted by high soil pH.

Reducing Soil pH

Reducing soil alkalinity often is a never-ending challenge, especially if high pH water is used for irrigation. Along with high pH irrigation water, most soils are highly buffered and thus resist dramatic, sudden changes in pH. Managers must constantly regulate and adjust their management programs to compensate for alkalinity. The most economically efficient method of lowering pH is the continued use of ammonium-based fertilizers such as ammonium sulfate and sulfur-coated urea. These materials are sometimes used to reduce soil pH due to the limited hydrogen ions produced via nitrification, but they do not generally contain enough sulfur or supply enough hydrogen ions to quickly or completely correct alkalinity problems. They can, however, gradually reduce or regulate pH if used long-term.

Where alkaline soil is an extreme problem, elemental sulfur and aluminum sulfate are materials which rapidly reduce pH. Elemental sulfur (S) is usually the most efficient and practical of these sources. The granular elemental sulfur source (90% powdered sulfur plus 10% bentonite clay) is preferred for spreading with conventional fertilizer spreaders. Oxidation of elemental sulfur produces acidity, in the form of sulfuric acid, to reduce soil pH.

Sulfur Oxidation

$$\underset{\text{sulfur}}{2S} + \underset{\text{oxygen}}{3O_2} + \underset{\text{water}}{2H_2O} \rightarrow \underset{\text{sulfate}}{2SO_4^{2-}} + \underset{(\downarrow pH)}{4H^+}$$

Due to the production of sulfuric acid (H_2SO_4), S has a high burn potential leading to severe plant injury and death. When using S, soil pH reduction can be too rapid in a narrow soil band. Therefore by using the soil as a buffer, drastic changes in soil pH can be minimized with proper incorporation.

Elemental (or granular) sulfur ranges from 99% to 20% purity, or less, with the lower contents in low-grade deposits containing clay and other materials. It is a yellow, inert, water-insoluble crystalline solid and is immobile in soil. Applied elemental sulfur is oxidized by soil microorganisms, the prominent group being bacteria in the *Thiobacillus* species, into sulfuric acid. When applied to the soil surface, the downward movement of the oxidized form of sulfur into the root zone is slow, with a dramatic pH decrease in the thatch layer occurring and minimal effect within the root zone.

Sulfuric acid (H_2SO_4) is considered a 'strong' acid since it readily dissociates, releasing its hydrogen ions which lowers the soil pH. The conversion of elemental sulfur to sulfuric acid, because it is a biological reaction involving microorganisms, increases with increasing temperature. This conversion does not occur readily when soil temperatures are below 40°F (4.4°C). A steady increase in oxidation occurs above 40°F; however, a sharp increase occurs at temperatures above 70°F (21.1°C). Similar to liming materials, smaller-particle-sized sulfur materials react faster than larger particles.

After application, elemental sulfur should be thoroughly mixed into the top six to eight inches of soil. Best results follow thorough mixing either by a power rototiller or by running a disk in several directions across the treated area. Adequate soil moisture (though not saturation) is necessary for this conversion to occur. Excessive soil moisture, however, reduces the degree of soil aeration needed for oxidation, thus sulfur conversion is reduced. Irrigation should therefore begin immediately after sulfur incorporation and continue at regular intervals for as long as oxidation is desired to maintain moisture levels near field capacity. This process may take several months, especially if initial soil pH is high, if high levels of salts are present, or if soil temperatures are cool. It is recommended to check soil pH more frequently to avoid overacidification, especially on sand-based putting greens, which have minimal buffering capacity. Prior to S application, evaluate the environmental conditions to ensure optimum efficiency.

In addition to lowering soil pH, other benefits are associated with sulfur applications. Sulfur is required as one of the 16 essential elements for plant growth. It is necessary for root growth, chlorophyll production, protein synthesis, and tissue development. Turfgrasses require almost as much sulfur, for example, as they do phosphorous. For nutritional purposes, turfgrasses require approximately one pound of sulfur per 1,000 ft^2 (48.9 kg ha^{-1}) per year.

Sulfur also sometimes reduces the incidence of several plant diseases, especially 'patch' diseases, and annual bluegrass (*Poa annua*) levels. Research indicates that 0.5 pounds of elemental sulfur per 1,000 ft^2 (24 kg ha^{-1}) on golf greens, and 2 lb per 1,000 ft^2 (97.7 kg ha^{-1}) on higher-cut turfgrass, reduces several patch diseases. Rates of 3.5 lb per 1,000 ft^2 (171.0 kg ha^{-1}) per year also has gradually reduced annual bluegrass stands. Superintendents should test the soil regularly to ensure that the soil pH is not drastically reduced after sulfur application in a short period of time. Refer to Chapter 7 for sulfur rates and sources used to lower soil pH.

Acid-Injection. A third method of reducing soil alkalinity is the injection of sulfuric acid or sulfur dioxide into irrigation water. If the soil pH is raised by excessive sodium or bicarbonate levels in the irrigation source, then a sulfur-injection system may be used to maintain or lower water pH. Reducing soil pH also helps dissolve insoluble carbonates (salts) into much more soluble bicarbonates to help flush and thus remove various salts from the soil surface. Refer to Chapter 2 for detailed information regarding acid injection into irrigation sources.

Established Turf. Once turf is established, significantly reducing soil pH becomes more difficult due to the plant-tissue burn that can occur when using high rates of acidifying materials. Care must be taken not to create too acidic a layer near the turfgrass crown. To minimize the injury potential, and to facilitate sulfur's acidifying effects in the turfgrass root zone, it is suggested that elemental sulfur application be in conjunction with turf coring or aerification.

If a soil is inherently alkaline, the turf manager basically has two methods of reducing pH once the site has been established in grass. One is to use ammonia-based fertilizers, such as ammonium nitrate or ammonium sulfate, as discussed previously. The other procedure is to add small, frequent applications of sulfur to the turf. Only elemental sulfur or sulfur compounds that can be oxidized to sulfate ions produce the desired acidification. Up to 5 pounds of elemental sulfur may be applied per 1,000 ft^2 (244.0 kg ha^{-1}) on taller maintained grasses, such as fairways or roughs. Applications to putting greens should be no greater than 0.5 pounds per 1,000 ft^2 (24.4 kg ha^{-1}). Applications should be spaced at least three to four weeks apart. Application during hot weather also should be avoided, as should application to wet leaf surfaces, and each application should be followed by irrigation. Total application of elemental sulfur should not exceed 10 pounds per 1,000 ft^2 (488.5 kg ha^{-1}) yearly.

Excessive amounts of sulfur and/or excessive watering (e.g., lack of soil oxygen) can result in hydrogen sulfide (H_2S) formation, which reacts with trace metal ions and precipitates in soils as compounds such as pyrite (FeS_2) and FeS, instead of escaping as a gas. Also, in a two-step, microbial mediated reaction, ferrous sulfate ($FeSO_4$) may form. Ferrous sulfate is very soluble, while FeS and FeS_2 are not; thus, these typically combine to form black layer one to two inches below the soil surface.

Formation of Ferrous Sulfate in Soils

$$\tfrac{1}{2}Fe_2O_3 + e^- + H^+ \rightarrow Fe^{+2} + \tfrac{3}{2}H_2O + SO_4^{+2} \rightarrow FeSO_4 + \tfrac{3}{2}H_2O$$

ferric oxide   ferrous   sulfate   ferrous
                      iron   sulfate

Other toxic components associated with soils of low oxygen content include carbon dioxide (CO_2) and methane (CH_4). Proper aerification and irrigation management minimizes the chance of such conditions. Applications during winter may not produce the desired results until spring when temperatures are warm enough to drive the microbial mediated reaction.

CATION EXCHANGE AND BASE SATURATION

Many soil nutrients occur naturally as complex, insoluble compounds which may not be readily available for plant use. Over time, as weathering occurs, these elements slowly enter the soil solution and become plant-available. Organic matter also may be degraded by the soil microbial population, releasing its nutrient constituents for possible plant uptake.

As soils are formed during the weathering processes, some minerals and organic matter are broken down to extremely small particles called **colloids.** Colloids are primarily responsible for the chemical reactivity of soils. Developed during the formation process, colloids from clay and organic matter sources typically have a net negative ($-$) charge. Therefore, colloids attract and hold (a process called **ionic bonding**) positively ($+$) charged particles (including many nutrients) on binding sites. This phenomenon is similar to the attraction between two opposite poles of a magnet and is referred to as **cation exchange.**

One of the most important parameters affecting turf management is a soil's ability to hold and release nutrients. Plant nutrients are taken up from the soil solution as charged, simple, soluble forms called **ions.** Positively charged ions are called **cations** while negatively charged ions are called **anions.** Potassium, for example, is absorbed by plants as a cation (K^+), whereas nitrogen is absorbed primarily as a compound anion (NO_3^-). Major cations retained on the soil's cation exchange sites include calcium (Ca^{+2}), magnesium (Mg^{+2}), potassium (K^+), sodium (Na^+), aluminum (Al^{+3}), and hydrogen (H^+). Absorbed in lesser amounts are iron (Fe^{+2}), zinc (Zn^{+2}), copper (Cu^{+2}), manganese (Mn^{+2}), and ammonium (NH_4^+).

Cation exchange involves a reversible process where cations in solution are exchanged (or replaced by other cations) with another cation on the soil's negatively charged exchange sites. In soil, the significant exchange sites are located on clay and organic matter. Exchangeable cations are not readily leached until they are replaced (or exchanged). Ions more strongly attracted to the cation exchange sites can replace the less tightly bound cations. For example, potassium can be exchanged for calcium or hydrogen. Also, this exchange may occur when the soil solution concentration is altered and is not in equilibrium with cations on the exchange sites. This occurs, for example, when excessive amounts of one cation (e.g., Ca^{+2}) are applied over another (e.g., K^+). Usually, a cation with a high charge density of 2 or 3 (e.g., Ca^{+2}) is preferentially held over cations with lesser charge (e.g., K^+). Due to hydrogen bonding, however, H^+ is an exception. Also, smaller ions (e.g., H^+) have greater affinity for soil exchange sites than larger ones. The following illustrates the general order of bonding strength of exchangeable cations.

General Order of Bonding Strength of Exchangeable Cations

$$H^+ > Al^{+3} > Ca^{+2} > Mg^{+2} > NH_4^+ > K^+ \geq Na^+$$

In soils, exchange reactions between the exchange complex on the clay or organic fractions and the cations in the soil solution occur constantly. The following equation illustrates a possible exchange reaction in soil.

$$Clay - 2H^+ + Ca^{+2} \rightarrow Clay - Ca^{+2} + 2H^+$$

The clay particle (on the left-hand side of the equation) has two negative charges satisfied by hydrogen ions. When calcium is added to the solution, one calcium ion (Ca^{+2}) can replace the two hydrogen ions on the exchange site, which then go into solution (right-hand side of the equation).

Equivalent Weight. Cations also are adsorbed and exchanged on a chemically equivalent weight (eq) basis. An **equivalent weight** is the amount (or weight) of an ion needed to equal the amount (or weight) of another ion (refer to Chapter 1). Equivalent weights are calculated by dividing the atomic weight of a cation by its valence, regardless of the sign. For example, 1 equivalent of Ca^{+2} is calculated by dividing the atomic weight of calcium (40 g mole^{-1}) by the valence of calcium (+2) to obtain 20 g. Likewise, 1 equivalent of K^+ is calculated by dividing the atomic weight of potassium (39 g mole^{-1}) by the valence of potassium (+1) to obtain 39 g. Therefore, for 1 equivalent of Ca^{+2} to equal 1 equivalent of K^+, it takes only 20 g of calcium compared to 39 g of potassium. Calculating milliequivalent weight (meq) is the same, only the amounts are in milligrams (mg) instead of grams (g). For further demonstration of equivalents see the following example. Also, Table 5-5 lists equivalent and milliequivalent weights of common cations.

Example:

How many milliequivalents (meq) of K^+ are in 78 mg of K^+?

TABLE 5-5. Equivalent and Milliequivalent Weights of Common Soil Cations

Cation	Molecular Weight	Valence	Equivalent Weight (g)	Milliequivalent Weight (mg)
Hydrogen (H^+)	1	1	1	1
Aluminum (Al^{+3})	27	3	9	9
Calcium (Ca^{+2})	40	2	20	20
Magnesium (Mg^{+2})	24	2	12	12
Potassium (K^+)	39	1	39	39
Sodium (Na^+)	23	1	23	23

Step 1: Determine the mass of K^+ in 1 meq of K^+. From the periodic table, potassium has an atomic mass of 39 mg/mmol (millimole). The single positive sign on the cation (K^+) indicates potassium has a valence of one. With this information, meq can be calculated by dividing the atomic mass by the valence. For potassium 1 meq of K^+ weighs 39 mg.

$$1 \text{ meq } K^+ = \frac{39 \text{ mg/mmol}}{1} = 39 \text{ mg}$$

Step 2: To determine the number of meq K^+ in 78 mg of K^+ it is easiest to set up a ratio. 1 meq K^+ is 39 mg, therefore 78 mg must equal 2 meq K^+.

$$\frac{1 \text{ meq } K^+}{39 \text{ mg}} = \frac{X \text{ meq } K^+}{78 \text{ mg}}$$

$$X \text{ meq } K^+ = \frac{78 \text{ mg}}{39 \text{ mg}} = 2$$

The concept of cation exchange is based on moles of charge. Recall, one **mole** of an element is the quantity of it having a mass in grams equal to the atomic weight. For example, the atomic weight of sodium is 23, so one mole of sodium weighs 23 grams. One mole of an element contains Avogadro's number (6.022×10^{23}) of atoms of the element. Therefore, one mole of charge is 6.022×10^{23} charges. So, if sodium exists as a cation (Na^+), then a solution containing one mole of sodium would contain 6.022×10^{23} positive charges and weigh 23 grams. In the case of a divalent cation (having 2 positive charges per mole) like Ca^{+2}, only half of its mass would be needed to equal the same amount of charge as a monovalent cation. Trivalent cations (e.g., Al^{+3}) would require a third as much.

The total number of exchangeable cations a soil can hold (or in other words, the amount of a soil's negative charge) is its **cation exchange capacity (CEC)**. Cation exchange capacity is calculated by summing the exchangeable cations (CEC = $H^+ + Al^{+3} + Ca^{+2} + Mg^{+2} + K^+ + Na^+$) and is expressed in units of milliequivalents per 100 grams of soil (meq/100 g) or centimoles of charge per kilogram of soil ($cmol_c/kg$). Numerically, meq/100 g and $cmol_c/kg$ are the same (see **Proof 1**). The next example determines the CEC of a given soil.

Proof 1

$$\frac{1 \text{ meq } H^+}{100 \text{ g soil}} \Rightarrow \frac{1 \text{ mg } H^+/\text{mmol}}{100 \text{ g soil}} \Rightarrow \frac{0.001 \text{ g } H^+/\text{mol}}{100 \text{ g soil}}$$

$$\Rightarrow \frac{1 \times 10^{-5} \text{ g } H^+/\text{mol}}{\text{g soil}} \times \frac{1,000 \text{ g soil}}{1 \text{ kg soil}}$$

$$\Rightarrow \frac{0.01 \text{ g } H^+/1 \text{ g charge}}{1 \text{ kg soil}}$$

Therefore,

$$\frac{0.01 \text{ g charge/mol}}{1 \text{ kg soil}} \Rightarrow 1 \text{ cmol}_c/\text{kg soil}$$

Example 2:

Calculate the CEC of a soil using the following information:

Cation	Atomic Weight (g mole^{-1})	Amt. on Exchange Sites (ppm)
Calcium (Ca^{+2})	40	4000
Magnesium (Mg^{+2})	24	840
Potassium (K$^+$)	39	78
Sodium (Na$^+$)	23	69
Aluminum (Al^{+3})	27	630
Hydrogen (H$^+$)	1	40

Step 1: First recall that 1 ppm = 1 mg/kg, therefore

Cation	Atomic Wt. (g mole^{-1})	Amt. on Exchange Sites (ppm)	Amt. on Exchange Sites (mg kg^{-1})
Calcium (Ca^{+2})	40	4,000	4,000
Magnesium (Mg^{+2})	24	840	840
Potassium (K$^+$)	39	78	78
Sodium (Na$^+$)	23	69	69
Aluminum (Al^{+3})	27	630	630
Hydrogen (H$^+$)	1	40	40

Step 2: Since CEC is generally expressed in milliequivalents (meq) 100 g^{-1} soil, convert mg kg^{-1} soil by multiplying by 0.1 (100 g divided by 1,000 g/kg).

Cation	Atomic Wt. (g mole^{-1})	Amt. on Exchange Sites (mg kg^{-1})	Amt. on Exchange Sites (mg 100 g^{-1})
Calcium (Ca^{+2})	40	4,000	400
Magnesium (Mg^{+2})	24	840	84
Potassium (K$^+$)	39	78	7.8
Sodium (Na$^+$)	23	69	6.9
Aluminum (Al^{+3})	27	630	63
Hydrogen (H$^+$)	1	40	4

Step 3: Now calculate the mass of meq for each cation. Recall, meq are equal to the atomic weight divided by the valence (e.g., Ca^{+2} has a valence of 2 while K$^+$ has a valence of one). Therefore, 1 meq of Ca^{+2} is equal to the atomic weight (40 g mole^{-1}) divided by the valence (2), and thus 1 meq of Ca^{+2} has a mass of 20 mg.

Cation	Atomic Weight (g mole^{-1})	Mass of 1 meq of Cation (mg)	Amt. on Exchange Sites (mg 100 g^{-1})	Amt. on Exchange Sites (meq 100 g^{-1})
Calcium (Ca^{+2})	40	20	400	20.0
Magnesium (Mg^{+2})	24	12	84	7.0
Potassium (K$^+$)	39	39	7.8	0.2
Sodium (Na$^+$)	23	23	6.9	0.3
Aluminum (Al^{+3})	27	9	63	7.0
Hydrogen (H$^+$)	1	1	4	4.0

Step 4: To calculate the meq of cation on the exchange site, divide the amount on the exchange site by the mass of 1 meq of the cation (e.g., for Ca^{+2}, divide 400 mg 100 g^{-1} soil by 20 mg to find 20.0 meq Ca^{+2} 100 g^{-1} soil).

Cation	Atomic Weight (g mole^{-1})	Mass of 1 meq of Cation (mg)	Amt. on Exchange Sites (mg 100 g^{-1})	Amt. on Exchange Sites (meq 100 g^{-1})
Calcium (Ca+2)	40	20	400	20.0
Magnesium (Mg^{+2})	24	12	84	7.0
Potassium (K$^+$)	39	39	7.8	0.2
Sodium (Na$^+$)	23	23	6.9	0.3
Aluminum (Al^{+3})	27	9	63	7.0
Hydrogen (H$^+$)	1	1	4	4.0

Step 5: To calculate the CEC, sum the amount of cations on the exchange site in meq 100 g^{-1} soil (e.g., CEC = Ca^{+2} [20.0] + Mg^{+2} [7.0] + K$^+$ [0.2] + Na$^+$ [0.3] + Al^{+3} [7.0] + H$^+$ [4.0] → 38.5 meq 100 g^{-1}.

Cation	Atomic Weight (g mole^{-1})	Mass of 1 meq of Cation (mg)	Amount on Exchange Sites (mg 100 g^{-1})	Amount on Exchange Sites (meq 100 g^{-1})
Calcium (Ca^{+2})	40	20	400	20.0
Magnesium (Mg^{+2})	24	12	84	7.0
Potassium (K^{+})	39	39	7.8	0.2
Sodium (Na^{+})	23	23	6.9	0.3
Aluminum (Al^{+3})	27	9	63	7.0
Hydrogen (H^{+})	1	1	4	4.0
CEC				**38.5**

Soils low in CEC retain nutrients poorly, so nutrients may readily leach through the soil profile. Leaching causes inefficient use of applied nutrients and a possible negative environmental impact on underlying water sources. In general, soils with high CECs are more fertile than soils with low CEC, because high CEC soils retain more exchangeable plant nutrients. A high Ca^{+2} level is desirable as well, because it reflects low concentrations of other potentially troublesome cations, like Al^{+3} and H^{+} in acidic soils and Na^{+} in sodic (saline) soils. Liming a soil with a calcium-containing product is a cation exchange reaction where most of the exchangeable Al^{+3} and H^{+} are neutralized. However, excessive amounts of one cation over another may result in an imbalance of nutrients. For example, excessive calcium may replace potassium ions on soil exchange sites, causing potassium deficiency for plants.

Flocculation and Dispersion

As discussed, the type of cation bound to exchange sites on soil colloids is important in determining the fertility and pH of a soil. The greater the quantity of Ca^{+2}, K^{+}, Mg^{+}, Fe^{+2}, and other secondary plant minerals, the more fertile the soil. Also, the more Al^{3+} and H^{+} held by the soil, the more acidic the soil. Cations can also influence the interactions of soil colloids and soil structure. The term **flocculation** describes the attraction of soil colloids to one another (Figure 5-3). Clay particles have an electronegative charge on their surface and therefore have the ability to attract cations. When cations swarm to these negative charges they provide a bridging for clays to form structure. Cations, such as Ca^{+2}, Fe^{+2}, and Al^{3+}, with a high charge density and/or a small hydrated radius promote flocculation or clay structure. These cations suppress the negative charge of the clays, allowing them to attract one another, hence improving soil structure.

Some cations disperse clay particles rather than attract. This process is referred to as **dispersion.** Dispersion is common in arid and semiarid regions where sodium (Na^{+}) accumulates in soils because of low rainfall. Sodium (Na^{+}) is responsible for dispersion since the large hydrated radius of a sodium ion does not allow it to get close enough to the clay particle to completely neutralize the electronegative charge. Sodium is also monovalent which only reacts with one exchange site, hence failing to create a bridge for clay attraction. The lack of colloid attraction degrades soil structure. Soils with poor structure fail to sustain plant growth effectively by reducing drainage and oxygenation. Dispersed soils can be amended with appli-

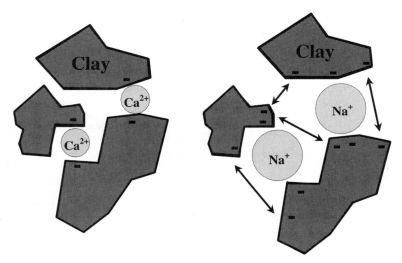

Figure 5-3. Shown are flocculated and dispersed soil clay particles. Calcium with the high charge density and small hydrated radius is able to attract soil colloids. Sodium has a larger radius and low charge density that does not satisfy the electronegativity of clays, causing repulsion of colloids and reducing soil structure.

cations of gypsum which is calcium sulfate ($CaSO_4$). Gypsum improves flocculation by replacing the Na^+ ion with Ca^{2+}. Soil dispersion is generally not a problem in sand-based golf greens because of the absence of electrochemical charges on sand particles. However, sodium can cause other problems in sand-based soils as discussed in Chapter Two.

Origins of Soil CEC

Cation exchange capacity originates from either isomorphic substitution or broken bonds (pH dependent charge). **Isomorphic substitution** occurs during formation of the clay mineral and is when a cation (commonly Fe^{+3}, Fe^{+2}, Mg^{+2}, or Zn^{+2}) substitutes for structural Al^{+3}. This is considered a permanent negative charge and is always present regardless of changes in soil pH. Clays with a high amount of isomorphic substitution are referred to as high-activity clays and generally have higher relative CECs. CEC from broken bonds are the result of a charge deficit on the clay surface and are dependent on soil pH. The CEC of the soil exchange complex (organic matter and clay) generally increases as the soil pH increases due to the dissociation of hydrogen ions from surface sites. These clay minerals are referred to as low activity clays and have lower relative exchange capacities.

The surface charge and expandability of clays are important in CEC values (Table 5-5). Due to their small size, clay particles expose a relatively large external surface area, which can hold ions at the edges of the clay mineral. In addition, certain types of clay (e.g., montmorillonite) have relatively extensive internal surface areas due to their expanding crystal units. These clays swell in the presence of water, increasing their surface area and allowing replacement of cations. For example, hydrogen ions can replace potassium ions within clay sheets when they expand. Montmorillonite also has some isomorphic substitution that further increases CEC values.

Conversely, nonexpanding clays (e.g., kaolinite) have less surface area and are not able to replace ions within its structure. Therefore, the CEC of these low-activity clays originates from broken bonds. Also, kaolinite has almost no isomorphic substitution within its structure, further decreasing its relative CEC.

The CEC on organic matter comes exclusively from broken bonds (ionization of H^+ from carboxyl, COOH, and phenolic, R-OH, groups on humus); there is no isomorphic substitution. However, organic matter, or humus, has a CEC many times greater than clay on a dry weight basis. Therefore, adding a little organic matter can exert a much greater influence on soil CEC than several times more clay. The effective CEC of humus is near zero at pH 4, increasing continuously with a maximum at about pH 10. Hydrogen ions tend to be held strongly to pH-dependent charges but less so to permanent charges.

Soil Type. The CEC of a soil can be estimated from its texture because of the direct relationship between soil texture and clay mineral content, and the indirect relationship of texture and soil organic matter (generally the sandier the soil, the lower its organic matter content). Clay minerals usually range from 4 to 140 meq/100 g, while organic matter can range from 150 to 350 meq/100 g in CEC values (Table 5-5).

Sandy soils generally have low CEC values due to their relatively small surface areas, resulting in less exposed negative charges to attract or hold cations. Sandy soils also contain relatively little organic matter or clay. This results in soils of low CEC, which are relatively infertile and have low water-retention potential, leading to potential nutrient leaching from the root zone. Most of the essential plant nutrients must, therefore, be applied via the turf nutrient-maintenance program. These soils generally benefit from additions of clay or organic matter. The following examples demonstrate how CEC can be calculated if the amount and type of organic matter and clay are known.

Example:

A sample from an 85:15 (sand:sphagnum peat by volume) putting green mix is oxidized (burned) and determined to have 1% organic matter by weight. Calculate a CEC for the mixture; assume the CEC of the peat alone is 125 meq $100 \ g^{-1}$.

Due to relatively low surface area and lack of surface negative charges to retain cations, the CEC contribution of the sand in the mix can be considered negligible. Therefore, the peat will be responsible for nutrient retention and thus the calculation is simple. CEC is determined by multiplying the amount, by weight, of organic matter (1%) by the CEC of the organic matter (125 meq/100 g). Thus, the CEC of the 85:15 mix is 1.25 meq/100 g.

CEC of 85:15 greens mix = 0.01×125 meq/100 g = 1.25 meq/100 g.

Example:

A fairway soil contains 40% clay and 5% humus. Determine the CEC of the soil, assume the clay is kaolinite. Refer to Table 5-4 for CEC values of the individual components.

Step 1: Determine the CEC contribution of the kaolinite clay. Since Table 5-4 lists a range of 4–6 meq 100 g^{-1}, an average of 5 meq 100 g^{-1} is used. The CEC of the clay contribution is determined by multiplying the percent clay (40%) by the CEC of pure kaolinite (5 meq 100 g^{-1}) to obtain 2 meq 100 g^{-1}.

CEC contribution of the clay = 0.4 × 5 meq 100 g^{-1} = 2 meq 100 g^{-1}

Step 2: Determine the CEC contribution of the humus. Since Table 5-4 lists a range of 150–350 meq 100 g^{-1}, an average of 250 meq 100 g^{-1} is used. The CEC of the humus contribution is determined by multiplying the percent humus (5%) by the CEC of pure humus (250 meq 100 g^{-1}) to obtain 12.5 meq 100 g^{-1}.

CEC contribution of the humus = 0.05 × 250 meq 100 g^{-1} = 12.5 meq 100 g^{-1}

Step 3: To determine the CEC of the fairway soil, sum the contribution of each component.

CEC of fairway soil = 2 meq 100 g^{-1} (from clay) + 12.5 meq 100 g^{-1} (from humus)

= 14.5 meq 100 g^{-1}

Increasing Soil CEC. Increasing CEC by adding clay or organic matter to soil is difficult due to the large amount of material needed. For example, to increase the CEC of a soil 1 meq/100 g, its clay or organic matter content must be increased 460 pounds per 1,000 ft^2 of soil (assuming a CEC of 100 meq/100 g for the clay or organic matter and incorporation 6 inches deep). Adding this much material would increase the clay or organic matter content of the soil 1%. As discussed, organic matter generally has a greater potential to increase CEC than clay. For example, a 5% content of organic matter by weight equals the CEC provided by a 30% content of illitic clay. Although additions of clay and organic matter may increase the CEC of sandy soils, excessive increases in these materials may adversely affect soil physical properties such as infiltration and percolation rate.

Base Saturation of the Cation Exchange Capacity. The degree to which the exchange sites are saturated with basic cations such as calcium, magnesium, sodium, and potassium as opposed to acidic cations (H^+ and Al^{+3}), is referred to as the **base saturation** of a soil. In general, the pH and fertility of a soil increase as the percentage base saturation increases. Higher base saturation increases the ease with which cations are absorbed by plants. Greatest availability of most nutrients to plants is in the soil pH range 6 to 7. In highly acidic soils (pH <5.0), exchangeable Al^{+3} may be present and, along with Mg^{+2} and/or H^+ ions, can suppress plant uptake of Ca^{+2} or K^+. However, toxic aluminum becomes less prevalent and therefore less detrimental to plants, as base saturation increases. The following example demonstrates base saturation calculation.

Example:

From the following data, calculate the percent base saturation: Ca^{+2} − 20, Mg^{+2} − 7.0, K^+ − 0.2 and Na^+ − 0.3, Al^{+3} − 7.0, H^+ − 4.0 meq/100 g:

Recall the base saturation is the sum of the basic cation Ca^{+2}, Mg^{+2}, K^+, and Na^+. Therefore, the calculation is the sum of the basic cations divided by the CEC and then multiplied by 100.

$$\% \text{ Base Saturation} = ([20.0 + 7.0 + 0.2 + 0.3]/38.5) \times 100 = 71.4\%$$

Exchangeable Acidity

The degree to which exchange sites are saturated with acidic cations such as H^+ and Al^{+3} is referred to as the **exchangeable acidity.** In general, the pH of a soil decreases (in other words, becomes more acidic) as the percentage exchangeable acidity increases.

Example:

From the data in Example 2, calculate the percent exchangeable acidity.
Recall the amount of exchangeable acidity is the sum of the acidic cations (Al^{+3} and H^+). Therefore, the calculation is the sum of the acidic cations divided by the CEC and then multiplied by 100.

$$\% \text{ Exchangeable Acidity} = ([7.0 + 4.0]/38.5) \times 100 \Rightarrow 8.6\%$$

Note: To check the calculations, remember that the sum of the % Base Saturation and % Exchange Acidity should equal 100% (e.g., 71.4% + 28.6% = 100%).

Measuring Soil CEC

Cation exchange capacity can be estimated or measured by several different methods. Since the direct measurement of CEC is costly and time-consuming, most soil testing laboratories routinely estimate CEC by measuring the predominant extractable cations (Ca^{2+}, Mg^{2+}, K^+, Na^+) and estimating extractable acidity (H^+ and Al^{3+}) from soil pH and buffer pH. This method will give erroneously high CEC values when soil nutrient levels are high and actual soil CEC is low, such as a sand-based green that is recently fertilized. In natural soils with normal nutrient levels, routine laboratory estimates of CEC are realistic.

Direct measurements of CEC may be obtained from some soil-testing laboratories. Methods utilized vary primarily in the pH at which CEC is measured. Soil pH has a large effect on measurement of CEC in soils where the CEC originates mostly from organic matter and low activity clays. The method that determines soil CEC at a pH closest to the pH of the soil as it is used is the most useful method. Soil CEC measured by different methods or estimated by different methods are not directly comparable.

Anion Exchange Capacity

In addition to the nutrient cations, major anions (negatively charged ions) present in soils include nitrate (NO_3^-), phosphate ($H_2PO_4^-$), sulfate (SO_4^{-2}), chloride (Cl^-), and carbonates (HCO_3^- and CO_3^{-2}). These anions generally are present in lower concentrations than the major cations and tend to leach from low CEC sandy soils since sandy soils lack adequate positive charges to retain them. Of these anions, phosphate, sulfate, and nitrate are important nutrient sources for plants. Sulfate, chloride, and carbonate salts tend to accumulate in saline soils including those near the coast. Carbonate anions often are added by the application of liming materials and in irrigation waters but unlike sodic (Na^+) dominant soils, the pH in soils containing free carbonate materials does not exceed 8.3.

Anion exchange capacity is highly dependent on soil pH and only occurs to an appreciable extent at pH <5.0. Since surface soil pH is usually maintained at higher levels, little anion exchange occurs in the root zone of soils used for turf production. Anion exchange, however, may occur in the subsoil of some turf soils.

Turf managers should remember the primary form of nitrogen available to plants in warm soils is nitrate (NO_3^-). Turfgrasses also can utilize ammonium nitrogen (NH_4^+) but due to typically high soil temperatures, ammonium nitrogen is often converted by microorganisms to nitrate nitrogen. Nitrate, which has moved below the root zone, will leach to lower depths or will be denitrified to gas. Other forms of nitrogen in the soil are generally held as insoluble organic matter compounds. Relatively small, frequent nitrogen applications are, therefore, generally more efficient for plant use compared to heavy, infrequent applications. Slow-release nitrogen sources help to reduce the amount of nitrogen leached because of the more gradual release of the nutrients into the soil solution.

Phosphate and sulfate anions are retained in soils by mechanisms other than anion exchange. Retention of these ions is favored by presence of certain cations such as high iron and aluminum oxide content and low pH. The strength of the bonding between these anions and the soil, particularly in the case of phosphate, may be quite strong and result in little of each nutrient remaining plant available. In addition, there is little downward movement of phosphate in most soils, except in extremely sandy soils and with high application rates of phosphate. Sulfate is retained much more weakly than phosphate, therefore retention of sulfate does not occur in the presence of phosphate. Leaching of sulfate from soil layers containing high levels of phosphorus readily occurs. Retention of sulfate, however, will occur when the leaching sulfate encounters low-phosphorus soil.

PRACTICE PROBLEMS

1. A sample from a putting green was analyzed and found to have 0.01 ppm (mg/kg) of H^+. What would be the pH of the soil? (*pH = 5.0*).

2. Name a method/material of increasing and decreasing pH and explain when these materials would be applied. (*Liming is a method of increasing soil pH. A liming material (e.g., calcitic limestone and dolomitic limestone) should be applied when soil pH falls below the optimum range (generally 5.5) for turfgrass growth. A soil should be limed to neutralize exchangeable aluminum, not to neutrality (pH 7.0). To reduce soil pH, use of ammonium-based fertilizers (e.g., ammonium sulfate and sulfur-coated urea) are recommended in less severe cases. However, in extreme cases, elemental sulfur and aluminum sulfate may be used but a potential for turfgrass burn exists.*

3. What adverse effects does soil pH have on soil properties and plant growth? (*nutrient availability [toxicity, exclusions, and deficiencies], rooting, pesticide effectiveness, and microbial activity*).

4. As a liming agent, 1,000 g of $CaCO_3$ is equivalent to how many grams of CaO? (*560 g of CaO*).

5. If an acidic soil can be corrected with 2,000 lb/a of $CaCO_3$, how many pounds per acre of $MgCO_3$ would be needed to accomplish the same thing? (*1,680 lb/a*).

6. Use the following data for calculations;

$$
\begin{aligned}
Ca^{+2} &= 3.5 \text{ meq}/100 \text{ g soil} \\
Mg^{+2} &= 0.5 \text{ meq}/100 \text{ g soil} \\
K^{+} &= 0.2 \text{ meq}/100 \text{ g soil} \\
Na^{+} &= 0.1 \text{ meq}/100 \text{ g soil} \\
Al^{+3} &= 1.2 \text{ meq}/100 \text{ g soil} \\
H^{+} &= 0.2 \text{ meq}/100 \text{ g soil}
\end{aligned}
$$

(a) Calculate the total CEC. (*CEC = 5.7 meq/100 g soil*).
(b) Calculate the percent base saturation. (*% base saturation = 75%*).
(c) Calculate the percent exchangeable acidity. (*25%*).
(d) How many meq/100 g soil of Ca^{+2} would be required to replace all the acidic cations? (*1.4 meq Ca^{+2}/100 g soil*).

7. A soil has a CEC of 5.4 meq/100 g. How many pounds of K^+ can be exchanged in an acre of soil to a depth of 12 cm? (The bulk density is assumed 1.5 g/cm^3.) (*3,377 lbs K^+*).

8. Describe the terms flocculation and dispersion in soils. What cations are responsible for both and why? (*Flocculation describes the attraction of soil colloids to one another and is caused by cations such as Ca^{2+}, Fe^{2+}, and Al^{3+}, with a high charge density and/or a small hydrated radius creating a bridge between soil colloids/clays. Dispersion is the repulsion of clay particles caused by excessive Na^+. Sodium's large hydrated radius and monovalent charge fails to satisfy the electrochemical charge of the clay/colloid, hence failing to create a bridge for clay attraction.*)

9. A limestone analysis shows the CCE at 90% and the fineness report shows 5% retained on 8-mesh, 5% retained on 40-mesh, 25% retained on 60-mesh, and 65% passing 60-mesh. Find the ECC and the quantity of lime necessary to apply 1,000 lb of pure $CaCO_3$ per acre. (*ECC = 73.1%; 1,368 lb lime/ A to properly apply 1,000 lb of $CaCO_3$*).

10. A soil contains 20% clay; 15% of the clay is kaolinite and 5% is montmorillonite. The organic matter content is 2%. Estimate the CEC. (*9.75 meq/ 100 g soil*).

11. Convert 40 mg of Ca^{+2} to milliequivalent weight. (*2 meq*).

12. How many milligrams are in 3 meq of Al^{+3}? (*27 mg*).

13. Name the two origins of CEC. Which has a permanent charge and which has pH dependent charges? (*Isomorphic substitution [permanent charge] and broken bonds [pH dependent charges]*).

CHAPTER 6

PLANT NUTRITION AND
TURF FERTILIZERS

INTRODUCTION

Proper fertilization is essential for maintaining high-quality turfgrasses. Fertilization provides plants with nutrients necessary to carry out physiological processes. The availability of nutrients affects turfgrass color, density, and vigor, and also allows turf plants to better resist diseases, weeds, insects, and extremes in climate conditions. There are currently 16 elements (17, for plants requiring sodium, Na) which are known to be essential to plant growth. These **essential elements** are classified into two categories based on their concentrations in plant tissue: **macronutrients**, and **micronutrients**. Macronutrients are found in concentrations greater than 500 to 1,000 parts per million (ppm), and micronutrients are found at concentrations of less than 100 parts per million. The 16 essential elements are described and classified in Table 6-1.

The three most abundant macronutrients in plant tissues are oxygen (O), carbon (C), and hydrogen (H). These nutrients are obtained from air and water, and are combined to form carbohydrates in the presence of light and chlorophyll through the process of photosynthesis.

Photosynthesis Reaction

$$\underset{\text{carbon}}{6CO_2} + \underset{\text{water}}{12H_2O} \xrightarrow[\text{chlorophyll}]{\text{light}} \underset{\substack{\text{carbohydrates} \\ \text{(or sugars)}}}{C_6H_{12}O_6} + \underset{\text{oxygen}}{6O_2} + \underset{\text{water}}{6H_2O}$$

Carbon dioxide is absorbed through leaf stomata and water is absorbed through roots. Therefore, fertilizer practices affecting root growth and function, as well as stomata opening and closing, indirectly influence a plant's ability to produce carbohydrates by photosynthesis. Carbohydrates produced from photosynthesis are used to generate more complex compounds such as starch and amino acids that

TABLE 6-1. Elements, Their Most Common Available Forms for Plant Uptake, and Primary Functions in Turfgrass Growth (McCarty, 2001)

Element (chemical symbol)	Most Common Used Form(s)	Function in Plant Growth
Macronutrients Obtained from air and water	Oxygen (O)	CO_2	Through photosynthesis, these elements are converted to simple carbohydrates and finally into amino acids, proteins, protoplasm, enzymes, and lipids.
	Carbon (C)	CO_2	
	Hydrogen (H)	H_2O	
Macronutrients Obtained primarily from fertilization	Nitrogen (N)	NO_3^- (nitrate) NH_4^+ (ammonium)	A mobile element within the plant. Used in the formation of amino acids, enzymes, proteins, nucleic acids, and chlorophyll. Generally increases color and shoot growth. Conversely, excessive N generally reduces heat, cold and drought hardiness; disease and nematode resistance; wear tolerance; and root growth.
	Phosphorus (P)	$H_2PO_4^-$ HPO_4^{-2} (phosphates)	A mobile element which is a constituent of phospholipids and nucleic acids. Involved in a carbohydrate transport system which moves energy to all parts of the plant for vital growth processes. This function in root development is most vital. P also hastens plant maturity, and is needed for glycolysis, amino acid metabolism, fat metabolism, sulfur metabolism, biological oxidation, and photosynthesis. In addition, P influences maturation, establishment, and seed production.
	Potassium (K)	K^+	A mobile element that is used by plants in large quantities, second only to nitrogen. K is essential for control and regulation of various minerals; adjustment of stomatal movements and water relation; promotion of meristematic tissue and rooting; activation of various enzymes; synthesis of proteins; and carbohydrate metabolism. K helps increase heat, cold, and drought hardiness; wear tolerance; and increases disease and nematode resistance.

TABLE 6-1. Elements, Their Most Common Available Forms for Plant Uptake, and Primary Functions in Turfgrass Growth (McCarty, 2001) (*Continued*)

Element (chemical symbol)	Most Common Used Form(s)	Function in Plant Growth
Secondary Nutrients Present in some fertilizer formulations; available in most soils, and/or as part of conditioners such as lime, dolomitic lime, and gypsum.		
Calcium (Ca)	Ca^{+2}	Immobile. Required for cell division (mitosis); important in cell membrane permeability; activates certain enzymes; provides chromosome stability and structure; and enhances carbohydrate translocation, formation, and increases protein content of mitochondria. Influences absorption of other plant nutrients. Also strongly influences soil pH and can improve soil structure, water retention, and infiltration by releasing sodium ions.
Magnesium (Mg)	Mg^{+2}	A mobile element that is a component of chlorophyll; assists in the stabilization of ribosome particles, and activates several plant enzyme systems such as carbohydrate and phosphate metabolism and cell respiration. Serves as a specific activator for a number of enzymes.
Sulfur (S)	SO_4^{-2}	A partially mobile element that is required for the synthesis of sulfur-containing amino acids—cystine, cysteine, and methionine; required for protein synthesis and activation of certain enzymes and two hormone constituents.
Micronutrients Most premium fertilizers contain these.		
Iron (Fe)	Fe^{+2} (ferrous) Fe^{+3} (ferric) $Fe(OH)_2^{+}$	Immobile. Necessary for chlorophyll, heme, and cytochrome production and in ferredoxin which participates in cellular respiratory (oxidation-reduction reactions) mechanism; an essential component of iron enzymes and carriers. Generally, increases color, shoot and root growth.
Manganese (Mn)	Mn^{+2}, organic salts	Immobile. Activates Mangano-enzyme; needed in Photosystem II of photosynthesis; connected with carbohydrate (nitrogen) metabolism, chlorophyll synthesis, oxidation-reduction process, phosphorylation reaction, and the citric acid (or TCA) cycle.

Element	Ion	Description
Copper (Cu)	Cu^{+2} (cupric) Cu^+ (cuprous)	Immobile. Connected with the light reaction during photosynthesis as a constituent of oxidation-reduction enzymes; found in cytochrome oxidase which is essential for plant (carbohydrate) metabolism and is used for production of the enzyme polyphenol oxidase; used as catalysts in plant metabolism.
Chlorine (Cl)	Cl^- (chloride)	Immobile. Possibly required for photosynthesis of isolated chloroplasts and as a bromide substitute. Believed to influence osmotic pressure and in balancing cell cationic charges. Also affects root growth.
Zinc (Zn)	Zn^{+2} $Zn(OH)^+$	Mobile. Component of the enzyme dehydrogenase which is needed for RNA and cytoplasmic ribosomes in cells, proteinases, peptidases and IAA (auxin) synthesis. Involved in the conversion of ammonium to amino nitrogen. Necessary for chlorophyll production, promotes seed maturation and production.
Boron (B)	H_3BO_3 (boric acid) HBO_3^{-2} $B_4O_7^{-2}$ BO_3^{-3}	Immobile. Facilitates sugar transport through membranes; involved in auxin metabolism in root elongation, protein and phosphate utilization; influences cell division (growth) by control of polysaccharide formation. B is a nonmetal.
Molybdenum (Mo)	MoO_4^{-2} (molybdate)	Required for the assimilation and reduction processes in nitrogen fixation to produce amino acids and proteins.
Sodium (Na)	Na^+	Regulates stomatal opening and nitrate reductase. Toxic levels are generally more of a problem than deficiencies.

require other essential elements, which are mainly absorbed by roots in the form of ions.

Mineral Mobility and Deficiencies

Nutrients are **mobile** if the plant can transport them from one tissue to another. Deficiency symptoms of mobile elements tend to develop in older tissues first as plants relocate nutrients from older tissues to support new growth. Mobile elements include nitrogen, phosphorus, potassium, magnesium, sulfur (limited mobility), and zinc. Deficiency symptoms of **immobile** elements appear in new growth as the plant is unable to relocate them from older tissues. Immobile elements include calcium, iron, boron, manganese, and copper.

Nutrient deficiencies are often due to external conditions that prevent their uptake from the soil, rather than actually being absent in the soil. Soil and tissue testing should be used to determine if sufficient nutrients are in the soil and if plant tissues are able to attain them. Restricted root and tissue growth from improper soil pH, inadequate or excessive moisture, or temperatures outside optimum ranges are several common reasons nutrient deficiencies may occur even though tests may indicate adequate levels in the soil.

PRIMARY NUTRIENTS AND FERTILIZERS

Nitrogen, phosphorus, and potassium fertilizers receive the greatest attention because they are most typically deficient and must be applied regularly. These elements are also required in the greatest amounts, and are referred to as the **primary** nutrients or elements. **Secondary** elements consist of calcium, magnesium, and sulfur. The remaining **micronutrients** are essential elements that are required in smaller amounts by plants.

Nitrogen

Nitrogen (N) is required by turf plants in larger quantities than any other element except C, H, and O. Turfgrass N tissue concentrations typically range from 2 to 6% (20 to 60 g N per kg) of total dry matter. Mobile within the plant, N is essential for the formation of amino acids, enzymes, proteins, nucleic acids, and chlorophyll. Nitrogen fertilizer application generally increases color and shoot growth. Although N must be applied to turfgrasses more than any other element, excessive N fertilization can lead to reduced heat, cold, drought, disease, nematode, and wear tolerance. Nitrogen can be detrimental to root growth as flushes of shoot growth diminish carbohydrates stored in roots. Excessive N fertilization can also lead to adverse environmental effects such as nitrate leaching into ground and surface waters.

Nitrogen Deficiency. When N is deficient in plants, chlorophyll production is reduced, resulting in an overall pale yellow-green coloration called **chlorosis**. Since N is mobile within plants, chlorosis due to insufficient N usually occurs first on the lower (older) leaves. In addition to chlorosis, N deficiency in turf causes slower growth rates and lower shoot density, resulting in lower recuperative ability. Chlorosis and thinning are not necessarily signs of N deficiency. Other factors can cause similar symptoms. Chlorosis may also be caused by iron, sulfur, or manganese deficiencies, and nematodes and other pests or diseases may cause thinning. Therefore, turf managers should determine the cause of these symptoms before indiscriminately applying N fertilizers.

Origins and Losses. Turfgrasses may obtain N from organic matter decomposition and, to a small degree, from air as N that has been oxidized by lightning and dispersed by rainfall (Figure 6-1). Additional N is typically applied as commercial fertilizers to maintain high-quality turfgrass. In soil, ammonium (NH_4^+), nitrate (NO_3^-), and nitrite (NO_2^-) forms are the most important compounds. Ammonium and nitrate forms of N are the only ones used by turf plants. While N may be applied in many forms, it must be changed to one of these two forms for plant use.

Soil microorganisms can break down or transform organic and some slow release fertilizer sources of N into nitrate or ammonium forms through the process of **mineralization**. This process involves three steps: **aminization**, **ammonification**, and **nitrification**. Aminization and ammonification are steps of mineralization in which proteins, amines, and amino acids (usually from organic matter or humus), are converted to ammonium. Ammonium N is the preferred N source because it does not require extra energy input by plants for assimilation and is less likely to leach or be subject to denitrification. Mineralization is described as the following:

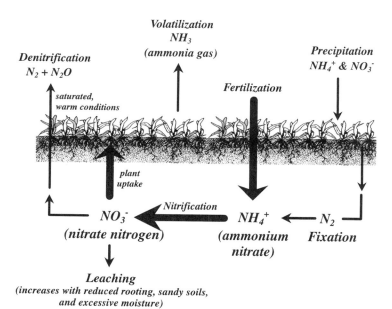

Figure 6-1. The turfgrass nitrogen cycle involving nitrogen additions, losses, and changes. The larger arrows represent more important and likely pathways.

Mineralization (Aminization and Ammonification)

$$R\text{—}NH_2 + H_2O \xrightarrow{\text{microorganisms}} NH_4^+ + R\text{—}OH + 275 \text{ kJ}$$

organic   water   ammonium   hydroxyl   energy
nitrogen   nitrogen   group

Nitrification is the transformation of ammonium to nitrate by soil microorganisms. It is favored by warm soil temperatures, adequate soil moisture, and soil oxygen. Nitrification does not readily occur under extreme temperatures (e.g., below freezing or above 105°F), in saturated or poorly aerated soil, in excessively dry soil, or in low pH (<4.8) soil. If nitrification does not occur, ammonium may accumulate to a point at which it becomes toxic to plants. Nitrate N is readily soluble in water and may be repelled by negatively charged exchange sites of the soil colloids. Therefore, unless grasses rapidly utilize this form, it may be lost through leaching. In addition to nitrate and water, hydrogen ions (H^+) are also produced during nitrification, which may then reduce soil pH. Nitrification is described as the following:

Nitrification

$$NH_4^+ + 1\tfrac{1}{2}O_2 \xrightarrow[\substack{\text{warm}\\\text{temperatures}}]{\substack{\text{Nitrosomonas}\\\text{bacteria}}} NO_2^- + 2H^+ + H_2O \xrightarrow[+\,\tfrac{1}{2}O_2]{\text{Nitrobacteria}}$$

ammonium   nitrite
nitrogen   nitrogen

$$NO_3^- + H_2O + 76 \text{ kJ energy}$$

nitrate
nitrogen

In addition to N losses from leaching and plant consumption, soil N can also be reduced through the processes of **denitrification** and **volatilization**. Denitrification is the conversion of nitrate under anaerobic conditions to gaseous N which can be lost to the atmosphere. Certain anaerobic soil microorganisms obtain oxygen from nitrates and nitrites, resulting in a release of nitrous oxide and nitrogen gas:

Denitrification

Numbers in parentheses represent valence or oxidation state.

$$2NO_3^- \xrightarrow{\uparrow O_2} 2NO_2^- \xrightarrow{\uparrow O_2} 2NO \xrightarrow{\uparrow O} N_2O\uparrow \xrightarrow{\uparrow O} N_2\uparrow$$

nitrate nitrogen   nitrate nitrogen   nitric oxide   nitrous oxide   gaseous
(+5)   (+3)   (+2)   (+1)   nitrogen (0)

Volatilization is the conversion of ammonium to ammonia gas, which can be lost to the atmosphere. If ammonium comes into direct contact with free calcium carbonate in the soil, ammonium bicarbonate will be formed. Ammonium bicarbonate is a relatively unstable compound. Upon exposure to the sun, it will decompose into ammonia, carbon dioxide, and water:

Ammonia Volatilization

$$NH_4^+ \quad + \quad CaCO_3 \quad \rightarrow \quad NH_3\uparrow \quad + \quad HCO_3^- \quad + \quad Ca^{+2}$$

ammonium nitrogen	calcium carbonate	ammonia gas	bicarbonate	calcium
(surface application)	(lime)			

Volatilization of ammonia can usually be avoided by incorporation of ammonium fertilizers into the soil. Irrigating with approximately ¼- to ½-inch water after ammonium fertilizer application also helps to minimize this potential N loss.

Calculating Nutrient Percentages

To determine the percentage of a particular nutrient in a fertilizer, the fertilizer formula and nutrient (chemical) atomic weights are needed. For example, to determine the percentage of N and P in diammonium phosphate (DAP), one needs to know the fertilizer formula $[(NH_4)_2HPO_4]$ and atomic weights of N (14), H (1), P (31), and O (17). The percentage of N and P are then calculated by adding up the total atomic weight of DAP and determining what percentage of this total is N and P.

For N:

$$\%N = \frac{2\,N}{(NH_4)_2HPO_4} \times 100$$

$$= \frac{2 \times 14}{2[14 + (4 \times 1)] + 1 + 31 + (4 \times 17)} \times 100 = 21\%$$

For P:

$$\%P = \frac{P}{(NH_4)_2HPO_4} \times 100$$

$$= \frac{31}{2[14 + (4 \times 1)] + 1 + 31 + (4 \times 17)} \times 100 = 23\%$$

Nitrogen Carriers

Synthetic N fertilizers are produced by reacting atmospheric N_2 and hydrogen gas (H_2) under heat and pressure to form ammonia (NH_3). The ammonia produced may then be further processed to form various inorganic fertilizers (Figure 6-2). Chemically, N sources are classified as either **quick-release (soluble)** or **slow-release (water-insoluble)**. Table 6-2 lists the most widely used N turf fertilizers and their characteristics.

Soluble N Sources. Soluble or quick-release forms of N fertilizers are available as liquids or granules. These forms are readily available to turf plants and result in a rapid color and growth response approximately 2 days after application. Sol-

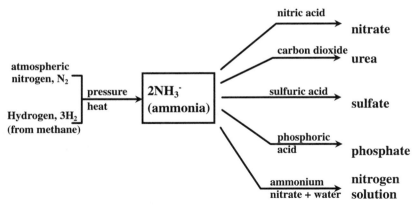

Figure 6-2. Manufacturing process of synthesizing various nitrogen fertilizers by reacting ammonia nitrogen with various chemicals.

uble sources of N are in either the ammonium or nitrate form. Nitrate forms are more prone to leaching while ammonium forms are prone to volatilization.

Soluble N sources dissolve in water to form cations and anions. This salt-like characteristic results in a greater plant tissue burn potential of the fertilizer. Burn potential can be reduced by making applications only to dry turf surfaces and when air temperatures are cooler than 80°F. Watering-in soluble N fertilizers immediately following application can also reduce the potential for burn. Some N fertilizer solutions available include: methylol urea + urea (30-0-0); methylene ureas + urea (28-0-0); triazones + urea (28-0-0); ammonium polyphosphate (10-34-0); and ammonium thiosulfate (12-0-0).

Urea is a white crystalline solid formed by reacting ammonia gas with carbon dioxide.

$$\underset{\text{carbon dioxide}}{CO_2} \quad + \quad \underset{\text{ammonia}}{2NH_3} \quad \rightarrow \quad \underset{\text{urea}}{CO(NH_2)_2} + \underset{\text{water}}{H_2O}$$

Urea is very soluble in water and has a 45% N content. Urea is unavailable to plants until it is converted to ammonium. Once applied, urea is broken down into ammonium carbonate by the enzyme **urease** which is present on plant tissue and organic matter. Direct applications of urea to the turf surface can result in conversion of the ammonium carbonate to ammonia and carbon dioxide, resulting in excess loss by volatilization. Volatilization can be avoided by irrigating after application to incorporate the nitrogen. Urea volatilization is described as:

Urea Volatilization

$$\underset{\text{urea}}{(NH_2)_2CO} \underset{H_2O}{\xrightarrow{\text{urease}}} \quad \underset{\text{ammonia bicarbonate}}{(NH_4)_2CO_3} \quad \rightarrow\rightarrow \quad \underset{\text{ammonia}}{NH_3\uparrow} + \quad \underset{\text{carbon dioxide}}{CO_2}$$

Ammonium sulfate/nitrate, ammonium phosphate, potassium nitrate, and cal-

TABLE 6-2. Primary Nutrient Sources and Characteristics Used in Turf Fertilizers (Modified from McCarty, 2001)

Nutrient Source [formula]	Approximate Nutrient Percentage				Salt Index (Foliar Burn Potential)		Acidifying Effect	Comment
	N	P_2O_5	K_2O	Water-Insoluble N	Per Nutrient Unit[a]	Relative to Sodium Nitrate (100)		
Synthetic Inorganic								
Ammonium nitrate [NH_4NO_3]	33	0	0	0	3.0 (high)	105	Medium	Water soluble; half N content is in the ammonium form, the other half in the nitrate form; high burn potential; potential fire and explosive hazard. Very hygroscopic (water loving) unless coated.
Ammonium sulfate [$(NH_4)_2SO_4$]	21	0	0	0	3.3 (high)	69	High	Water soluble; contains 24% S; has greatest acidifying effect of listed sources. Often used in flooded soils.
Calcium nitrate [$Ca(NO_3)_2$]	16	0	0	0	4.1 (v. high)	—	Basic	Very hygroscopic unless in airtight containers; contains 19% Ca and 1.5% Mg; fast-acting with high burn potential; N release is not temperature dependent; used on sodic soils to displace sodium.
Potassium nitrate [KNO_3]	13	0	44	0	1.6 (high)	74	Basic	Also known as saltpeter or nitre. Water soluble K source with supplemental N; low salt concentration, low chloride, fire hazard. Has alkalinity effect.
Nitrate of soda (sodium nitrate) [$NaNO_3$]	16	0	0	0	6.1 (v. high)	100	Basic	Water soluble; has highest burn potential of all materials. Has alkalinity effect.
Synthetic Organics								
Urea [$CO(NH_2)_2$]	45	0	0	0	1.6 (high)	75	Medium	Water soluble; rapid release; may volatilize if surface applied, especially under alkaline conditions; may leach rapidly if rainfall occurs immediately after application.

TABLE 6-2. Primary Nutrient Sources and Characteristics Used in Turf Fertilizers (Modified from McCarty, 2001) *(Continued)*

Nutrient Source [formula]	Approximate Nutrient Percentage				Salt Index (Foliar Burn Potential)		Acidifying Effect	Comment
	N	P_2O_5	K_2O	Water-Insoluble N	Per Nutrient Unit[a]	Relative to Sodium Nitrate (100)		
Urea formaldehyde (or UF) [CO(NH₂)₂ CH₂]ₙCO(NH₂)₂]	18–40 (38)	0	0	12–35 (27)	0.3 (low)	—	Low	Slowly soluble; N release rate is temperature and formulation dependent. Urea form contains 38-0-0 (27% water-insoluble), methylene ureas are 40-0-0 (~15% water-insoluble).
Isobutylidene Diurea (or IBDU) [CO(NH₂)₂]₂C₄H₈]	31	0	0	27	0.2 (low)	—	Low	Slowly soluble; N release rate is not temperature dependent but depends on moisture availability and particle size. Fine particle sizes contain 26% water insoluble N while coarse particles contain 28% water-insoluble N.
Coated								
Sulfur-coated urea (or SCU) [CO(NH₂)₂ + S]	15–45 (32)	0	0	—	0.7 (low)	—	Medium	Slowly soluble; contains 10-20% S; N release rate is temperature and coating thickness dependent. Has minor acidifying effect.
Plastic or Poly resin-coated urea	10–44	0	0	—	— (low)	—	Low	Slowly soluble; N release rate is temperature and coating thickness dependent.
Natural Organics								
Milorganite	6	4	0	5.5	0.6 (low)	3	Low	Activated sewage sludge; N release rate increases with higher temperatures; contains micronutrients, especially Fe.
Ringer Turf, Nature Safe, Red Rooster, Sustane, Actinite, Hynite + others	5–18	1–6	5–6	—	varies (low)	~3.5	Low	Nitrogen is from urea, methylene ureas, ammoniacal sources, water and hydrolyzed poultry feather meal, bone meal, leather tankage, fish meal, and blood.

[a] Based on 20 pounds of plant nutrients. Generally, the higher the salt index/unit of nutrient, the higher the burn potential of the particular fertilizer material.

cium nitrate are other commonly used water-soluble N sources collectively referred to as **inorganic salts**. Once dissolved, ammonium ions can be converted by nitrobacteria into nitrate, which is the main available form to plants. Unlike ammonium sulfate and phosphate, potassium nitrate and calcium nitrate fertilizers do not need to undergo conversion by nitrobacteria since their N source is already in the form of nitrate.

Slow-Release N Sources. Many slow- or control-release N fertilizers have been developed to overcome some of the disadvantages of soluble N sources (Figure 6-3). These slow-release N fertilizers are either slowly soluble, slowly released, or held in a natural organic form. Advantages of these slow-release forms include a more uniform growth response, less potential for N loss, and lower salt burn potential. There are, however, some drawbacks to slow-release N sources. Slow-release sources have higher per unit costs than soluble sources due to increased manufacturing processes, slower initial plant response, and are not adaptable to liquid application systems. In addition, application rates at which these sources release N may vary with fertilizer timing, source, temperature, moisture, pH, and particle size. To be considered a slow-release fertilizer, at least 15% of the nutrient in a fertilizer is released slowly over a period of time. General characteristics of several slow-release N sources are listed in Table 6-3.

Sulfur-Coated Urea (SCU). Sulfur-coated urea is manufactured by passing granulated or prilled urea pellets through a pressurized stream of molten sulfur in a rotating drum. Coated particles are then sealed with a microcrystalline wax which protects the surface from microbial degradation, strengthens the sulfur shell, and decreases the initial release of urea. After cooling, a diatomaceous earth or vermiculite clay coating is added to reduce cracking. The urea is gradually released by diffusion through cracks, holes, and imperfections in the coating surface.

The nonuniform coatings crack at different times, resulting in variable N release rates. The rate at which urea diffuses through the sulfur coating also depends on soil conditions. Nitrogen release is more rapid in soils with warm temperatures, good moisture, and neutral pH, all of which favor soil microorganism activity. A slow-release pattern is the result of the average release of individual particles. Some particles release N immediately, others with release somewhat delayed, and the remainder releasing after considerable delay.

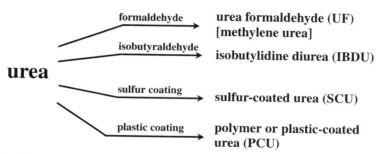

Figure 6-3. Manufacturing process of slow-release nitrogen fertilizers by reacting urea with various chemicals.

TABLE 6-3. General Characteristics of Several Slow-Release Nitrogen Sources (McCarty, 2001)

Characteristic	Sulfur Coated Urea (SCU)	Polymer Coated Urea (PCU)	Urea Formaldehyde (UF)	Methylene Urea (MU)	Isobutylidene Diurea (IBDU)	Natural Organic
Percent N	39% N	41–42% N	38% N	40% N	31% N	2–10% N
Immediately available N	3.9% N	0% N	11% N	26% N	3.1% N	10% N
Release time	12–16 weeks	8–16 weeks	2 years	8–12 weeks	12–16 weeks	8–52 weeks
Release mechanism	coating breakdown	osmosis	microbial	microbial	hydrolysis	microbial
Release requirements	moisture	moisture	moisture & soil temperature	moisture & soil temperature	moisture	moisture & soil temperature
Best response season	all seasons	summer	summer	summer	spring & fall	summer
Initial response	medium	slow	medium-slow	medium	medium-slow	slow
Residual effect	extended	extended	extended	extended	extended	extended
Water solubility	low	low	medium-low	medium	medium-low	low
Foliar burn potential	low	low	low	low	low	low
Soil temperature release dependence	low	medium	high	medium	low	high

Sulfur-coated urea particles are subject to damage, which can result in an immediate release of N. The granules can be damaged during transport, blending, and application, or from the weight of mowers, rollers, or wheels. While heavier sulfur coatings release N more slowly, problems can occur with mower crushing or pickup. Finer microprills or miniprills should therefore be used for greens application, and SCU handling should be kept to a minimum as a general rule.

Polymer-Coated Urea or Plastic/Resin-Coated Urea. In a similar technology to SCU, urea or other soluble N sources can be coated with a resin or polymer plastic material. Resin coatings rely on osmosis rather than coating imperfections to release N. Once inside the coating, water dissolves some of the solid fertilizer, creating a concentrated solution which then diffuses back through the coating and out into the soil. As the particles swell, urea may also be released by pellet cracking. The process of controlled diffusion is essentially constant over time.

Resin-coated fertilizers have a more predictable controlled-release characteristic than sulfur-coated products. Release rates vary from 70 to 270 days, depending on coating thickness and water dissolution into the prill. Higher temperatures can increase release rates and decrease longevity. The major disadvantage of resin-coated fertilizers is cost when compared to other slow-release fertilizers.

Several variations of resin coatings are available. Sulfur-coated urea may be additionally coated with a polymer. This secondary coating protects the prill, decreases dust when handling, and controls the release of nutrients along with the sulfur layer. Another coating method involves a thin double coating of resin followed by a sulfur coating. Although thin, the two resin coats together form a strong shell. This type of product appears to be less affected by temperature. Examples include: *PolyPlus, Poly-S, Poly-XPRO, Poly NS-52,* and *TriKote.* A newer process involves a coating of diphenylmethane diisocyanate followed by a polyol coating, which combined form a layer of polyurethane. These products also rely on diffusion for N release, with longevity of release depending on coating thickness. Examples of poly-coated fertilizers include: *PolyOn; Osmocote; Sierra; Agriform; ProKote; ScottKote, Meister; V-Cote;* and *MultiCote.*

Controlled-Release Synthetic N Sources (Noncoated). **Isobutelene diurea (IBDU)** is formed by reacting isobutyraldehyde with urea in an acid solution to form a single-molecule material containing 31% N, of which 90% is insoluble. Water facilitates the hydrolysis of IBDU back to urea and butyric acid.

$$\begin{array}{c}CH_3 \\ \diagdown \\ CHCHO \\ \diagup \\ CH_3\end{array} + 2NH_2\text{-}CO\text{-}NH_2 \longrightarrow \begin{array}{c}CH_3 \qquad NHCONH_2 \\ \diagdown \quad \diagup \\ CHCH \\ \diagup \quad \diagdown \\ CH_3 \qquad NHCONH_2\end{array} + H_2O$$

isobutyraldehyde   urea   isobutylidene diurea (or IBDU)

The N release of IBDU is primarily dependent on particle size and soil moisture and is not as dependent on temperature. This allows for a faster release of N in winter months when compared to other controlled-release fertilizers which are dependent on microbial activity. IBDU is affected by soil pH, with optimum release ranging from pH 5 to 8. Particle size has the greatest influence on N release with smaller particles providing greater surface area and thus increasing the rate of hydrolysis.

Ureaformaldehyde (UF) or ureaform is a generic designation for several methylene urea polymers formed by reacting urea with formaldehyde to first form monomethylol urea and then form soluble methylene urea and ureaform. Ureaform fertilizers contain 38% N.

1. $CO(NH_2)_2 + CH_2O \qquad\qquad \rightarrow NH_2-CO-NH-CH_2-OH$
   urea   formaldehyde   methylol urea

2. $CO(NH_2)_2 + NH_2-CO-NH-CH_2-OH \rightarrow NH_2-CO-NH-CH_2-NH-CO-NH_2 + H_2O$
   urea   methylol urea   methylene diurea   water
                                            (or urea formaldehyde, UF)

These products have varying length polymers of methylene urea depending on the proportion of ureas and formaldehyde in the initial reaction. Chain length determines solubility. Longer polymers have less solubility. The smaller the ratio of urea to formaldehyde, the longer the chain of polymers formed and the longer the residual time of N release. Manufacturers alter the proportions of urea and formaldehyde to meet the desired qualities of a particular use. Nitrogen in UF sources are classified as:

1. **Cold-water-soluble N (CWSN):** readily available and can be in liquid formulation.
2. **Cold-water-insoluble N (CWIN** at 20° to 25°C): available over several weeks by microbial degradation.
3. **Hot-water-insoluble N (HWIN** at 98° to 100°C): available over several months by slow microbial degradation.

All UF products depend on microbial degradation for N availability. Therefore, conditions favoring microbial activity promote N release. Shorter-chained polymers are more readily digested by microorganisms. Nitrogen from UF is mineralized to ammonium throughout the growing season.

Natural Organic N Sources. Composted or waste materials of human or animal origin have been adapted for use as slow-release N fertilizers. These sources include manure, sludges, bone meal, humates, and composted plant residues. The nutrient contents of these materials are usually low, and are described in Table 6-4. Organic N forms are converted to ammonium and then to nitrate by soil microorganisms. Advantages of organic N sources are limited burn potential, little effect on pH, and low leaching losses. Other nutrients are usually included in addition to N, and some sources may also improve the physical condition of sandy soils.

Milorganite. Milorganite is the most widely used commercial organic N source for turf. It is an activated sewage sludge from the Milwaukee Sewage Commission.

TABLE 6-4. Approximate Amounts of Macronutrients Often Found in Common Organic Fertilizer Sources (Modified from McCarty, 2001)

Nutrient Source	N	P_2O_5	K_2O
		%	
Animal By-products			
Dried blood	13	2	1
Bone meal, steamed	3	25	0
Dried fish meal	10	7	0
Fish emulsion	4–5	2–4	1–2
Tankage, animal	7	10	1
Excreta			
Guano, bat	8.5	5	1.5
Guano, bird	8–13	8–15	2
Cattle manure	2–5	1.5	2
Horse manure	2–8	1–3	2–7
Poultry manure	5–15	3	1.5
Sewage sludge, dried	2	2	—
Sewage sludge, activated	6	3	0.5
Swine manure	7	4	6
Plant Residues			
Cottonseed meal	7	3	2
Garbage tankage	2.5	3	1
Linseed meal	5.5	2	1.5
Rapeseed meal	5.5	2.5	1.5
Soybean meal	7	1.5	2.5
Tobacco stems	2	0.5	6
Alfalfa meal	3	1	2
Peat	1–3	0.25–0.5	0.5–1
Seaweed kelp extract	1–2	0–1	5–13
Wood ashes	0	1–2	3–7
Compost	1–3	0.5–1	1–3

Raw sewage is inoculated with microorganisms, aerated, filtered, dried, ground, screened, and sterilized. The result is a product containing approximately 6% N which is 92% soluble. Milorganite also contains 2% phosphorus as P_2O_5 and an array of micronutrients.

Advantages of Milorganite include low burn potential and a uniform release of N over 3 to 4 weeks with little effect on soil pH and salinity. Milorganite also provides iron, copper, and zinc, and has low leaching and volatilization losses. Disadvantages include a higher cost per unit N, a lack of potassium, and dependence on soil microorganisms for release. Its dark color can, however, serve as a soil warmer in cooler weather, which can increase microbial activity. Other notable commercial organic N sources include *Actinite* and *Hynite*.

Phosphorus

Phosphorus (P) is the second most likely deficient nutrient for plant growth. Turf tissue P concentrations typically range from 0.1 to 1% by dry weight. Phosphorus concentrations of less than 0.2% are considered deficient and levels above 1% are considered excessive for turf. Highest tissue concentrations of P are typically found in new leaves and growing points. Phosphorous plays an essential role as a component of adenosine triphosphate (ATP), the molecule responsible for the transfer of energy during metabolic processes. It is also an essential component of deoxyribonucleic acid (DNA), ribonucleic acid (RNA), and phospholipid cellular membranes.

Phosphorus Deficiency

Phosphorus is mobile in plants, therefore P deficiency symptoms typically appear first in older tissues. Symptoms include overall slow growth, and weak, stunted plants with dark green lower leaves. Lower leaves may eventually turn reddish purple along leaf margins. Severe P deficiency is evidenced by reddish leaf tips which may develop into streaks down the blades. Roots are used for energy storage in the form of carbohydrates, and are very dependent on adequate P levels. When root growth is slowed, soil P is not readily encountered. Therefore, P deficiencies most often occur under conditions which restrict root growth such as low soil temperatures, low soil oxygen, and during establishment.

Soil Phosphorus and Plant Uptake. Phosphorus is relatively insoluble in soils and is predominately absorbed by plants in the orthophosphate ion forms of $H_2PO_4^-$ and HPO_4^{-2} from the soil solution. The availability of soil P is highly pH dependent. Extremes in soil pH can result in precipitation of P in insoluble forms. Soils should therefore be managed to maintain a pH between 5.5 and 6.5 to get maximum benefit from applied P. The equilibrium between forms of soil P is illustrated by:

Phosphorus Forms at Various Soil pH Levels

$$H_2PO_4^- \quad \leftrightarrow \quad H_2O + HPO_4^- \quad \leftrightarrow \quad H_2O + PO_4^{-3}$$

(acid conditions − soil pH <6.0)　　(neutral soils − pH 7.0)　　(alkaline conditions–soil pH > 8.0)

Although negatively charged, phosphate ($H_2PO_4^-$) does not readily leach in acid soil due to its binding to cationic metals such as calcium, iron, or aluminum (CA^{+2}, Fe^{+2}, Fe^{+3}, Al^{+3}) that are associated with negatively charged colloids (clays or organic matter). This interaction forms colloid-metal-phosphate complexes, which bind the phosphate to the colloid. Phosphate also binds to cations in the soil solution to form insoluble calcium, iron, and aluminum phosphates. Due to its low solubility, P is not as prone to leaching and P applications are not needed as often as N applications. Excessive P applications can affect the availability of iron (Fe) as it may form insoluble complexes. Soil tests are recommended to ascertain the need for P fertilizers.

Phosphorus Fertilizers. The most common forms of P fertilizers are the superphosphates and ammonium phosphates. The primary forms of P fertilizers are described in Table 6-5. Superphosphates contain monocalcium phosphate as the primary P source and are manufactured by treating rock phosphate with acids.

TABLE 6-5. Primary Phosphorus Sources and Characteristics Used in Turf Fertilizers (Modified from McCarty, 2001)

Source	Approximate Nutrient Percentage			Salt Index (Foliar Burn Potential)		Acidifying Effect	Comment
	N	P_2O_5	K_2O	Per Nutrient Unit[a]	Relative to Sodium Nitrate (100)		
Phosphorus (P) Carriers [formulas]							
Monoammonium phosphate (MAP) [$(NH_4)H_2PO_4$]	11	48	0	0.5 (low)	30	Medium	Soluble P source which also provides N and reduces soil pH that is used in many fertilizers. Preferred to DAP when applied to alkaline soils.
Diammonium phosphate (DAP) [$(NH_4)_2HPO_4$]	18–21	46–53	0	0.6 (low)	34	Medium	Soluble P source containing higher N than MAP and also reduces soil pH. Significant ammonia losses on alkaline soils can occur.
Superphosphate [$Ca(H_2PO_4)_2 + CaSO_4$]	0	20	0	0.4 (low)	8	Neutral	Soluble P source often used in mixed fertilizers; contains Ca (18 to 21%) and S (12%) as gypsum. Has little acidity effect.
Triple (or treble) superphosphate [$Ca(H_2PO_4)_2.H_2O$]	0	46	0	0.2 (low)	10	Neutral	Concentrated P source containing Ca (13%).
Ammonium polyphosphate [$NH_4H_2PO_4 + (NH_4)_3HP_2O_7$]	10	34	0	—	—	—	A P and N liquid solution source. Used in fluid fertilizers.
Milorganite	6	4	0	0.6 (low)	3	Low	Activated sewage sludge; N release rate increases with higher temperatures; contain micronutrients, especially Fe.
Colloidal phosphate	0	≈8	0	low	—	Neutral	Contains 20% Ca. Low P availability. Best used as a powder on acid soils.

[a]Generally, the higher the salt index/unit of nutrient, the higher the burn potential of the particular fertilizer material.

243

Superphosphate is made using sulfuric acid and triple superphosphate is made using phosphoric acid. Ammonium phosphates are produced by reacting ammonia with phosphoric acid.

Other lesser-used P sources include bone meal (15–34% P_2O_5), basic slag (10–18% P_2O_5), ammonium polyphosphate (37% P_2O_5), and calcium metaphosphate (62–65% P_2O_5). Available P in fertilizers is expressed as P_2O_5. Actual P content in a bag of fertilizer must be converted from the percent of P_2O_5 listed in the fertilizer analysis as follows:

$$\% \ P_2O_5 \text{ on bag} \times 0.43 = \% \ P \text{ in fertilizer}$$

For example, a bag of fertilizer with analysis 16-4-8 (16% N − 4% P_2O_5 − 8% K_2O) would contain

$$4\% \ P_2O_5 \times 0.43 = \textbf{1.72\% P}$$

Potassium

Potassium (K) is found in concentration second only to N in plants. Turf K tissue concentrations typically range from 1 to 5% by dry weight. Potassium is essential for osmotic regulation in plants and is directly responsible for regulating turgor pressure in guard cells which open or close stomata. Potassium is also responsible for regulation of more than 60 enzymes within plants. Potassium is often called the "health element" because an ample supply helps increase turf tolerance to heat, cold, drought, diseases, and wear.

Potassium Deficiency. Potassium deficiency occurs when concentrations are below 1% in tissue. Deficiency symptoms include interveinal chlorosis and rolling and burning (**necrosis**) of leaf tips. Leaf veins finally turn yellow and margins become scorched. Potassium is mobile within plants and therefore deficiency symptoms usually occur first in older leaves.

Most plants can absorb more K than needed, which is referred to as **luxury consumption**. Luxury consumption can lead to deficiencies of magnesium (Mg) and calcium (Ca). When K levels become high, Mg deficiency symptoms show, followed by Ca deficiency symptoms at higher K levels.

Soil Potassium and Uptake. Potassium is absorbed from the soil solution in the monovalent cation form (K^+). Potassium is highly soluble and is subject to leaching, especially in sandy soils. Soil colloid exchange sites are capable of adsorbing K ions, maintaining an equilibrium in the soil solution. Soils high in 2:1 type clays are capable of fixing K, rendering it unavailable to plants. Soils high in Mg or Ca may require greater applications of K due to competition for uptake by roots. As a general rule, K should be applied in a 2:1 or 1:1 ratio of N to K to maintain adequate K levels.

Potassium Fertilizers. Potassium fertilizers are often referred to as "potash" after the process of producing potassium carbonate needed for making soap by filtering water through wood ashes. Potassium fertilizer sources are described in Table 6-6.

TABLE 6-6. Primary Potassium Sources and Characteristics Used in Turf Fertilizers (Modified from McCarty, 2001)

Source [formulas]	Approximate Nutrient Percentage			Salt Index (Foliar Burn Potential)		Acidifying Effect	Comment
	N	P_2O_5	K_2O	Per Nutrient Unit[a]	Relative to Calcium Nitrate (100)		
Muriate of potash (potassium chloride) [KCl]	0	0	50–60	2.2 (high)	116	Neutral	Most common K source; soluble; high burn potential; contains 44% Cl.
Sulfate of potash (potassium sulfate) [K_2SO_4]	0	0	45–50	0.9 (low)	46	Neutral	Contains 17% S; used instead of KCl where Cl is not desirable, to reduce foliage burn potential, and to provide S; may not leach as rapidly as KCl.
Potassium-magnesium sulfate (or K-Mag) [$K_2SO_4 \cdot 2MgSO_4$]	0	0	18–22	2.0 (high)	43	Neutral	Contains 11% Mg and 23% S. Also known as langbeinite.
Potassium nitrate [KNO_3]	13	0	37–44	1.6 (high)	74	Basic	Also known as salt-peter or nitre. K source with supplemental N; water soluble; low salt concentration, low chloride, fire hazard. Has alkalinity effect.

[a]Generally, the higher the salt index/unit of nutrient, the higher the burn potential of the particular fertilizer material.

Muriate of potash (KCl) is the most often used K fertilizer. It is mined from K salt deposits formed by the evaporation of seawater. Reaction of KCl with sulfuric or nitric acids form **sulfate of potash** or **potassium nitrate**. In addition to providing S or N along with K, these forms are used to reduce the salt index in comparison to KCl.

Soluble K content in a fertilizer is expressed as K_2O. Conversion from K_2O to actual K content is as follows:

$$\% \ K_2O \text{ on bag} \times 0.83 = \% \ K \text{ in fertilizer}$$

For example: a bag of fertilizer with analysis 8-10-10 (8% N—10% P_2O_5—10% K_2O) would contain

$$10\% \ K_2O \times 0.83 = \textbf{8.3\% K}$$

SECONDARY PLANT NUTRIENTS

Calcium

Calcium (Ca) is essential for plant growth as it strengthens cell walls, enhances cell division, encourages protein synthesis, facilitates carbohydrate synthesis, and promotes root formation and growth. Calcium is also important for maintaining cellular pH and acts as a regulator for many enzymatic reactions. Calcium is utilized by plants in the divalent cation form (Ca^{+2}).

Calcium deficiency symptoms include twisted or deformed leaves with reddish brown margins. Leaves eventually turn rose-red and die and roots may become short and bunched. Calcium is immobile in plants. Therefore, deficiency symptoms occur in younger leaves. Deficiencies most often occur in sandy soils, extremely acidic (pH < 5) soils, or sodic soils. Excessive Ca may interfere with the availability of other nutrients, especially in the cases of potassium and magnesium and to a lesser extent with phosphorus, manganese, iron, zinc, and boron.

Calcium occurs naturally in high-pH soils, and is added as lime in acidic soils. Commercial sources of Ca include calcitic and dolomitic limestone, gypsum, superphosphates, calcium nitrate, shells, slags, and water treatment residue (Table 6-7).

Magnesium

Magnesium (Mg) is the central component of chlorophyll molecules. Magnesium also plays a role in energy transfer, enzyme activation, and nutrient transport and uptake.

Magnesium deficiency symptoms include general chlorosis leading to interveinal chlorosis. Interveinal chlorosis may be followed by blotchy red margins and necrosis. Magnesium is mobile within plants. Therefore, deficiency symptoms occur first in older tissues. Deficiencies are most common in acidic sandy soils with low

TABLE 6-7. Primary Calcium and Magnesium Sources and Characteristics Used in Turf Fertilizers (McCarty, 2001)

Source	Approximate Nutrient Percentage			Comment
	N	P_2O_5	K_2O	
Calcium (Ca) Carriers [formulas]				
Gypsum (calcium sulfate) [$CaSO_4 \cdot 2H_2O$]				
− anhydrite	0	0	0	Contains 24% S and 41% calcium oxide; has little effect on soil pH.
− hydrated	0	0	0	Contains 19% S and 33% calcium oxide; has little effect on soil pH.
Calcium nitrate [$Ca(NO_3)_2$]	16	0	0	Very hygroscopic; contains 19% Ca and 1.5% Mg; fast acting with high burn potential; N release is not temperature dependent; used on sodic soils to displace sodium.
Dolomitic limestone [$CaMg(CO_3)_2$]	0	0	0	Used to increase soil pH; contains 22% Ca and 11% Mg. Very slowly available. Low salt hazard.
Superphosphate [$Ca(H_2PO_4)_2$ + $CaSO_4$]	0	20	0	Soluble P source often used in mixed fertilizers; contains Ca (18 to 21%) and S (12%) as gypsum.
Triple (or treble) super-phosphate [$Ca(H_2PO_4)_2H_2O$]	0	46	0	Concentrated P source containing Ca (13%).
Magnesium (Mg) Carriers				
Magnesium sulfate (or Epsom salt) [$MgSO_4$]	0	0	0	Contains 13-23% S and 10-17% Mg; water soluble; neutral salt with little effect on soil pH.
Potassium magnesium sulfate [$K_2SO_4 \cdot 2MgSO_4$]	0	0	18–22	Contains 23% S and 11% Mg; water soluble.
Dolomitic limestone [$CaMg(CO_3)_2$]	0	0	0	Increases soil pH; contains 22% Ca and 11% Mg. Very slowly available. Low salt hazard.

*a*Generally, the higher the salt index/unit of nutrient, the higher the burn potential of the particular fertilizer material.

CEC or soils of extremely high pH. High Ca and K levels in the soil tend to reduce Mg uptake. Application of 1 pound of Epsom salts (magnesium sulfate) in 3 to 4 gallons of water over 1,000 square feet is a simple test for Mg deficiency. If the turf greens up within about 24 hours, Mg deficiency should be suspected.

Magnesium sources include dolomitic limestone, sulfates of potash and magnesium, magnesium sulfate (Epsom salts), oxide, and chelates (Table 6-7).

Sulfur

Sulfur (S) is found in a turf tissue concentration range of 0.15 to 0.5% of dry weight. Sulfur is essential for the formation of amino acids, proteins, and chlorophyll, and reduces the incidence of disease. Sulfur is absorbed by roots in the form of the divalent anion SO_4^{-2}.

Sulfur deficiency symptoms include general chlorosis and yellowing in interveinal areas with scorched leaf tips. Roots become abnormally long and stems become woody. Symptoms are often confused with N deficiency and may necessitate tissue testing to distinguish. Although sulfur is mobile in plants, deficiency symptoms may occur either in older or younger tissues. Remobilization and translocation of S is dependent on N status. Sulfur deficiency accompanied by low N will become evident in older leaves first.

Over 90% of available S exists in organic matter, which has about a 10 to 1 nitrogen to sulfur ratio. When the N to S ratio exceeds 20 to 1, deficiency is more likely. At high pH, S may precipitate as calcium sulfate, or may be complexed by aluminum and/or iron oxides at lower pH levels. Sulfur sources include gypsum, elemental sulfur, ferrous sulfate, liquid ammonium thiosulfate, potassium magnesium sulfate, ammonium sulfate, SCU, and potassium sulfate (Table 6-8).

In poorly drained waterlogged soils which become anaerobic, SO_4^{-2} and sulfur-containing organic matter can be reduced by bacteria to toxic hydrogen sulfide (H_2S). This condition is encouraged by excessive applications of elemental sulfur. Insoluble sulfides may also form by reacting with iron or manganese:

Sulfide Formation

$$Fe^{+2} \quad + \quad S^{-2} \rightarrow \quad FeS$$

dissolved ferrous iron   sulfide   iron sulfide (solid)

Turf soils containing toxic levels of hydrogen sulfide or iron sulfate are acidic and commonly form a black layer several inches below the soil surface. They typically are characterized by the distinct smell of rotten eggs. Low soil oxygen can result in reduced forms of manganese, copper, and iron and result in gray and blue colored ("gumbo") subsoils.

MICRONUTRIENTS

Micronutrients are essential elements needed in small (<100 parts per million) amounts. These include **boron** (B), **chlorine** (Cl), **copper** (Cu), **iron** (Fe), **manganese** (Mn), **molybdenum** (Mo), and **zinc** (Zn) (Table 6-1). Sodium (Na) is also a micronutrient for certain plants. Micronutrient deficiency symptoms can easily be confused with pest occurrence or other stresses. General micronutrient deficiency symptoms are described in Table 6-9. Many soils contain adequate levels of these nutrients and some are also found as impurities in fertilizers.

Micronutrient deficiencies are most common in sandy, peat, or muck soils, high pH soils, phosphoric soils, and poorly drained soils. Many micronutrients may also become toxic if applied excessively such as Mn, Zn, Cu, and B. Regular soil and tissue testing is the best preventative approach to micronutrient management. In

TABLE 6-8. Primary Sulfur Sources and Characteristics Used for Turf Fertilizer

Source [formulas]	Approximate Nutrient Percentages		Comment
	Sulfur (S)	Others	
Gypsum (calcium sulfate) [CaSO$_4$·2H$_2$O]	16–24	20% Ca	A neutral salt with little acidifying effect. Commonly used on sodic soil.
Elemental sulfur [S]	up to 99	—	Oxidizes to sulfuric acid and lowers pH; foliage burn potential; available as a granular or liquid; slow acting; requires microbial oxidation; eye irritant.
Epsom salts (magnesium sulfate) [MgSO$_4$]	13–223	10–17% Mg	Neutral salt with little acidifying effect.
Ferrous sulfate [FeSO$_4$·7H$_2$O]	19	21% Fe	Water soluble; usually applied foliarly.
Ferrous ammonium sulfate [(NH$_4$)$_2$ FeSO$_4$·6H$_2$O]	15	14% Fe + 7% N	Water soluble; usually applied foliarly.
Ammonium thiosulfate [(NH$_4$)$_2$S$_2$O$_3$ + H$_2$O]	26	12% N	Most widely used S source in clear liquid fertilizers; foliage burn potential.
Potassium magnesium sulfate (or K-mag) [K$_2$SO$_4$·2MgSO$_4$]	22	22% K$_2$O + 11% Mg	Commonly used on alkaline soils.
Ammonium sulfate [NH$_4$)$_2$SO$_4$]	24	21% N	Water soluble; high acidifying potential.
Sulfur-coated urea (or SCU) [CO(NH$_2$)$_2$ + S]	10–20	32% N	Slowly soluble.
Superphosphate [Ca(H$_2$PO$_4$)$_2$ + CaSO$_4$]	12	20% P$_2$O$_5$ + 20% Ca	Soluble P which contain gypsum (calcium sulfate). Has little acidifying effect.
Potassium sulfate (or sulfate of potash) [K$_2$SO$_4$]	17	50% K$_2$O	Used instead of KCL to reduce foliage burn potential and to supply S.

TABLE 6-9. Micronutrient Forms, Deficiencies, and Sources for Turf Managers

Nutrient	Deficiency Occurrence	Deficiency Symptoms	Fertilizer Sources
Iron (Fe)	Fe levels in soils often are sufficient; however, soil conditions often render them unavailable. Deficiency occurs with excessive soil pH (>7.0), Ca, Zn, Mn, P, Cu, and bicarbonates (HCO_3) levels in irrigation water; Poor rooting, poor soil drainage, and cold soils also are associated with deficiency. At low soil pH, P can combine with Fe to form insoluble (unavailable) iron phosphate while at high pH, excessive P uptake by plants may inactivate absorbed Fe. For each increase in pH, there is a 100-fold decrease in soluble Fe^{+2}. A plant tissue ratio of P to Fe at 29 to 1 also provides healthy turf while a P:Fe ratio of 40:1 often expresses Fe deficiency. A Fe:Mn ratio of 2:1 in plant tissue also has been suggested. Heavy metals and/or bicarbonates from effluent water or sewage sludge as a soil amendment may also compete with Fe for plant uptake. Deficiency symptoms are most severe during warm days/cool nights (e.g., early spring and fall) when root growth is insufficient to support shoot growth.	Chlorosis resembling N deficiency except Fe chlorosis is interveinal (i.e., between leaf veins) and first occurs in the youngest leaves since Fe is immobile within the plant. Older leaves are affected later. N deficiency causes the entire leaf, including veins, to yellow simultaneously. Fe deficient leaves finally turn white. Fe chlorosis tends to be in random-scattered spots, creating a mottled appearance and appears more severe when mowed closely. N deficiency develops uniformly over a large area and appears unaffected by mowing. Management practices to reduce P deficiency are to lower the soil pH, improve drainage, reduce P fertilization, and use one of the listed foliar sprays.	**Ferrous sulfate** [$FeSO_4 \cdot 7H_2O$]: (19–21% Fe and 19% S); usually foliarly applied; low acidifying effect; water soluble. **Ferrous ammonium sulfate** [$FeSO_4 \cdot (NH_4)_2SO_4$]: (5–14% Fe, 16% S, and 7% N); usually foliarly applied; also provides some N; medium acidifying effect; water soluble. **Chelated iron** [Fe salts of -EDTA, -HEDTA, -EDDHA, or -DTPA]: (5–14% Fe); longer greening effect than the other Fe sources; low acidifying effect. **Iron frits** (14% Fe).

Zinc (Zn)	Alkaline soils decrease solubility and availability, as does excessive soil Cu^{+2}, Fe^{+2}, and Mn^{+2} and excessive soil moisture, nitrogen, and phosphates. Zn solubility increases 100-fold for each decreased pH unit. Above pH 7.7, Zn becomes $Zn(OH)^+$. Lower light intensities reduce root uptake. Sands also are likely to have lower Zn levels than clays.	**Zinc sulfate** $[ZnSO_4 \cdot H_2O]$; (35% Zn and 12% S); water soluble, foliarly applied. **Zinc chelate** [ZnEDTA]; (9–14% Zn); foliar applied. **Zinc oxide** [ZnO]; (78% Zn); water soluble, foliar applied. **Zinc frits** (4–7% Zn).
	Interveinal chlorosis in both younger and some older leaves. Mottled-chlorotic leaves, rolled and thin leaf blades; stunted, shortened internode growth; dark, desiccated-looking leaves (starting with the youngest ones); leaves finally turn white in appearance.	
Manganese (Mn)	Deficiencies occur in sand, peat, and muck soils (insoluble complexes are formed), alkaline soils high in Ca (for each increase in pH, there is a 100-fold decrease in soluble Mn^{+2}); at low temperatures; and in poor drainage. Excess Fe, Cu, Zn, K, and Na can reduce Mn adsorption. A Fe to Mn ratio in leaf tissue should be at least 2 to 1. Adjusting soil pH to below 7.0 usually reduces Mn deficiencies.	**Manganese sulfate** $[MnSO_4 \cdot H_2O]$ (26–28% Mn and 13%S); applied foliarly. **Manganese oxide** [MnO] (33–77% Mn). **Mancozeb fungicides** (16% Mn and 2% Zn). **Manganese chelates** (5–12% Mn). **Tecmangam** (20% Mn). **Manganese frits** (3–6% Mn).
	Yellowing (chlorosis) between veins (interveinal) of youngest leaves with veins remaining dark green to olive green color since Mn is an immobile element within the plant; small, distinct necrotic leaf spots develop on older leaves; leaf tips may turn grey to white, droop, and wither. On closely mowed turf, mottled or blotchy appearance develops, with little or no response to N occurring.	

TABLE 6-9. **Micronutrient Forms, Deficiencies, and Sources for Turf Managers** (*Continued*)

Nutrient	Deficiency Occurrence	Deficiency Symptoms	Fertilizer Sources
Copper (Cu)	Deficiency is mostly in sand, peat, muck, and high organic soils due to tight binding properties of these for Cu. Excess Fe, N, P, and Zn and high soil pH encourage deficiency. Toxic levels can result from excess sewage sludge applications, use of poultry manures, copper sulfate, and copper containing pesticides such as Bordeau mixture. Liming to pH 7.0 is often the simplest means of overcoming Cu phytotoxicity. Reducing N fertilization may also help.	Deficiencies are rare. Deficiency symptoms include yellowing and chlorosis of younger leaf margins; leaf tips initially turn bluish, wither and droop, eventually turning yellow and die; youngest leaves become light green and necrotic; plant dwarfing with inward rolling of leaves which develop a blue-green appearance; symptoms progress from the leaf tips to the base of the plant. Toxicity symptoms of excessive levels include reduced shoot vigor, poorly developed and discolored root systems, and leaf chlorosis resembling iron deficiency.	**Copper sulfate** [$CuSO_4 \cdot 5H_2O$] (13–53% Cu and 13% S); foliar or soil applied. **Copper oxide** [CuO] (40% Cu); foliar or soil applied. **Copper chelates** [CuEDTA] (9–13% Cu); foliar applied.
Boron (B)	Organic matter is the principal source of B; availability increases with decreasing soil pH; deficiencies are most common in high pH, leached, or very dry, sandy soils. Ca also decreases translocation of B in plants. Liming acidic soils frequently causes a B deficiency.	Thickening, curling, and chlorotic leaves develop on dwarf (rosette) plants; chlorotic streaks develop in the interveinal areas. Leaf tips turn pale green. Plants develop a "bronze" tint. B is immobile within the plant; symptoms, therefore, first appear in meristematic tissues and young leaves. Deficiencies are infrequent in turf.	**Borax** [$Na_2B_4O_7 \cdot 10H_2O$]; (11% B and 9% Na). **Boric acid** [H_3BO_3]: 17% B. **Fertilizer borate** [sodium tetraborate, $Na_2B_4O_7 \cdot 5H_2O$, 14–21% B; sodium pentaborate, $Na_2B_{10}O_{16} \cdot 5H_2O$, 18% B] **Solubor** (20% soluble B).

Element			Sources
Molybdenum (Mo)	Availability increases with increasing soil pH; deficiencies are most common in acid sands or highly weathered soils; excess Cu, Fe, Mn, or sulfate may reduce Mo utilization by plants. Deficiencies often occur in ironstone soils of Australia, New Zealand, and the Netherlands.	Resembles mild N deficiency with pale yellow-green stunted plants; mottled yellowing of interveinal areas then appear in older leaves. Deficiencies are rare. Lime acid soils.	**Ammonium molybdate** $[(NH_4)_2MoO_4]$; (54% Mo) liquid. **Sodium molybdate** $[Na_2MoO_4 \cdot H_2O]$ (40% Mo). **Molybdenum trioxide** $[MoO_3]$ (66% Mo). **Molybdic oxide** (47% Mo).
Chlorine (Cl)	Less available in alkaline soils, or soils high in NO_3^- and SO_4^{-2}; very mobile in acid to neutral soils. Toxic levels reduce water availability to plants, causes premature leaf yellowing, leaf tip and margin burning, and leaf bronzing and abscission.	Chlorosis of younger leaves and wilting of plants; not mobile within plants and accumulates in older parts. Deficiencies are rare. Chlorine is most commonly applied in large quantities along with the potassium source in fertilizers.	**Ammonium chloride** $[NH_4Cl]$ (66% Cl, 25% N). Acid-forming fertilizer. **Calcium chloride** $[CaCl_2]$ (65% Cl). **Magnesium chloride** $[MgCl_2]$ (74% Cl). **Potassium chloride** $[KCl]$ (47% Cl, 60% K). **Sodium chloride** $[NaCl]$ (60% Cl, 40% Na).

TABLE 6-10. Solution Used to Spot Treat for Micronutrient Deficiencies

Deficient Micronutrient	Fertilizer Source	Rate	
		oz/gal	lb Element/1,000 sq ft
Fe	iron sulfate	⅔	0.025
Mn	manganese sulfate	½	0.025
Zn	zinc sulfate	½	0.010
Cu	copper sulfate	½	0.003
B	borax	0.1	0.001
Mo	sodium molybdate	0.01	0.001

some cases, high-surface-area glasslike beads called **frits** are applied to provide B, Cu, Zn, and other micronutrients. Frits gradually weather in soil, slowly releasing nutrients. Many micronutrients may also be applied as foliar sprays. Table 6-10 offers a starting guideline for spot treatment of micronutrients when sprayed on the foliage to the drip point.

Some micronutrients, such as iron, copper, zinc, and manganese, are normally nonsoluble. **Chelates**, **chelating agents**, or **sequestering agents** are used to make these nutrients soluble so they can enter the soil solution. Chelates are organic molecules which combine with a nonsoluble metal atom to become a water-soluble compound available for plant uptake (see Figure 6-4). Chelates also help avoid the formation of nonsoluble complexes with other soil chemicals. Commercially available chelating agents include ethylenediaminetetraacetic acid (**EDTA**), diethyl-enetriaminepentaacetic acid (**DTPA**), cyclohexanediaminetetraacetic acid (**CDTA**), ethylenediaminedi (*o*-hydroxyphenylacetic acid) (**EDDHA**), **citrate**, and **gluconate**. These range from 5 to 14% iron.

LIQUID FERTILIZATION

Foliar liquid fertilization, or **foliar feeding**, involves the application of soluble nutrients directly to the leaf surface. This method of fertilization allows for rapid nutrient absorption and utilization. Foliar feeding is most commonly used for micronutrient applications due to the small amounts required. Foliar application of N,

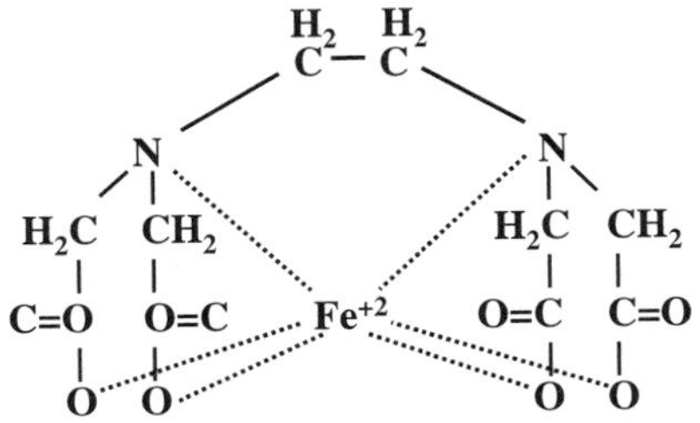

Figure 6-4. Chelating agents allow normally insoluble ions to be in a soluble form for plant absorption. Shown is a Fe-EDTA (ethylenediaminetetraacetic acid) complex ion, which allows Fe^{+2} ions to be available for plant use.

P, and K is more difficult due to burn potential. Low rates of urea can be used to apply N foliarly under low light and mild ($< 85°F$) conditions.

Fertigation is the application of nutrients through an irrigation system. This method uses frequent, light applications of nutrients through sprinkler heads referred to as **spoon-feeding**. Fertigation is most often used to apply N and S to maintain a more even color and avoid growth surges associated with heavier granular applications. Spoon-feeding is especially useful on sandy soils in which heavier applications are more prone to leaching. Proper design, calibration, and maintenance of the irrigation system is necessary to provide even fertilization.

Several types of fluid fertilizers are used (Table 6-11). Three main categories of fluid fertilizers include:

1. **Clear liquid.** These are true solutions, free of solids, clear enough to see through, and are limited to low analyses since salting-out will occur at low temperatures when fertilizer grades are high.

2. **Suspension fertilizer.** These are higher concentration mixtures of liquids and finely divided solids when the solids do not settle rapidly and can be redispersed readily by agitation to give a uniform mixture. Certain types of clays usually are added at 1 to 2% as suspending agents. Suspension fertilizer's advantage over clear liquid are: (i) higher analysis grades can be produced; (ii) costs are lower because less pure products can be used: (iii) larger quantities of micronutrients can be suspended; and (iv) powdered forms of pesticides can normally be suspended and used.

3. **Slurry fertilizers.** These are mixtures of liquids and finely divided solids that settle rapidly in the absence of agitation and form a firm layer in the bottom of the tank. This layer is difficult to resuspend and may cause line or emitter plugging.

A main difference between liquid and dry fertilizers is related to solubility of the phosphorus. In dry fertilizer, the phosphorus sources may vary in water solubility from 30% in some highly ammoniated superphosphates to almost 100% in diammonium or monoammonium phosphate. Granular phosphorus fertilizers, therefore, should supplement fertigation fertilizer use. Practically all potassium and inorganic nitrogen in both fluid and dry fertilizer is 100% water soluble.

Manufacturing of Liquid Fertilizers. There are two general methods of manufacturing liquid-mixed fertilizers. The simplest method is known as the batch or suspension process and consists merely of dissolving the correct proportions of the solid plant-food carriers, such as ammonium phosphates, urea, or potassium chloride in water to give the desired grade of final product. The weighed constituents are dissolved in the proper amount of water with a suitable mixing device. The solution may be heated to aid in the dissolving process since many dry fertilizer products absorb heat from the water when mixed. The relatively higher cost of raw materials generally limits this to small operations or to companies engaged in manufacturing specialty grades. Solution grade forms of these products are used.

The second and most widely used method is based on the neutralization of phosphoric acid with ammonia to produce ammonium polyphosphates. Anhydrous or aqueous ammonia, or ammonia-ammonium nitrate or ammonia-urea type nitro-

TABLE 6-11. Foliar (Liquid) Nitrogen Solutions and Their Properties

Fertilizer Source	N	P	K	Water Insoluble N (WIN)	Other Nutrients	Examples
	%					
Solutions						
Methylol urea + urea (formaldehyde + urea)	30	0	0	0	—	RESI-GROW GP-4340; GR-4341 (30-0-2); & 4318; FLUF; Form-U-Sol; Homogesol-27; Slo-Release; Flormolene; CoRoN (28-0-0); Nitro-26
Triazones + urea (formaldehyde + ammonia + urea)	28	0	0	0	—	N-Sure; Trisert; Formolene-Plus
Ammonium polyphosphate	10	34	0	0	—	—
Ammonium thiosulfate	12	0	0	0	26% S	—
Ammonium nitrate	20	0	0	0	—	—
Aqueous (or Aqua) ammonia	23	0	0	0	—	—
Urea-ammonium nitrate solution	32	0	0	0	—	—
Urea-ammonium nitrate solution	32	0	0	0	—	—
Calcium ammonium lnitrate	17	0	0	0	9% Ca	—
Urea solution	23	0	0	0	—	—
Urea sulfuric acid	10–28	0	0	0	9–18%	—
Suspensions						
Methylene ureas	18	0	0	5	—	—
Sprayable Powders						
Methylene ureas	40	0	0	12–14	—	Triaform; Nutralene; Scotts MU40; METH-EX40; Chip
Urea j(urea formaldehyde)	38	0	0	25	—	Nitroform; Powder Blue; Slo-Release
Isobutylidene urea (IBDU)	31	0	0	21	—	IBDU

gen solutions, are reacted with phosphoric acid solutions followed by the addition of solid sources of nitrogen and/or potash. Potassium chloride is the usual source of potash. Polyphosphates also can sequester certain micronutrients and thus allow these to be added in fluid fertilizer. Aqueous ammonia also is reacted with sulfate and elemental S to form 12-0-0-26S ammonium thiosulfate. It can be used in a wide variety of N-P-K-S formulations and is essentially noncorrosive. It should, however, not come in contact with tin, copper, or brass. The density of most common liquid mixtures will approximate 10 pounds per gallon.

Soluble Sources. The liquid application form in foliar feeding enters plants directly by penetrating leaf cuticles or stomata, and then enters the cells. This method provides quicker utilization of nutrients than through soil treatment. Research also has shown that the physical form of the nutrient, dry or fluid, has no measurable effect on its agronomic properties, such as total amount of plant growth. Quickly available nitrogen sources denote rapid or quick availability of nitrogen to the turfgrass plant after fertilizer application. These quickly available nitrogen sources have a high potential for foliar burn. This results from their salt-like characteristics dissolving readily in water to form cations (positive ions) and anions (negative ions). These ions are hydrophilic (water-loving) and when in direct contact with the leaf surface, they quickly absorb moisture from the plant, resulting with a brown burn appearance. The more free cations and anions in soil solution or on the plant surface, the greater is the potential for fertilizer burn. This is a problem when quickly available liquid nitrogen forms, generally in excess of 1 lb N per 1,000 sq.ft., are used. Most recommendations call for foliar fertilization to occur during periods of low temperature and relatively high humidity during early morning or late evening hours. New liquid fertilizer technology will hopefully minimize some of these problems.

Because of its water solubility, urea is the most widely used fertilizer material and is often mixed with ammonium nitrate or potassium nitrate (Table 6-11). Liquid urea is characterized by a quick response in terms of turf color and a medium to high burn potential. Low rates, applied more frequently, are required to promote even turf growth and color and to minimize burn potential when using liquid urea. A fine, powder form of urea formaldehyde (*Powder Blue*) also can be used for liquid fertilization. Powder Blue is a 38-0-0 with its nitrogen divided as 27% insoluble and 13% soluble. Other quickly available liquid-nitrogen carriers include ammonium sulfate, ammonium polyphosphate, and ammonium thiosulfate.

The remaining soluble nitrogen sources are mixtures of urea and water-soluble short-chain methylene ureas. Nitrogen release from this methylene urea is by rapid microbial degradation. This provides a quick plant response, but has less potential for foliar fertilizer burn. These also are sometimes called controlled-release nitrogen forms.

An aqueous nitrogen solution which contains more than half of its nitrogen as monomethylol urea with the remaining being free urea and ammonia is marketed as *Formolene*. Formolene is formulated as a 30-0-2 and contains $3\frac{1}{4}$ pounds of nitrogen per gallon. This is basically a soluble nitrogen source but has a lower salt index than urea. Other quick-release urea and methylene urea nitrogen carriers include *Form-U-Sol* and *Nitro-26*. Form-U-Sol contains 28% nitrogen, of which 67% is urea and 33% methylol urea. *Nitro-26* contains 26% nitrogen with 30% urea and 70% methylol urea.

Slow-Release Sources. Several new materials which have better slow-release characteristics are now commercially available. These allow heavier rates to be applied less frequently without undesirable surges in growth or color and minimize turf foliar burn potential. To be classified as a slow-release source, this fact must be identified on the label and comprise at least 15% of the total nitrogen.

CoRoN. CoRoN is a aqueous solution of a number (approximately 70%) of poly-methylene ureas and amine-modified polymethylene ureas. CoRoN consists primarily of a straight chain, amine-modified polymethylene urea containing 2 to 4 urea units amounting to about 30% of the contained nitrogen. Small amounts of methylene diurea and dimethylene triurea are also present while cyclic urea formaldehyde products, such as triazones, are not. No free ammonia and little methylol urea are included as a part of CoRoN. CoRoN contains a small amount of sodium bicarbonate to protect its near-neutral pH and sufficient water to safely maintain its 28-0-0 formulation in water. Its nitrogen release is dependent upon microbial action, but due to the relatively high urea content, it has been shown to be effective in winter months. It tends not to last as long as a dry slow-release nitrogen source, but its initial greenup is quicker. *GP4340* and *GP4341* are additional liquid methylol urea solutions.

N-Sure. N-Sure is a liquid nitrogen fertilizer containing triazones combined with urea in a ratio of 0.48 to 1.0. N-Sure may contain methylene diurea and methylol urea amounting to 6% by weight. Triazones are stable heterocyclic nitrogen-carbon ring compounds made, usually, under low pH conditions, from urea, formaldehyde, and ammonia. N-Sure contains 30% nitrogen and its nitrogen release rate is microbial dependent. It has been demonstrated to be effective during cool temperature but its response does not last as long as a solid slow-release nitrogen source. *Trisert* and *Formolene-Plus* are other triazone and urea liquid products.

FLUF. FLUF (Flowable Liquid Urea Formaldehyde) is another slow-release nitrogen solution source. It consists of cold water soluble free urea and methylene diurea, cold water insoluble-hot water soluble polymethylene ureas, and small amounts of hot water insoluble polymethylene ureas. Several formulations are available including 10-0-10, 16-2-4, and 18-0-0. *Slo-Release* is another liquid UF suspension source.

PRACTICE PROBLEMS

1. Where are the first signs of mobile and immobile plant nutrient deficiencies most likely to occur? (*Symptoms of mobile nutrient deficiencies tend to develop in older tissues first as plants relocate nutrients to developing tissues. Immobile nutrient deficiencies appear in new growth as the plant is unable to relocate them from older tissues.*)

2. What are some consequences of excessive nitrogen fertilization? (*Excessive N fertilization can lead to reduced heat, cold, drought, disease, nematode, and wear tolerance. Nitrogen can be detrimental to root growth as flushes*

of shoot growth diminish carbohydrates stored in roots. Excessive N fertilization can also lead to adverse environmental effects such as nitrate leaching into ground and surface waters.)

3. What are some advantages and disadvantages of using a natural organic N source such as Milorganite?

   Advantages:
   - limited burn potential
   - uniform N release
   - little pH or salinity effects
   - provides micronutrients
   - low leaching and volatilization potential

   Disadvantages:
   - higher cost per unit N
   - no K
   - depends on soil microorganism activity

4. Why is phosphorous essential to plant growth? (*Phosphorous plays an essential role as a component of ATP, the molecule responsible for the transfer of energy during metabolic processes. It is also an essential component of DNA, RNA, and phospholipid membranes.*)

5. How is root growth related to phosphorous deficiencies? (*Phosphorous is not very mobile in soils. When root growth is slowed, soil P is not readily encountered. Therefore, P deficiencies most often occur under conditions which restrict root growth such as low soil temperatures, low soil oxygen, and during establishment.*)

6. What are the primary roles of potassium and why is it called the "health" element? (*Potassium is essential for osmotic regulation in plants and is directly responsible for regulating turgor in guard cells which open or close stomata. Potassium is also responsible for regulation of more than 60 plant enzymes. It is often called the "health" element because an ample supply helps increase turf tolerance to heat, cold, drought, diseases, and wear.*)

7. Describe turf potassium deficiency symptoms. (*Potassium deficiency in turf is characterized by interveinal chlorosis and rolling necrotic leaf tips. Leaf veins finally turn yellow and margins become scorched. Potassium is mobile in plants and therefore symptoms occur first in older leaves.*)

8. What is a chelate? (*Chelates are organic molecules which combine with a non-soluble metal atom to form a water-soluble compound available for plant uptake.*)

9. What is foliar feeding and when is it most likely to be used? (*Foliar feeding is the application of soluble nutrients directly to the leaf surface, This method of fertilization allows for rapid nutrient absorption and utilization. Foliar feeding is most commonly used for micronutrient applications, due to the small amounts required.*)

10. Describe the three main types of fluid fertilizers. (*Clear liquid fertilizers are true solutions which are limited to lower concentrations to prevent the precipitation of salts. Suspension fluid fertilizers contain higher concentrations of nutrients and are a mixture of liquids and finely divided solids which easily remain suspended if agitated. Slurry fertilizers are liquid and fine solid mixtures which settle rapidly if not agitated constantly.*)

CHAPTER 7

PLANT TISSUE AND SOIL TESTING

TISSUE TESTING

Nutrient deficiencies in plants can be difficult to correctly diagnose. Several nutrient deficiencies exhibit symptoms that are easily confused, depending on severity. Tissue and soil analyses can be helpful tools in diagnosing nutrition problems and in determining the effectiveness of fertilization programs. Tissue analysis is especially useful in diagnosing micronutrient deficiencies. Potential deficiencies may be detected by tissue analysis before visual symptoms appear. Tissue analysis also provides information on nutrient levels available to turf plants compared to soil test levels and to possibly determine what may interfere with uptake.

Tissue nutrient levels are usually expressed as content (often referred to as concentration) per unit dry weight of leaves. Tissue analysis involves laboratory techniques and specialized equipment. For these reasons, managers typically turn to state extension or commercial laboratories for tissue analysis.

Sampling. The tissue sampled in plants is primarily the leaves. Sample collection can be done by hand or by the use of catch baskets during mowing operations. Care should be taken to ensure that no soil or other contaminants are included in the samples. Unhealthy turf or turf showing severe signs of deficiency should not be directly sampled. Nutrient levels may become skewed by the onset of stress. When deficiency is severe, healthier samples collected from adjoining plants in the same area will usually allow for proper diagnosis.

Tissue Preparation. Leaves collected in the field often have films of dust or spray residues such as copper containing fungicides which may affect analysis. Rinsing fresh samples in pure water or a mild detergent solution may be necessary to remove heavy films. Once rinsed, turf tissue should be refrigerated until it can be received by the laboratory and oven-dried. Tissue samples are typically oven-dried for 48 hours at 70°C in a forced-air oven. The drying process stops physiological processes such as respiration by removing moisture and degrading enzymes. Drying is also necessary since nutrient content is expressed on a dry-weight basis.

Once dried, tissue samples are chopped or ground to a uniform fine-particle size. This process is usually performed using a cyclone-type grinding mill with an abrasive action. The result is a fine, powder-like sample. At this point a sample is ready for laboratory preparation.

Organic Matter Destruction

Before determining nutrient content, the organic portions of plant tissues must be destroyed (digested), which frees the nutrients and transforms them into a soluble form. The technique used for digestion depends on the nutrients to be measured. The two most commonly used methods are **acid digestion** and **dry ashing**.

The most common method use for nitrogen content determination is an acid digestion technique referred to as the **Kjeldahl** procedure. This method involves the digestion of tissue in sulfuric acid (H_2SO_4) at 360 to 410°C using a specialized digestion block. Copper and potassium salts are added as catalysts in this procedure. As N bonds are broken by the heat, the SO_4 atmosphere traps N in the form of ammonium sulfate, NH_4SO_4. The samples turn clear as the tissue digests. Once cooled, the samples are diluted with deionized water and are then ready for analysis by specialized equipment.

The dry ashing procedure can be used to determine the content of most of the remaining nutrients. This method oxidizes the organic components of turf tissue by heating dry samples to 500°C for 4 to 8 hours. The remaining ash is dissolved in water plus hydrochloric acid (HCl) and/or nitric acid (HNO_3) and is then ready for analysis.

Elemental Analysis

Determining the actual amounts of dissolved minerals in prepared tissue solutions involves the use of specialized equipment. **Atomic absorption spectrophotometry** (AAS) can be used to analyze solutions for the plant nutrients K, Ca, Mg, Zn, Fe, Cu, Mn, and Na. The AAS instrument operates on the principle of ground-state energy levels of atoms. When atoms are at a ground-state, they can absorb electromagnetic radiation of certain wavelengths. The wavelengths absorbed are specific for each element. Hollow cathode lamps are used to emit light of the corresponding wavelengths. The element used in the lamp corresponds to the element to be tested for. Electric current causes the lamp element to emit light of a wavelength which will be absorbed by the ground-state atoms of that element from the solution. Fine droplets of the sample solution are passed through an air-acetylene flame. The high-temperature flame produces ground-state atoms of the elements in solution. Atoms specific to the lamp in use absorb light from the lamp. Monochromator measurements indicate how much of the light was absorbed. This measurement is used to quantify the amount of the element in solution when readings are compared to standardized solutions. An AAS system is used to measure **atomic emission** when analyzing for K. In this case, K atoms release light energy when returned to the ground-state by the flame.

Inductively coupled argon plasma (ICAP) emission spectrometry is becoming more widely used to analyze for P, K, Ca, Mg, Zn, Fe, Cu, Mn, and B. An ICAP instrument is used to measure the emission of radiant energy from excited atoms. An ICAP instrument uses a stream of extremely hot argon gas called a "plasma" to excite atoms. Atoms from the solution enter the plasma and become excited and completely vaporized. As the atoms leave the plasma, their energized electrons move back to lower ground-state energy orbits, resulting in the emission of electromagnetic energy of wavelengths specific for each element in the solution. A detection system in the ICAP instrument quantifies these emissions. The intensity of these characteristic emissions is directly proportional to the element concentration in the solution.

Nutrient Concentrations

Primary and secondary nutrients occur in relatively large quantities within plants and are usually expressed in grams (g) of the element per kilogram (kg) of plant dry weight. Micronutrients occur in smaller quantities and are usually expressed in milligrams (mg) of the element per kilogram of dry weight. Table 7-1 provides general guidelines for nutrient levels in turfgrass leaf analysis. Some laboratories report concentration of primary nutrients as a percentage. To obtain a percentage, divide the g/kg values by 10.

SOIL TESTING

An important tool for establishing and maintaining high-quality turf is soil testing. Soil tests will quantify many soil characteristics such as pH, cation exchange capacity (CEC), and soil nutrient levels, which would otherwise be difficult to determine. Soil sample analyses involve specialized techniques and equipment, and are usually performed by a County Cooperative Extension Service or commercial laboratory. Soil tests should be conducted prior to turf establishment so any needed amendments may be added prior to planting. On established stands of turfgrass, soils are typically sampled yearly, or when the turf appears to have a nutritional problem.

Variations often occur between testing laboratories because of different extraction and analysis techniques. The ranking of the nutrient level, however, should be similar regardless of the extractant. It is recommended turf managers pick a particular laboratory and stick with it, as chances of the lab switching analysis techniques are minimized. In most cases, these laboratories use university extraction and analysis techniques and fertility recommendations for a specific region or soil type. Managers should be careful the laboratory chosen uses information on calibration of soil test results for the plant material being grown. Recommendations based on responses of plants other than turfgrass may provide inaccurate results since turfgrass needs differ from most crops. For example, laboratories not specializing in turfgrass tend to overestimate phosphorus recommendations and underestimate potassium requirements. Also, laboratories use varying extraction techniques, depending on its geographical location (soil type). Turf managers should know the specific techniques used by labs and not compare results from

TABLE 7-1. Adequate or Sufficiency Ranges for Nutrients from Tissue Analysis (Modified from McCarty, 2001; Jones et al., 1991)

Element		General	Bermudagrass		Creeping Bentgrass	Perennial Ryegrass
			Greens/Tees	Fairways		
		g/kg	%			
Primary Nutrients	Nitrogen (N)	27–35	4.00–6.00	3.00–5.00	4.50–6.00	4.50–5.00
	Phosphorus (P)	3–5.5	0.25–0.60	0.15–0.50	0.30–0.60	0.35–0.40
	Potassium (K)	10–25	1.50–4.00	1.00–4.00	2.20–2.60	2.00–2.50
Secondary Nutrients	Calcium (Ca)	5–12.5	0.50–1.00	0.50–1.00	0.50–0.75	0.25–0.30
	Magnesium (Mg)	2–6	0.13–0.40	0.13–0.50	0.25–0.30	0.16–0.20
	Sulfur (S)	2–4.5	0.20–0.50	0.15–0.50	0.30–0.70	0.27–0.32
			mg/kg or ppm			
Micronutrients	Iron (Fe)	35–100	50–350	50–350	100–300	40–60
	Manganese (Mn)	25–150	25–300	25–300	50–100	2–10
	Zinc (Zn)	20–55	20–250	20–250	25–75	14–20
	Copper (Cu)	5–20	5–50	5–50	8–30	6–7
	Boron (B)	10–60	6–30	6–30	8–20	9–17
	Molybdenum (Mo)	~2–8	0.10–1.20	0.10–1.20	no data	0.5–1.00

Element		St. Augustinegrass	Tall Fescue	Kentucky Bluegrass
			%	
Primary Nutrients	Nitrogen (N)	1.90–3.00	3.40–3.80	2.60–3.50
	Phosphorus (P)	0.20–0.50	0.34–0.45	0.28–0.40
	Potassium (K)	2.50–4.00	3.00–4.00	2.00–3.00
Secondary Nutrients	Calcium (Ca)	0.30–0.50	no data	no data
	Magnesium (Mg)	0.15–0.25		
	Sulfur (S)	no data		
		– mg/kg or ppm –		
Micronutrients	Iron (Fe)	50–300	no data	no data
	Manganese (Mn)	40–250		
	Zinc (Zn)	20–100		
	Copper (Cu)	10–20		
	Boron (B)	5–10		
	Molybdenum (Mo)	no data		

labs using different extraction techniques. Table 7-2 lists various extraction techniques used for specific nutrients and soil types.

Sampling. Soil should be collected to give a representative sample of the area of turf in question. This can be achieved by taking 15 to 20 small plugs at random over the entire area (Figure 7-1). Since most turf roots are located in the top 6 inches of soil, sampling depth should be limited to 6 inches. Collected plugs should be mixed thoroughly, and approximately 1 pint is required for testing. Soil samples should not be placed in metal containers because nutrients from these may dissolve and provide erroneous soil nutrient levels. The County Extension Service or other testing labs can supply additional information on the proper techniques for sampling and submitting a soil sample.

Soil pH and Lime Requirement

Soil pH is a measurement of the hydrogen ion (H^+) activity in the soil solution. Solution pH is measured using a glass electrode which measures the electrical potential and compares it to standard values. A pH value is the negative logarithm of H^+ activity and is measured on a scale of 0 to 14 with values below 7.0 acidic, 7.0 being neutral, and values above 7.0 alkaline. Soil samples are mixed with deionized water, usually in a 1:1 ratio, and a soil acidity is measured with an electrode meter. This pH represents the **active acidity**.

Soil nutrients are generally more available to plants in the pH range of 6.0 to 7.0. Soil organisms also function best in this range. When soil pH is higher than 7.0, several nutrients such as P, Fe, Mn, B, Cu, and Zn become less available (Figure 7-2). Certain nutrients such as P, K, Ca, and Mg become less available below a pH of 6.0. Below soil pH of 5.5, some micronutrients such as Mn and some non-nutrients such as Al become toxic. The recommended soil pH range for optimum turf growth is 5.5 to 6.5.

If a soil pH is too acidic for optimum turf growth, lime may be applied to increase pH. A soil's active acidity is insufficient information to determine the amount of lime required to increase the pH of the soil by a desired amount. This is due to the **buffering capacity** of the soil. Exchangeable H^+ and Al^{+3} ions on soil colloids and not soil solution represent **potential** or **exchangeable acidity**. While H^+ contributes directly to acidity, one Al^{+3} ion can contribute three H^+ ions to acidity by reacting with water. This three-step reaction results in the formation of a nonreactive Al compound (gibbsite) and is referred to as the hydrolysis of Al^{+3} (Figure 7-3). When bases such as lime are added to neutralize active acidity, exchangeable acidity is released from soil exchange sites to maintain an equilibrium of H^+ in solution. Calcium ions from the liming material displace Al^{+3} adsorbed to the exchange sites and allow for it to be neutralized in the soil solution (Figure 7-4). Soils with high exchangeable acidities are said to be well buffered and will resist changes in pH. Therefore, it is necessary to determine the buffering capacity of a soil to determine the liming requirement.

A common method of determining the amount of lime needed is based on the pH change of a buffered solution compared to the soil active acidity. An acidic soil will lower the pH of the buffer solution as acidic cations are removed from the exchange complex. The resulting pH is known as the **buffer pH**. Soil pH (in water)

TABLE 7-2. Extraction Techniques Used to Determine Soil Nutrient Levels for Various Locations and Soil Types

Extraction Techniques[a]	Comments
Ammonium acetate (NH_4OAc), pH 7.0	Widely used in the Midwest and far-western USA for CEC and K. At pH 4.8, extracts more Ca and Mg.
Ammonium acetate + acetic acid	Used to extract sulfate (sulfur).
Ammonium bicarbonate (NH_4HCO_3) or Sodium bicarbonate ($NaHCO_3$)	Used in central western USA states on calcareous soils.
Bray P1	Extracts relatively soluble CaP, FeP, and AlP; some organic P.
Mehlich I (dilute double acid method; $HCl + H_2SO_4$)	Used in the clayey soils of the southeastern USA for relatively soluble CaP, FeP, and AlP; excessive P in calcareous soils. Also used to extract micronutrients Cu, Mn, B, and Zn. Also used to extract Na to determine CEC and base saturation.
Mehlich II	Extracts relatively soluble CaP, FeP, and AlP; some organic P; superior on volcanic ash or loess-derived soils.
Mehlich III	Used to extract P and cations.
Morgan	Used in northeastern and northwestern USA; extracts P dissolved by carbon dioxide.
Olsen	Extracts CaP fractions and some FeP. Better on calcareous soils than acid extractants.
Water	Extracts sulfur in arid and semiarid regions.
Dilute acid or salt	Extracts sulfur in humid regions.
DTPA-TEA (diethylenetriaminepenataacetic acid-triethanolamine, pH 7.3)	Most widely used extractant for the micronutrients Fe, Mn, Zn, and Cu.
Glass electrode pH meter on a 1:1 (v/v) basis of soil: deionized water	Soil pH
Buffer solution, pH 8.0 + glass electrode and pH meter	Buffer pH (exchangeable or potential acidity)

[a] After extraction, nutrient concentrations are often determined by inductively coupled plasma (ICP) emission spectrometry.

265

X = sample site

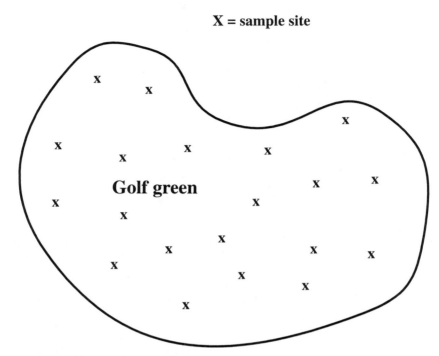

Figure 7-1. Sampling at random to give a representative soil sample on a golf green. Samples should be combined, placed in a paper bag that is properly marked, and submitted to an analytical laboratory.

and buffer pH are highly correlated. Based on empirical data from a wide range of soils, a soil laboratory can use the soil and buffer pH to determine the amount of lime required to raise the pH of a soil to target levels (6.5 for many plants). The lower the buffer pH, the higher the lime requirement.

Soil Basicity or Alkalinity

If a soil is too alkaline (has a high pH), determine whether it is due to an inherent soil characteristic or previous excessive application of liming materials. It is quite difficult, if not impossible, to appreciably change the pH of naturally occurring alkaline soils such as those found in coastal areas or fill soil containing marl, shell, or limestone by use of sulfur, ammonium sulfate, or similar acid-forming materials. If a high pH is due to applied lime or other alkaline additive, then these acid-forming materials may be effective in reducing soil pH if applied at the proper rate, frequency, and duration.

Granular, super-fine dust, or wettable sulfur or aluminum sulfate may be used to decrease soil pH (Table 7-3). Granular sulfur is best for home lawn situations due to the ease of application with cyclone fertilizer spreaders and the reduced possibility of foliar burn from the granules.

Thoroughly water-in sulfur after application, taking care to wash off all above-ground plant parts. It takes approximately one-third the amount of **sulfur** to de-

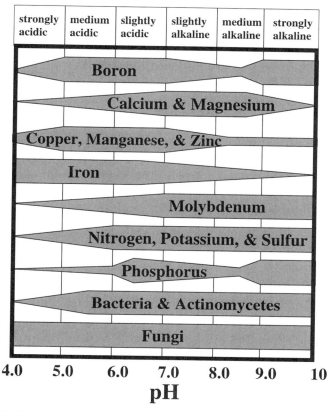

Figure 7-2. pH effects on soil nutrient availability and soil microbial populations. The relative availability of each element at a specific soil pH is indicated by the width of the bar.

crease the soil pH 1 unit as it does **calcic lime** to **increase** the soil pH 1 unit (Table 7-4). On established turf, do not apply more than 5 to 10 pounds of elemental sulfur per 1,000 square feet per application. Repeat applications of sulfur should not be made more often than once every 2 to 3 months and only when temperatures are cool (<75°F), and should be watered-in immediately after application. Remember that sulfur oxidizes in the soil and mixes with water to form a strong acid (sulfuric acid) that can severely damage plant roots—use with caution.

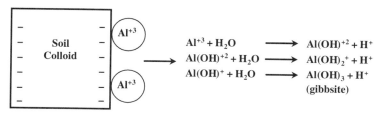

Figure 7-3. Increased acidity due to the hydrolysis of exchangeable aluminum.

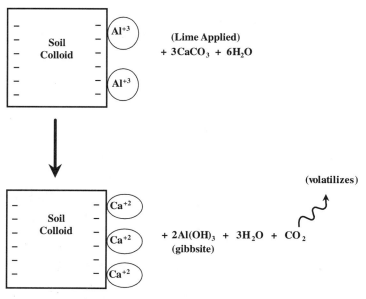

Figure 7-4. Overall reaction of liming.

Buffer pH (Lime Index) vs. Soil pH

As mentioned, **soil pH** (also called **active acidity**) reflects the actual hydrogen (H^+) concentration in the soil solution and can be measured with an indicator solution or a pH meter. Exchangeable hydrogen and aluminum ions on soil colloids represent **potential** or **exchangeable acidity**. When bases like lime are added to neutralize active acidity, potential acidity is released from the exchange sites to maintain an equilibrium between the two forms of acidity. Soils containing appreciable amounts of clay, organic matter, and humus (with high CEC values) tend to have high potential acidities. They resist pH changes when limed, and are said to be **well-buffered**. Another example involves comparing two soil types, a clay loam soil and a sandy soil. It would require more lime to raise the pH of the clay loam soil than with the sandy soil (Table 7-4). Thus, the clay soil has a higher buffering capacity than the sandy soil.

A common method of determining the amount of lime needed is based on the pH change of a buffered solution compared to the pH as a soil-water suspension. An acid soil will lower the pH of the buffer. By calibrating pH changes in the buffered solution which accompany the addition of known amounts of acid, the amount of lime required to bring a soil to a particular pH can be determined and this is the soil's **buffer pH** (also called **lime index**).

A lime recommendation is based on a calculation of the difference between the soil (or active) pH and the buffer (or exchangeable) pH. A lower buffer pH value means higher acid reserves exist in the soil, thus the soil is well buffered and will require higher lime rates to increase its pH. Typically a sandy soil has a higher buffer pH than a clay because of its lower buffering capacity. This indicates that similar amounts of lime will increase the soil pH more for a sandy soil compared to a clay, thus sandy soils require a relatively low amount of lime compared to a clay or high organic matter containing soil (Table 7-5).

TABLE 7-3. Sulfur-Containing Compounds Which Produce an Acidifying Effect (Modified from *The Sulphur Institute*)

Material	Form	Chemical Formula	Sulfur (%)	Sulfur Content (lb/ton)	Nitrogen (%)	Other (%)
Aluminum sulfate	granular	$Al_2(SO_4)_3 \cdot 18H_2O$	14	288	0	11(Al)
Ammonia-sulfur solution	solution	$NH_3 + S$	10	200	74	—
Ammonium bisulfite solution	solution	$NH_4HSO_3 + H_2O$	17	340	9	—
Ammonium polysulfide solution	solution	NH_4S_x	40	800	20	—
Ammonium sulfate[a]	granular	$(NH_4)_2SO_4$	24	484	21	—
Ammonium thiosulfate solution	solution	$(NH_4)_2S_2O_3 + H_2O$	26	520	12	—
Aqua-sulfur solution	solution	$S + H_2O$	5	100	20	—
Ferrous sulfate	solution	$FeSO_4 \cdot H_2O$	19	376	0	33(Fe)
Lime sulfur (dry)	granular	CaS_x	57	1140	0	43(Ca)
Lime sulfur (solution)	solution	$CaS_x + Ca_2SO_4A5H_2O$	23–24	480	0	9(Ca)
Sulfuric acid (100%)	solution	H_2SO_4	33	654	0	—
Sulfuric acid (66° Be=93%)	solution	H_2SO_4	30	608	0	—
Sulfur (elemental)	granular	S	100	2000	0	—
Sulfur dioxide	gas→solution	SO_2	50	1000	0	—

[a] Ammonium sulfate liquid can be formed by adding ammonia and sulfuric acid to irrigation water.

TABLE 7-4. Amount of Aluminum Sulfate [Al$_2$(SO$_4$)$_3$ · 18H$_2$O] (14% S) Required to Lower Soil pH of a Loamy Soil Before Turf Establishment.[a] Reduce Amounts Indicated by One-third for Sandy Soils and Increase by One-half for Clayey Soils

Current pH	Desired pH				
	6.5	6.0	5.5	5.0	4.5
	Pounds of aluminum sulfate to add per 1,000 sq. ft.				
8.0	180	240	330	420	480
7.5	120	210	270	360	420
7.0	60	120	210	300	360
6.5	—	60	150	240	270
6.0	—	—	60	150	210

[a] If elemental sulfur (99% S) is used, multiply table values by 0.15 to convert.
If ammonium sulfate [(NH$_4$)$_2$SO$_4$] (24% S) is used, multiply table values by 0.29 to convert.
If ferrous sulfate (FeSO$_4$ · 7H$_2$O) (19% S) is used, multiply table values by 1.26 to convert.
If lime sulfur solution (24% S) [CaS$_5$ + CaSO$_4$ · 5H$_2$O] is used, multiply table values by 0.61 to convert.
If sulfuric acid (100% H$_2$SO$_4$) is used, multiply table values by 0.43 to convert.

Lime and Fertilizer Recommendations

Usually at the end of a soil test analysis report, lime, fertilizer and other amendment recommendations, based on the test results, are listed. These typically are self-explanatory and expressed in pounds of product needed per 1,000 square feet of grass. The goal of the recommendations are three-fold: (1) to satisfy immediately the plant nutritional needs; (2) to build soil-nutrients reserves to optimal levels; and (3) to reduce over-abundant nutrients.

Cation Exchange Capacity. The total number of exchangeable cations a soil can hold is known as its cation exchange capacity (CEC) and is generally expressed in units of milliequivalents per 100 grams of soil (meq/100 g) or centimoles per kilogram (cmol/kg) of soil. Higher CEC values usually represent better soils in terms of fertility because the soil can hold more nutrients such as K^+, Mg^{+2}, Cu^{+2}, Mn^{+2}, Zn^{+2}, and Fe^{+3}. Soil constituents which attract cations, such as organic matter and clay, have higher CEC values than less fertile sandy soil (Table 7-6).

To measure soil CEC, a sample is saturated with a solution of cations which will replace the cations on exchange sites and force them into solution. The soil

TABLE 7-5. Examples of Rates of Dolomitic Limestone or Calcium Carbonate Required to Raise pH of Sand, Loam, Clay, or Muck Soil to 6.5

Current pH	Pounds Required per 1,000 sq. ft. to Raise Soil pH to 6.5		
	Sand	Loam	Clay or Muck
6.0	20	35	50
5.5	45	75	100
5.0	65	110	150
4.5	80	150	200
4.0	100	175	230

TABLE 7-6. Cation Exchange Capacity (CEC) Examples of Various Soils

Soil	CEC (meq/100 g)	Relative Level
Sand	0–6	Very low
Sandy loam	6–12	Low
Loam	12–30	Medium
Silt loam	10–50	Medium
Clay loams	15–30	Medium
Clays	18–150	High

solution is then collected, filtered, and titrated to determine the amount of cations that were displaced.

Base Saturation (or Cation Saturation). The degree to which the total CEC sites are saturated with the base-forming cations calcium, magnesium, and potassium and sodium as opposed to the acid-forming cations hydrogen and aluminum is referred to as the **base saturation** of a soil (Table 7-7). In general, the pH and fertility of a soil increase as the percentage base saturation increases. Higher base saturation generally increases the ease with which cations are absorbed by plants. Greatest availability of most nutrients to plants is in the soil pH range 6 to 7. In highly acidic soils (pH < 5.5), exchangeable aluminum may be present and, along with magnesium and/or hydrogen ions, can suppress plant uptake of calcium or potassium. However, toxic aluminum becomes less prevalent and therefore less detrimental to the plant, as the base saturation increases.

Nutrients. A typical soil analysis will include the P, K, Ca, Mg, S, B, Cu, Fe, Mn, Zn, and Na status of the soil. Soil N is not determined due to its readily changing nature in the soil. Since ionic forms of nutrients in solution exist in an equilibrium with exchangeable forms on soil colloids, methods must be used to extract these exchangeable forms to give a true measure of an element's availability to plants. Extraction methods usually involve the use of concentrated ionic solutions. The ions in the extractant displace the exchangeable ions into solution. This resulting solution can then be analyzed using methods similar to those described in the tissue analysis section of this chapter.

Most soil analysis reports list nutrient levels as parts per million (ppm) or milliequivalents (meq) per 100 grams of soil (Table 7-8). Results for the major ele-

TABLE 7-7. Desired Cation Exchangeable Capacities (CEC) and Percent Base Saturation Range in Soils

Cation	% Cation Exchange Capacity	% Base Saturation
Calcium (Ca^{+2})	60 to 70	50 to 80
Magnesium (Mg^{+2})	10 to 20	8 to 22
Potassium (K^+)	5 to 10	1 to 9
Sodium (Na^+)	0 to 1	0 to 1
Hydrogen (H^+)	0 to 10[a]	0

[a] A hydrogen percentage above 15% may indicate a nutrient imbalance.

TABLE 7-8. Relative Response Range of Soil Elements Analyzed by Mehlich-I Extractant[a] (Modified from McCarty, 2001; Carrow et al., 2001)

Analysis	Acceptable Ranges	Comments
Nitrogen/Organic Matter	≤5%	Due to its readily changing status in soils, nitrogen availability is hard to predict. Many times the percent organic matter serves as a reserve for many essential nutrients, especially nitrogen. Labs, therefore, list an Estimated Nitrogen Release figure based on the percentage of organic matter present to estimate the nitrogen that will be released over the season in pounds per acre.
Phosphorus	5–30 ppm	Phosphorus absorption is greatest between a soil pH of 5.5 to 6.5. Values for other extractant procedures include:
Potassium	see comment	Generally, higher K levels are required in high-clay- or organic-matter-containing soils. Soils with high levels of Mg may also require higher K applications. Sandy soils require more frequent, light K applications compared to heavier ones. Due to luxury consumption and leaching loss, levels above medium as reported by soil testing are mostly unnecessary. Values for various extractant procedures include:

Phosphorus:

Extraction Technique	Very Low	Low	Medium	High
			ppm P	
Bray P1	0–4	5–15	16–30	>31
Mehlich III	0–12	13–26	27–54	>55
Olsen	0–6	7–12	13–28	>29

Potassium:

Extraction Technique	Very Low	Low	Medium	High
			ppm K	
1M NH4OAc (pH 7.0)				
Sands/most soils	0–40	41–75	76–175	>176
Fine-textured (>35% clay)	0–55	56–100	101–235	>235
Mehlich III				
Sands/most soils	0–25	26–50	51–116	>116
Fine-textured (>35% clay)	0–40	41–75	76–175	>176
Mehlich I				
Sands/most soils	0–30	31–60	61–140	>140
Fine-textured (>35% clay)	0–45	46–90	91–200	>201

Calcium	5–50 ppm (see comment)	With most soils, liming with dolomite to insure an adequate soil pH for proper plant growth will provide more-than-adequate concentrations of Ca and Mg. Their deficiencies are more common in sandy, acidic, and/or low organic matter containing soils. Use gypsum (calcium sulfate) if calcium is needed when soil pH is too high. Consider using magnesium oxide, magnesium sulfate or sulfate or potash-magnesia if soil tests are low in Mg and lime is not required. Ca deficiencies are uncommon, however, Mg deficiencies often occur in acidic soils low in CEC and subject to frequent leaching. Heavy liming with calcium carbonate (also called calcite) lime or heavy use of K also may induce Mg deficiency. Apply magnesium sulfate (Epsom salts) to test for Mg deficiency. Guidelines for Mg:K and Ca:K ratios based on saturation percentages on the soil CEC include:
Magnesium	5–20 ppm (see comment)	

Ca:K	<10:1	Ca deficiency may occur
	>30:1	K deficiency may occur
Mg:K	<2:1	Mg deficiency may occur
	>10:1	K deficiency may occur
Ca:Mg	<3:1	Ca deficiency may occur
	>3:1	Mg deficiency may occur

Soil pH	5.5–6.5	Soil pH less than 5.5 becomes highly acidic and can produce toxic elements to the turf. Alkaline soil pH (>7.0) often limits availability of many minor elements.
Cation Exchange Capacity (CEC)	5 to 35 meq/ 100 g	CEC measures a soil's ability to hold the cations Ca, Mg, K, H, and Na. Increasing CEC generally occurs with increasing soil organic matter or clay content. Generally, the higher the CEC value, the more productive the soil. A suggested range of the total makeup of a soil's CEC is 65 to 75% Ca, 12 to 18% Mg, and 3 to 5% K.
Percent Base Saturation	(see comment)	Percent base saturation refers to the proportion of the CEC occupied by the cations Ca, Mg, K, H, and Na. With sandy soils, base saturation percentages have little value when determining nutrient levels.

273

TABLE 7-8. Relative Response Range of Soil Elements Analyzed by Mehlich-I Extractant[a] (Modified from McCarty, 2001; Carrow et al., 2001) (Continued)

Analysis	Acceptable Ranges	Comments
Iron	12–25 ppm	Soil pH and relative levels of other elements such as P are important when interpreting Fe soil test. Generally, Fe becomes less available in alkaline or extremely acidic soils, and soils with excessive P or moisture levels. See Copper.
Manganese	2–10 ppm	Levels where a plant response to applied Mn may occur include: 3–5, 5–7, 7–9 ppm for mineral or organic soils with pH 5.5–6.0, 6.0–6.5, 6.5–7.0, respectively. Deficiencies are more prone on coarse, sandy, acid soils that receive excessive water. See Copper.
Zinc	1–3 ppm	Levels where a plant response to applied Zn may occur include: 0.5, 0.5–1.0, 1–3 ppm for soils with pH 5.5–6.0, 6.0–6.5, 6.5–7.0, respectively. Zinc interactions with P and soil pH can alter needed application rates. See Copper.
Copper	0.1–0.5 ppm	Levels where a plant response to applied Cu may occur include: 0.1–0.3, 0.3–0.5, 0.5 ppm for **mineral soils only** with pH 5.5–6.0, 6.0–6.5, 6.5–7.0, respectively. Copper deficiencies can occur on alkaline soils, high organic matter (peat and muck) soils, soils fertilized heavy with N, P, and Zn, and when flatwood soils are first cultivated. Toxic conditions may exist when Cu levels exceed 2–3, 3–5, and 5 ppm in mineral soils with pH of 5.5–6.0, 6.0–6.5, and 6.5–7.0, respectively. Additional levels used by many laboratories for micronutrient availability include:

Extraction Technique Micronutrient	Low (Deficient)	Medium	High (Sufficient)
		ppm	
DTPA			
Fe	<2.5	2.6–5.0	>5.0
Mn	<1.0	1–2	>2
Zn	<0.5	0.6–1.0	>1
Cu	<0.2	0.2–0.4	>0.4
Mehlich III			
Fe	<50	50–100	>100
Mn	<4.0 (pH 6.0)	4.0–6.0	>6.0
Zn	<8.0 (pH 7.0)	8.0–12.0	>12.0
	<1.0	1.1–2.0	>2.0
Cu	<0.3	0.3–2.5	>2.5

Boron	1–1.5 ppm	Boron deficiencies occur more commonly on sandy, low organic matter soils, and alkaline soils. Boron is most soluble (available) under acid soil conditions.
Sulfur	see comment	Soil S levels, like N, are dependent on soil organic matter levels and are erratic to measure and often results are meaningless. Soils which are low in organic matter, well drained, have low CEC values, and are fertilized with excessive nitrogen, can develop low S levels. Foliar application of magnesium sulfate (Epsom salt) will indicate if S deficiencies exist by greening up within 48 hours after application.

[a] Acceptable ranges represent typical values generated by the Mehlich-I soil nutrient extractant procedure. Values may vary if other extractant procedures are used which are typically performed for various soil types and geographical regions. Refer to the specific soil testing facility and report to determine which nutrient extractant procedure was used and what the generated values actually represent.

TABLE 7-9. An Example of a Soil and Tissue Analysis Laboratory Report

Grower:	Received:	Processed:	Sample ID:
Grass:	Phone:	Fax:	E-mail:

P = Plant   S = Soil

Element	Plant Tissue	Soil (lb/a)	Test Ratings — Deficient / Low / Medium / High
Nitrogen (N)	3.13 %	—	PPPPPPPPPPPPPPPPPPPP
Phosphorus (P)	0.32 %	129	PPPPPPPPPPPPPPPPPPPPPPPPPP SSSSSSSSSSSSSSSSSSSSSSSSSS
Potassium (K)	1.61 %	111	PPPPPPPP SSSSSSSSSSSSSSSSSSSSSSS
Calcium (Ca)	0.47 %	584	PPPPPPPPPPPPPPPPPPPPPPPPPP SSSSSSSSSSSSSSSSSSSS
Magnesium (Mg)	0.35 %	196	PPPPPPPPPPPPPPPPPPPPPP SSSSSSSSSSSSSSSSSSSSSSSSSSSSSSSSSS
Sulfur (S)	0.12 %	46	PPPPPPPP SSSSSSSSSSSSSSSSSSSSSSSSSS
Boron (B)	5 ppm	0.20	PPPPPPPPPPPPPPPPPPPPPPPP SSSSSSSSSS
Copper (Cu)	7 ppm	0.80	PPPPPPPPPPPPPPPPPPPPPPPP SSSSSSSSSSSSSSSSSSSS
Iron (Fe)	106 ppm	103	PPPPPPPPPPPPPPPPPPPPPPPPPPP SSSSSSSSSSSSSSSSSSSSSSSSSSSSSSSSSS
Manganese (Mn)	38 ppm	10	PPPPPPPPPPPPPPPPPPPPPPPPPP SSSSSSSSSSSS
Zinc (Zn)	24 ppm	4.00	PPPPPPPPPPPPPPPP SSSSSSSSSSSSSSSSSSSSSSSSSS

Grower: Received: Sample ID:

Grass: Phone: E-mail:

Processed:

Fax:

Element	Plant Tissue	Soil (lb/a)	Deficient	Low	Medium	High
			P = Plant			S = Soil
			Deficient	Low	Medium	High
Sodium (Na)	—	11 ppm	SSS			
Soluble Salts	—	0.080 mmho/cm	SSS			
Soil pH (or active acidity)		6.7				
Buffer pH (or lime index)		7.9				
Organic Matter		1.1%				
Calculated Cation Exchange Capacity		6.0 meq/100 g				
			%K	−2.5	%H	−66.7
			%Ca	−24.0	%Na	−0.8
			%Mg	−6.5		

Lime and Fertilizer Recommendations:

1. Lime (lb/1,000 sq. ft.) _____ 3. Phosphate (lb P_2O_5/1,000 sq. ft.) _____ 5. Other _____

2. Nitrogen (lb N/1,000 sq. ft.) _____ 4. Potash (lb K_2O/1,000 sq. ft.) _____

ments and micronutrients are most commonly reported in ppm on an elemental basis. However, many labs are now reporting this as units of pounds of nutrient per acre. This unit is based on the assumption that the surface 6-inch of soil in an acre weighs approximately 2 million pounds. Therefore, to convert ppm to approximate pounds per acre, multiply by two. If the desire is to know the approximate pounds of nutrients present on a per 1,000 square foot basis, then divide the pounds per acre value by 4. From these reported nutrient levels, most soil test readings are given a fertility rating index of very low (VL), low (L), medium (M), high (H), or very high (VH). Usually, the division between medium and high is the critical value. Above this point there is no expected plant response to added fertilizer, while below this, increasing amounts of fertilizer are needed with decreasing levels.

Interpreting a Soil Analysis Report

A soil analysis report supplies a wealth of information concerning the nutritional status of a soil and may aid in the detection of potential problems which could limit turfgrass growth or color. A typical soil analysis supplies information relative to cation exchange capacity, soil acidity, lime requirements, and the phosphorus, potassium, calcium, and magnesium status of the soil. Nitrogen is not determined because of its readily changing nature. Additional information can be requested from lab reports, such as soil organic matter content, soluble salts, and irrigation water analysis. Table 7-9 lists the results from a typical soil and plant tissue report. Recommendations, in terms of lime and nutrients, are typically listed at the end of the report.

PRACTICE PROBLEMS

1. What plant parts and locations should be collected for turfgrass tissue analysis? (*Turfgrass leaves are the primary tissue sampled. Unhealthy turf or turf showing severe signs of deficiency should not be directly sampled because nutrient levels may become skewed due to stress. Healthier samples from adjoining plants should be taken when deficiencies are severe.*)

2. Why must organic matter in tissue samples be destroyed? (*Organic matter must be destroyed to free the nutrients so that they may be dissolved and quantified. The two most commonly used methods are acid digestion and dry ashing.*)

3. What is atomic absorption spectrophotometry (AAS) used for, and what principle is it based on? (*AAS can be used to analyze solutions for K, Ca, Mg, Zn, Fe, Cu, Mn, and Na. This instrument operates on the principle of ground-state energy levels of atoms.*)

4. What types of information can be gained from soil tests? (*Soil testing can quantify soil characteristics such as nutrient levels, pH, CEC, and base saturation.*)

5. When should a soil be tested? (*Soil tests should be conducted prior to turf establishment so that any needed amendments may be added prior to planting. On established turf, soils are typically sampled yearly, or when the turf appears to have a nutritional problem.*)

6. How should soil samples be collected? (*Soil should be collected so as to give a representative sample of the area in question. This is achieved by taking many small plugs at random across a location, then mixing them thoroughly. Sampling depth should be limited to the top six inches of soil since this is where the majority of turf roots are located.*)

7. What is the difference between active and exchangeable acidity? (*Active acidity is the acidity of a soil mixed with water and is a direct measurement of H^+ in solution. Exchangeable acidity depends on Al^{+3} and H^+ adsorbed on soil exchange sites which are responsible for a soil's ability to resist changes in* pH.)

8. What is the relationship between soil pH and nutrient availability? (*Soil nutrients are generally most available to plants in the pH range of 6.0 to 7.0. At a pH greater than 7.0, the nutrients P, Fe, Mn, B, Cu, and Zn become less available. Nutrients such as P, K, Ca, and Mg become less available below a pH of 6.0.*)

9. Describe CEC. (*CEC [cation-exchange capacity] is a measurement of the total number of exchangeable cations a soil can hold. CEC is expressed in milliequivalents per 100 g of soil. Higher CEC values represent better soils in terms of fertility as the soil can hold more cation nutrients. Organic matter and clay are responsible for soil CEC.*)

10. What does a soil's base saturation represent? (*Base saturation refers to the degree to which soil exchange sites are saturated with basic cations such as Ca^{+2}, Mg^{+2}, Na^+, and K^+. In general, the pH and fertility of a soil increase as the percentage base saturation increases. A higher base saturation increases the ease of cation absorption by plants.*)

CHAPTER 8

PESTICIDE CHEMISTRY AND FATE IN THE ENVIRONMENT

INTRODUCTION

Pesticides in the environment have received much media and scientific attention in recent years. Turf stands have repeatedly been shown to minimize pesticide and nutrient leaching and runoff and are often recommended for such purposes along the perimeter of agriculture production fields. Turfgrasses are unique systems due to the extremely high density of plants, with communities containing up to 2,500 plants per square foot. Turfgrasses also produce a thatch layer high in organic matter which acts as a filter and binds many pesticides before they can reach the soil. It has been estimated that a 150-acre golf course has the capacity to absorb 12 million gallons of water during a 3-inch downpour. This water infiltrates and is absorbed by the turf/thatch/soil profile before it moves horizontally as runoff. Thatch also harbors high populations of microorganisms that use pesticides and nutrients as energy sources as they break down these compounds into simple molecules. Turfgrasses also possess dense, fibrous root systems that are capable of adsorbing pesticides.

PESTICIDE NOMENCLATURE

A **pesticide** is defined as any substance or mixture of substances intended for preventing, destroying, repelling, or mitigating any pest, and any substance or mixture of substances intended for use as a plant regulator, defoliant, or desiccant. Three types of names normally are associated with a pesticide. The **chemical name** describes the chemistry of the compound. These usually are a technical and lengthy description of the chemical. The **common name** is a generic term assigned to the chemical and often is a simpler version of the chemical name. Chemical and common names must be approved by an appropriate authority. The **trade name** is used for marketing purposes to promote the sale of a specific product. It often is the most recognizable pesticide name. A pesticide with one common name can have a number of trade names. For example, Fungo, Cleary 3336, and SysTec 1998 are **trade names** for the fungicide thiophanate methyl. Thiophanate methyl is the **common name** while the **chemical name** is dimethyl 4,4'-o-phenylenebis[3-thioallophanate]. Due to the number of trade names and their constant change, most scientific journals and university publications refer to the common name of a pesticide.

PESTICIDE REGISTRATION

Registering a new pesticide is a time-consuming, complicated, and expensive venture. Only one successful pesticide reaches the market out of every 20,000 compounds tested. Developing a new pesticide costs $35 million to $50 million with an additional $40 million to $100 million required to build a production plant. Eight to 10 years of testing normally are required before a compound reaches the market. Since a patent protects a compound for 17 years, less than 10 years of exclusive marketing can be expected to protect the investment of development and continued research.

Much of the money needed for pesticide development is used to generate required data from extensive and rigorous testing. Testing for crop safety, pest control efficacy, environmental hazards, and a wide array of toxicological tests is performed. These increasing costs and regulations have significantly reduced the number of companies developing new pesticides.

Pesticide Classification

General-use pesticides are those that will not cause unreasonable adverse effects to the environment and may be purchased and applied by the general public when used according to label directions. However, in some states, anyone applying any pesticide for monetary compensation or to public property (including golf courses) must have a license or be directly supervised by someone with a license. **Restricted-use** pesticides are pesticides that pose some risk to the environment or human health even when used according to the label. These pesticides must be applied by certified applicators, or persons under their direct supervision, who have shown the ability to use these materials safely and properly. Persons handling restricted-use pesticides also must wear approved protective clothing. The pesticide label will indicate whether a pesticide is classified as a restricted-use product. A third category, **mixed-use,** covers pesticides which are classified as 'general' for certain purposes and 'restricted' for others.

PESTICIDE FORMULATIONS AND CARRIERS

Pesticides are not sold to end-users as pure chemicals, but are formulated or combined with appropriate solvents, diluents, or adjuvants to form a material called a **formulation**. The primary function of formulating a pesticide is to permit uniform application. However, formulations also extend the stability and storage life of pesticides, enhance pesticide activity, allow pesticides to be packaged in convenient containers, and allow for safer use. Pesticides are available in a variety of formulations and often the same pesticide is sold as several different formulations (Table 8-1). A **Material Safety Data Sheet** (**MSDS**) for each formulation of a pesticide should be obtained and cataloged. These sheets provide information on:

(1) Chemical product/company identification
(2) Composition/information on ingredients
(3) Hazardous identification
(4) First-aid measures
(5) Fire-fighting measures
(6) Accidental release measures
(7) Handling and storage
(8) Exposure controls/personal protection
(9) Physical and chemical properties
(10) Stability and reactivity
(11) Toxicological information
(12) Ecological information
(13) Disposal considerations
(14) Transportation information
(15) Regulatory information
(16) Other information

MSDS for each pesticide formulation must be kept readily available for workers to read prior to handling the pesticide and to refer to in emergency situations.

Technical Information Bulletins

It has become quite common for some golf courses to submit pesticide use plans to Water Management Districts or other state agencies. In most cases, the information required may either be found on the label or on the MSDS for the pesticide. However, some information may only be found in technical bulletins. These also are written by the company manufacturing the product, but normally are *not* provided to the pesticide user. If a specific piece of information cannot be located on the label or MSDS, contact the company representative (salesperson, sales manager, technical research & development representative, website, etc.) and request a technical bulletin.

Labeling Is the Law

It is extremely important to remember that the pesticide label is the *law*. Pesticides may not be used in a manner not permitted by the labeling. Pesticide uses inconsistent with the label include:

(1) Applying pesticides to plants, animals, or sites not specified in the directions for use. If the label does not state it is for use on turfgrass, then it is not legal to use on turfgrass.

(2) Using higher dosages, higher concentrations, or more frequent applications than specified on the label.

(3) Not following the directions for use, safety, diluting, storage, and disposal. This also includes any restrictions on course reentry, not only for employees but for golfers as well.

The law does allow you to:

TABLE 8-1. Comparisons of Pesticide Formulations (Read Individual Labels for Product Specific Information) (McCarty, 2001)

Formulation (Abbreviation)	Mixing/Loading Hazards	Plant Phytotoxicity	Effect on Application Equipment	Agitation Required	Visible Residues	Compatible with Other Formulations
Dry flowables/water dispersible granules (DF or WDG)	minimum	safe	abrasive	yes	yes	good
Emulsifiable concentrates (EC)	spills & splashes	maybe	may affect rubber pump parts	yes	no	fair
Flowables (F)	spills & splashes	maybe	may affect rubber pump parts; also abrasive	yes	yes	fair
Dusts (D)	severe inhalation hazards	safe	—	yes	yes	—
Granules (G) & pellets (P or Ps)	minimum	safe	—	no	no	—
Microencapsulated (M)	spills & splashes	safe	none	yes	—	fair
Solutions (S)	spills & splashes	safe	nonabrasive	no	no	fair
Soluble powders (SP)	dust inhalation	safe	nonabrasive	no	some	fair
Wettable powders (WP)	dust inhalation	safe	abrasive	yes	yes	highly

(1) Apply pesticides at dosages, concentrations, and frequencies that are less than those listed on the label if you obtain expert opinion or have data to justify the lower rate.

(2) Apply a pesticide against any target pest not listed on the label *if* the application is to a crop/plant, animal, or site that is listed on the label. In other words, if a new weed suddenly appears, it is legal to use a herbicide for control as long as turfgrass is listed on the label and you know the material will control the weed.

(3) Mix a pesticide with a fertilizer if the mixture is not prohibited by the label.

(4) Mix two or more pesticides together if all the dosages are at or below the labeled rate(s), and the mixture is not prohibited by any of the labels.

Read the *entire* label of any pesticide before you buy, mix, apply, store, or dispose of it. If you have questions on how to use a pesticide, it is quite likely that other applicators have the same questions. Be a good consumer and tell the manufacturer your concerns. They may not realize there are problems or questions with label directions. The label must contain the items listed below.

(1) Trade name
(2) Ingredient statement
   (a) Active ingredient (chemical name; common name may be present)
   (b) Inert ingredient(s)
(3) Type of pesticide (herbicide, insecticide, nematicide, fungicide, etc.)
(4) Net contents
(5) Name and address of manufacturer—establishment number
(6) EPA registration number—indicates label is approved by EPA
(7) Signal words and symbols
   (a) Danger—highly toxic; some products also may carry the word 'Poison' printed in red plus the skull and crossbones symbol (category I)
   (b) Warning—moderately toxic (category II)
   (c) Caution—slightly toxic (categories III and IV)
(8) Precautionary statements
   (a) Route of entry [to the body] statements
   (b) Specific action statements [to prevent poisoning accidents]
   (c) Protective clothing and equipment statements
   (d) Other statements may be listed in regard to precautions to take while handling the product
(9) Statement of practical treatment in case of poisoning
(10) Environment hazards
   (a) Special toxicity statements (e.g., toxic to bees, fish, etc.)
   (b) General environmental statements
(11) Physical or chemical hazards
(12) Classification statement: general- or restricted- use pesticide
(13) Reentry statement

(14) Storage and disposal
(15) Directions for use

CARRIERS

Pesticides are applied to the target site with the use of a carrier. A carrier is a gas, liquid, or solid substance used to propel, dilute, or suspend a pesticide during its application. Water is the most commonly used liquid carrier, although fluid fertilizers also may be used. Granules and pellets that consist of clay, corncobs, ground nut hulls, sand, or dry fertilizer serve as carriers for dry pesticide formulations.

Sprayable Formulations

Sprayable formulations are applied with liquid carriers, usually water. The amount of liquid carrier required to cover the turfgrass uniformly will be indicated on the label. Use the label recommendation for each pesticide you apply, because amounts above the label rate are illegal and those below the label rate may be ineffective.

A. Water-Soluble Formulations

Aerosols (A).   Aerosols contain one or more active ingredients and a solvent. Most aerosols contain a very low percentage of active ingredient. There are two types of aerosol formulations: the ready-to-use type and those made for use in smoke or fog generators. Insecticides are the pesticides most often used as aerosols.

Water-Soluble Liquids (S or SL). A water-soluble pesticide formulation typically consists of the pesticide, water as solvent for the pesticide, selected surfactants to improve wetting and penetration, and possibly an antifreeze. These form true solutions (completely dissolved) when mixed with water and are nonabrasive and do not plug screens or nozzles. The resulting solution can be clear or colored and is stable, requiring no agitation once initially mixed.

Water-Soluble Powders (SP or WSP). Water-soluble powders are finely divided dry solids that look like wettable powders; however, they completely dissolve in water to form true solutions requiring no agitation once initially mixed. Wettable powders, however, do not form true solutions and must be constantly agitated. Water-soluble powders possess all advantages of wettable powders with none of the disadvantages except inhalation hazard during mixing.

B. Emulsifiable Formulations

Emulsifiable Concentrates (E or EC).   Emulsifiable concentrates are oily (or non-polar) liquids that form emulsions (droplets of oil surrounded by water) in water (polar) instead of forming true solutions. The *emulsifying agent* acts as a binder-coupler between the oil-water surface, reducing interfacial tension and allowing the tiny droplets of oil to remain in suspension. This allows water-insoluble pesticide to be uniformly dispersed in water, even though each maintains its original identity.

After EC compounds are added to water, the resulting emulsions are milky colored and require mild agitation to keep the pesticide uniformly suspended in the spray tank. Each EC gallon usually contains 25 to 75% (2 to 6 pounds) active ingredient. Emulsions present few problems in mixing, pumping, or spraying. They are not abrasive, do not plug screens or nozzles, and leave little visible residue.

C. Dry Solids Suspended in Water

Wettable Powders (W or WP).   Wettable powders are finely ground solids that look like dust and consist of a dry diluent (usually a hydrophilic clay such as bentonite or attapulgite) plus the pesticide and perhaps adjuvants. Usually, pesticides make up 50 to 80% (by weight) of a wettable powder formulation. The various adjuvants in the formulation prevent lumpiness or flocculation of the finely ground materials and improve mixing in the spray tank. Wettable powders do not dissolve in water; rather, they form unstable suspensions in water, giving it a cloudy appearance, and require vigorous agitation to prevent settling of the suspended particles. Inhalation hazards also exist when pouring and mixing the powder. Wettable powders formulations also cause rapid nozzle wear, often clog nozzles and screens, and may leave visible residues.

Dispersible Granules or Dry Flowable (DG or DF or WDG). These finely ground solids are formulated as water-dispersible granules and form a suspension in water. These are similar to wettable powder formulations, except they are granule-sized particles. Once in solution, the granules break apart into a fine powder. Agitation is required to prevent settling of the suspended particles and nozzle wear is similar to flowables. Granules are made up of finely ground solids combined with suspending and dispersing agents. Their chief advantage over wettable powders and flowables is ease of measurement and handling and they are less susceptible to inhalation and wind blowing. Note: These formulations are always applied with a liquid (water or fluid fertilizer) carrier.

Water-Soluble Bags/Packs. Some pesticides are being sold with a premeasured amount of the pesticide formulation (usually a wettable powder or dry flowable) packaged inside a water-soluble bag. This bag will dissolve when placed in a tank of water, releasing the pesticide. This eliminates the need to handle the pesticide directly, thus reducing worker exposure to the pesticide. These bags are not to be broken before placing in the tank. Exact sprayer calibration is necessary since parts or pieces of a bag cannot be used.

D. Liquid Suspensions (L or F) Dispersed in Water

Flowables or Aqueous Suspensions (F or AS).   Also designated as **liquids (L)** or **water-dispersible liquids (WDL)**. These are highly viscous liquids (not easily poured) containing finely ground solids suspended in a liquid system. The particles are smaller than those of the wettable powders. These formulations form a suspension in water and require agitation to remain distributed. These also settle out when in storage, therefore requiring vigorous shaking before use but have less mixing and dust exposure problems typical of wettable powders. They may leave a visible residue. Nozzle wear is intermediate between WP and EC, more similar to WP.

Emulsions of a Water-dissolved Pesticide of Oil (EO). These are fine globules of pesticide in water dispersed within an oil. **Emulsion of an Oil-dissolved Pesticide in Water (EW)**—This is pesticide in fine globules of oil dispersed within water. Unlike emulsifiable concentrates which consist of a single oil-based phase, emulsions are packaged in two phases, water and oil. This allows the mixing of two unlike or incompatible formulations in the same package.

Microencapsulated (M). These are particles of pesticides (liquid or dry) surrounded by a plastic coating. The formulated product is mixed with water and applied as a spray. Once applied, the capsule slowly releases the pesticide. Advantages of microencapsulated pesticides are increased safety to applicator, ease of mixing and handling, and controlled release, thus extending the period of pest control. It also reduces volatilization and leaching. Constant agitation is necessary to maintain the solution.

Dry Formulations

Dry pesticide formulations are not applied with liquid carriers but are applied as purchased. Normally the pesticide is formulated in relatively low concentrations on the dry carrier to aid in uniform distribution.

Granules (G). Small granular particles (<10 μm^3) are applied in the dry state. These consist of the pesticide plus a dry carrier such as clay, vermiculite, walnut shells, sand, or corncobs. The active material either coats the outside of the granules or is absorbed into them. Pesticide concentrations typically range from 2 to 10%. Advantages of granules include: (a) ready to use—water not needed for application, (b) they are generally quicker to apply than liquid applications, (c) they can be combined with fertilizer to combine two steps and thus reduce costs, and (d) public perception is usually more favorable toward using granules compared to liquid applications. Granular formulations require slightly more rainfall for activation than sprayable formulations and tend to be more expensive. Uniform application can also be a problem and application equipment is harder to calibrate. When combined with fertilizer, proper timing of pest control and appropriate plant fertilization timing needs should coincide.

Pellets (P). Pellets are similar to granules except particles usually are larger. Pellets are frequently used for spot applications, applied 'by hand' from shaker cans or with hand spreaders. These usually contain low active-ingredient concentrations, approximately 5 to 20%. See the above comments for granules.

Dusts (D). Dusts are popular homeowner formulations of insecticides and fungicides requiring simple equipment and are effective in hard-to-reach areas. Most formulations are ready-to-use and contain between 1/2 to 10% active ingredient plus a fine, dry, inert carrier such as talc, chalk, clay, or ash. Due to drift hazards, few herbicides are currently formulated as dust.

Spray Additives

Most pesticides require a spray additive to enhance its performance or handling of that material. An **adjuvant** is a spray additive that enhances the performance, safety, or handling characteristics of a pesticide. 'Adjuvant' is a broad term and includes **surfactants, crop oils, crop oil concentrates, anti-foaming agents, drift control agents, pH modifiers** and **compatibility agents** (Table 8-2). These help modify the surface properties of liquids by enhancing and facilitating emulsifying, dispersal, wetting, spreading, sticking, and penetrating of liquids into plants and soil. Surfactants, crop oils and crop oil concentrates are added according to label directions since indiscriminate use may cause severe plant injury or decreased pesticide performance. Some pesticides, such as postemergence herbicides, and a few fungicides, have surfactants included in their formulation and additional surfactant is unnecessary. Always read the pesticide label before adding any adjuvants. Look for recommendations as to the type of adjuvant to add. Use only the recommended rates as too much of some adjuvants can cause an unsprayable tank mix. Surfactants are most often used in liquid (soluble, emulsifiable) and dry (wettable powders, others) formulations applied in aqueous sprays.

Surfactants. Substances without affinity for each other (such as water and leaf wax) tend to repel. To 'bind' the two surfaces, surfactants with a lipophilic (oil-loving) portion and a hydrophilic (water-loving) portion on the same molecule, are used. The term **surfactant** is an acronym for **surface-active agents** to indicate the changes they produce at surfaces. At low concentrations, surfactants reduce surface tension between spray droplet and waxy leaf surface, allowing the spray droplet to spread out and contact a greater portion of the leaf. This aids penetration and helps prevent droplets from rolling off the leaf. At higher concentrations, surfactants help dissolve the wax in the leaf cuticles, allowing easier penetration of the leaf by the pesticide. However, this also accounts for undesirable phytotoxicity if excessive rates are used.

Three major types of surfactants include **emulsifiers, stickers,** and **wetting agents. Emulsifiers** stabilize the dispersal of oil-soluble pesticides in water so that the pesticide will not settle out. These allow petroleum-based formulations such as emulsifiable concentrates to mix with water. These usually are added by the chemical company during the pesticide formulation process. **Invert emulsifiers** allow water-based pesticides to mix with petroleum-based carriers. **Stickers** (or **adhe-**

TABLE 8-2. Various Pesticide Mixture Spray Additives

• Acidifier	• Emulsifier
• Activator	• Fertilizer
• Adjuvant	• Penetrant
• Buffer	• Safener
• Compatibility agent	• Spreader
• Crop oil concentrate	• Sticker
• Defoamer	• Surfactant
• Drift control agent	• Wetting agent

sives) cause the spray droplet to adhere to the leaf surface and reduces spray runoff during application and washoff by rain or irrigation. Stickers often are combined with wetting agents (spreader-stickers) to increase adhesion and spray droplet coverage.

Wetting agents help the spray droplet to spread over the leaf surface by reducing the interfacial tension between the leaf surface and spray droplets. Wetting agents also allow wettable powders to mix with water. The three types of wetting agents (**nonionic, cationic,** and **anionic**) are classified based on how they ionize or separate into charged particles in water. Nonionic surfactants do not ionize and thus remain uncharged. This is the most commonly used type of surfactant and is compatible with most pesticides. They are unaffected by water containing high levels of calcium, magnesium, or ferric ions. They also can be used in strong acid solutions. **Anionic** ionizes with water to form a negative charge while **cationic** ionizes with water to form a positive charge. These are only occasionally used. A pesticide mixed with an anionic surfactant will stick to the leaf tissue but often is not absorbed by the plant. These should be used with pesticides that remain on the plant surface (contact pesticides).

A pesticide mixed with a nonionic surfactant will help a pesticide penetrate plant cuticles. These are best used with systemic pesticides that need to be absorbed by the plant to be effective. Cationic surfactants are extremely phytotoxic. Do not use them unless it is specifically stated on a pesticide label.

Crop Oils. **Crop oils** and **crop oil concentrates** are nonphytotoxic light oils that contain varying percentages of surfactants and primarily emulsifiers. These are phytobland petroleum or vegetable oils that increase pesticide absorption through leaf cuticles (or waxy layer). Crop oils contain 1 to 10% surfactant and commonly are used at concentrations of 1 gallon per acre. Crop oil concentrates contain 17 to 20% surfactant and are generally used at concentrations of 1 quart per acre. Crop oil concentrates have replaced crop oils since reduced amounts of the adjuvant is required.

Miscellaneous Adjuvants. The use of **antifoaming agents** (or defoamers) are used to minimize air entrapment during agitation and may be necessary if excessive foaming occurs in the spray tank. **Drift control agents** (or thickeners) reduce spray droplet drift by reducing the percentage of very fine spray particles in the spray mist. **Compatibility agents** are added to fluid fertilizer and pesticide mixtures to prevent these individual components from separating or clumping. Follow label directions closely for mixing compatibility agents. However, before adding any such mixture to a spray tank, *test* the mixture in a small jar to ensure there will be no clumping or separation (see procedure below).

Penetrants allow pesticides to enter the outer surface of plants while **spreaders** allow a uniform coating layer over the treated surface.

Some pesticides will be inactivated if the pH is too high or too low. **Modifiers** are compounds, either buffers or acidifiers, available to adjust the pH of the water to be used as the pesticide carrier. Buffers change the pH to a desired level, and then keep it relatively constant. Acidifiers neutralize alkaline solutions (lower the pH) but will not maintain the pH at that level as well as buffers do. Use an acidifier to lower solution pH after the pesticide is added to the tank. Ask your sales representative to provide you with the manufacturer's recommendation for the pH of the carrier.

Fertilizer. Liquid fertilizer, most often ammonium sulfate, is sometimes added at 2 to 5% concentration to enhance pesticide uptake and activity. The fertilizer appears to enhance pesticide absorption presumably by partially dissolving plant cuticles. Results are generally best for controlling annual weeds with herbicides. Perennial weed control is more erratic, presumably due to rapid burn-down of topgrowth by the fertilizer before sufficient herbicide uptake and translocation can occur to underground reproductive plant parts.

Pesticide Compatibility

Two or more pesticides, or one that can be mixed with fertilizer, are compatible if no adverse effects occur as a result of the mixture. Possible effects of mixing incompatible chemicals include:

- Effectiveness of one or both compounds may be reduced.
- A precipitate may form in the tank, clogging screens and nozzles of application equipment.
- Plant phytotoxicity, stunting, or reduced seed germination and production may occur.
- Excessive residues.
- Excessive runoff.

Compatibility Test. A compatibility test (the Jar Test) should be made well before mixing chemicals for application:

1. Place 1 teaspoon of each chemical in a quart jar containing about a pint of water.
2. Close the lid tightly, shake vigorously, and observe the mixture for settling out, layering, formation of gels, flakes, or other precipitates, or a change in temperature of the mixture (e.g., rapid heating).
3. If any of these effects are seen, the chemicals are not compatible and should not be used together. If nothing happens, let the jar stand for about 30 minutes and reobserve.

Mixing Compatible Chemicals. Mixing some pesticides require premixing in a smaller, separate container or tank.

1. Always add a wettable powder first. Make a slurry with it in a separate container by adding a small amount of water until it forms a gravy-like consistency. Slowly add this slurry to the tank with the spray tank agitator running.

2. Dry flowable or water-dispersible granules are added second. Flowables should be premixed (1 part flowable to 1 part water) and poured slowly into the tank.

3. Liquid flowables should be added third. Liquids should also be premixed (1 part liquid chemical to 2 parts water or liquid fertilizer) before blending in the tank. Many labels provide the proper mixing sequence.

4. Emulsifiable concentrates and water soluble liquids should be combined last.

Proper Order for Tank Mixing Various Pesticide Formulations:

$$WP \rightarrow DF \rightarrow F \rightarrow EC \rightarrow S$$

Acid Equivalents

When determining the dosage rate of a pesticide, the amount of "active ingredient" applied per given area (e.g., lb ai/acre) or within its solution (e.g., lb ai/gal) is often used. However, with some pesticides, most notably herbicides, its molecule has been altered to impose some additional characteristic to it, such as increased solubility, increased plant penetration, or increased translocation within plants, without destroying or adding to its pest-control properties. Most often a carboxyl (COOH) group (an acidic group) is altered by substitution of the hydrogen ion (H^+) of the carboxyl group with another ion, such as sodium (Na^+) or ammonia (NH_4^+), to form a salt or reaction of the carboxyl group with an alcohol to form an ester. The **acid equivalent** of a salt or ester form of a pesticide is that portion of the molecule that represents the original acid form of the molecule. Acid equivalents are needed only when working with those pesticides that are acids and their respective salts and esters. Nonacidic pesticides do not have salt or ester forms; thus, acid equivalents are not needed.

When determining the amount of pesticide to apply based on its acid equivalent, this is adjusted to take into account the heavier weight of the respective salt or ester, as compared to its acid form. These recommendations applied as salts or esters are based only on the pesticidal (parent acid) portion of the salt or ester molecule involved, excluding the portion of the molecule that is inactive. This allows the comparison of pesticides based on equal numbers of molecules rather than on the equal weights of chemical applied. To apply an equal number of molecules of a compound, a greater amount (weight) of a salt formulation would be needed compared to the acid form of a pesticide.

To determine acid equivalents of a pesticide, the acid equivalent of its parent acid form is always 100% while that of its salt or ester form is always less than 100%. The acid equivalent of a salt or ester form of a pesticide is determined by dividing the molecular weight of the acid form minus by a value of 1 which represents the loss of the H^+ ion when the carboxyl group is altered, by the molecular weight of its salt or ester and multiplied by 100.

acid equivalent of salt

$$\textbf{or ester form (\%)} = \frac{\text{molecular weight of acid form} - 1}{\text{molecular weight of salt or ester form}} \times 100$$

Examples:

1. The molecular weight of 2,4-D herbicide is 221 g while the molecular weight of its sodium salt is 243. Determine the acid equivalent of the sodium salt of 2,4-D.

$$\text{acid equivalent} = \frac{221 \text{ g} - 1}{243 \text{ g}} \times 100 = 90.5\%$$

2. Determine the acid equivalent of the isopropyl ester of 2,4-D (molecular weight 263 g).

$$\text{acid equivalent} = \frac{221 \text{ g} - 1}{263 \text{ g}} \times 100 = 83.7\%$$

To determine the acid equivalent of a pesticide formulation based on the number of pounds per gallon of a salt or ester of a pesticide, multiply the number of pounds per gallon of the salt or ester form present by the acid equivalent of the pesticide.

Examples:

1. How many pounds per gallon of acid equivalent does a 4 lb/gal of the diethanolamine salt of 2,4-D contain? (the molecular weight of diethanolamine salt of 2,4-D is 326 g).

Step 1: determine the acid equivalent of the diethanolamine salt of 2,4-D as shown above:

$$\text{acid equivalent} = \frac{221 \text{ g} - 1}{326 \text{ g}} \times 100 = 67.5\%$$

Step 2: now multiply the pounds per gallon of the salt applied by its acid equivalent.

4 lb/gal of diethanolamine salt × 0.675 = 2.70 lb/gal acid equivalent

2. A herbicide formulation contains 2 lb/gal of the methyl ester of 2,4-D. How many pounds per gallon of acid equivalent does it contain? (acid equivalent of methyl ester of 2,4-D is 93.6%)

2 lb/gal of methyl ester of 2,4-D × 0.936 = 1.87 lb/gal acid equivalent.

To determine the acid equivalent of a pesticide treatment applied as so many pounds per acre of a salt or ester form of the pesticide, multiply the pounds per acre of the salt or ester applied by the predetermined acid equivalent of the respective salt or ester form.

Examples:

1. Two pounds per acre of the dimethylamine salt formulation of 2,4-D was applied. How many pounds per acre of the acid equivalent were applied?

Step 1: determine the acid equivalent of the dimethylamine salt of 2,4-D as shown above:

$$\text{acid equivalent} = \frac{221 \text{ g} - 1}{266 \text{ g}} \times 100 = 82.7\%$$

Step 2: now multiply the pounds per acre of the salt applied by its acid equivalent.

2 lb/acre of dimethylamine salt × 0.827 = 1.65 lb/acre acid equivalent

2. The butyl ester of 2,4-D was applied at the rate of 0.75 lb/a. How many pounds of the acid equivalent were applied? (acid equivalent of butyl ester of 2,4-D is 79.4%).

0.75 lb/a of butyl ester of 2,4-D × 0.794 = 0.60 lb/acre acid equivalent.

PESTICIDES IN THE ENVIRONMENT

Fate of Pesticides

Environmentally introduced pesticides and nutrients experience numerous fates and routes of decomposition following application. Most pesticides pose little, if any, threat when used according to the label. This is due to the numerous means by which they are absorbed and broken down by natural entities in the environment. Major avenues of pesticide dissipation include (Figure 8-1):

- Sorption in thatch and soil mineral (clay and silt) and organic matter,
- Volatilization and evaporation (these are minor),
- Photodegradation by ultraviolet light from the sun (this is minor),
- Chemical and microbial decay,
- Plant uptake.

Pesticides typically have functional groups or linkages such as hydroxyl (OH), alkyl (e.g., CH_3, a methyl group), amino (NH_2), nitro (NO_2), chloro (Cl), carboxyl (COOH), and thio (SH) groups. These groups are susceptible to enzymatic or chemical activity. Chemical and microbial degradation are similar in that pesticides are broken down through the processes of **hydrolysis, oxidation, reduction,** and others to carbon dioxide (CO_2), water (H_2O), and miscellaneous inorganic products such as nitrogen (N), sulfur (S), and phosphorus (P). Hydrolysis involves cleavage of a

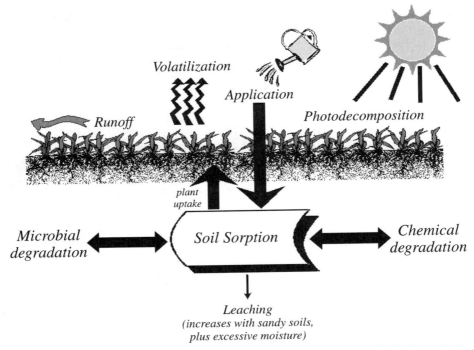

Figure 8-1. Many forces act to decompose pesticides once they are applied. These include photodecomposition, volatization, microbial and chemical degradation, and soil sorption.

bond by adding water to a product to form different, and most often, less active compounds. Chemical bonds are broken and either of the ions (H^+ or OH^-) of water becomes attached to the pesticide molecule. The resulting substitution renders the molecule inactive.

Oxidation involves a compound losing electrons while reduction is when a compound is degraded (made less stable) by gaining electrons. Oxidation reactions include **dealkylation** (removal of an aliphatic chain), **decarboxylation** (removal of a carboxyl group to produce CO_2), **dehalogenation** (removal of fluorine, chlorine, iodine, or bromine), **hydroxylation** of an aromatic ring, **cleavage** of an aromatic ring, and **conjugation** (combining of two molecules). Soil microbes can use pesticides as a food source and this rate of degradation is influenced by the pesticide present, temperature, soil water content, pH, oxygen levels, organic matter, and prior pesticide use.

Pesticide persistence is often expressed as **half-life** (indicated as DT_{50}) which is the time (days or weeks) required for 50% of the original pesticide to break down into other products. Half-life values change according to the location and site being treated and thus are guidelines instead of absolute values. A pesticide with a DT_{50} of <30 days is considered non-persistent. A DT_{50} of 30 to 120 days is moderately persistent, but usually breaks down rapidly (Table 8-3). A DT_{50} greater than 120 days is considered persistent. Most pesticides have a half-life less than 120 days. Pesticides composed of aromatic (ring) structures and halogen (chlorine, bromine, fluorine, and iodine) substitutions tend to persist longer than straight chain mate-

TABLE 8-3. Relative Persistence of Pesticides in Relation to Their Half-lives (DT$_{50}$)

Half-life (DT$_{50}$), days	Persistence
<30	nonpersistent
30 to 120	moderately persistent
>120	persistent

rials. Also, the more chlorinated a compound is in a series of analogous compounds, the longer it persists.

Residual Buildup. A common misconception is pesticides "buildup" in soil after consecutive yearly use. A theoretical example would involve an herbicide with a 120 days half-life. If applied yearly for consecutive years and it is degraded yearly to one-third (120 day half-life divided by 365 days per year) of the maximum use rate (1 lb/a), the maximum amount remaining after six years of consecutive use at the 1 pound rate would be approximately one-half the initial application rate (Figure 8-2).

Fate of Pesticides. Once a pesticide leaves the nozzle or spreader, there are four major places it can go: (1) air, (2) plants, (3) soil, and (4) water.

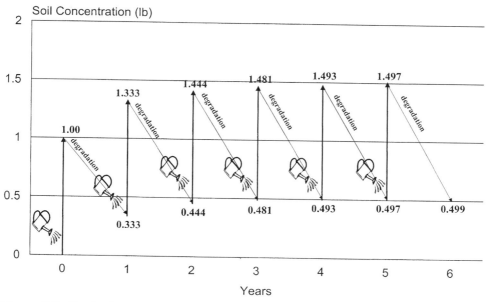

Figure 8-2. Yearly degradation curve of an herbicide applied annually at 1 lb, and one-third of the original concentration remains at the end of each season (after Ross and Lembi, 1999). After six years of consecutive use, only approximately one-half of the annual 1 lb application rate remains.

I. Atmosphere. When using traditional applicators, the air is the first place a pesticide goes before it hits a target. Losses of pesticides to the air can occur. Here are some factors in these losses:

(A) **Volatilization. Volatilization** and **evaporation** of pesticides involve the process where the chemicals are transformed from a solid or liquid phase into a gas. This tendency to volatilize is expressed in units of vapor pressure. **Vapor pressure** (or **volatility**) is the measure of the intramolecular bonding forces of a compound and is usually expressed as mm Hg (mercury) at 25° C (Table 8-4). Compounds possessing weak intramolecular forces readily volatilize and can easily change from a solid or liquid form to a gaseous form at room temperature. Problems have usually involved pesticides with vapor pressures greater than 1.0×10^{-4} mm Hg at 25° C. These materials are usually incorporated into the soil or applied as granules or slow-release formulations.

Volatilization increases with the inherent vapor pressure of a chemical, with increasing temperature, increasing air movement, and the absence of incorporation. Losses to volatilization typically range from 5 to 20% but can be higher when a volatile compound is surface-applied on a hot, windy day. Some of the factors in volatilization are:

(1) *Soil Placement:* Pesticides incorporated by being irrigated-in or injected have a much lower rate of volatilization compared to those surface applied.

(2) *Soil Organic Matter and Clay Content:* Higher soil organic matter or clay contents will increase the adsorption of a pesticide, which in turn reduces the amount available for volatilization.

(3) *Soil Moisture:* Since moisture effectively competes for soil adsorption or binding sites, higher moisture contents can work to slow pesticide adsorption to soil particles, which then encourages volatilization.

(4) *Temperature:* Increasing temperatures can increase volatilization, but the relationship is not direct because changes in moisture usually accompany temperature changes. That is, it usually is not raining when it is very hot.

(5) *Wind:* Increasing wind speed will increase volatile losses, although a rough surface such as turf can greatly reduce these effects.

TABLE 8-4. Vapor Pressure as a Degree of Volatility

Volatility	Vapor pressure range at 20° to 30°C (mm Hg)
Very highly volatile	$>10^{-3}$
Highly volatile	10^{-4} to 10^{-3}
Moderately volatile	10^{-5} to 10^{-4}
Low volatility	10^{-6} to 10^{-5}
Very low volatility	10^{-7} to 10^{-6}
Extremely low volatility	$<10^{-7}$

As discussed, volatility is highly dependent on temperature, moisture, soil texture, and the properties of a specific herbicide, and is extremely important in determining how a particular herbicide can be used. For example, compounds with high volatility are applied and incorporated by watering-in to prevent loss through volatilization to the air. Solids and liquids increase vaporization as the temperature increases. Pesticides formulated as esters also have a greater potential for volatility than do amine formulations (Table 8-5). 2,4-D, for example, in its acid form is only slightly soluble. However, it can be reacted with bases to form salts or with alcohols to form high volatile esters (Figure 8-3). Common salts that are formed include sodium, potassium, ammonium, and several amine salts, with amine salts being the most commonly used salt formulation. These ionize (dissociate) in water to form charged particles. These are not soluble in oil and are used with wetting agents and formulated as water-soluble liquids. One of the best ways to reduce volatilization is to use a pesticide's salt formulation.

Ester formulations are nonpolar molecules and do not ionize, thus are insoluble in water. They are highly soluble in oil and readily wet and penetrate plant cuticles. Ester formulations, however, tend to be volatile, thus are formulated as heavier, long-chained lower volatile alcohols (emulsifiable concentrates).

(B) **Drift**. Most pesticide applications are liquid sprays applied several feet or more above the soil or turf. This creates an opportunity for wind to carry a portion of the spray away from the target. Under worst-case conditions (high winds, small droplets), portions of the spray can be carried downwind. Several factors are critical.

(1) *Wind:* The amount of drift is directly related to wind speed. Spraying in windy conditions (greater than 10 miles per hour wind speed) may cause drift away from the target. Highly turbulent winds, which occur during inversions or on hot afternoons, are more likely to cause drift.

(2) *Droplet Size:* Nozzles which produce a significant number of small droplets (e.g., <100 microns) can significantly increase drift. There is always a tradeoff between the improved coverage of small droplets and the risk of drift. Larger droplets (e.g., >200 microns) are least likely to drift but may reduce coverage.

(3) *Adjuvants:* Tank additives have been shown to reduce drift primarily by reducing the proportion of droplets in the smallest sizes. Not all adjuvants work well for these purposes.

(4) *Boom Height:* The farther the boom is from the intended target, the greater the chance of drift.

(C) **Environmental Impacts of Pesticides in the Atmosphere:** The most immediate impact of pesticide losses to the atmosphere is the reduction of pest control. If one pound of product is recommended to control a pest and half of it is lost to the atmosphere, the pest is probably not going to be controlled. The second possible impact is on adjacent property, where the pesticide could cause significant damage. Damage could be in the form of injured crops, residues on crops with no label for that pesticide, or negative wildlife impacts such as on fish or bees.

TABLE 8-5. Chemical Properties of Various Salt, Acid, and Ester Formulations of Various Herbicides (Wauchope et al., 1992)

Herbicide	Solubility (mg L^{-1})	Half-life (days)	K_{OC} (mL g^{-1})	Vapor Pressure (mm Hg)	pK$_a$
Dicamba, DMA salt	850,000	14	2	3.4 x 10^{-5} (acid)	1.91
2,4-D acid	890	10	20	8 x 10^{-6}	2.80
2,4-D DMA salt	796,000	10	20	0	2.80
2,4-D esters	100	10	100	2.3 x 10^{-3} (methyl ester) 3 x 10^{-6} (3-butoxy propyl ester)	2.80
2,4-DP ester	50	10	1,000	3 x 10^{-6}	2.86
2,4-DP acid	71	10	170	<10^{-7}	2.86
MCPP, DMA salt	660,000	21	20	0	3.11
MCPP, acid	620	21	20	<10^{-7}	3.11
MCPA, DMA salt	866,000	25	20	0	3.12
Triclopyr, amine salt	210,000	46	20	0	2.68
Triclopyr acid	430	46	20	1.2 x 10^{-6}	2.68
Clopyralid, amine salt	300,000	40	6	0	2.30

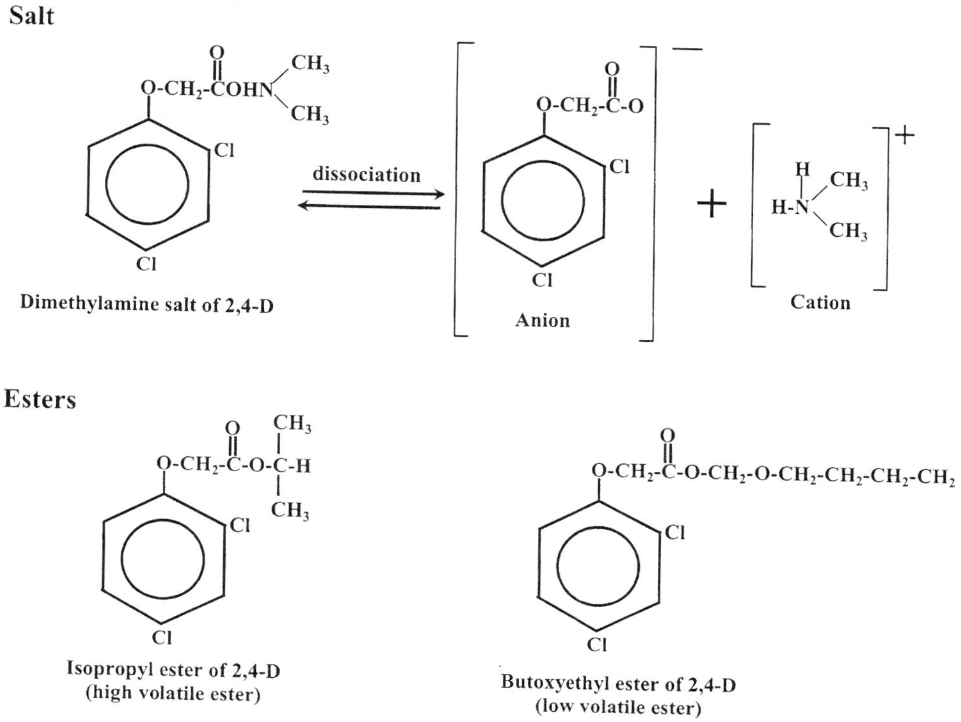

Salt

Dimethylamine salt of 2,4-D

dissociation

Anion   Cation

Esters

Isopropyl ester of 2,4-D
(high volatile ester)

Butoxyethyl ester of 2,4-D
(low volatile ester)

Figure 8-3. Salt and ester forms of 2,4-dichlorophenoxy acetic acid (2,4-D). The salt formulation dissociates into an anion (soluble) and cation, while ester formulations range from high volatile with low molecular weight and relatively short side carbon chain alcohols. Low volatile ester formulations are heavier in molecular weight, with longer-chained alcohols with an ether linkage.

II. Plants. The most important target of most pesticide applications is the turf itself. A number of fates await a pesticide once it lands on the turf:

(A) **Photolysis**. The sun provides a wide spectrum of radiation beyond the narrow band called light. The higher-energy ultraviolet radiation is sufficiently strong to cause some pesticides to break apart. This is the case for residues which are exposed on the plant (or soil) surface.

(B) **Plant Absorption**. Absorption of a pesticide by a plant can be either through the leaf or the roots. Getting through the leaf is difficult due to leaf hairs and a waxy cuticle blocking entry. One way to improve coverage and penetration is by using an adjuvant or spray additive which allows the droplets to spread on the leaf surface without beading up.

(C) **Effects of Plants on Pesticides in the Environment**. Uptake and metabolism of pesticides by plants are important in a turf environment due to high percentage of ground covered. Much of the applied pesticides still ends up in the thatch and soil, however. The impacts of plants are still quite important. A turf cover significantly reduces drift through interception and increased surface 'roughness' which slows wind. The canopy can reduce surface temperatures 10 to 20°, which slows volatilization. Turf also creates a more porous soil, allowing more water to infiltrate and slowing runoff.

III. Soil. The majority of applied pesticides end up in the thatch and soil. Even when the pesticide reaches a leaf, it is likely that most of it will be washed off and soak into the thatch and soil. Applied pesticides are largely processed and disposed of in the thatch and soil. A very serious environmental contamination problem would exist if this did not occur. However, a spill on the ground is a different situation. Concentrated chemicals that occur in a spill usually overwhelm normal soil processes and leach into deeper layers, possibly to groundwater. Mixing and loading on a hard surface where spills can be easily cleaned up or recycling rinseates avoids this type of problem. In the absence of a spill, pesticide fate in the soil/thatch region of the turfgrass is dictated by adsorption, chemical and biological degradation, and leaching (Figure 8-1).

(A) **Soil Adsorption**. Soil sorption is the affinity a chemical has to adhere to soils. Electrostatic sorption mechanisms include hydrogen bonding, van der Waals' forces, ion exchange, and partitioning (or hydrogen bonding). The term **sorption** includes the processes of adsorption and absorption. **Adsorption** is the binding of a chemical onto the surface of a soil particle while **absorption** is the binding of a chemical into a soil particle. Adsorption is generally the more important means of binding a chemical to the soil surface. This is greatly influenced by the chemical and physical characteristics of the chemical (e.g., anionic, cationic, or nonionic), the soil characteristics or composition, and the nature of the soil solution (Table 8-6).

Ionizable pesticides can be sorbed through ion exchange mechanisms with the charged species. As discussed in Chapter 2, the tendency of an acid, in aqueous solution, to donate protons (H^+) is the dissociation (or ionization) constant (K_a). The pK_a value of a pesticide determines the ability of a molecule to undergo ion exchange; in other words, its ability to dissolve in solution. The pK_a is the negative log of the ionization constant of the acid (K_a) and for the dissociation of typical weak acid (HA) is determined by:

TABLE 8-6. Soil Retention Characteristics of Charged Pesticides

Pesticide Charge	Soil Sorption Characteristics
Cationic (positively)	Strongly held to negatively charged soil by ionic bonds; e.g., diquat (Reward) and paraquat
Anionic (negatively)	Poorly held to negatively charged soil particles unless positively charged soil colloids are present like hydrous oxides of calcium, iron and aluminum; e.g., 2,4-D, bentazon (Basagran)
Nonionic (neutrally)	Often weakly held at the soil surfaces through weak physical forces; e.g., dinitroanilines.

$$HA \quad \leftrightharpoons H^+ \quad + A^-$$
$$\text{(acids)} \quad \text{(proton)} \quad \text{(base)}$$

$$K_a = \frac{[H^+]\,[A^-]}{[HA]}$$

$$pK_a = -\log\,[K_a] = -\log\frac{[H^+]\,[A^-]}{[HA]} = pH - \log\frac{[A^-]}{[HA]}$$

Acidic pesticides contain carboxylic (–COOH) or phenolic groups which may ionize to produce organic anions (–COO⁻). Their tendency to ionize (dissolve) in aqueous solution is described by their acid dissociation constant (K_a).

$$R-COOH \leftrightharpoons RCOO^- + H^+$$

$$pK_a = pH - \log\frac{[R-COO^-]}{[R-COOH]}$$

The pK_a equation is useful for calculating the pH of known solutions or relative strengths of an acid (Table 8-7). At the point of dissociation, the concentration of the undissociated acid ([HA]) and its anion ([A⁻]) are equal and pH = pK_a. At higher pH, the equilibrium will shift toward the dissociated species, releasing more [H⁺] . For example, from Table 8-5, the pK_a value for 2,4-D (acid) is 2.80. 2,4-D, therefore, is a moderately strong organic acid (Table 8-7). At a pH of 2.80, the concentration of the undissociated ([HA]) and associated species ([A⁻]) are equal. At pHs above 2.80, the equilibrium shifts toward the associated ([A⁻]) species and dissociated H⁺. At a normal 6 to 7.5 soil pH, the 2,4-D would exist primarily as the dissociated, charged species (A⁻) . Since soil colloids have overall negative charges, 2,4-D is repelled from most soils making it mobile. At low soil pH, adsorption of the uncharged form of 2,4-D is to be expected but as soil pH increases, adsorption will decrease.

The major soil characteristics affecting pesticides are soil texture, permeability, and organic matter content. Coarse, sandy soil textures tend to have low cation exchange capacities (CECs) and high permeability rates, and thus hold applied materials poorly. Increases in organic matter and certain clays tend to increase a soil's ability to hold applied materials. This is one reason organic matter should be

TABLE 8-7. Classification for Pesticide Acidic Properties

Acidity	K_a	pK_a
Very strong	$>10^{-1}$	<1
Strong	10^{-1} to 10^{-3}	1 to 3
Moderate	10^{-3} to 10^{-5}	3 to 5
Weak	10^{-5} to 10^{-7}	5 to 7
Very weak	10^{-7} to 10^{-9}	7 to 9
Extremely weak	$<10^{-9}$	>9

considered in turf soil construction. Clay soils are least likely to allow leaching, but are most likely to have runoff. Most insecticides readily adsorb to soil and thatch, which is why they are rarely detected in groundwater. The majority of fungicides and herbicides are also tightly bound by soil, but some do have the potential to leach to groundwater.

Partition (or Adsorption) Coefficient. The constant used to measure the tendency of a chemical to sorb to the soil organic matter is called the **partition** or **adsorption coefficient,** reported as K_{OC}. For an organic compound, the larger the K_{OC} value, the more strongly it will be sorbed to organic matter in soils, therefore less likely to leach or volatilize. A partition coefficient less than 100 is considered low and the chemical has a greater tendency to leach in low organic-matter-containing soil (Table 8-8). Values between 100 and 1,000 indicate that a pesticide is moderately mobile and that mobility is determined by other parameters such as soil type (sandy vs. loam) and pesticide persistence (DT_{50}). A K_{OC} value of 1,000 or greater usually indicates an immobile pesticide, such as with most preemergence herbicides.

Pesticides that do bind tightly to soil may be preferred from an environmental perspective since this reduces the movement of the pesticide. This can be a problem, however, because a pesticide may not be active if it is highly bound to soil. A good example is the herbicide glyphosate (Roundup Pro), which is inactivated in soil through tight binding to clays.

(B) **Degradation**. Pesticides are often quickly degraded once they reach the thatch and soil layers. The sun can break them down through photolysis just as on plant surfaces. Acids commonly found in the soil can sever parts of the pesticide in a process called hydrolysis. The most important factor, however, is the organisms living in soil which use them as food sources. Bacteria are the main degraders in soil and thatch. Most turf pesticides will be degraded in thatch and soil in a matter of days or weeks. This is good if one wants to minimize the possibility of the pesticide reaching ground or

TABLE 8-8. Pesticide Characteristics Influencing the Potential for Groundwater and Surface Water Contamination (Balogh and Walker, 1992)

Chemical Characteristic	Range for Potential Contamination
Water solubility	>30 ppm
K_d	<5, usually <1
K_{OC} (mL/g)	<300 to 500
Henry's law constant[a]	<10^{-2} atm per m^{-3} mol
Hydrolysis half-life	>175 days
Photolysis half-life	>7 days
Field dissipation half-life	>21 days

[a]Henry's law describes the influence of pressure on the solubility of a gas. Specifically, the solubility of a gas is directly proportional to the pressure of the gas above the solution and involves the equation, $P_a = K_h C_a$. P_a is the partial vapor pressure of the pesticide in the vapor phase, C_a is the pesticide concentration in the soil solution, and K_h is a constant characteristic of the gas referred to as the Henry's law constant.

surface water. Of course, this also means that the length of effectiveness of the pesticide is also reduced. Pesticide chemists developing new products are always confronted with this dilemma: a chemical that persists may be effective longer but may have an increased risk of contaminating water. The EPA will not allow a new chemical on the market if it poses undue risk of contaminating water.

(C) **Leaching**. A pesticide that is not bound to the soil and is not degraded can move through the soil with the infiltrating water. Leaching is dependent on these primary factors: (1) the chemical properties of the pesticide (e.g., DT_{50}); (2) chemical properties of the soil (e.g., K_{OC}); and (3) timing and amount of water applied following pesticide use. As chemicals move downward in the soil, both the amount of adsorption and the rate of degradation decline rapidly. There is little organic matter or bacterial activity once past the root zone. Fortunately, the adsorption and degradation processes handle all or nearly all of the pesticide before it can reach the lower layers.

Solubility is the extent a chemical will dissolve in water (Table 8-9). Generally the higher a liquid's solubility, the greater the chance it may move from the site of application. Although solubility is normally a good indicator of the likelihood a chemical may be mobile, its sorption to soil also must be considered. Highly soluble pesticides, however, often are readily susceptible to microbial degradation and thus may not persist long enough to leach. Leaching is generally greater when highly water soluble, long-lived pesticides are used in low organic matter containing soils followed by heavy rainfall.

Overall, specific parameters influencing leaching are sorption (Koc) and persistence (half-life or DT_{50}). Nonpersistent pesticides having half-lives (<30 days) are less likely to leach regardless of strength of adsorption because of their short residual time in soil. Leaching of more persistent pesticides is dependent on their sorption coefficients. Those with large (>500) Koc values are unlikely to leach unless their half-life values are quite long (e.g., >100 days). An example of this is atrazine with an estimated half-life of 60 days combined with a Koc value of 100. Atrazine, therefore, is moderately persistent and has moderate sorption, thus small amounts (typically, <5%) may leach.

IV. Pesticides in Water. Much of the bad press pesticides have received is from detections in ground and surface water used for drinking water supplies. Surveys

TABLE 8-9. Solubility Rankings of a Compound Based on Water Solubilities

Water Solubility (ppm)	Relative Solubility
> 10,000 (1%)	Very highly soluble
1,000 to 10,000	Highly soluble
100 to 1,000	Moderately soluble
10 to 100	Low solubility
1 to 10	Very low solubility
0.1 to 1	Extremely low solubility

of ground and surface water have found pesticides in some areas of the country. The extent of the contamination is becoming reasonably well defined, but the source or sources of contamination are often quite elusive. The sources and problems associated with groundwater and surface water contamination are quite different and will be dealt with separately in the following.

(A) **Surface Water:** Most pesticide contamination of streams, lakes, and estuaries occurs as runoff from agricultural and urban areas. Runoff carries with it a mix of suspended soil particles and any pesticides which were either attached to the particles or dissolved in surface moisture just before runoff began. The amount of pesticide loss to runoff is affected by the following factors:

1. *Rain Intensity*—Heavy downpours result in minimal infiltration and maximum runoff.

2. *Surface Conditions*—Recently tilled soil and soil with a good ground cover have the most resistance to runoff since water infiltrates relatively easily and the surface is 'rough' enough to break up water flow. Maximum runoff is expected during the month after planting, since the soil is exposed and the turf has not grown large enough to intercept rain and reduce its impact energy.

3. *Magnitude and Length of Slope*—The steeper and longer the slope, the greater the chance of runoff picking up energy and soil.

4. *Method of Application*—Pesticides tilled or injected into the soil are less likely to be lost in runoff, although the disturbance of the soil itself may increase soil (and attached pesticide) losses. Foliar pesticides can suffer large losses in runoff if a heavy downpour occurs soon after application.

5. *Timing*—As mentioned above, if a runoff event occurs soon after the pesticide is applied substantial losses can occur.

Losses of pesticides to runoff generally are found at 1 to 5% of that applied, depending on the various factors. Losses are usually the greatest in the 1 to 2 weeks after application and are highly dependent on storm events.

The effects of providing untreated grassed borders can be quite substantial, with reductions of pesticide movement into adjoining streams of 80 to 90% (Baird et al., 1997). The combination of infiltration, reduced overland flow rates, and adsorption in these zones can be quite effective in keeping pollutants in the fields from getting into the waterways. The role of forested buffers is likely quite similar.

It is important to emphasize that buffers function only when the waters they receive are spread across the strip. Runoff which moves through a buffer in a ditch or channel has little opportunity to degrade or adsorb before it intercepts surface water.

Once organic chemicals like pesticides enter surface water, their rate of degradation slows considerably compared to soil degradation rates. A portion of the pesticide will partition onto the sediment and remain there until a flood event moves the sediment back into the moving water. This is thought to be the explanation for why low levels of pesticides can be detected long after the application season.

(B) **Groundwater.** Groundwater is water located beneath the earth's surface. It is often erroneously perceived that groundwater occurs in vast underground lakes, rivers, or streams. Groundwater usually occurs in aquifers composed of pore spaces and cracks in rock and soil. An **aquifer** may be defined as a formation that contains sufficient saturated permeable material to yield significant quantities of water to wells and springs. Aquifers, such as unconsolidated sands and gravels, can store and transmit water. They are quite extensive and may be confined above or below by a confining bed, a relatively impermeable material such as clay or sandy clay.

Unconsolidated aquifers are sand and gravel deposits which can be relatively shallow, often only 10 to 20 feet below the surface. The pores within these deposits are filled with water if they are below the water table. These aquifers are mostly located in coastal plain areas within 200 miles of the coast. Recharge of these aquifers is usually local but there may be several layered on top of each other, with lower aquifers recharging some distance away. Wells drilled into the first or top layer, or superficial aquifer, are the most susceptible to contamination.

Groundwater moves very slowly through irregular spaces within otherwise solid rock or seeps between particles of sand, clay, and gravel. An exception is in limestone areas, where groundwater may, in fact, flow through large underground channels or caverns.

Groundwater is recharged (replaced) mostly from rain or snow that enters the soil. Water moving downward in the soil is either absorbed by plants, is held in the upper layers of soil, or moves down through the root zone until it reaches a zone saturated with water. This saturated zone is the uppermost layer of groundwater. The **water table** is the 'dividing line' between the groundwater and the unsaturated rock or soil above it. Spring and fall generally are the times when the water table is closest to the soil surface.

The following are major factors determining whether a pesticide moving through the soil will reach the groundwater:

(A) **Soil type:** sandy soils leach more than loamy or heavier soils,

(B) **Pesticide characteristics:** how tightly it binds to soil and thatch; how long it lasts in the soil,

(C) **Weather:** cool, wet conditions can push the pesticide deep in the soil before it can degrade or bind,

(D) **Depth to groundwater:** the deeper the groundwater, the more time a pesticide has to break down.

Most rural residents get their water from wells placed in groundwater tables. The water which is found in those aquifers may come from the nearby area or many miles away, depending on the type of aquifer. The water may have been in the aquifer for several years or many decades.

Sources of Contamination

Point-Source. Environmental contamination originates either as **point-source** or **nonpoint-source**. Point-source pollution comes from a specific, identifiable point.

A pesticide spill into a well, sinkhole, or storm sewer are examples of identifiable point-source pollution. Sewage treatment plants and concentrated animal production facilities also are potential point-sources. Other point-source pollution comes from improper disposal of pesticide containers and water from rinseates, leaks, and spills at the site of pesticide storage facilities, and spills that occur during mixing and loading pesticides into application equipment. Groundwater can be contaminated directly in many ways. Some of the most serious include back siphoning, surface water movement into wells, or drainage into limestone channels. These contamination problems can nearly always be prevented. Once they occur, however, the point of entry becomes a point-source for contamination. A plume of contamination moves slowly away from the source and can spread to contaminate many wells downgradient.

Nonpoint. Nonpoint-source pollution generally involves contamination from a normal application over a wide surface area(s). This can occur if nutrients or pesticides leach through the soil and reach groundwater, or if they wash off in runoff and enter lakes or streams. Leaching through the soil profile and movement with runoff water are believed to be two major sources of nonpoint pollution. However, if used according to the pesticide label, it is believed that nonpoint-source pollution is actually very minor and contributes little to the overall pollution problem. Problems normally develop only when an intense rainfall occurs almost immediately after application, before the pesticide has been absorbed by the plant or soil.

Chemical properties of pesticides also influence the likelihood of groundwater contamination. These properties include solubility, adsorption and absorption capability, and persistence. Chemicals with high solubility, low adsorption capability, and extended persistence have more potential of becoming nonpoint-source polluters (Table 8-10).

Research indicates that a solid ground coverage by turf is probably the best "filter" in preventing both lateral and horizontal movement of applied pesticides,

TABLE 8-10. Parameters Which Minimize the Risk for Groundwater and Surface Water Contamination from Pesticide Use

Pesticide or Site Characteristic	Parameters Which Minimize Off-site Movement
Pesticide properties	(1) Low solubility, (2) High soil adsorption (K_{OC}), (3) Short half-life or little persistence, (4) High volatility.
Soil properties	(1) Finer textured soil, (2) Higher organic matter content.
Site characteristics	(1) Deep water table, (2) Flat vs. sloping land, (3) Adequate distance from surface water, sink holes, or abandoned wells, (4) Soil completely covered with turf, mulch, or ground cover.
Management planning	(1) Adequate planning and consideration for impending weather events, (2) Proper application and timing, (3) Proper incorporation through irrigation following application.

fertilizers, and soil sediments (Fig. 8-4). Untreated turf buffer zones around sensitive areas, such as ponds, lakes, or streams, also provide the best assurance of preventing unwanted lateral pesticide movement. Turf plants also directly absorb pesticides and, when actively growing, can reduce the likelihood of leaching of water-soluble pesticides.

BEST ENVIRONMENTAL TURFGRASS MANAGEMENT SUMMARY

Nutrient and pesticide movement or soil sediment erosion could negatively affect environmental quality if allowed to enter lakes or streams in an uncontrolled manner or in significant amounts. Best Management Practices are plans to reduce this possibility by: (1) growing a solid turf stand which reduces the off-site transport of sediment, nutrients, and pesticides, (2) controlling the rate, method, and type of chemicals being applied, and (3) reducing the total chemical load by using economic thresholds, alternate pest control, and fertility testing. Following the labeling directions exactly is the best way to preventing contaminating groundwater. In addition, the following should be remembered:

1. Avoid disturbing sensitive wildlife areas and wetlands during the initial design and construction of a turf area.
2. Select plant species that are locally adapted and require minimum inputs.

Figure 8-4. Research indicates growing a healthy, thick turf is one of the best methods of preventing unwanted lateral movement of applied materials such as pesticides or nutrients.

3. During construction, all necessary steps of preventing soil erosion and managing stormwater runoff on disturbed areas should be implemented such as installing silt fencing, hay protection, sodding highly erodible areas, etc.

4. Maintain the turf to encourage a deep, actively growing root system which is better able to recover applied nutrients and thereby prevent leaching.

5. When possible, select pesticides based on the following:

    (a) Lowest toxicity to humans, mammals, fish, birds, and bees.

    (b) Rapidity of degradation and lowest leaching potential.

    (c) Highest soil adsorption.

    (d) Lowest volatility.

6. Using the appropriate pesticide and nutrient rates (not excessive, especially for nitrogen and phosphorus).

7. Use the least amount of soluble nutrient sources commensurate with acceptable turfgrass quality.

8. Use the best application method to minimize any special risks.

9. Prevent back-siphoning of the pesticide into your water source by keeping the end of the fill hose above the spray tank's water level.

10. Locate mix-load sites and equipment-rinsing sites at least 100 feet from surface water or from wells or sinkholes that have direct links to groundwater.

11. Dispose all pesticide waste in accordance with local, state, and federal laws to prevent contaminating groundwater through proper disposal of unused pesticides, pesticide containers, and container rinse water.

12. Use ponds or basins, vegetation strips, riparian zones (e.g., bottomland hardwood, floodplain forests), and channels containing vegetation to filter or assimilate nutrients from drainage water.

13. Spread drainage in grassed or natural areas.

14. Use a natural or constructed waterway or outlet maintained with vegetative cover to prevent soil erosion and to filter nutrients.

15. Maintain an untreated (no spray) vegetative buffer zone of 10 to 50 feet adjacent to all water sources to help filter nutrients or pesticides from runoff.

16. Manage a decline in dissolve oxygen levels in water by controlling algae, nutrient runoff, and by providing adequate aeration.

17. Test soil and tissues to optimize fertilization with the growth and use by turfgrasses to prevent excess use and possible runoff.

18. Prevent runoff by using irrigation water management so application rates do not exceed the infiltration capacity of the soil.

19. Avoid pesticide or nutrient applications just prior to anticipated rainfall events.

20. Do not apply pesticides or nutrients to an area in excess than can be quickly and efficiently watered-in.

21. Return grass clippings when practical as they are a source of most major nutrients and by returning them after mowing, this aids in recycling.

22. Follow IPM practices in addition to the proper storage, mixing, application and disposal of pesticides, their containers and rinseates.

23. Frequently check and calibrate all pesticide and fertilizer applicators.
24. Install a well-balanced landscape with a mix of shrubs, trees, grass areas, and water features that sustains and encourages wildlife and a diversity of plants.
25. Keep detailed, accurate records on nutrient and pesticide applications.
26. Provide periodic pesticide handling and use training and updating sessions for all employees.

PRACTICE PROBLEMS

1. Define a pesticide and indicate the three types of names normally associated with one. (*"Any substance or mixture intending for preventing, destroying, repelling, or mitigating any pest or for use as a plant regulator, defoliant, or desiccant:" chemical name, common name, and trade name.*)
2. List and define the two classes of pesticide. (***General-use,*** *which do not cause unreasonable adverse effects to the environment and may be bought and used by the general public;* ***restricted-use,*** *which pose some risk to the environment or human health even when used according to the label. Applicators must be certified and approved protective clothing worn.*)
3. What are the most common carriers for liquid and dry formulated pesticides? (*Liquid is water followed by liquid fertilizer; dry is clay, corncobs, ground nut hulls, sand, or dry fertilizer.*)
4. What is an emulsifying agent and emulsifiable concentrate (EC) pesticide formulation? (*An emulsifying agent acts as a binder-couplet between an oil-water surface, reducing interfacial tension, allowing tiny droplets of oil to remain in suspension. EC are oily [nor nonpolar] liquids that form emulsions [droplets of oil surrounded by water] in water [polar] and are not true solutions.*)
5. Indicate if spray tank agitation is required to keep the following formulations in suspension.
   a. dry flowable/water dispersible granules (*yes*)
   b. emulsifiable concentrates (*yes*)
   c. flowables (*yes*)
   d. solutions (*no*)
   e. soluble powders (*no*)
   f. wettable powders (*yes*)
6. Define adjuvant and surfactant and list three types of surfactants. (***Adjuvant***—*a spray additive that enhances the performance, safety, or handling characteristics of a pesticide.* ***Surfactant***—*surface-active agents which lower the surface tension between a polar and nonpolar molecule. Emulsifiers, stickers, and wetting agents.*)
7. Define half-life. (*Time in days or weeks required for 50% of an original material to break down into other products.*)

8. Distinguish between adsorption and absorption. (*Adsorption is binding of a chemical onto a surface; absorption is binding of a chemical into a surface.*)

9. Distinguish between point-source and nonpoint-source contamination. (***Point-source pollution*** *originates from a specific, identifiable source or point such as a spill or leak;* ***nonpoint-source*** *originates from a wide surface area such as leaching of a normal treatment.*)

10. List the three main means of Best Management Practices to help reduce nutrient and pesticide pollution potential. (*1. Promote growing a solid turf stand to reduce off-site movement of sediments, nutrients, and pesticides; 2. promote controlling the rate, method, and types of chemicals being applied; 3. promote the reduction of total chemical use by implementing economic thresholds, alternative pest control, and fertility testing (IPM)*).

APPENDIXES

APPENDIX A

ELECTRON (ORBITAL) PAIRS

Two electrons spin on their axes in opposite directions. This opposite spin creates magnetic fields which allow paired electrons to attract each other. Two electrons in an atom which differ only in having opposite spins are called an **electron** or **orbital pair.** The region occupied by this pair of electrons is called an **orbital.** In the first shell (designated as K or 1), only one orbital (called an s orbital) is possible, and this shell is therefore filled by the two electrons of the atom. Orbitals are designated by the letters "s," "p," "d," and "f," from the names *sharp, principal, diffuse,* and *fundamental,* which describe the shape of the various orbitals and thus helps describe the shape and structure of molecules. Only four different shaped orbitals are used since the number of known elements have sufficient electrons to fill four orbitals. For most elements in biology, however, the "f" subshell is not utilized and only up to the $4p$ level is important.

$1s$ $\qquad$ $2s$ $\qquad$ $2p$ $\qquad$ $3s$ $\qquad$ $3p$ $\qquad$ $4s$ $\qquad$ $3d$ $\qquad$ $4p$

Because of the close spacing of the higher energy-orbitals, overlapping and "criss-crossing" of orbitals occurs. Therefore, a strict sequence of energy levels does not occur but rather an "order of filling" occurs. The $4s$ subshell, for example, fills before $3d$.

Several important points with electron orientation include:

1. The outer shell of an atom never contains more than eight electrons.
2. The number of orbitals existing in any principal shell is the same as the number of the shell. For example, shell 1 (or "K") has one orbital designated as "s"; shell 2 (or "L") has two different shaped orbitals designated as "s" and "p"; shell 3 (or "M") has three different shaped orbitals designated as "s," "p," and "d"; shell 4 (or "N") has four different shaped orbitals designated as "s," "p," "d," and "f."

3. The number of "s," "p," "d," and "f" orbitals in any energy level if sufficient electrons are present follows the pattern of 1s orbital, 3p orbitals, 5d orbitals, and 7f orbitals (odd numbers).

4. The total number of orbitals for any energy level (or shell) is determined by the formula $(n)^2$ where "n" is the number of the shell. For shell 1 (or K), only one orbital is available. For shell 2 (or M), four orbitals are available, one "s" and three "p" orbitals. For shell 3 (or N), nine orbitals are available, one "s," three "p," and five "d" orbitals. For shell 4 (or O), seven "f" orbitals occur following the odd-numbering pattern.

5. In any energy level, the "s" orbital is filled first with two electrons if available. The three "p" orbitals are filled by placing one electron in each orbital and if additional electrons are available, electrons pair up in the orbitals until they are filled. The same procedure is used if "d" and "f" orbitals are available.

6. The maximum number of electrons in a principal shell is equal to $2(n)^2$, where n is the shell number (or principal quantum number). Shell 2 (or L), therefore, can hold no more than eight electrons ($2 \times 2^2 = 8$); shell 4 (or N), no more than 32 ($2 \times 4^2 = 32$). There is parallelism between the $(n)^2$ formula in number 4 above and the $2(n)^2$ formula in this statement since an orbital may contain a maximum of two electrons.

In orbital notation, one electron occupying a space orbital is represented as ↑. Two electrons occupying a space orbital is represented as ↑↓ while an unoccupied space orbital is represented as __. Two electrons in an orbital have opposite spin, one up and one down. For example, the orbital diagram for the carbon atom with six electrons in its ground state is written:

$$ \text{C} \quad \uparrow\downarrow \quad \uparrow\downarrow \quad \uparrow\ \uparrow\ \_ $$
$$ 1s^2 \qquad 2s^2 \qquad 2p^2 $$

The number of electrons in each orbital is indicated by a superscript as illustrated above. Other examples of orbital notation include:

Element	Atomic Number	Electron Configuration and Designation
H	1	↑ $1s^1$
He	2	↑↓ $1s^2$
N	7	↑↓ $1s^2$ ↑↓ $2s^2$ ↑ ↑ ↑ $2p^3$
O	8	↑↓ $1s^2$ ↑↓ $2s^2$ ↑↓ ↑ ↑ $2p^4$
Na	11	↑↓ $1s^2$ ↑↓ $2s^2$ ↑↓ ↑↓ ↑↓ $2p^6$ ↑ $3s^1$
Ca	20	↑↓ $1s^2$ ↑↓ $2s^2$ ↑↓ ↑↓ ↑↓ $2p^6$ ↑↓ $3s^2$ ↑↓ ↑↓ ↑↓ $3p^6$ ↑↓ $4s^2$
Zn	30	↑↓ $1s^2$ ↑↓ $2s^2$ ↑↓ ↑↓ ↑↓ $2p^6$ ↑↓ $3s^2$ ↑↓ ↑↓ ↑↓ $3p^6$ ↑↓ $4s^2$ ↑↓ ↑↓ ↑↓ ↑↓ ↑↓ $3d^{10}$

For additional information on orbitals, quantum theory, and hybridization, a chemistry text should be consulted.

The **Lewis-Dot system** (or **electron-dot system**) was developed to indicate the valence (outer shell) electrons in their lowest energy state (ground state) and higher energy state (excited state). Using this system, the electron arrangement in their orbitals is shown in a more useful manner. Two dots, if present, are placed on the top of the symbol to represent an "*s*" shaped orbital. The remaining dots representing electrons are then placed singly on each of the remaining surfaces of the element if the number of electrons is sufficient. These three surfaces represent three "*p*" shaped orbitals. The remaining electrons are then paired on these faces if available. The Lewis-Dot system is discussed in more detail in Chapter 1.

APPENDIX B

NAMING INORGANIC COMPOUNDS

Turfgrass and agricultural students and managers should be able to recognize chemical formulas and their names. Almost all home and garden products produced and sold contain labels listing their ingredients. By comparing labels, consumers can almost always find the same product at a more favorable price. Another important consideration for understanding ingredients is for the safe use and storage of the product. Writing chemical formulas and naming them correctly is one of the major keys to success for chemistry students.

Compounds may be classified from a classical standpoint as **acids, bases,** and **salts.** Acids contain hydrogen (H^+) as the positive element; bases contain the hydroxide ion (OH^-); and salts do not contain hydrogen as the positive element nor hydroxide as the negative ion. Acids have hydrogen as the positive element followed by either a nonmetal or polyatomic ion. For example, the molecular formula for phosphoric acid, H_3PO_4, indicates $3H^+$ forms in solution:

$$H_3PO_4(aq) \rightarrow 3H^+(aq) + PO_4^{-3}(aq)$$

Bases normally have a formula which begins with a metal or NH_4^+ (ammonium) and ends with OH^- such as $Ba(OH)_2$ or NH_4OH:

$$Ba(OH)_2 \rightarrow Ba^{+2} + 2OH^-$$
$$NH_3 + H_2O \rightarrow NH_4^+ + OH^-$$

Other examples of bases include $Sr(OH)_2$, and CH_3NH_2.

Salts have a formula which begins with a metal or NH_4^+ and ends with a nonmetal or polyatomic ion other than hydroxide. For example, $(NH_4)_2CO_3$, $AgNO_3$, $NaCl$, $CuCl_2$, K_2SO_4, NH_4NO_3, and Na_3PO_4 are all salts. The word salt is a generic compound that includes more additional compounds than ordinary table salt, $NaCl$.

When an acid reacts with a base, neutralization occurs, leading to the formation of water and a salt. For example:

$$\underset{\text{acid}}{H_2SO_4} + \underset{\text{base}}{2KOH} \rightarrow \underset{\text{salt}}{K_2SO_4} + \underset{\text{water}}{2H_2O}$$

Binary Compounds. Chemical formulas are classified into two main groups—*binary* and *ternary* compounds. The simplest compounds are those made up of two elements and are called binary compounds. In naming binary compounds, the element that has a positive oxidation number appears first, followed by the name of the negative element where the ending is changed to *–ide* (**Chart B-1**). For example, Cu_2O is copper(I) oxide, CuO is copper(II) oxide, $AlCl_3$ is aluminum chloride, and $SnCl_4$ is tin(IV) chloride.

Compounds composed of elements with variable oxidation numbers have the roman numeral as part of the compound name. For example, $Cu(C_2H_3O_2)_2$ is called copper(II) acetate, not just copper acetate.

If one of the two elements is a metal and the other a nonmetal, the name of the metal is used first. If a compound is composed of two nonmetals, the element that is less electronegative (to the left of a family or to the bottom of a group in the periodic table) is given a positive oxidation number and the name of the first nonmetal is used. When naming the second element, it is named normally as any other binary compound with its ending changed to *–ide*. The primary exception is when hydroxide is attached to a positively charged element to form a base. The polyatomic hydroxide (hydroxyl) ion (OH^-) consist of two elements. When it combines with a metal, a base is formed. Confusion sometimes results as it ends in *-ide*, the same ending as binary salts. For example, the compound of sodium (Na^+) and chlorine (Cl^-) is called sodium chlor*ide* or NaCl (cation, anion); NaCl = sodium chlor *ide* to form sodium chloride. Other examples include the compound of magnesium and oxygen (MgO) being called magnesium ox*ide*; HCl is hydrogen chlor*ide*; H_2S is hydrogen sulf*ide*; AgCl is silver chlor*ide*; Al_2O_3 is aluminum ox*ide*; $MgBr_2$ is magnesium brom*ide*; CaS is calcium sulf*ide*; $CaCl_2$ is calcium chlor*ide*; Na_2O is sodium ox*ide*; and, BrCl is bromine chlor*ide*.

In writing the correct formula, the *-ide* means only two different elements are included (except for hydroxide). First, find the correct symbol of the two elements and then find the ionic charge of the elements by using the periodic table. Every chemical compound, regardless if it is binary or ternary, must have a total charge of zero (the sum of the oxidation numbers must be algebraically equal to zero). To accomplish this, use subscripts to balance the charge if necessary.

Examples:

1. What is the correct formula and name for a compound consisting of sodium and chlorine? $Na^{+1}Cl^{-1}$; $(+1,$ from $Na^{+1}) + (-1,$ from $Cl^{-1}) = 0$, thus the correct formula is NaCl or sodium chlor*ide*.
2. What is the correct formula and name for a compound consisting of magnesium and chlorine? $Mg^{+2}Cl^{-1}$, $(+2,$ from $Mg+^2) + (-1,$ from $Cl^{-1}) \neq 0$, thus 2 Cl ions are needed to equal zero: to check this; $Mg_1^{+2}Cl_2^{-1}$, $(+2) + (-2) = 0$; the correct formula is $MgCl_2$, or magnesium chlor*ide* (note that the subscript '$_1$' is omitted with Mg as the symbol Mg represents one atom).

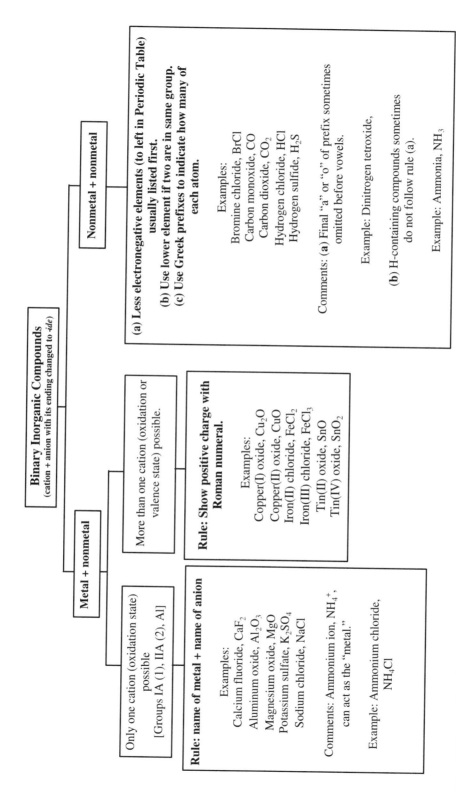

Binary Inorganic Compounds
(cation + anion with its ending changed to *-ide*)

Metal + nonmetal

Only one cation (oxidation state) possible
[Groups IA (1), IIA (2), Al]

Rule: name of metal + name of anion

Examples:
Calcium fluoride, CaF$_2$
Aluminum oxide, Al$_2$O$_3$
Magnesium oxide, MgO
Potassium sulfate, K$_2$SO$_4$
Sodium chloride, NaCl

Comments: Ammonium ion, NH$_4^+$, can act as the "metal."

Example: Ammonium chloride, NH$_4$Cl

More than one cation (oxidation or valence state) possible.

Rule: Show positive charge with Roman numeral.

Examples:
Copper(I) oxide, Cu$_2$O
Copper(II) oxide, CuO
Iron(II) chloride, FeCl$_2$
Iron(III) chloride, FeCl$_3$
Tin(II) oxide, SnO
Tin(IV) oxide, SnO$_2$

Nonmetal + nonmetal

(a) Less electronegative elements (to left in Periodic Table) usually listed first.
(b) Use lower element if two are in same group.
(c) Use Greek prefixes to indicate how many of each atom.

Examples:
Bromine chloride, BrCl
Carbon monoxide, CO
Carbon dioxide, CO$_2$
Hydrogen chloride, HCl
Hydrogen sulfide, H$_2$S

Comments: **(a)** Final "a" or "o" of prefix sometimes omitted before vowels.

Example: Dinitrogen tetroxide,

(b) H-containing compounds sometimes do not follow rule (a).

Example: Ammonia, NH$_3$

Chart B-1. An abbreviated overview of the current United States rules for naming binary inorganic compounds.

If two nonmetals form more than one compound with each other, a Greek prefix may be used to indicate the number of atoms of the elements in the formula (Chart B-1). The usual prefixes are: *mono–*, 1; *di–*, 2; *tri–*, 3; *tetra–*, 4; *pent(a)–*, 5; *hexa–*, 6; *hepta–*, 7; *octa–*, 8; *nona–*, 9; and, *deca–*, 10. All prefixes except *mono–* are used with the first element as well; e.g., P_2O_5 is *di*phosphorous *pent*oxide; CO, carbon *mon*oxide; CO_2, carbon *di*oxide. The prefix enables one to distinguish compounds of the same elements combined in different proportions, and also gives a clue to the formula of the compound. This is particularly true when two nonmetals form the compound. Other examples include: PI_3 is phosphorus *tri*iodide; ICl is iodine *mono*chloride; IF_5 is iodine *penta*fluoride; and, N_2O_4 is *di*nitrogen *tetr*oxide. The final '*a*' or '*o*' of a prefix is sometimes omitted before vowels. For example, N_2O_4 is dinitrogen *tetr*oxide not tetraoxide; and CO is carbon *mon*oxide not monooxide.

Names of common binary compounds composed of two nonmetals.

Binary Compound	Name
CO	carbon *mon*oxide
CO_2	carbon *di*oxide
NO_2	nitrogen *di*oxide
SO_2	sulfur *di*oxide
SO_3	sulfur *tri*oxide
CCl_4	carbon *tetra*chloride
CS_2	carbon *di*sulfide
P_2O_5	*di*phosphorus *pent*oxide

Binary Acids. An acid is a substance that produces hydronium ions (H_3O^+) in aqueous solution. If the compound begins with hydrogen and is dissolved in water, it is an acid. Binary acids contain hydrogen as the positive element and a nonmetallic element as the negative element. A binary acid in the **anhydrous** or dry state is named in the same way as any binary compound, with hydrogen treated as the positive element. In water, however, these compounds are named by using the prefix *hydro–* to represent the hydrogen atom and the ending of the nonmetallic element is changed to *–ic*, followed by the word *acid*. Pronunciation restraints sometimes require modification; e.g., HCl is called *hydro*chloric *acid*; H_2S is *hydro*sulfuric *acid*. The prefix *hydro–* is used only in naming binary acids and not ternary acids.

Examples of Binary Acids

Formula	Name of Pure (or Anhydrous or Dry) Substance ___*ide*	Name of Acid (Water Solution) *hydro*___*ic*
HF	hydrogen fluor*ide*	*hydro*fluor*ic* acid
HCl	hydrogen chlor*ide*	*hydro*chlor*ic* acid
HBr	hydrogen brom*ide*	*hydro*brom*ic* acid
HI	hydrogen iod*ide*	*hydr*iod*ic* acid
HCN	hydrogen cyan*ide*	*hydro*cyan*ic* acid
H_2S	hydrogen sulf*ide*	*hydro*sulfur*ic* acid

Most binary acids are prepared by dissolving the gas represented by the formula into water to produce an aqueous (water) solution. It is generally understood that the formula represents an acid unless the gaseous state of matter is indicated by using (g). The gas is then named as any binary salt; e.g., HCl(g) is hydrogen chlor*ide*, HCl(aq) is hydrochlor*ic acid*; HCN(g) is hydrogen cyan*ide*, but HCN(aq) is hydrocyan*ic acid*; H_2S(g) is hydrogen sulf*ide*.

In the past, atoms whose oxidation (or valence) numbers vary traditionally added the suffix *-ous* to the root name for the lower valence state, and the suffix *-ic* for the higher valence state. For example, for iron (Fe), the ferr*ous* ion is Fe^{+2} and the ferr*ic* iron is Fe^{+3} or Cu^{+2} is cupr*ous* and Cu^{+3} is cupr*ic*. However, when an element had more than one valence state, confusion often occurred. To reduce this confusion, a Roman numeral is now used in parentheses to indicate the valence number following the name of the element. For example, Fe^{+2} is now referred to as iron(II) and Fe^{+3} as iron(III). Other examples include: CuCl, copper(I) chloride; $CuCl_2$, copper(II) chloride; $FeCl_2$, iron(II) chloride; $FeCl_3$, iron(III) chloride; $SnCl_2$, tin(II) chloride; $SnCl_4$, tin(IV) chloride.

Example:

What is the systematic name of each of the following two oxide forms of copper, Cu_2O and CuO? From Table 1-3 it is found that the charge of an oxide ion (O^{-2}) is -2. Since Cu_2O is a compound, its net charge must be equal to zero. For the net charge to be zero, the total charge of the two copper ions must be $+2$ since the charge on the O ion is -2. Therefore, the charge on each copper ion is $+1$ and its name is copper(I) oxide.

For the net charge on CuO to be zero, the charge on the copper ion must be $+2$. The name of this oxide of copper is copper(II) oxide.

Polyatomic Ions. A group of elements with an excess charge may have a single name, for example: sulfate (SO_4^{-2}), nitrate (NO_3^-), carbonate (CO_3^{-2}), hydroxide (OH^-), phosphate (PO_4^{-3}), and ammonium (NH_4^+). Each of these groups act as a charged unit and is called a polyatomic ion.

Ternary Compounds. Ternary compounds have three or more elements and usually contain a polyatomic ion (an ion composed of more than one kind of atoms). It is important to remember the symbol and charge of the common polyatomic ions and that it ends with *–ate*. The method of naming chemical compounds containing these ions is similar to binary compounds except the *-ide* ending change is not necessary. The name of the polyatomic ion is used instead. For example, SO_4^{-2} is called sulf*ate* ion. A few polyatomic ions end in *–ide*; the most common are the hydrox*ide* ion (OH^-), and the cyan*ide* ion (CN^-). In naming compounds containing polyatomic ions, the name of the cation is listed first, followed by the name of the anion. For example, NH_4CN is ammonium cyan*ide* while $BaSO_4$ is barium sulf*ate*.

Polyatomic ions may have different forms. Polyatomic ions are treated as if they were a single element and if subscripts are needed, the whole ion must be placed in parentheses with the subscript placed outside and to the right.

Example:

Write the correct formula of magnesium (Mg) chlorate (ClO_3): From Table 1-3, the oxidation values of magnesium and chlorate is shown: $Mg^{+2}ClO_3^{-1}$, $(+2) + (-1) \neq 0$, therefore, the ClO_3 is placed in parentheses and the subscript '2' is placed to the right to give the 2 ions a net charge of -2 to form $Mg^{+2}(ClO_3)_2^{-1}$, $(+2) + (-2) = 0$. The correct formula is $Mg(ClO_3)_2$

Names of three element compounds (ternary) often end in -*ate*. For example, $CuSO_4$ is copper(II) sulf*ate*; KNO_3 is potassium nitr*ate*; $(NH_4)_2CO_3$ is ammonium carbon*ate,* and $Ca_3(PO_4)_2$ is calcium phosph*ate*. The only common polyatomic ion with a positive oxidation number is the ammonium ion, NH_4^+. Its compounds are named in the same way as compounds of positive elements: NH_4Cl – ammonium chlor*ide*; $(NH_4)_2S$ – ammonium sulf*ide*; NH_4NO_3 – ammonium nitr*ate*.

Different forms of the polyatomic ions exist in nature. The chemical process known as neutralization of an acid and base provides an excellent format for mastering both the recognition of these ions and their use in formulas. Students should master the basic process in which an acid and base mix together to produce a salt and water. Water is formed when the hydrogen ion removed from the acid is combined with a hydroxide ion from the base. The remaining ions form the salt.

acid	+ base	→ salt	+ water
$HClO_3$	+ NaOH	→ $NaClO_3$	+ H_2O
chloric acid	sodium hydroxide	sodium chlorate	water

The ternary acids and their salts are named in a systematic manner based in part on the neutralization process. The polyatomic ion, chlorate (ClO_3^{-1}) in the above acid, has three other forms as do the salts that form the chlorate ion. They are identified and named in the following manner:

$HClO_4$	*perchloric* acid	$NaClO_4$	sodium *perchlorate*
$HClO_3$	**chloric acid**	**$NaClO_3$**	**sodium chlorate**
$HClO_2$	chlor*ous* acid	$NaClO_2$	sodium chlor*ite*
$HClO$	*hypochlorous* acid	$NaClO$	sodium *hypochlorite*

The oxidation state of the polyatomic ion (-1) remains the same and there is a similarity in naming both the acid and salt. If the common polyatomic ions in their -*ate* form are known, the formula or correct name from all the other forms of the ion can be determined. This reduces learning four different forms of each –*ate* ion. The most common -*ate* polyatomic ions include: chlor*ate* (ClO_3^-), sulf*ate* (SO_4^{-2}), carbon*ate* (CO_3^{-2}), nitr*ate* (NO_3^-), and phosph*ate* (PO_4^{-3}). Always start with the correct –*ate* ion form and note the number of O atoms either increase or decrease as all of the forms are derived.

Ternary Acids. When hydrogen is the positive element in a ternary compound, the water solution of this compound is an acid. The names of these acids are related to the names of the polyatomic ions in a definite way. If the name of the polyatomic ion ends in *–ate*, the name of the acid ends in *–ic*; if the polyatomic ion ends in *–ite*, the acid ends in *–ous*. Review the previous example and note that prefixes "per" and "hypo" are also used.

Conjugate Base	Acid
*Per*_____*ate*	*Per*_____*ic*
example: *per*chlor*ate* (ClO_3^-)	*per*chlor*ic* acid ($HClO_4$)
_____*ate*	_____*ic*
examples: chlor*ate* (ClO_3^-) sulf*ate* (SO_4^{-2}) nitr*ate* (NO_3^-)	chlor*ic* acid ($HClO_3$) sulfur*ic* acid (H_2SO_4) nitr*ic* acid (HNO_3)
_____*ite*	_____*ous*
examples: chlor*ite* (ClO_2^-) sulf*ite* (SO_3^{-2}) nitr*ite* (NO_2^-)	chlor*ous* acid ($HClO$) sulfur*ous* acid (H_2SO_3) nitr*ous* acid (HNO_2)
*Hypo*_____*ite*	*Hypo*_____*ous*
example: *hypo*chlor*ite* (ClO_2^-)	*hypo*chlor*ous* acid ($HClO$)

Names of common ternary acids.

Formula	Name of Acid
$HClO$	*hypo*chlor*ous* acid
$HClO_2$	chlor*ous* acid
$HClO_3$	chlor*ic* acid
$HClO_4$	*per*chlor*ic* acid
$HBrO_3$	brom*ic* acid
H_2CO_3	carbon*ic* acid
H_3BO_3	bor*ic* acid
HNO_2	nitr*ous* acid
HNO_3	nitr*ic* acid
H_2SO_3	sulfur*ous* acid
H_2SO_4	sulfur*ic* acid
$H_2S_2O_3$	thiosulfur*ic* acid
H_3PO_3	phosphor*ous* acid
H_3PO_4	phosphor*ic* acid

Ternary Salts. When the hydrogen of a ternary acid is replaced by a metallic element, the resulting compound is called a ternary salt of that acid. All *-ic* ternary acids form *-ate* salts, and all *–ous* ternary acids form *–ite* salts. The endings *-ic* and *–ate* indicate one more oxygen atom in the polyatomic ion than the endings *–ous* and *–ite*. Binary salts have the ending *–ide* while ternary acids use *–ic* and *–ous* and salts use *–ite* and *–ate*.

Names of common ternary salts.

Formula	Name of Salt
$NaNO_3$	sodium nitr*ate*
$NaNO_2$	sodium nitr*ite*
Na_2SO_4	sodium sulf*ate*
Na_2SO_3	sodium sulf*ite*
$NaHCO_3$	sodium bicarbon*ate* (baking soda)
K_2CO_3	potassium carbon*ate* (potash)
Cu_2SO_4 and $CuSO_4$	copper(I and II) sulf*ate*

Bases. Common inorganic bases are known as hydroxides and contain the hydroxyl ion, OH^-. Hydroxides react with acids to form water and salts. In naming bases, the word "hydroxide" is preceded by the name of the positive ion. Only ternary bases exist (no binary bases) because three elements are found in the formula.

Names of common inorganic bases.

Formula	Name
KOH	potassium *hydro*xide
$Fe(OH)_2$	iron(II) *hydro*xide or ferrous *hydro*xide
NH_4OH	ammonium *hydro*xide
NaOH	sodium *hydro*xide
$Mg(OH)_2$	magnesium *hydro*xide (or milk of magnesia)
$Ca(OH)_2$	calcium *hydro*xide

Additional Considerations. The Prefixes *per–* and *hypo–*. The prefix *per–* usually indicates that an element is combined with a larger than usual amount (one more than normal) of oxygen. Examples include: *per*oxide (O_2^{-2}); hydrogen *per*oxide (H_2O_2); and, potassium *per*manganate ($KMnO_4$).

The prefix *hypo–* is used to name an ion and acid with two less oxygen atoms than the *–ate* ion. For example, chlorine (Cl) forms four different ions with oxygen, all having the oxidation number of −1: ClO^-, ClO_2^-, ClO_3^-, ClO_4^-. Because the ClO_3^- ion is the most common of these, it is named chlor*ate*, and its corresponding acid is $HClO_3$, chlor*ic* acid. The ion with one less oxygen atom, ClO_2^-, is the chlor*ite* ion; its acid is chlor*ous* acid. The name of the ion with one more oxygen atom per molecule than the chlorate ion has the prefix *per–*. ClO_4^- is the *per*chlorate ion and $HClO_4$ is *per*chloric acid.

Hydrates. Some ionic crystals contain water molecules attached to their structure when they are formed. This water is referred to as *water of hydration* and is shown in the formula for the crystal as ·H_2O. (the period means "contains"). Copper(II) sulfate is one such crystal where five molecules of water are combined with each molecule of copper sulfate and the formula is $CuSO_4 \cdot 5H_2O$. This structure is named copper(II) sulfate pentahydrate. The name of the compound is used and a prefix representing the number of water molecules precedes hydrate (water).

Copper(II) sulfate pentahydrate is used in the turf and agricultural industries to control algae in standing water. The crystals are blue; however, if the water of hydration is removed by heating (becomes anhydrous or dry state), the substance changes its crystalline form and become a grayish-white powder. If water is added to this anhydrous copper(II) sulfate, crystals of $CuSO_4 \cdot 5H_2O$ are formed again and the blue color returns. Using lower concentrations of the blue crystal lessens their adverse impact on the environment.

Examples:

1. Name the following compounds:

$NaHCO_3$	*sodium bicarbonate or sodium hydrogen carbonate*
$CuCl$	*copper(I) chloride*
$Mg(C_2H_3O_2)_2$	*magnesium acetate*
$ZnSO_4$	*zinc sulfate*
$PbCO_3$	*lead(II) carbonate*
$Fe(OH)_3$	*iron(III) hydroxide*
$AgNO_3$	*silver nitrate*
$K_2Cr_2O_7$	*potassium dichromate*
$Al(ClO_3)_3$	*aluminum chlorate*

2. Write the formula for the following compounds:

sodium sulfite	Na_2SO_3
mercury(I) chloride	Hg_2Cl_2
ammonium hydroxide	NH_4OH
iron(II) sulfate	$FeSO_4$
calcium bromide	$CaBr_2$
aluminum nitrite	$Al(NO_2)_3$
lead(II) sulfide	PbS
potassium hydrogen carbonate	$KHCO_3$
sodium peroxide	Na_2O_2
silver chromate	Ag_2CrO4

3. Name the following compounds:

Al_2O_3	*(aluminum oxide)*
$Cr(C_2H_3O_2)_3$	*(chromium(III) acetate)*
$Fe(OH)_3$	*(iron(III) hydroxide)*
Fe_2O_3	*(iron(III) oxide)*
$AgNO_3$	*(silver nitrate)*
K_2SO_4	*(potassium sulfate)*
$Al(ClO_3)_3$	*(aluminum chlorate)*
$Ba_3(PO_4)_2$	*(barium phosphate)*
BaI_2	*(barium iodide)*
Ag_2S	*(silver sulfide)*
Ag_2SO_4	*(silver sulfate)*
$Cu(OH)_2$	*(copper(II) hydroxide)*
CuO	*(copper(II) oxide)*
Cu_2O	*(copper(I) oxide)*
SO_3	*(sulfur trioxide)*

4. Write the formula for the following compounds:

nickel(II) sulfite	$(NiSO_3)$
nickel(II) sulfide	(NiS)
sodium peroxide	(Na_2O_2)
silver acetate	$(AgC_2H_3O_2)$
iron(II) dichromate	$(FeCr_2O_7)$
sodium sulfide	(Na_2S)
mercury(I) chloride	$(HgCl)$
ammonium hydroxide	(NH_4OH)
iron(II) sulfate	$(FeSO_4)$
calcium bromide	$(CaBr_2)$
magnesium bicarbonate	$[Mg(HCO_3)_2]$

5. Write the formula for the following binary and ternary acids.

chlorous acid	$(HClO_2)$
hydriodic acid	(HI)
pernitric acid	(HNO_4)
sulfurous acid	(H_2SO_3)
hydrosulfuric acid	(H_2S)
carbonous acid	(H_2CO_2)

APPENDIX C

THE METRIC SYSTEM

In the English System of measurement used in the United States, neither the names nor the sizes of the units have a logical relationship to one another. There are 12 inches in a foot, 3 feet in a yard, 1,760 yards in a mile, and so forth. The metric system, however, is a simple one based on the decimal relationships of the numbers in our number system. Because of the decimal relationships between units, calculations and changes from one unit to another are easily made. It simply means moving the decimal point or adding or removing zeros from the original numeral. In this system, the names of relatively few basic units need to be learned. Units of other sizes are then formed by adding prefixes to the basic unit. The main disadvantage of the metric system in everyday usage is that metric units lack the practical sizes of English units. The following is a list of those prefixes more commonly used:

Metric Prefix Definitions (basic metric unit = 1)

tera = 10^{12}	deci = 10^{-1}
giga = 10^{9}	centi = 10^{-2}
mega = 10^{6}	milli = 10^{-3}
kilo = 10^{3}	micro = 10^{-6}
hecto = 10^{2}	nano = 10^{-9}
deca = 10^{1}	pico = 10^{-12}

Therefore, a kilometer (km) is 1,000 meters; a milligram (mg) is 1/1,000 gram; and a nanosecond (nsec) is 1/1,000,000 second. *Milli-*, *centi-*, and *kilo-* are the prefixes used most. Metric units are used almost exclusively in chemistry.

Some of the more important derived units in the metric system are:

Length. The basic unit of length is the meter (m). A meter (m) = 3.28 feet = 39.4 inches = 100 cm = 1.094 yds = 1,000 mm. The meter, centimeter, and millimeter are much too large for conveniently expressing dimensions on the molecular or atomic scale. For this purpose the micron, millimicron, and the Ångstrom (Å) are more useful. The atomic diameters of atoms range from 1 to about 5 Ångstrom units. For long distances, kilometer (km) is used, which is about 0.6 miles. For short measurements, centimeter (cm) or millimeter (mm) is used.

English and metric units used in various measurements are the following:

Measurement	English Unit	Metric Unit	Relationship
length	inch (in)	centimeter (cm)	2.54 cm/in.
length	yard (yd)	meter (m)	0.91 m/yd
length	mile (mi)	kilometer (km)	1.61 km/mi
Mass	ounce (oz)	gram (g)	28.4 g/oz
Mass	pound (lb)	gram (g)	454 g/lb
Mass	pound (lb)	kilogram (kg)	2.21 lb/kg
Volume	cubic inch (in.^{3})	milliliter (mL)	16.4 mL/in.^{3}
Volume	quart (qt)	liter (L)	0.95 L/qt

Mass (or weight). The standard of mass is the kilogram (kg). The basic unit of mass is the gram (g), which is one one-thousandth of mass as kg. 1 gram = 1,000 mg = 0.0353 oz = 0.001 kg = 0.002205 lb. One kilogram is about 2.2 pounds and 1,000 g.

Volume. The basic unit of volume is the liter, which is about 1.06 quarts. It is defined as one thousand cubic centimeters. One cubic centimeter (cc) and one milliliter (mL) are equal. 1 liter (l) = 2.113 pts. = 1,000 mL = 1.06 qts. = 33.8 fl.oz. = 0.26 gal.

To convert from one unit to another requires only moving the decimal point the correct number of places (often three). For example, 250 mL = 0.250 liter since milliliters are smaller than liters. In general, the larger the size of each one of a unit, the fewer there will be of them. Conversely, the smaller the unit, the more of them. For example, 2 m = 2,000 mm, since a lot of small units (mm in this case) make up the 2 large meters. Some other examples include:

0.250 m = 250 mm
29 g = 0.029 kg
520 cc = 520 mL = 0.520 L
$1 \mu g$ = 0.000001 g (or 1×10^{-6} g)

Metric Units

Size		Mass	Length	Volume
1,000 units	10^3	kilogram (kg)	kilometer (km)	kiloliter (kL)
1	1.0	gram (g)	meter (m)	liter (L)
1/10	0.1	decigram (dg)	decameter (dm)	deciliter (dc)
1/100	0.01	centigram (cg)	centimeter (cm)	centiliter (cL)
1/1,000	0.001 or 10^{-3}	milligram (mg)	millimeter (mm)	milliliter (mL)
1/1,000,000	10^{-6}	microgram (mcg)	micrometer (μm)	microliter (λ) (lambda)
1/1,000,000,000	10^{-9}	nanogram (ng)	nanometer (nm)	nanoliter (nL)

Temperature Scales

In temperature measurements, a long, narrow tube, the thermometer, is most often used. The thermometer most often contains mercury which expands (like most substances) when its temperature rises and contracts when its temperature falls. The scale on the thermometer used to measure temperature change is either Fahrenheit (F) or Celsius (also referred to as centigrade, C). On the centigrade scale, the freezing point of water is zero °C, and the boiling point, 100°C. To convert between F and C, the following equations are used:

$$\text{degrees Centigrade} = (°F - 32) \times 5/9$$

$$\text{degrees Fahrenheit} = (°C \times 9/5) + 32$$

Therefore, to change C to F: multiply C by 9/5 (or 1.8) and add 32. To change F to C, subtract 32 and multiply by 5/9 (or 0.556).

Examples:

Convert 86°F to C.

$$C = (F - 32) \times \frac{5°C}{9°F}$$
$$= (86 - 32) \times 5 \, C/9$$
$$= 54 \times 5/9$$
$$= 30°C$$

Convert 46°C to F.

$$F = \left[C \times \frac{9 \, F}{5 \, C} \right] + 32$$
$$= [46 \times 9 \, F/5] + 32$$
$$= 115°F$$

APPENDIX D

UNIT ANALYSIS

Units are necessary to describe the extent numbers exist. It does no good to say than an item has a mass of seven without describing the units, for example, 7 g, 7 kg, or 7 mg. Just as numbers can be multiplied and divided, so can units. For example, to determine the distance one goes by traveling at a speed of 50 cm/sec for 3 seconds is determined as:

$$\frac{50 \text{ cm}}{\text{sec}} \times 3 \text{ sec} = 150 \text{ cm}$$

This is an example of canceling of units common to both numerators and denominators and removed from the expression where,

$$\frac{ax}{a} = x$$

Examples:

(1) How many oranges can be bought for 75 cents if one dozen costs 50 cents?

$$\text{number of oranges} = 75 \text{ cents} \times \frac{1 \text{ dozen}}{50 \text{ cents}} \times \frac{12 \text{ oranges}}{\text{dozen}}$$

$$= 18$$

(2) Find the number of feet in 1.8 miles (1 mile = 5,280 feet).

$$\text{feet} = 1.8 \text{ mi} \times \frac{5,280 \text{ ft}}{\text{mi}} = 9,504 \text{ feet}$$

(3) Convert 5/16 inch to mm.

$$\frac{5 \text{ in}}{16} \times \frac{2.54 \text{ cm}}{\text{in}} \times \frac{10 \text{ mm}}{\text{cm}} = 8 \text{ mm}$$

(4) Convert 212°F to C.

$$C = (F - 32) \times \frac{5°C}{9 \text{ F}}$$

$$= (212 - 32) \times 5 \text{ C}/9$$

$$= 54 \times 5/9$$

$$= 100°C \text{ (or boiling)}$$

(5) Convert 0°C to F.

$$F = \left[C \times \frac{9°F}{5 \text{ C}} \right] + 32$$

$$= [0 \times 9 \text{ F}/5] + 32$$

$$= 32°F \text{ (or freezing)}$$

(6) If a car gets 30 miles/gallon of gas, how many kilometers could it travel on 1 liter? (1 mile = 1.61 km; 1 gal = 4 qt; and 1.06 qt = 1 L).

$$\frac{30 \text{ miles}}{\text{gal}} \times \frac{1.62 \text{ km}}{1 \text{ mile}} \times \frac{1 \text{ gal}}{4 \text{ qt}} \times \frac{1.06 \text{ qt}}{1 \text{ L}} = 12.8 \text{ km/L}$$

Using Powers of 10—Exponentials

In most measurements of everyday affairs, we do not deal with very large or very small numbers. Our units of measurement have been chosen so that most measurements come out in numbers of convenient size. In scientific work, however, measurements can vary over an enormous range of sizes. The mass of an atom would be a decimal fraction with a similarly large number of zeros to the right of the decimal point. It is clearly impractical to work with such numbers written out in full, and scientists therefore use powers of 10 to abbreviate them. An example is the number 1026. This number may be written: 1.026×10^3. The symbol 10^3 means "multiply by 10 three times": $1.026 \times 10^3 = 1.026 \times 10 \times 10 \times 10$ or $1.026 \times 1,000 = 1,026$. Another way of interpreting this notation is to say that 10^3 means "move the decimal point three places to the right." Note that $1.026 \times 10^3 = 10.26 \times 10^2 = 102.6 \times 10^1 = 1026$. Each time the decimal point is moved one place to the right, you reduce the power of 10 by 1. Moving the decimal point to the left increases the power of 10: $1.026 \times 10^3 = 0.1026 \times 10^4$.

When dealing with the use of exponents to express powers of numbers of algebra (x^a, etc.), measurements expressed in powers of 10 can be multiplied together or divided by one another in accordance with the rules of exponents in algebra. For example:

5.0×10^9 multiplied by $3.0 \times 10^3 = 15 \times 10^{12} = 1.5 \times 10^{13}$
2.4×10^8 divided by $8.0 \times 10^5 = 0.30 \times 10^3 = 3.0 \times 10^2$
2.0×10^{-24} divided by $4 \times 10^{-35} = 0.5 \times 10^{11} = 5.0 \times 10^{10}$

To add or subtract quantities expressed as powers of 10, all quantities must be converted to the same power of 10. For example, to add 2.7×10^4 and 3.8×10^5, change the second number to 38×10^4. You can then add them to get 30.8×10^4.

Some Common Exponential Notations

$$x^0 = 1$$
$$x^{-a} = 1 \div x^a$$
$$x^a x^b = x^{a+b}$$
$$(xy)^a = x^a y^a$$
$$(x^a)^b = x^{ab}$$
$$x^a \div x^b = x^{a-b}$$

Examples:

$$3^2 = 3 \times 3 \qquad\qquad = 9$$
$$3^4 = 3 \times 3 \times 3 \times 3 = 81$$
$$(\tfrac{1}{3})^3 = \tfrac{1}{3} \times \tfrac{1}{3} \times \tfrac{1}{3} \quad = \frac{1}{9} = 0.111$$

$$10^{-3} = \frac{1}{10} \times \frac{1}{10} \times \frac{1}{10} = \frac{1}{1,000} = 0.001$$
$$10^{-2} = \frac{1}{10} \times \frac{1}{10} \qquad = \frac{1}{100} = 0.01$$
$$10^{-1} = \frac{1}{10} \qquad\qquad = \frac{1}{10} = 0.1$$

$$10^0 = 1$$
$$10^1 = 10$$
$$10^2 = 10 \times 10 = 100$$
$$10^3 = 10 \times 10 \times 10 = 1,000$$

$$3 \times 2^3 = 3 \times (2 \times 2 \times 2) \qquad = 24$$
$$4.1 \times 10^3 = 4.1 \times (10 \times 10 \times 10) = 4,100$$

$$12,345 = 12.345 \times 10^3 = 123.45 \times 10^2 \quad = 1234.5 \times 10^1$$
$$= 12,345 \times 10^0 = 123,450 \times 10^{-1} = 1,234,500 \times 10^{-2}$$

APPENDIX E

CONJUGATE ACIDS AND BASES

The classical definition of acid is a substance that increases the concentration of hydrogen ions (H^+), and a base increases the concentration of hydroxyl (OH^-) ions when dissolved in water. The Brønsted-Lowry definition accounts for reactions in the gas phase, thus an acid is now any species that can donate a H^+ (proton) ion, while a base is any species that can accept a proton. Classical acids and bases are included under the Brønsted-Lowry definition plus many more species as well.

Summary of Definitions of Acids and Bases.

Definition	Acid	Bases
Classical	Increases $[H^+]$	Increases $[OH^-]$
Brønsted-Lowry	Proton donor	Proton acceptor
Lewis	Electron pair acceptor	Electron pair donor

Brønsted-Lowry. An acid-base reaction under the Brønsted-Lowry definition consists of the transfer of a proton from an acid to a base. Every acid-base reaction has an acid and a base for reactants and an acid and a base for products. For example, water acts as a Brønsted-Lowry (B-L) base when it reacts with the weak acid, HF, in the forward reaction,

$$\underset{\text{B-L acid}_1}{HF} + \underset{\text{B-L base}_2}{H_2O} \rightleftharpoons \underset{\text{B-L acid}_2}{H_3O^+} + \underset{\text{B-L base}_1}{F^-}$$

The F^- ion is a B-L base because it accepts a proton from the acid H_3O^+ in the reverse reaction. Acid and bases that are related by loss or gain of H^+ are called **conjugate acid-base pairs**. In this reaction, the acid HF and the base F^- are a conjugate acid-base pair as are the base H_2O and the acid it forms, H_3O^+.

The base remaining after an acid donates its proton is called the **conjugate base** of the acid. Each acid has a corresponding base, called a conjugate base, that is formed when the acid loses a hydrogen ion. Suppose an acid gives up (or donates) a proton (H^+). The remainder of the acid particle itself is then capable of accepting a proton. Therefore, this remaining particle may be considered to be a base, its conjugate base. Considering the following general reaction, A^- is the conjugate base of HA; while for the reverse reaction, H_2O is the conjugate base of H_3O^+. The acid resulting when a base accepts a proton is called the **conjugate acid** of the base. The only difference between the members of a conjugate pair is a single proton. The acid has one more hydrogen than the base.

$$HA + H_2O \rightleftharpoons H_3O^+ + A^-$$
$$\text{acid}_1 \quad \text{base}_2 \quad \text{acid}_2 \quad \text{base}_1$$

↑conjugate pair↑

↑_____conjugate pair_____↑

base_1 is the conjugate base of acid_1

acid_1 is the conjugate acid of base_1

acid_2 is the conjugate acid of base_2

base_2 is the conjugate base of acid_2

Again, from the reaction, H_3O^+ is the conjugate acid of H_2O; while for the reverse reaction, HA is the conjugate acid of A^-. Each acid has one more proton than its conjugate base. The stronger an acid, the weaker its conjugate base; the stronger a base, the weaker its conjugate acid. Water and bicarbonate (HCO_3^-) can act as either an acid or base and are said to be **amphoteric**. The following are examples of conjugate acids and bases.

For example,

Acid₁		**Base₂**		**Acid₂**		**Base₁**
HSO_4^-	+	H_2O	$\rightleftharpoons$	H_3O^+	+	SO_4^{-2}
$H_2SO_4^-$	+	H_2O	$\rightleftharpoons$	H_3O^+	+	HSO_4^-
HCl	+	H_2O	$\rightleftharpoons$	H_3O^+	+	Cl^-
HCl	+	$NaOH$	$\rightleftharpoons$	$NaCl$	+	H_2O
H_2O	+	NH_3	$\rightleftharpoons$	NH_4^+	+	OH^-
H_2O	+	CO_3^{-2}	$\rightleftharpoons$	HCO_3^-	+	OH^-
HCO_3^-	+	OH^-	$\rightleftharpoons$	H_2O	+	CO_3^{-2}
HCO_3^-	+	Cl^-	$\rightleftharpoons$	HCl	+	HCO_3^-

For HSO_4^-, for example, the SO_4^{-2} ion is the remainder of the HSO_4^- ion after its proton (H^+) has been removed. It is the conjugate base of the acid HSO_4^-. The SO_4^{-2} ion, as a base, can accept a proton from H_3O^+ and the acid HSO_4^- is formed.

$$H_3O^+ + SO_4^{-2} \rightleftharpoons HSO_4^- + H_2O$$
$$\text{Acid}_1 \quad \text{Base}_2 \quad \text{Acid}_2 \quad \text{Base}_1$$

The HSO_4^- ion is the conjugate acid of the base SO_4^{-2}. A conjugate acid is the species formed when a base accepts a proton. Thus, in the example, the HSO_4^- ion and the SO_4^{-2} ion are a conjugate acid-base pair. Likewise, the H_2O molecule and the H_3O^+ ion make up the second conjugate acid-base pair in the reaction.

Lewis Acids. In other reactions resembling acid-base reactions but not involving the transfer of a proton, a broader definition than Brønsted-Lowry was proposed by Lewis. A **Lewis acid** is a species that accepts an electron pair to form a covalent bond; thus, an empty valence orbital must be available to accept the electron pair from the Lewis base. A Lewis base is a electron pair donor.

Example:

Identify the Lewis acid and base in each of the following reactions:

a. $Cd^{+2} + 4CN^- \rightleftharpoons Cd(CN)_4^{-2}$

Metal ions typically have an empty valence orbital to accept an electron pair, thus the Cd^{+2} is the acid. Anions typically have one or more unshared electron pairs to donate, thus the $4CH^-$ is the base.

b. $Zn(OH)_2 + 2OH^- \rightleftharpoons ZN(OH)_4^{-2}$

Again, as in example A, metal ions typically have an empty valence orbital to accept an electron pair, thus the Zn is the acid. Anions typically have one or more unshared electron pairs to donate, thus the $4OH^-$ is the base.

c. $SO_3 + H_2O \rightleftharpoons H_2SO_4$

Water has two unshared pairs of valence electrons, thus cannot create an empty valence orbital, thus is a base. SO_3 can create an empty valence orbital by converting one double-bonded oxygen to a single bond, thus is a acid.

GLOSSARY

Abscisic acid   a plant hormone responsible for bud dormancy, seed dormancy, and stomatal closing, among other effects.

Absorption   taking up or into by capillary, osmotic, chemical, or solvent action; as a sponge absorbs water.

Absorption spectrum   the spectrum of light waves absorbed by a particular pigment.

Accuracy   nearness of a measurement to its real or accepted value.

Acid   (1) substance which donates hydrogen (or proton) ions when dissolved in water; (2) also an electron-pair acceptor.

Acid anhydride   oxide that reacts with water to form an acid, or that is formed by the removal of water from an acid.

Acid cation   hydrogen (H^+) and aluminum (Al^{+3}) ions which contribute to an acid soil pH.

Acid equivalent (ae)   amount of parent acid from the active ingredient content of a pesticide formulation.

Acid pesticide   pesticide whose molecular form becomes negatively charged as the pH is increased.

Acid rain   rainwater with a pH below 5.6.

Acidifier   an additive which lowers the pH of a spray mixture.

Activated charcoal   charcoal, which has had its surface treated, usually by super-heating, to provide maximum surface area for adsorption.

Activation energy   energy required to start a chemical reaction by causing a collision between molecules.

Activator   a spray additive that increases the effectiveness of another material, such as a pesticide.

Active acidity   hydrogen and aluminum ions in the soil solution, measured by pH.

Adenine a purine base present in DNA, RNA, and nucleotide derivatives, such as ADP and ATP.

Adenosine triphosphate (ATP) a nucleotide consisting of adenine, ribose sugar, and three phosphate groups that is the major source of usable chemical energy in metabolism. Upon hydrolysis, ATP loses one phosphate and releases useable energy to become **adenosine diphosphate** (**ADP**).

Adjuvant any additive that enhances the performance or handling of another material.

ADP *see* adenosine triphosphate.

Adsorption adhesion of dissolved substances or liquids to the surfaces of solid bodies.

Alcohol organic hydroxyl compound formed by replacing one or more hydrogen atoms of a hydrocarbon with an equal number of hydroxyl (OH) groups. A *primary* alcohol contains a —CH_2OH group while a *secondary* alcohol contains a —CHOH— group.

Aldehyde organic compound formed by dehydrating oxidized alcohol; contains —CHO (formyl) group.

Alicyclic compound organic compound arranged in a ring structure, e.g., cyclo-propane (C_3H_6).

Aliphatic compound an organic compound consisting of straight or branched chains, e.g., propane (C_3H_8).

Alkali a strong base, such as sodium hydroxide or potassium hydroxide.

Alkaloid a basic (alkaline), bitter-tasting, nitrogen-containing compound in plants that produces a variety of physiological reactions; includes morphine, cocaine, caffeine, nicotine, and atropine.

Alkane straight- or branched-chain hydrocarbon where the carbon atoms are connected by only single covalent bonds.

Alkene straight- or branched-chain hydrocarbon where two carbon atoms in each molecule are connected by double covalent bonds.

Alkyl a group obtained from a saturated hydrocarbon (alkane) by removing one hydrogen atom.

Alkyne a straight- or branched-chain hydrocarbon where two carbon atoms in each molecule are connected by a triple covalent bond.

Alloy a substance composed of two or more metals which may be chemically combined or in a mixture.

Amide an organic compound containing the amide functional group —CON—.

Amine a compound derived from ammonia by substituting one or more hydro-carbon groups for hydrogen atoms; example: CH_3NH_2.

Amino acid an organic compound containing a carboxylic acid (—COOH) group and an amino (—NH_2) group from which protein molecules are synthesized.

Amorphous lacking a definite crystalline shape.

Amphoteric able to act either as an acid or a base; e.g., $Al(OH)_3$.

Anhydride a compound without water derived from another compound.

Anhydrous containing no water.

Anion   negatively charged ion, such as Cl^-, OH^-, NO_3^-, SO_4^{-2}, $H_2PO_4^-$, PO_4^{-3}.

Antenna complex   portion of photosynthesis consisting of pigment molecules that gather light and "funnel" it to the reaction center.

Anthocyanin   a water-soluble blue or red pigment which aids in light harvesting during photosynthesis.

Antioxidants   chemicals which reduce oxidation.

Apical dominance   the influence exerted by a terminal bud in suppressing the growth of lateral, or axillary, buds.

Aquifer   a water-containing layer of rock, sand, or gravel that yields useable supplies of water.

Aromatic compounds   organic compounds whose structure is related to that of benzene (C_6H_6), the simplest aromatic compound.

Aromatic hydrocarbon   a hydrocarbon with alternating single and double covalent bonds in six-membered carbon rings; often aromatic in smell, hence the name.

Aryl   group obtained from a ring hydrocarbon by removing one hydrogen atom from the ring.

Atmosphere   body of gases surrounding the earth.

Atom   smallest particle of an element able to enter into a chemical reaction; e.g., to combine with atoms of other elements.

Atomic number   total number of protons in the nucleus of an atom.

Atomic theory of matter   all matter is composed of small particles called atoms which cannot be divided, created, or destroyed.

Atomic weight   weight of an atom of an element compared to 12 for carbon.

ATP   *see* adenosine triphosphate.

Auxin   a class of plant hormones that primarily control cell elongation.

Avogadro's number   number of atoms in 12 grams of carbon; 6.022045×10^{23}.

Balanced equation   an equation containing the same number of atoms of each of the elements among both the reactants and products.

Base   (1) a substance which produces hydroxyl (OH) ions when dissolved in water such as Ca^{+2}, Mg^{+2}, K^+, Na^+; (2) a proton acceptor; (3) an electron-pair donor.

Base exchange   the replacement of one cation by another on the soil cation exchange capacity.

Base saturation   relative amount of the basic cations, Ca^{+2}, Mg^{+2}, Na^+, and K^+ in a soil compared to acidic cations, H^+ and Al^{+3}. Mathematically, base saturation is a sum of the basic cations divided by the total cations present:

$$\text{Base saturation} = \frac{Ca^{+2} + Mg^{+2} + Na^+ + K^+}{\text{CEC}}$$

Basic pesticide   a pesticide whose molecular form becomes positively charged as pH is lowered.

Benzene series   family of aromatic hydrocarbons with the formula C_nH_{2n-6}; e.g., benzene, C_6H_6.

Binary compound   a compound consisting of only two elements.

Biochemical oxygen demand (BOD)   quantity of dissolved oxygen used in the biochemical oxidation of organic matter. It is a measure of organic matter quantity in wastewater, such as sewage, decomposed by bacteria.

Biochemistry   the study of the chemistry of living systems.

Biodegradable   a substance that can be converted by microorganisms into simpler substances naturally found in the environment.

Bond   an attraction between atoms or ions from gaining, losing, or sharing electrons by atoms.

Bond energy   energy needed to break a chemical bond and form a neutral atom.

Boyle's law   volume of gas varies inversely with its pressure at a given temperature and quantity (moles) of gas.

Branch-chain   an organic group attached as a side chain to one of the carbon atoms of a continuous straight carbon molecule.

Brimstone   an ancient name for sulfur.

Brine   a concentrated salt or ocean water solution.

Brownian movement   erratic, zigzag motion of colloidal particles from their impact with particles of a dispersion medium such as water.

Buffer   a substance that resists any change in pH.

Buffer pH   used to determine buffering capacity of a soil for lime requirements.

Buffer solution   solution to which a small amount of acid or base can be added without appreciably changing its pH (or hydrogen ion concentration).

Buffering capacity   ability of soils to resist chemical change caused by the high cation exchange capacity and in some cases, free calcium carbonate.

Bulk flow   movement of water or other liquid induced by gravity, pressure, or a combination of both.

Bundle sheath   layer of cells surrounding a vascular bundle consisting of parenchyma and/or sclerenchyma cells.

C_3 plants   plants using only the Calvin (or C_3) cycle or pathway in the fixation of CO_2; the first stable product is the 3-carbon compound, 3-phosphoglycerate (3-PGA).

C_3 cycle or **pathway**   *see* Calvin cycle.

C_4 plants   plants where the first product of CO_2 fixation is a 4-carbon compound, oxaloacetate (or OAA) where both the Calvin (or C_3) cycle and the C_4 pathway are used.

C_4 cycle (Hatch-Slack) or **pathway**   reactions where carbon dioxide is fixed to phosphoenolpyruvate (or PEP) to yield a 4-carbon compound, oxaloacetate (or OAA).

Calcium carbonate equivalent (CCE)   a relative measurement of the purity of a liming material compared to 100 for calcium carbonate ($CaCO_3$).

Calorie   amount of heat necessary to raise the temperature of one gram of water one degree centigrade.

Calvin cycle   series of reactions during photosynthesis where carbon dioxide is reduced to 3-phosphoglyceraldehyde (or 3PGA) and the carbon dioxide acceptor, ribulose 1,5-bisphosphate (RuBP), is regenerated.

Carbohydrate a compound of carbon, hydrogen, and oxygen, usually with a H:O ratio of 2:1; e.g., sugars, starch, glycogen, and cellulose.

Carbonate a compound containing CO_3^{-2} ions.

Carbon fixation the conversion of carbon dioxide into organic compounds during photosynthesis.

Carbonyl group the $-C=O$ group.

Carboxyl group the $R-COOH$ group, characteristic of the organic acids, carboxylic acids; e.g., acetic acid, CH_3COOH.

Carboxylic acid a organic compound containing the $-COOH$ group.

Carcinogen a cancer-causing substance.

Carotene (or **carotenoid**) a yellow or orange pigment belonging to the carotenoid group.

Casparian strip a bandlike region of primary wall containing suberin and lignin found in radial and transverse walls of endodermal and exodermal cells.

Catalyst a substance which speeds up a reaction by reducing the reaction's energy of activation but is itself left unchanged; an example is enzymes.

Cation a positively charged ion, such as Fe^{+3}, Ca^{+2}, Mg^{+2}, K^+, H^+, Al^{+3}, NH_4^+.

Cation exchange capacity sum of exchangeable cations a soil can absorb and retain against leaching; expressed as centimoles per kg (cm kg^{-1}) or milliequivalents per 100 grams (meq/100 g) of soil.

Cationic pesticide a very strong, basic pesticide whose positive charge is independent of pH.

Cellulose a carbohydrate that is the chief component of plant cell walls. It consists of glucose molecules attached end to end.

Chain structure a series of consecutive carbon atoms of an organic compound held together by chemical bonds. The chains may be straight or branched.

Chelate an organic compound which forms a ring structure where a metal cation can be held, keeping it more available in the soil or plant uptake; e.g., EDTA, DTPA.

Chemical bond linkage between atoms produced by the transfer or sharing of electrons.

Chemical equation the condensed facts of a chemical reaction including the formulas of reacting substances and the products of the reaction including any special conditions (heat, electricity, etc.) needed to bring about a reaction.

Chemical formula a sequence of chemical symbols and subscripts showing the elements and their ratios present in a compound. H_2O is the chemical formula for water, indicating two molecules of hydrogen (H_2) occur for each molecule of oxygen (O).

Chemistry the science that studies the composition of substances and the changes they undergo.

Chlorophyll the green pigment of plant cells which is the receptor of light energy during photosynthesis.

Chloroplast a plastid in plant cells which holds chlorophyll and is the site of photosynthesis.

Chromosomes   long molecules of DNA that carry genes.

Coalesce   to join together or collect into a whole.

Coenzyme   a nonprotein organic molecule that plays an accessory role in enzyme-catalyzed processes, often by acting as an electron donor or acceptor; e.g., NAD^+ and FAD.

Cofactor   nonprotein components required by enzymes in order to work; many are metal ions, while others are coenzymes.

Colchicine   an alkaloid derived from the autumn crocus plant (*Colchicum autumnale*) which is used to induce changes in cellular chromosome number. It arrests the formation of the cell plate, thus allows the chromosome number of the treated plant cells to double.

Colloid   a mixture made up of particles of one substance dispersed throughout another with particle size between that of solutions and suspensions.

Combustion   the chemical action that produces heat and light.

Compatibility agent   an additive that facilitates the mixing or suspension of two or more formulations. Often used when a liquid fertilizer is the carrier solution for a pesticide.

Compound   a substance composed of chemically united elements in definite proportions by weight.

Concentration   the amount of solute per unit volume of solvent.

Conjugate acid   species formed when a base acquires a proton.

Conjugate base   species that remain after an acid has donated a proton.

Covalence   kind of chemical bond in which one or more pairs of electrons are shared by different atoms.

Covalent bonding   bonding where atoms share electrons.

Crop oil concentrate   oil-based spray additive that enhances leaf cuticle penetration of a pesticide.

Cutin   fatty substances deposited on the surface of many plant cells where it forms a cuticle which acts as a barrier to water loss, pathogen invasion, and other functions.

Cyclic compound   organic compounds whose carbon atoms form rings.

Cytokinin   class of plant hormones that primarily promote cell division.

Decarboxylation   removal of a carboxyl group, —COOH, from a compound.

Defoamer   an additive that reduces foam in a spray tank.

Degradation   transformation by chemical or biological means of an original parent compound into one or more different compounds including degradates, intermediates, and metabolites.

Dehydrate   removal of water from a substance.

Dehydrogenation   removal of hydrogen; opposite of hydrogenation.

Deionizing (water)   purifying water of dissolved salts by passing it through synthetic resins.

Denatured alcohol   ethyl alcohol with an additive for industrial use and not for consumption.

Density   mass per unit volume of a material.

Deoxyribonucleic acid (DNA)   carrier of genetic information (or code) in cells. It is composed of chains of phosphate, purines, and pyrimidines, and sugar (deoxyribose).

Deoxyribose   a 5-carbon sugar with one less atom of oxygen than ribose; a component of DNA.

Desalination   removal of salts by one of several methods such as evaporation, reverse osmosis, etc.

Desorption   the detachment of a pesticide from a soil particle.

Deuterium   an isotope of hydrogen (often called heavy hydrogen or ^2H) with atomic weight of 2.

Dew point   highest temperature at which water vapor condenses from air.

Diatomic molecule   a particle composed of two covalently bonded atoms.

Diffusion   tendency of gases or liquids to mix freely, spread, or intermingle of their own accord, usually from a region of greater concentration to one of lesser concentration.

Dilute   to cause little solute in solution compared with amount of solvent.

Diploid   having two sets (2*n*) of chromosomes.

Dipole   *see* polar molecule.

Diprotic   an acid capable of donating two protons per molecule.

Disaccharide   a sugar formed from the covalent bonding of two simpler sugar molecules; e.g., sucrose.

Displacement   one element taking the place of another in a compound.

Dissociation   the separation of ions of an electrovalent compound due to the action of a solvent.

Distillation   the process of vaporizing a liquid and then condensing it into a liquid, leaving behind nonvolatile impurities.

DNA   *see* deoxyribonucleic acid.

Double bond   a bond between atoms involving two electron pairs; in organic chemistry—*unsaturated*.

Drift control agent   an additive which reduces spray drift of a liquid spray mixture.

'Dry Ice'   solid carbon dioxide.

Ductility   a substance, usually a metal, which can be drawn into a wire.

Effective calcium carbonate (ECC)   measurement of limestone quality from multiplying calcium carbonate equivalent of a liming material by its fineness or particle size.

Electrolysis   a chemical reaction (decomposition) brought about by electricity.

Electrolyte   a substance whose water solution conducts an electrical current.

Electron   the smallest negative-charged unit found in an atom. Electrons orbit the positively charged nucleus of atoms and determine the atom's chemical properties.

Electron cloud   part of an atom outside the nucleus where electrons are most probably found.

Electron pair   two electrons of opposite spin in the same space orbital.

Electron shell   spheres surrounding atoms of increasing energy levels occupied by the electrons.

Electron structure   distribution of electrons in an atom's quantum shells.

Electron transport   movement of electrons down an energy chain such as during the Z-scheme of photosynthesis and electron transport chain of respiration. As electrons move down the chain, the energy released is used to form ATP from ADP plus phosphate.

Electron transport chain   a series of energy-releasing redox reactions in cells which provide the electrons for ATP production.

Electronegativity   the tendency of atoms to attract a shared electron pair or to form an ionic bond with another atom.

Element   building blocks of which matter is composed consisting of only one kind of atom.

Empirical (molecular) formula   a formula showing the numbers and kinds of atoms; e.g., CH_4 for methane.

Emulsifier   an additive that promotes the suspension of one liquid in another.

Emulsifying agent   a colloidal substance which forms a film around immiscible particles to obtain a suspension.

Emulsion   a suspension of fine particles or droplets of one liquid in another. The droplets are surrounded by a emulsifying agent.

Endothermic   a chemical reaction in which heat is necessary (or absorbed) for it to occur.

Energy   the ability to do work.

Energy level   a specific amount of energy possessed by an electron or group of electrons in an atom.

Energy of activation   the amount of energy possessed by atoms or molecules needed to produce a chemical change.

Entropy   the property which describes the disorder of a system.

Enzyme   an organic catalyst that lowers the activation energy required for specific chemical reactions.

Equation   a shorthand method of showing the changes in a chemical reaction.

Equilibrium   a state of dynamic balance where forward and reverse reactions are equal.

Equivalent   the amount of material that reacts with or provides one gram formula weight of hydrogen.

Equivalent weight   the amounts of substances that are equivalent to each other in chemical reactions. Determined in an acid as that weight of substance that furnishes 1 mole of hydrogen ions while in a base, that weight which furnishes 1 mole of hydroxide (OH^-) ions. Also measured as the change in oxidation (valence) atoms undergo in a chemical reaction.

$$\text{equivalent weight} = \frac{\text{molecular weight}}{\text{number of H or OH per molecule}} \quad \text{or} \quad \frac{\text{molecular weight}}{\text{valence}}$$

Ester   an organic compound containing a —O— group formed by the reaction between an acid and an alcohol; e.g., diethyl ether, $(C_2H_5)_2O$.

Ether   an organic oxide with the general structure R-O-R where R is a hydrocarbon group, either aliphatic or aromatic.

Ethylene   a gaseous plant hormone involved in fruit ripening and other growth events.

Evaporation   a process where a liquid forms a vapor.

Exchangeable sodium percentage   the degree of saturation of the cation exchange capacity with sodium; calculated by:

$$ESP = \frac{\text{exchangeable sodium (meq/100 g)}}{\text{cation exchange capacity (meq/100 g)}} \times 100$$

Excited atoms   atoms that absorbed a photon (energy).

Exogonic   a chemical reaction where energy is released; *see* exothermic.

Exothermic   a chemical reaction where heat is given off, such as the burning of paper.

Family   in chemistry, a group of elements with common characteristics or properties.

Fat   ester of glycerol and three long-carbon-chain (fatty) acids that are solids at ordinary temperatures. Liquid fats are called oils.

Fatty acid   a carboxylic acid having a long hydrocarbon chain.

Ferredoxin   electron-transferring proteins with high iron content; often involved with photosynthesis.

Flavonoids   phenolic compounds which are water-soluble pigments found in plant cell vacuoles.

Fluid-mosaic model   a membrane structure composed of a lipid bilayer embedded with protein molecules.

Formal solution   one gram formula weight of a substance in one liter of solution.

Formula   a combination of symbols and subscript numbers used to show the composition of a substance.

Formula weight   the sum of atomic weights of all atoms expressed by a formula.

Formyl group   the —COH group.

Free radical   an electrically neutral fragment of a molecule having an unshared electron or an unused chemical bond.

Functional group   a group of atoms which characterizes certain types of organic compounds, such as —OH for alcohols.

Galvanize   to coat iron or steel with zinc.

Gas   a state of matter lacking definite shape or volume.

Gel   a colloidal dispersion of liquid in a solid.

Gene   a unit of heredity consisting of a sequence of DNA nucleotides that codes for a protein, tRNA, or rRNA molecule, or regulates the transcription of such a sequence.

Gibberellins a class of plant hormones best known for being responsible for cell elongation.

Glucose a common 6-carbon monosaccharide sugar ($C_6H_{12}O_6$) in plants.

Glyceride an ester of glycerine; e.g., fats and oils.

Glycerol a 3-carbon molecule which combines with fatty acids to form fats or oils.

Glycogen a carbohydrate similar to starch which serves as the food reserves in organisms besides plants.

Glycolysis a metabolic process where carbohydrates are converted to pyruvic acid with the production of ATP.

Gram a unit of weight in the metric system; the weight of 1 mL of water at 4°C.

Gram-atom *see* gram-atomic weight.

Gram-atomic weight the atomic weight in grams of one mole (6.023×10^{-23}) of atoms of an element.

Gram-formula weight the formula weight in grams of one mole of a substance.

Gram-molecular volume the volume occupied by one gram-molecular weight of any gaseous substance, 22.4 L at STP.

Gram-molecular weight the molecular weight in grams of one mole of molecules of a substance.

Grana (singular, granum) a series of stacked thylakoids in plant chloroplasts where the light reactions of photosynthesis occur.

Groundwater subsurface water in the zone of saturation that moves freely, often horizontally.

Group in chemistry, the vertical column in the periodic table containing elements with similar properties.

Guanine a purine base found in DNA and RNA.

Half-life the time required for half of the atoms of a given radioactive substance to be changed to another substance.

Halogen a salt producer; any member of the chlorine family.

Halogen family the elements in Group VII on the periodic table; reactive non-metals, each with seven electrons in its outer energy level.

Hard water water containing Ca, Mg, or ferrous ions, which forms a precipitate with soap.

Hatch-Slack cycle or **pathway** *see* C_4 cycle.

Heat energy transferred between objects because of a difference in temperature, from high to low.

Heat of vaporization quantity of heat needed to vaporize 1 gram of a substance; for water at 100°C, 540 calories.

Hemicellulose a polysaccharide in cell walls resembling cellulose but more soluble and less ordered.

Henry's law At a given temperature, the solubility of a gas in a liquid is in direct proportion to the pressure above the solution.

$$C_g = kp_{gas}$$

where C_g = concentration of the dissolved gas,
    k = constant characteristic of the gas,
    p_{gas} = pressure of the gas above the solution.

Heterocyclic compounds   organic ring molecule which incorporates atoms such as O, N, S, P and others into its ring system; e.g., nucleic acids and ethylene oxide (C_2H_4O).

Heterogeneous   having parts with different properties.

Hill reaction (or Z-scheme)   Z-shaped photosynthetic reaction where excited electrons flow down an energy gradient with energy released to drive carbohydrate formation.

Homogeneous   uniform; having similar properties throughout.

Homologous   a series of compounds, such as hydrocarbons, where each member differs from the next by the same group.

Hormone   an organic substance produced in minute quantities in one part of a plant and transferred to another and which solicits a specific growth response; a specific chemical signal.

Humidity   the amount of moisture in the air.

Humus   well-decomposed, relatively stable, dark-colored colloidal soil organic matter containing no recognizable plant parts, that contributes significantly to the cation exchange capacity of organic matter.

Hydrate   a crystalline compound, usually a salt, loosely combined with a definite number of water molecules; e.g., $CuSO_4 \cdot 5H_2O$.

Hydrated ion   solute ion with water molecules attached.

Hydride   any binary compound containing hydrogen.

Hydrocarbon   a binary organic compound of hydrogen and carbon.

Hydrogen bond   a weak bond between a hydrogen atom in one polar molecule and a very electronegative atom in a second polar molecule, usually an oxygen or nitrogen atom.

Hydrogenation   the process in which hydrogen is combined with another substance, usually organic, in the presence of a catalyst.

Hydrolysis   the splitting of a molecule or bond by the addition of hydrogen (H^+) and hydroxyl (OH^-) ions from water. For example, the action of water in the presence of a catalyst upon one carbohydrate to form simpler carbohydrates. In salts, a reaction involving the splitting of water into its ions by the formation of a weak acid or weak base, or both.

Hydronium ion   hydrated hydrogen ion, H_3O^+; when an extra hydrogen ion combines with a water molecule.

Hydrophilic   water-loving colloids, they tend to be quite stable.

Hydrophobic   water-hating colloids, they tend to precipitate easily.

Hydroxyl (hydroxide)   referring to the $-OH^-$ group formed by the dissociation of a water molecule.

Hydroxides   compounds where the hydroxyl group (OH) is present as the hydroxide ion (OH^-); e.g., sodium hydroxide or NaOH.

Hygroscopic   readily takes up and retains moisture from the atmosphere.

Hypothesis   a possible or proposed explanation of the nature of an action, it is not as developed as a theory.

IAA   *see* indoleacetic acid.

Immiscible   liquids which are not soluble in each other or do not mix.

Indicator   a substance that changes color on the passage from acidity to alkalinity, or the reverse.

Indoleacetic acid (IAA)   a plant hormone from naturally occurring auxin that promotes cell elongation.

Induction   the process of charging one body by bringing it into the electric field of another charged body.

Inert   does not react.

Inorganic   materials not possessing carbon.

Inorganic chemistry   chemistry of noncarbon-containing compounds.

Ion   an atom or group of combined atoms that has lost or gained one or more electrons, thus carries one or more electric charges; e.g., NH_4^+, OH^-.

Ion-exchange   (1) a chemical reaction where two ionic compounds exchange ions; e.g., the reaction of sodium chloride with silver nitrate to produce sodium nitrate and silver chloride. (2) The removal of ions from solution by replacing these with other ions from certain minerals and synthetic resins. Used in softening hard water and in the production of deionized water.

Ionic bond   the electrostatic bond resulting when electrons are transferred from one atom to another; e.g., Na^+Cl^-.

Ionic equation   an equation showing reaction among ions.

Ionization   the process in which ions are formed from neutral atoms.

Ionization energy   the energy required to remove an electron from an atom. Electron removal causes an atom to become a positive ion.

Ionization equation   the equation showing the ions set free from an electrolyte.

Isomerization   rearranging atoms in a molecule to form another of the same molecular formula (isomers).

Isomers   compounds having the same percentage composition but different structures; e.g., glucose and fructose.

Isomorphous substitution   the replacement of one atom by another of similar size in a soil's crystal lattice without changing the crystal structure of the mineral.

Isotope   one of two or more forms of the same element differing in atomic weight (number of neutrons) but having the same atomic number and the same chemical properties.

Joule (J)   a unit of work or energy; a newton meter.

Kelvin   the SI unit of temperature of absolute zero, $-273°C$.

Ketone   an organic compound containing the —CO— group; e.g., acetone, $(CH_3)_2CO$.

Kilocalorie (or **kilogram calorie**)   1,000 calories.

Kinetic energy   the energy of motion.

Kinetic-molecular theory   an explanation that all molecules are in motion; this motion is most rapid in gases, less rapid in liquids, and very slow in solids.

Kinetin   a purine which acts as a cytokinin in plants and promotes cell division.

K_d or Soil partition coefficient   a soil-specific description of the sorption tendency of a pesticide to a soil.

K_{OC} or Organic carbon partition coefficient   the constant used to describe the tendency of a compound (pesticide) to sorb to soil's organic fraction.

Kranz anatomy   a wreathlike arrangement of mesophyll cells around a layer of large bundle-sheath cells, forming two concentric layers around the vascular bundle which helps to conserve carbon dioxide for photosynthesis in C_4 plants.

Krebs cycle (or **TCA** or **Citric acid cycle**)   a cyclic series of reactions during respiration in the mitochondria which oxidizes pyruvate to hydrogen atoms, electrons, and carbon dioxide. This releases energy in the form of ATP and NADH which are used during oxidative phosphorylation to eventually form water.

Latent heat of vaporization   the amount of energy (heat) absorbed from the environment when a liquid evaporates (turns from a liquid to a vapor); e.g., 540 kcal when 1 kg of water evaporates at 20°C.

Law   in science, a generalization about the uniform behavior in natural processes.

Law of conservation   states energy or mass can change from one form to another, but cannot be created or destroyed in a chemical reaction.

Leaching   the downward movement of substances through the soil.

Lewis dot symbol   a dot structure showing the outer-shell (or valence) electrons of an atom.

Light reactions   photosynthetic reactions in light that cannot occur during the dark.

Lignin   a phenolic secondary wall constituent that provides strength and stiffness.

Lipase   an enzyme which acts as a catalyst in the digestion of fats to form glycerol and fatty acids.

Lipid   a nonpolar organic molecule that is insoluble in water but is soluble in other nonpolar solvents; e.g., fats, oils, steroids, phospholipids, and carotenoids.

Liquid   a state of matter having a constant volume but no definite shape.

Luminous   being able to emit light.

Luster   a shiny appearance, typical of metal elements.

Malleable   a property of metals where it can be hammered into sheets.

Mass   a definite quantity of matter, usually expressed in units of weight.

Mass number   (a) the nearest whole number to the atomic mass (weight) of the individual atoms of an isotope; (b) the sum of protons and neutrons in the nucleus of an atom.

Matter   anything that has weight and occupies space.

Melting   the change of state from solid to liquid. Also referred to as *fusion*.

Mesophyll   chloroplast-containing tissue located between layers of leaf epidermis.

Metallic bonding   the force holding metals together, characterized by the outer electrons of the atoms forming a common electron cloud distributed throughout the crystal.

Metalloid an element with metal and nonmetal properties; e.g., B, Si, As, Sb, Te, At, Ge.

Metals elements whose atoms generally have three or fewer electrons in their outer energy level; are shiny, conduct heat and electric current, and tend to lose electrons in reactions.

Micelle a structural unit composed of many molecules; e.g., the micelle unit formed by soaps during cleaning.

Micro (μ) 1/1,000,000 (one-millionth).

Milli (m) 1/1,000 (one-thousandth).

Milliequivalent (meq) one one-thousandth of an equivalent. One equivalent is 1 gram hydrogen in 1 liter of water while one milliequivalent is 0.001 gram (or 1 milligram) hydrogen in 1 liter of water.

Mineral an inorganic substance found in nature.

Mineralization the complete transformation or degradation of a substance into carbon dioxide, water, and other inorganic products.

Miscible liquids which are soluble in each other.

Mitochondrion (plural: mitochondria) a double-membraned organelle in cells that houses the Krebs cycle and the electron transport system where ATP is produced.

Mixture a material composed of two or more substances each which retains its own characteristic properties.

Molality the concentration of a solution expressed in moles of solute per 1,000 grams of solvent.

Molal solution a solution with one mole of solute in 1,000 grams of solvent.

Molarity (M) the concentration of a solution expressed in moles of solute per liter of solution.

Molar solution a solution with one mole of solute in 1,000 mL of solution.

Mole the amount of a substance containing the Avogadro's number (6.022×10^{23}) of any kind of chemical unit.

Molecular formula a chemical formula denoting the constituent elements of a molecular substance and the number of atoms of each element composing one molecule.

Molecular weight the sum of the atomic weights of all the atoms in a molecule of a substance.

Molecule the smallest particle of a substance (element or compound) that can exist in the free state.

Monomer the simple repeating unit in a polymer.

Monoprotic an acid capable of donating one proton (H^+) per molecule.

Monosaccharide a simple sugar, as $C_6H_{12}O_6$, that cannot be dissolved into simpler sugars.

Mutation abrupt inheritable change in organisms brought about by alterations in a gene or chromosome, or by an increase in chromosome number.

NAD$^+$ *see* nicotinamide adenine dinucleotide.

NADP$^+$ *see* nicotinamide adenine dinucleotide phosphate.

Neutralization the union of the hydrogen ion of an acid and the hydroxyl ion of a base to form water.

Neutron an electrically neutral particle that is within the nucleus of an atom.

Nicotinamide adenine dinucleotide (NAD$^+$) a coenzyme functioning as an electron acceptor in many oxidation reactions of respiration.

Nicotinamide adenine dinucleotide phosphate (NADP$^+$) a coenzyme functioning as an electron acceptor in many reduction reactions of biosynthesis; similar in structure to NAD$^+$ except it contains an extra phosphate group.

Nitrogenous base a nitrogen-containing purine or pyrimidine which is one of the building blocks of nucleic acids.

Noble gases elements in Group O (or 18) on the periodic table; all except helium have eight electrons in their outer energy level; are very stable, and occur as single atoms in nature.

Nomenclature an organized method of assigning names.

Nonelectrolyte a substance whose solution does not conduct a current of electricity.

Nonmetal an element with five or more electrons in the outer energy level; a poor conductor of heat and electricity; tends to gain electrons when it reacts with metals.

Nonpolar covalent bond a covalent bond where an equal attraction exists for the shared electrons and a resulting balanced distribution of charge.

Nonpolar molecule a molecule with all nonpolar bonds (electrical charges are evenly distributed with no regions of positive or negative charges). Nonpolar compounds are characterized as being hydrophobic (water-hating) and not very soluble in water but readily bound to organic matter.

Normal solution a solution containing 1 gram H$^+$, or its equivalent such as 17 g OH$^-$, 23 g Na$^+$, 20 g Ca^{+2}, etc., in 1 liter of solution.

Normality (N) concentration of a solution expressed in equivalents of solute per liter of solution.

Nuclear energy energy released by the fission, fusion, or disintegration of the nuclei of atoms.

Nucleic acid an organic acid (DNA or RNA) in the nuclei of cells consisting of joined nucleotide complexes that stores genetic information and directs the synthesis of proteins.

Nucleotide a single unit of nucleic acid composed of a phosphate, a 5-carbon sugar (either ribose or deoxyribose), and a purine or a pyrimidine.

Nucleus the central part or core of an atom.

Nuclide a variety of atom determined by the number of protons and neutrons in its nucleus.

Nutrient any substance which nourishes life.

Octet rule when atoms react so as to have eight electrons in their outer (or valence) shells.

Olefin "oil-former," another name for alkenes, as their halides are usually oily liquids.

Orbital   probable location about a nucleus where an electron is found.

Orbital pair   two electrons of opposite spin in an atomic orbital.

Ore   a natural mineral substance from which an element (usually a metal) may be obtained.

Organic acid   an organic compound containing the —COOH group.

Organic carbon partition coefficient   *see* K_{OC}.

Organic chemistry   the study of carbon-containing compounds.

Organic compound   a carbon-containing compound.

Oxidase   an enzyme that catalyzes oxidation-reduction reactions.

Oxidation   (a) a chemical union of oxygen with any substance; (b) a chemical reaction in which an element loses electrons, thus increases in oxidation number.

Oxidation number   (or state)   the charge which an ion has or which an atom appears to have when its electrons are counted.

Oxidation-reduction (redox) reaction   the chemical process where one element attains a more positive oxidation (loses an electron) state while an associated element attains a more negative oxidation state (gains an electron). These are important means of energy transfer.

Oxidative phosphorylation   the formation of ATP from ADP plus inorganic phosphate during respiration in the electron transport chain in the mitochondrion.

Oxide   a simple compound of oxygen plus another element where oxygen has an oxidation number of -2.

Oxidizing agent   a substance that gives up its oxygen readily, removes hydrogen from a compound, or takes electrons from an element.

Oxo acids   oxygen-containing acids; e.g., HOI, HOBr, HOCl.

Oxygenase   enzyme which catalyzes the reduction of oxygen.

Paraffin series   a term describing the methane series of hydrocarbons.

Parts per million (ppm)   a concentration term indicating the number of units of weight of a solute per million units of weight of solution, such as mg of solute per kg of solution.

Penetrant   an additive that enhances leaf cuticle penetration of a material such as a pesticide.

Peptide   two or more amino acids linked by peptide bonds.

Peptide bond   the bond formed between the carboxyl (—COOH) group and the amino (—NH$_2$) group of two amino acids. Water is removed during this process.

Percolation   the downward movement of water through a media such as soil.

Periodic table   an arrangement of the chemical elements in rows according to increasing atomic numbers, in vertical columns having similar properties.

Periods   in chemistry, the horizontal rows of the Periodic Table.

Peroxide   a compound with O_2 in the -1 oxidation state.

pH   a measure of hydrogen ions determined by the logarithm of the reciprocal of hydronium-ion concentration; $-\log [H^+]$. The scale is from 1 to 14 where values below 7 are acidic, neutral at 7.0, and values above 7 as alkaline.

Phenolics   a group of compounds having a hydroxyl group (—OH) attached to an aromatic ring (a ring of 6-carbons containing three double bonds) and which includes flavonoids, tannins, lignins, and salicylic acid.

Phenyl group   the C_6H_{5-} group.

Phospholipids   a lipid similar to a fat but with only two fatty acids attached to the glycerol backbone with the third space occupied by a phosphorus-containing molecule.

Phosphorylation   a reaction where a phosphorus is added to a compound; e.g., the formation of ATP from ADP plus inorganic phosphate.

Photon   a quantum unit of electromagnetic radiation energy.

Photophosphorylation   the formation of ATP in chloroplasts during photosynthesis.

Photosynthesis   a reaction in green plants which produces glucose (carbohydrates) from carbon dioxide and water under the catalytic action of chlorophyll in the presence of light.

Pigment   a light-absorbing substance, often selectively.

pK_a   a logarithmic measure of the strength of an acid as the number of hydrogen ions ionized (liberated) per mole of acid in solution; mathematically the $-\log[K_a]$.

Polar covalent bond   a bond in which electrons are closer to one atom than another; not equally shared.

Polar molecule   a molecule whose atoms are not arranged symmetrically, thus the electric charges are not uniformly distributed, resulting in positively and negatively charged regions on the molecule. Polar compounds are often hydrophilic (water-loving), thus readily soluble in water but not strongly bound to organic matter. Also referred to as *dipole*.

Polyatomic ion   a group of covalently bonded atoms that act together as one charged atom.

Polymer   a compound formed by two or more simpler molecules or radicals with repeating structural units.

Polymerization   the process of combining several molecules to form one large one such as glucose or nucleotides to form polymers such as starch or nucleic acid.

Polypeptide   amino acids linked together by peptide bonds but not as complex as a protein.

Polyploid   having more than two sets of chromosomes in a cell; e.g., triploid ($3n$) has three sets of chromosomes while a tetraploid ($4n$) has four.

Polyploidy   the number of chromosomes in a cell; e.g., haploid ($1n$) is one set, diploid ($2n$), two sets.

Polysaccharide   a large complex molecule which has the general formula $(C_6H_{10}O_5)_n$; e.g., glycogen, starch, and cellulose.

Polyunsaturated fatty acid   a fatty acid containing two or more carbon-carbon double bonds.

Potential energy   the energy due to the position of a body or to the configuration of its particles.

PPM   *see* parts per million.

Precipitate   an insoluble compound formed in the chemical reaction between substances in solution.

Precision the reproducibility of measured data.

Pressure the amount of force per unit area.

Primary structure amino acid bonding sequence to each other in a peptide chain.

Product an element or compound resulting from a chemical reaction.

Property a quality or characteristic used to describe a substance.

Protein large, complex organic molecules, with nitrogen, found in structures of plants and animals.

Proton a positively charged particle which acts as one of the units of atomic structure.

Proton acceptor a Brønsted-Lowry base.

Proton donor a Brønsted-Lowry acid.

Purine a larger nitrogenous base with a double-ring structure such as adenine or guanine found in DNA and RNA.

Pyrimidine a smaller nitrogenous base with single-ring structure, such as cytosine, thymine, or uracil found in DNA or RNA.

Qualitative analysis a term applied to the methods and procedures used in finding out any or all of the constituent parts of a substance.

Quantitative analysis a term applied to the methods and procedures used in finding out the definite quantity or percentage of any or all of the constituent parts of a substance.

Quantum the ultimate unit of light energy.

Quantum shell an electron shell surrounding an atomic nucleus.

Radical a chemical species that carries an unpaired electron.

Reactant an element or compound entering into a chemical reaction; substance left of an arrow sign ($\rightarrow$) in an equation.

Reaction indicating a chemical change has taken place and represented by an equation.

Reagent any chemical taking part in a reaction.

Redox pertaining to oxidation-reduction (electron transfer) reactions.

Reducing agent substance that loses its valence electrons to another element; a substance that is readily oxidized.

Reduction (a) a chemical reaction in which an element gains electrons and thereby decreases in valence; (b) a process in which oxygen is removed from a substance.

Reduction potential electrode potential associated with a reduction half-reaction.

Relative humidity the ratio, expressed in percent, of the amount of water vapor in the air and the amount the air can potentially hold when saturated at the same temperature.

Relative weights same as atomic weights; the average weight of an atom of an element compared with the weight of an atom of carbon, having an atomic weight of 12.

Reserve acidity acidity on the cation exchange capacity of the soil, measured by buffer pH determination; used to determine lime requirement of a soil.

Respiration   the complete breakdown (oxidation) of sugar or other organic compounds to carbon dioxide and water with the release of energy.

Reversible reaction   any reaction that reaches an equilibrium, or which can be made to proceed from right to left as well as from left to right.

Ribonucleic acid (RNA)   a type of nucleic acid formed on chromosomal DNA, and is involved in protein synthesis. RNA is composed of chains of phosphate, sugar molecules (ribose), and purines and pyrimidines.

Ribose   a 5-carbon sugar that is a component of RNA.

Ribosome   a small particle composed of protein plus RNA, and is the site of protein synthesis.

RNA   *see* ribonucleic acid.

Rubisco   the abbreviated name of RuBP carboxylase/oxygenase, an enzyme that catalyzes the fixation of carbon dioxide to ribulose 1,5-bisphosphate (RuBP) in the Calvin cycle.

Safener   an additive that reduces the toxicity of materials to plants by a physiological mechanism.

Saline-sodic soil   a soil containing both sufficient exchangeable sodium (ESP >15) to interfere with the growth of most plants, with an appreciable level of soluble salts.

Saline soil   a soil containing sufficient levels of soluble salts to interfere with plant growth, but sodium levels are not a problem.

Salt   a compound containing positive ions from a base and negative ions from an acid, or results from the direct combination of metal and nonmetal. It is made up from a cation other than H^+ and an anion other than OH^- or O^{-2}; e.g., NaCl breaks up into Na^+ and Cl^- in water.

Saponification   a reaction taking place when an alkali reacts with a fat or vegetable oil to form soap.

Saturated   (a) solution where the concentration of solute is the maximum possible; (b) an organic compound with only single covalent bonds between carbon atoms.

Science   the process of observing, studying, and attempting to explain our world.

Shell   in chemistry, the region about the nucleus of an atom where electrons move; an energy level.

Slag   the product formed when the flux reacts with the impurities of an ore in metallurgical processes.

Soap   the salt of a fatty acid made by heating an ester with a strong base; e.g., potassium palmitate, sodium stearate.

Sodic soil   a soil containing sufficient exchangeable sodium (ESP >15) that it interferes with the growth of most plants, without high levels of total soluble salts. The sodium causes soil physical problems.

Sodium adsorption ratio   the relative hazard of irrigation water expressing the activity of sodium ions to the levels of calcium and magnesium ions measured as millimoles of charge per liter (mmol/L).

Soil partition coefficient   *see* K_d.

Sol   the colloidal dispersion of a solid in a liquid.

Solid   the state of matter having a definite volume and shape.

Solubility   the weight in grams of a substance needed to saturate 100 grams of the solvent at a given temperature; the amount of solute dissolved in a given amount of solvent.

Soluble salt   a salt soluble in the soil water phase which contributes to salinity, including Na^+, Cl^-, K^+, NH_4^+, NO_3^-, and SO_4^{-2}.

Solute   a substance that is dissolved in a solvent to produce a solution.

Solution   a uniform mixture of a solute in a solvent.

Solvent   a liquid in which another substance (solute) is dissolved; e.g., sugar (solute) dissolved in water (solvent).

Sorption   a general term which includes both absorption and adsorption.

Spreader   in chemistry, a wetting agent that increases the area a spray mixture droplet will cover a target.

Starch   a polysaccharide with the general formula, $(C_6H_{10}O_5)_n$; when hydrolyzed in acid, it changes to glucose.

Stereochemistry   the three-dimension, spatial arrangements of the atoms of a molecule.

Steroid   a class of organic compounds with a structure of four fused carbon rings. Many hormones are steroids.

Sterol   an alcohol derivative of a steroid that retains the essential steroid structure; e.g., cholesterol.

Sticker   an additive that promotes spray droplet adhering to or sticking to the target. It reduces runoff during application and washoff by rain.

Strong acids (or **bases**)   acids (or bases) that completely break up into ions (has a high degree of ionization) in water solution.

Structural formula   pictured representation of the atomic arrangement of molecules.

Sublimation   change of a solid to a vapor (or reverse) without passing through the liquid phase.

Substance   a single kind of matter, element, or compound with one set of identifying or specific properties.

Substituent   atom(s) bonded to another atom that forms part of the carbon chain of an organic molecule.

Sugar   carbohydrates with a sweet taste. Also, the name for the most common sugar, sucrose, $C_{12}H_{22}O_{11}$.

Supersaturated   an unstable solution containing solute concentrations higher than when saturated.

Surfactant   an acronym for "*surf*ace *act*ive *agent*s" which are additives that improve the emulsifying, dispersing, spreading, wetting, or other surface modifying properties of liquids.

Suspension   a mixture of finely divided solid material in a liquid from which the solid settles on standing.

Symbol   letter(s) used to represent one atom of an element, such as H for hydrogen.

Synthesis   the union of two or more simpler substances to form a more complex compound.

Temperature   the measure of the ability of a system to transfer heat to, or acquire heat from, other systems.

Theory   an explanation used to interpret the mechanics of nature's actions.

Thylakoid   a saclike membranous structure in chloroplasts which stack to form grana and contain chlorophyll.

Thymine   a pyrimidine in DNA but not in RNA.

Transcription   the enzyme-catalyzed assembly of an RNA molecule complementary to a strand of DNA.

Transition elements   the elements in Groups 3 through 12 on the periodic table usually having two (incomplete) electrons in their outer energy levels.

Triatomic   composed of three atoms.

Triglyceride   a glycerol ester of fatty acids, the main constituent of fats and oils.

Triose   a 3-carbon sugar.

Triprotic   an acid capable of donating three protons per molecule; e.g., H_3PO_4, phosphoric acid.

Tritium   a rare unstable 'tripleweight' hydrogen isotope (^3H) having one proton and two neutrons in its nucleus.

Tyndall effect   the scattering of light by colloidal particles in a suspension.

Unit   a quantity adopted for measurement, as grams or centimeters.

Unsaturated   (a) an organic compound with one or more double or triple covalent bonds between carbons atoms; (b) a solution.

Unstable   reactive; nucleus emits a particle or radiation.

Uracil   a pyrimidine found in RNA but not in DNA.

Valence   the number of hydrogen atoms that are equivalent to one atom of the element.

Valence electron   one of the electrons in the outer shell of an atom.

Valence shell   the outermost energy level of an atom.

van der Waals forces   weak forces of attraction between molecules due to slightly positive and negative charges resulting from random molecule movement.

Vapor pressure   equilibrium pressure exerted at any temperature by the vapor coming from an evaporating substance. This indicates the tendency of a compound (solid or liquid) to volatilize or become a gas. Often measured as millimeters of mercury (mm Hg).

Vascular bundle   strands of xylem and phloem frequently enclosed by a bundle sheath or parenchyma or fibers.

Vinyl group   the CH_2=CH— group.

Viscosity   the property of a liquid that describes how it pours.

Volatile   referring to a substance that evaporates readily.

Volatility   a measure of the ease and speed of a substance's evaporation.

Volatilization   a process where chemicals transfer from a solid or liquid into a gas.

Water table   the top level of a permanent groundwater zone.

Weak acids (or **bases**)   acids (or bases) which show only a low degree of ionization in water solution.

Weak electrolyte   weak acid or base.

Weight   the measurement of force of attraction between an object and the earth.

Wetting agent   a material that decreases the surface tension of a liquid, causing it to spread out better.

Xanthophyll   a yellow chloroplast-located pigment that is a member of the carotenoids.

Zeatin   a cytokinin plant hormone isolated from maize.

Zeolite   in chemistry, a natural mineral, sodium silico-aluminate, used to soften water.

REFERENCES AND ADDITIONAL READING

Baird, J. H., N. T. Basta, R. I. Huhnke, M. E. Payton, G. V. Johnson, D. E. Storm, and M. D. Smolen. 1997. Influence of buffer length and mowing height on surface runoff of pesticides and nutrients from bermudagrass turf. *Agronomy Abstracts* 89:130.

Balogh, J. C. and W. J. Walker, (Eds.). 1992. *Golf Course Management and Construction: Environmental Issues.* Lewis Publishers, Chelsea, MI.

Branham, B. E. 1994. Herbicide fate in turf. pp.109–151 in A. J. Turgeon, Ed. *Turf Weeds and Their Control.* ASA and CSSA, Madison, WI.

Buchanan, B. B., W. Gruissem, and R. L. Jones. 2000. *Biochemistry and Molecular Biology of Plants.* American Society of Plant Physiologists, Rockville, MD.

Carrow, R. N., D. V. Waddington, and P. E. Rieke. 2001. *Turfgrass Soil Fertility and Chemical Problems.* Sleeping Bear Press, Chelsea, MI.

Farnham, D. S., R. F. Hasek, and J. L. Paul. 1985. Water quality: its effect on ornamental plants. University of California Cooperative Extension Publication 2995.

Jones J. B., Jr., B. Wolf, and H. A. Mills. 1991. *Plant Analysis Handbook.* Micro-Macro Publishing, Inc., Athens, GA.

Lea, P. J. and Leegood, R. C. 1999. *Plant Biochemistry and Molecular Biology, 2nd ed.* John Wiley and Sons, Ltd., West Sussex, England.

Mauseth, J. D. 1998. *Botany: An Introduction to Plant Biology.* Saunders College Publishing, Philadelphia, PA.

McCarty, L. B. 2001. *Best Golf Course Management Practices.* Prentice Hall, Upper Saddle River, NJ.

McCarty, L. B., R. J. Black, and K. C. Ruppert, Eds. 1995. *Florida Lawn Handbook.* Univ. Fla. (IFAS) SP-45, Gainesville, FL.

Raven, P. H., R. F. Evert, and S. E. Eichhorn. 1999. *Biology of Plants, 6th ed.* Freeman and Company. New York, NY.

Ross, M. A. and C. A. Lembi. 1999. *Applied Weed Science, 2nd ed.* Prentice-Hall, Upper Saddle River, NJ.

Tisdale, S. L., W. L. Nelson, and J. D. Beaton. 1985. *Soil Fertility and Fertilizers, 4th ed.* Macmillan Publishing, Inc. New York, NY.

Tortora, G. J., D. R. Cicero, and H. I. Parish. 1970. *The Chemical Organization of Plants.* The Macmillan Company, London.

Umland, J. B. and J. M. Bellama. 1999. *General Chemistry, 3rd ed.* Brooks/Cole Publishing Company. Pacific Grove, CA.

Voet, D. and J. G. Voet. 1995. *Biochemistry, 2nd ed.* John Wiley and Sons, Inc., New York, NY.

Wauchope, R. D., T. M. Butler, A. G. Hornsby, P. W. M. Augustyn-Beckers, and J. P. Burt. 1992. The SCS/ARS/CES pesticide properties database for environmental decision-making. *Environ. Contam. Toxicol.* 123:1–64.

Westcot, D. W. and R. S. Ayers. 1984. Irrigation water quality criteria. p. 3:1–3:37. In G.S. Pettygrove, and T. Asano Eds. *Irrigation with Reclaimed Municipal Wastewater—A Guidance Manual.* Report No. 84-1 wr. Calif. State Water Resources Control Board, Sacramento, CA.

Westerman, R. L., Ed. 1990. *Soil Testing and Plant Analysis, 3rd ed.* Soil Science Society of America, Inc. Madison, WI.

INDEX

A (aerosols), 285
AAS (atomic absorption spectrophotometry), 261
Abscisic acid (ABA), 191, 193
Absorption:
  plant, 299
  root toxicity, 119–120
  soil, 300
Acephate, 100
Acetic acid, 90, 135, 146
Acetylene, 139
Acids, 88–96
  binary, 320–321
  chemical properties of herbicide, 298
  in chemical reactions, 89
  classification of, 317
  conjugate, 336
  definitions of, 88–89
  dissociation of, 90, 91
  equivalent weights of, 54–55
  ionization constants of, 93–96
  naming of, 317, 320–323
  neutralization of, 90–92
  properties of, 90
  strengths of, 92–96
  ternary, 322–323
Acid anhydrides, 89
Acid-base pairs, conjugate, 335–337
Acid-base reaction, 335
Acid digestion, 261
Acid equivalents, 291–293
Acidifiers (in pesticide carriers), 289
Acid injection, 110, 112–114, 213
Acidity:
  and decomposition of organic matter, 199
  exchangeable, 223
  fertilizer effects on soil, 201–202
  in formula writing, 23–24
  industrial effects on soil, 202
  measurement of soil, 198
  microorganism effects on soil, 201
  neutralization of soil, 202–211
  origin of, 198–202
  plant growth effects on soil, 201
  soil, 196, 198–211
  soil testing of, 264, 266
  water's effect on soil, 199–201
Acid rain, 211
Actinides, 10
Actinite, 236, 241

Activation, energy of, 64–65, 127
Active acidity, 198, 264, 268
Addition reaction, 169
Additives, spray, 288–290
Adenine, 186
Adenosine diphosphate (ADP), 66, 155, 176
Adenosine triphosphate (ATP):
  in carbohydrate metabolism, 155
  in carbohydrate synthesis, 176
  in glycolysis, 177–178
  hydrolysis reaction of, 180, 181
  in Krebs Cycle, 178
  phosphorus in, 242
  in photorespiration, 179–180
  in photosynthesis, 66
Adhesives, 288, 289
Adhesive forces, 76
Adjuvants, 288–290, 297
ADP, see Adenosine diphosphate
Adsorption:
  sodium, 105–107, 110, 114, 115
  soil, 300–302
Adsorption coefficient (K_{OC}), 302
Aeration, 212
Aerification, 208, 210
Aerobic respiration, 170
Aerosols (A), 285
Affinity, 18, 19–20
Agitators, 34
Ag (silver), 20
Air:
  as dispersal medium, 33
  macronutrients obtained from, 227
  pesticides in, 296–299
Al, see Aluminum
Alcohols, 36, 135, 136, 139
Alcohol series, 134
Aldehydes, 146
Aliphatic hydrocarbons, 131–139
  location of substituents on, 134–135
  saturated, 132–137
  unsaturated, 137–139
Alkali family (Group IA (1)), 9
Alkaline-earth family (Group IIA (2)), 9
Alkalinity:
  acid-injection for reducing soil, 213
  on established turf, 213–214
  soil, 211–214

soil testing of, 266, 267, 269–270
sulfur for reducing soil, 212–214
Alkanes, 132–135
Alkanoic compounds, 135
Alkenes, 137–140
Alkyl group, 136–137
Alkynes, 137, 139, 140
Alpha (α)—glucose, 152, 154
Alpha carbon, 162
Aluminosilicates, 199
Aluminum (Al), 9
  and soil acidity, 196, 199–201, 203
  and soil pH, 264, 267
  in weathered soils, 210
Aluminum sulfate, 270
Amides, 148–149
Amines, 148
Aminization, 231, 232
Amino acids, 148, 159, 162–165
Amino group, 159
Ammonia, 96, 148
  covalent bonds in, 29
  volatilization of, 232–233
Ammoniacal based fertilizers, 201–202
Ammonia water, 97
Ammonification, 231, 232
Ammonium, 231–233
Ammonium nitrate, 235
Ammonium polyphosphate, 243, 244
Ammonium sulfate, 212, 235, 249, 290
Ammonium thiosulfate, 249
Amphoteric substances, 89, 148, 336
Amylases, 167
Amylopectin, 154
Amylose, 154
Analysis, unit, 331–333
Analytical chemistry, 1
-ane (suffix), 132, 140
Ångstrom, 328
Anhydrides:
  acid, 89
  basic, 96–97
Anhydrous state, 320
Anilines, 130, 148
Anions, 20–22, 199, 214, 223–224, 321
Anionic pesticides, 300
Anionic surfactants, 289
Anthocyanins, 171, 173
Anticodon, 190
Antifoaming agents, 289
Antifreeze, 136
Application, method of, 304
Aqueous ammonia, 257

The Periodic Table

Legend (example box):

1	H	hydrogen	1.008

= Atomic number
= Symbol
= Name
= Atomic weight

≈ International Numbering System
≈ USA Numbering System

Transition Elements — VIIIB

Period	1 IA	2 IIA	3 IIIB	4 IVB	5 VB	6 VIB	7 VIIB	8 VIIIB	9	10	11 IB	12 IIB	13 IIIA	14 IVA	15 VA	16 VIA	17 VIIA	18 0
1	1 H hydrogen 1.008																	2 He helium 4.003
2	3 Li lithium 6.941	4 Be beryllium 9.012											5 B boron 10.81	6 C carbon 12.01	7 N nitrogen 14.01	8 O oxygen 16.00	9 F fluorine 19.00	10 Ne neon 20.18
3	11 Na sodium 22.99	12 Mg magnesium 24.31											13 Al aluminum 26.98	14 Si silicon 28.09	15 P phosphorus 30.97	16 S sulfur 32.07	17 Cl chlorine 35.45	18 Ar argon 39.95
4	19 K potassium 39.10	20 Ca calcium 40.08	21 Sc scandium 44.96	22 Ti titanium 47.87	23 V vanadium 50.94	24 Cr chromium 52.00	25 Mn manganese 54.94	26 Fe iron 55.85	27 Co cobalt 58.93	28 Ni nickel 58.69	29 Cu copper 63.55	30 Zn zinc 65.39	31 Ga gadolinium 69.72	32 Ge germanium 72.61	33 As arsenic 74.92	34 Se selenium 78.96	35 Br bromine 79.90	36 Kr krypton 83.80
5	37 Rb rubidium 85.47	38 Sr strontium 87.62	39 Y yttrium 88.91	40 Zr zirconium 91.22	41 Nb niobium 92.91	42 Mo molybdenum 95.94	43 Tc technicium 98	44 Ru ruthenium 101.1	45 Rh rhodium 102.9	46 Pd palladium 106.4	47 Ag silver 107.9	48 Cd cadmium 112.4	49 In indium 114.8	50 Sn tin 118.7	51 Sb antimony 121.8	52 Te tellurium 127.6	53 I iodine 126.9	54 Xe xenon 131.3
6	55 Cs cesium 132.9	56 Ba barium 137.3	57 *Lu lutecium 175.0	72 Hf hafnium 178.5	73 Ta tantalum 180.9	74 W tungsten 183.8	75 Re rhenium 186.2	76 Os osmium 190.2	77 Ir iridium 192.2	78 Pt platinum 195.1	79 Au gold 197.0	80 Hg mercury 200.6	81 Tl thallium 204.4	82 Pb lead 207.2	83 Bi bismuth 209.0	84 Po polonium (209)	85 At astatine (210)	86 Rn radon (222)
7	87 Fr francium (223)	88 Ra radium (226)	89 †Ac actinium (227)	104 Rf rutherfordium (261)	105 Db dubnium (262)	106 Sg seaborgium (263)	107 Bh bohrium (264)	108 Hs hassium (265)	109 Mt mcincrnium (268)									

Noble gases 18 0 • Halogens 17 VIIA • Nonmetals ← • Metals ↓

* Lanthanides

58 Ce cerium 140.1	59 Pr praseodymium 140.9	60 Nd neodymium 144.2	61 Pm promethium (145)	62 Sm samarium 150.4	63 Eu europium 152.0	64 Gd gadolinium 157.3	65 Tb terbium 158.9	66 Dy dysprosium 162.5	67 Ho holmium 164.9	68 Er erbium 167.3	69 Tm thulium 168.9	70 Yb ytterbium 173.0	71 Lu lutecium 175.0

† Actinides

90 Th thorium 232.0	91 Pa protactinium 231.0	92 U uranium 238.0	93 Np neptunium (237)	94 Pu plutonium (244)	95 Am americium (243)	96 Cm curium (247)	97 Bk berkelium (247)	98 Cf californium (251)	99 Es einsteinium (254)	100 Fm fermium (257)	101 Md mendelevium (258)	102 No nobelium (259)	103 Lr lawrencium (260)

The periodic table of the elements is arranged so elements with similar properties are grouped together. The elements are arranged in rows in order of increasing atomic number. The atomic number represents the nuclear charge and the total number of electrons in a neutral atom of the element. The vertical columns have similar properties and called **groups** or **families**. The Roman numerals at the top of the columns indicate the number of electrons in the outermost shell of an atom. The elements in the farthest right column labeled 0 (He, Ne, Ar, Kr, Exe, and Rn) are called **noble (or inert) gases** because they are all unreactive gases.

The horizontal rows are called **periods**. The two rows at the bottom, the **lanthanide series** (atomic numbers 58–71) and the **actinide series** (90–103), are placed there to save space so the periodic table can fit on a page. Those elements with numbers in parentheses are radioactive elements that do not have a typical isotopic composition on earth. The mass given in parenthesis is the mass of the most stable isotope.

Most of the elements are **metals**. All are solids (except mercury) under ordinary conditions. **Nonmetals** have physical and chemical properties which vary greatly. Some nonmetals (hydrogen, nitrogen, oxygen, fluorine, chlorine, and the noble gases) are gases under ordinary conditions; others are solids (carbon, phosphorus, sulfur, and iodine). Only bromine is a liquid.

Macronutrients essential for plant growth found at concentrations >500 to 1,000 ppm (or mg/kg) in plants.

Micronutrients generally found at concentrations <100 ppm in plants. Some are toxic in excessive amounts. Cobalt (Co), nickel (Ni), selenium (Se), silicon (Si), sodium (Na), and vanadium (V) are essential nutrients only for certain plants, thus those boxes are not shaded.